THE

HISTORY OF CHRISTIANITY

VOLUME III

AMS PRESS
NEW YORK

THE

HISTORY OF CHRISTIANITY,

FROM THE BIRTH OF CHRIST TO THE ABOLITION OF
PAGANISM IN THE ROMAN EMPIRE.

By HENRY HART MILMAN, D.D.,

DEAN OF ST. PAUL'S.

IN THREE VOLUMES.—Vol. III.

A NEW AND REVISED EDITION.

LONDON:

JOHN MURRAY, ALBEMARLE STREET.

1863.

Library of Congress Cataloging in Publication Data

Milman, Henry Hart, 1791-1868.
    The history of Christianity.

    Reprinted of the 1863 ed. published by J. Murray,
London.
    Includes index.
    1. Church history—Primitive and early church,
ca. 30-600. I. Title.
BR162.M6   1978   209'.01   78-173733
ISBN 0-404-04350-X

Reprinted from the edition of 1863, London
First AMS edition published in 1978

International Standard Book Number:
Complete Set: 0-404-04350-X
Volume III: 0-404-04353-4

Manufactured in the United States of America

AMS PRESS INC.
NEW YORK, N.Y.

CONTENTS OF VOL. III.

BOOK III.—*continued.*

CHAPTER VI.—*continued.*

BOOK IV.

HISTORY OF CHRISTIANITY.

BOOK III.—*continued.*

CHAPTER VI.—*continued.*

Julian.

INSTEAD of the Christian hierarchy, Julian hastened to
environ himself with the most distinguished Philosophers.
of the Heathen philosophers. Most of these,
indeed, pretended to be a kind of priesthood. Intercessors between the deities and the world of man, they
wrought miracles, foresaw future events ; they possessed
the art of purifying the soul, so that it should be reunited to the Primal Spirit : the Divinity dwelt within
them.

The obscurity of the names which Julian thus set
up to rival in popular estimation an Athanasius or a
Gregory of Nazianzum, is not altogether to be ascribed to the final success of Christianity. The impartial verdict of posterity can scarcely award to these
men a higher appellation than that of sophists and
rhetoricians. The subtlety and ingenuity of these more
imaginative, perhaps, but far less profound, *schoolmen* of
Paganism, were wasted on idle reveries, on solemn
trifling, and questions which it was alike useless to
agitate and impossible to solve. The hand of death
was alike upon the religion, the philosophy, the elo-

quence, of Greece; and the temporary movement
which Julian excited was but a feeble quivering, a last
impotent struggle, preparatory to total dissolution.
Maximus appears, in his own time, to have been the
most eminent of his class. The writings of Libanius
and of Iamblichus alone survive, to any extent, the
general wreck of the later Grecian literature. The
genius and the language of Plato were alike wanting
in his degenerate disciples. Julian himself is, perhaps,
the best, because the plainest and most perspicuous,
writer of his time: and the "Cæsars" may rank as no
unsuccessful attempt at satiric irony.

Maximus was the most famous of the school. He
Maximus. had been among the early instructors of Julian. The Emperor had scarcely assumed the
throne, when he wrote to Maximus in the most urgent
and flattering terms: life was not life without him.[a]
Maximus obeyed the summons. On his journey through
Asia Minor, the cities vied with each other in doing
honour to the champion of Paganism. When the Emperor heard of his arrival in Constantinople, though
engaged in an important public ceremonial, he broke it
off at once and hastened to welcome his philosophic
guest. The roads to the metropolis were crowded
with sophists, hurrying to bask in the sunshine of imperial favour.[b] The privilege of travelling at the public
cost by the posting establishment of the empire, so
much abused by Constantius in favour of the bishops,
was now conceded to some of the philosophers. Chry-

---

[a] Epist. xv. The nameless person
to whom the first epistle is addressed
is declared superior to Pythagoras or
Plato. Epist. i. p. 372.

[b] The severe and grave Priscus despised the youths who embraced philosophy as a fashion. Κορυβαντιών-
των ἐπὶ σοφίᾳ μειρακίων. Vit.
Prisc. apud Eunap., Ed. Boisson.
p. 67.

santhius, another sophist of great reputation, was more modest and more prudent; he declined the dazzling honour, and preferred the philosophic quiet of his native town. Julian appointed him, with his wife, to the high-priesthood of Lydia; and Chrysanthius, with the prophetic discernment of worldly wisdom, kept on amicable terms with the Christians. Of Libanius, Julian writes in rapturous admiration. Iamblichus had united all that was excellent in the ancient philosophy and poetry; Pindar, Democritus, and Orpheus, were blended in his perfect and harmonious syncretism.[c] The wisdom of Iamblichus so much dazzled and overawed the Emperor that he dared not intrude too much of his correspondence on the awful sage. "One of his letters surpassed in value all the gold of Lydia." The influence of men over their own age may in general be estimated by the language of contemporary writers. The admiration they excite is the test of their power, at least with their own party. The idolatry of the philosophers is confined to the few initiate; and even with their own party, the philosophers disappointed the high expectations which they had excited of their dignified superiority to the baser interests and weaknesses of mankind. They were by no means proof against the intoxication of court favour; they betrayed their vanity, their love of pleasure. Maximus himself is accused of assuming the pomp and insolence of a favourite; the discarded eunuchs had been replaced, it was feared by a new, not less intriguing or more disinterested, race of courtiers.

To the Christians, Julian assumed the language of the most liberal toleration. His favourite orator thus

[c] Epist. xv.

described his policy. "He thought that neither fire
_{Toleration of} nor sword could change the faith of mankind;
_{Julian.} the heart disowns the hand which is com-
pelled by terror to sacrifice. Persecutions only make
hypocrites, who are unbelievers throughout life, or
martyrs honoured after death.[d] He strictly prohibited
the putting to death the Galileans (his favourite appellation of the Christians), as worthy rather of compassion
than of hatred.[e] "Leave them to punish themselves,
poor, blind, and misguided beings, who abandon the
most glorious privilege of mankind, the adoration of
the immortal gods, to worship the mouldering remains
and bones of the dead."[f] He did not perceive that it
was now too late to reassume the old Roman contempt
for the obscure and foreign religion. Christianity had
sate on the throne; and disdain now sounded like mor-
tified pride. And the language, even the edicts, of the
Emperor, under the smooth mask of gentleness and
pity, betrayed the bitterness of hostility. His conduct
was a perpetual sarcasm. It was the interest of Paganism to inflame, rather than to allay, the internal
feuds of Christianity. Julian revoked the sentence of
_{His sarcastic} banishment pronounced against Arians, Apolli-
_{tone.} narians, and Donatists. He determined, it is
said, to expose them to a sort of public exhibition of
intellectual gladiatorship. He summoned the advocates
of the several sects to dispute in his presence, and presided with mock solemnity over their debates. His own
voice was drowned in the clamour, till at length, as

---

[d] Liban. Orat. Parent. v. i. p. 562.

[e] He asserts, in his 7th epistle, that
he is willing neither to put to death,
nor to injure the Christians in any manner; but the worshippers of the gods

were on all occasions to be preferred—
προτιμᾶσθαι. Compare Epist. lii.

[f] His usual phrase was, "worshippers of the dead, and of the bones
of men."

though to contrast them, to their disadvantage, with the
wild barbarian warriors with whom he had been engaged,—"Hear me," exclaimed the Emperor; "the
Franks and the Alemanni have heard me." "No wild
beasts," he said, "are so savage and intractable as
Christian sectaries." He even endured personal insult.
The statue of the "Fortune of Constantinople," bearing
a cross in its hand, had been set up by Constantine.
Julian took away the cross, and removed the Deity into
a splendid temple. While he was employed in sacrifice,
he was interrupted by the remonstrances of Maris, the
Arian bishop of Chalcedon, to whom age and blindness
had added courage. "Peace," said the Emperor,
"blind old man, thy Galilean God will not restore thine
eyesight." "I thank my God," answered Maris, "for
my blindness, which spares me the pain of beholding
an apostate like thee." Julian calmly proceeded in his
sacrifice.[g]

The sagacity of Julian perceived the advantage to be
obtained by contrasting the wealth, the power, and the
lofty tone of the existing priesthood with the humility
of the primitive Christians. On the occasion of a dispute between the Arian and orthodox party in
Edessa, he confiscated their wealth, in order,
as he said, to reduce them to their becoming
and boasted poverty. "Wealth, according to their admirable law," he ironically says, "prevents them from
attaining the kingdom of heaven."[h]

Taunts their professions of poverty.

But his hostility was not confined to these indirect
and invidious measures, or to quiet or insulting
scorn. He began by abrogating all the exclusive privileges of the clergy; their immunity from

Privileges withdrawn.

---

[g] Socrates, iii. 12.   [h] Socrat. iii. 13.

taxation, and exemptions from public duties. He would
not allow Christians to be prefects, as their law prohibited their adjudging capital punishments. He resumed all the grants made on the revenues of the
municipalities, and the supplies of corn for their maintenance. It was an act of more unwarrantable yet
Exclusion politic tyranny to exclude them altogether
from public
education. from the public education. By a familiarity
with the great models of antiquity, the Christian had
risen at least to the level of the most correct and
elegant of the Heathen writers of the day. Though
something of Oriental expression, from the continual
adoption of language or of imagery from the Sacred
Writings, adhered to their style, yet even that gives
a kind of raciness and originality to their language,
which, however foreign to the purity of Attic Greek,
is more animating and attractive than the prolix and
languid periods of Libanius, or the vague metaphysics
of Iamblichus. Julian perceived the danger, and resented this usurpation, as it were, of the arms of
Paganism, and their employment against their legitimate parent. It is not, indeed, quite clear how far, or
in what manner, the prohibition of Julian affected the
Education of Christians. A general system of education,
the higher
classes. for the free and superior classes, had gradually
spread through the empire.[1] Each city maintained a
certain number of professors, according to its size and
population, who taught grammar, rhetoric, and philosophy. They were appointed by the magistracy, and
partly paid from the municipal funds. Vespasian first
assigned stipends to professors in Rome, the Antonines

---

[1] There is an essay on the professors | Monsieur Naudet, Mém. de l'Institut,
and general system of education, by | vol. x. p. 399.

extended the establishment to the other cities of the empire. They received two kinds of emoluments; the salary from the city, and a small fixed gratuity from their scholars. They enjoyed considerable immunities, exemption from military and civil service, and from all ordinary taxation. There can be no doubt that this education, as originally designed, was more or less intimately allied with the ancient religion. The grammarians, the poets,[k] the orators, the philosophers of Greece and Rome, were the writers whose works were explained and instilled into the youthful mind. "The vital principle, Julian asserted, in the writings of Homer, Hesiod, Demosthenes, Herodotus, Thucydides, Isocrates, Lysias, was the worship of the gods. Some of these writers had dedicated themselves to Mercury, some to the Muses. Mercury and the Muses were the tutelar deities of the Pagan schools." The Christians had glided imperceptibly into some of these offices, and perhaps some of the professors had embraced Christianity. But Julian declared that the Christians must be shameful hypocrites, or the most sordid of men, who, for a few drachms, would teach what they did not believe.[m] The Emperor might, with some plausibility, have insisted that the ministers of public instruction paid by the state, or from public funds, should at least not be hostile to the religion of the state. If the prohibition extended no farther than their exclusion from the public professorships, the measure might have worn some

---

[k] Homer, then considered, if not the parent, the great authority for the Pagan mythology, was the elementary school-book.

[m] When Christianity resumed the ascendancy, this act of intolerance was adduced in justification of the severities of Theodosius against Paganism. Petunt etiam, ut illis privilegia deferas, qui loquendi et docendi nostris communem usum Juliani lege proximâ denegarunt. Ambros. Epist. Resp. ad Symmach.

appearance of equity; but it was the avowed policy of
Julian to exclude them, if possible, from all advantages
derived from the liberal study of Greek letters. The
original edict disclaimed the intention of compelling the
Christians to attend the Pagan schools; but it contemptuously asserted the right of the government to
control men so completely out of their senses, and, at
the same time, affected condescension to their weakness
and obstinacy.[n] But if the Emperor did not compel
them to learn, he forbade them to teach. The interdict, no doubt, extended to their own private and
separate schools for Hellenic learning. They were not
to instruct in Greek letters without the sanction of the
municipal magistracy. He added insult to this narrow
prohibition: he taunted them with their former avowed
contempt for human learning; he would not permit
them to lay their profane hands on Homer and Plato.
" Let them be content to explain Matthew and Luke in
the churches of the Galileans."[o]   Some of the Christian
professors obeyed the imperial edict.[p]   Proæresius, who
taught rhetoric with great success at Rome, calmly
declined the overtures of the Emperor, and retired into
a private station.   Musonius, a rival of the great Proæresius, was silenced.   But they resorted to an expedient
which shows that they had full freedom of Christian
instruction.   A Christian Homer, a Christian Pindar,
and other works were composed in which Christian
sentiments and opinions were interwoven into the lan-

---

[n] Julian. Epist. xlii. p. 420. Socrates, v. 18.   Theodoret, iii. 8.
Sozomen, v. 18.   Greg. Naz. Or. iii.
p. 51, 96, 97.

[o] Julian. Epist. xlv.

[p] The more liberal Heathens were
disgusted and ashamed at this measure
of Julian. "Illud autem erat incle-
mens obruendum perenni silentio, quod
arcebat docere magistros, rhetoricos, et
grammaticos, ritûs Christiani cultores."
Amm. Marcell. xx. c. 10.

guage of the original poets. The piety of the age greatly admired these Christian parodies, which, however, do not seem to have maintained their ground even in the Christian schools.[q]

Julian is charged with employing unworthy or insidious arts to extort an involuntary assent to Paganism. Heathen symbols everywhere replaced those of Christianity. The medals display a great variety of deities, with their attributes. Jupiter is crowning the Emperor, Mars and Mercury inspire him with military skill and eloquence. The monogram of Christ disappeared from the Labarum, and on the standards were represented the gods of Paganism. As the troops defiled before the Emperor, each man was ordered to throw a few grains of frankincense upon an altar which stood before him. The Christians were horror-stricken, when they found that, instead of an act of legitimate respect to the Emperor, they had been betrayed into paying homage to idols. Some bitterly lamented their involuntary sacrilege, and indignantly threw down their arms; some of them are said to have surrounded the palace, and loudly avowing that they were Christians, reproached the Emperor with his treachery, and cast down the largess that they had received. For this breach of discipline and insult to the Emperor, they were led out to military execution. They vied with each other, it is said, for the honours of martyrdom.[r] But the bloody scene was interrupted

Arts of Julian to undermine Christianity.

---

[q] After the death of Julian, they were contemptuously thrown aside by the Christians themselves. Τῶν δὲ οἱ πόνοι ἐν τῷ ἴσῳ μὴ γραφῆναι λογίζονται. Socrates, E. H. iii. 16.

[r] Jovian, Valentinian, and Valens, the future Emperors, are said to have been among those who refused to serve in the army. Julian, however, declined to accept the resignation of the former.

by a messenger from the Emperor, who contented himself with expelling them from the army, and sending them into banishment.

Actual persecutions, though unauthorised by the imperial edicts, would take place in some parts from the collision of the two parties. The Pagans, now invested in authority, would not always be disposed to use that authority with discretion, and the Pagan populace would seize the opportunity of revenging the violation of their temples, or the interruption of their rites, by the more zealous Christians. No doubt the language of an address delivered to Constantius and Constans had expressed the sentiments of a large party among the Christians. "Destroy without fear, destroy ye, most religious Emperors, the ornaments of the temples. Coin the idols into money, or melt them into useful metal. Confiscate all their endowments for the advantage of the Emperor and of the government. God has sanctioned, by your recent victories, your hostility to the temples." The writer proceeds to thunder out the passages of the Mosaic law, which enforce the duty of the extirpation of idolaters.[s] No doubt, in many places, the eager fanaticism of the Christians had outstripped the tardy movements of imperial zeal. In many cases it would now be thought an act of religion to reject—in others, it would be impossible to satisfy—the demands for restitution. The best authenticated acts of direct persecution relate to these disputes. Nor can Julian himself be exculpated from the guilt, if not of conniving at, of faintly rebuking these tumultuous acts of revenge or of wanton outrage. In some of the Syrian towns, Gaza, Hierapolis, and Cæsarea, the Pagans

[s] Julius Firmicus Maternus, de Errore Profanorum Religionum, c. 29.

had perpetrated cruelties too horrible to detail. Not
content with massacring the Christians, with every kind
of indignity, they had treated their lifeless remains with
unprecedented outrage. They sprinkled the entrails
of their victims with barley, that the fowls might be
tempted to devour them. At Heliopolis, their cannibal
fury did not shrink from tasting the blood and the
inward parts of murdered priests and virgins. Julian
calmly expresses his regret that the restorers Restoration
of the temples of the gods have in some of temples.
instances exceeded his expressed intentions; which,
however, seem to have authorised the destruction of the
Christian churches, or at least some of their sacred places.[t]

Julian made an inauspicious choice in the battle-field
on which he attempted to decide his conflict Julian con-
with Christianity. Christianity predominated tends on
ill-chosen
to a greater extent in Constantinople and in ground.
Antioch than in any other cities of the empire. In
Rome he might have appealed to the antiquity of
Heathenism, and its eternal association with the glories
of the republic. In Athens, he would have combined
in more amicable confederacy the philosophy and the
religion. In Athens his accession had given a considerable impulse to Paganism; the temples with the
rest of the public buildings, had renewed their youth.[u]

---

[t] Greg. Nazianz. Socrates, iii. 14.
Sozomen, v. 9. Compare Gibbon,
vol. iv. p. 116, who has referred the
following passage in the Misopogon to
these scenes.

Οἱ τὰ μὲν τῶν θεῶν ἀνέστησαν
αὐτίκα τεμένη· τοὺς τάφους δέ τῶν
ἀθέων ἀνέτρεψαν πάντας ὑπὸ τοῦ
συνθήματος, ὃ δὴ δέδοται παρ' ἐμοῦ
πρώην, οὕτως ἐπάρθεντες τὸν νοῦν,

καὶ μετέωροι γενόμενοι τὴν διανοίαν,
ὡς καὶ πλέον ἐπεξελθεῖν τοῖς εἰς
τοὺς θεοὺς πλημμελοῦσιν ἢ βουλω-
μένῳ μοι ἦν. Misopogon, p. 361.

Did he mean by the τάφοι chapels,
like those built over the remains of
St. Babylas, in the Daphne, at Antioch,
or the churches in general?

[u] Mamertinus, probably, highly
paints the ruin, that he may exalt the

Eleusis, which had fallen into ruin, now reassumed its splendour, and might have been wisely made the centre of his new system. But in Constantinople all was modern and Christian. Piety to the imperial founder was closely connected with devotion to his religion. Julian could only restore the fanes of the tutelary gods of old Byzantium; he could strip the Fortune of the city of her Christian attributes; but he could not give a Pagan character to a city which had grown up under Christian auspices. Constantinople remained contumaciously and uniformly Christian. Antioch had been a chief seat of that mingled Oriental and Grecian worship of the Sun which had grown up in all the Hellenised parts of Asia; the name of Daphne given to the sacred grove, implied that the fictions of Greece had been domiciliated in Syria.

Antioch was now divided by two incongruous, but equally dominant passions—devotion to Christianity, and attachment to the games, the theatre, and every kind of public amusement. The bitter sarcasms of Julian on the latter subject are justified and confirmed by the grave and serious admonitions of Chrysostom. By a singular coincidence, Antioch came into collision with the strongest prejudices of Julian. His very virtues were fatal to his success in the re-establishment of Paganism; its connexion with the amusements of the people Julian repudiated with philosophic disdain. Instead of attempting to purify the degenerate taste, he had all the austerity of a Pagan monk. Public exhibitions were interdicted to his reformed priesthood;

---

restorer. "Ipsæ illæ bonarum artium magistræ et inventrices Athenæ omnem cultum publicè privatimque perdide- rant. In miserandam ruinam conci- derat Eleusinia." Mamert. Grat. Actio. ix. p. 147.

once, at the beginning of the year, the Emperor entered
the theatre, remained in undisguised weariness, and withdrew in disgust. He was equally impatient of wasting
his time as a spectator of the chariot race; he attended
occasionally, out of respect to the presiding deity of
the games; saw five or six courses, and retired.[x] Yet
Paganism might appear to welcome Julian to   Julian at
Antioch. It had still many followers, who   Antioch.
clung with fond attachment to its pomps and gay processions. The whole city poured forth to receive him; by
some he was hailed as a deity. It happened to be the
festival of Adonis; and the loud shouts of welcome to
the Emperor were mingled with the wild and shrill
cries of the women, wailing that Syrian symbol of the
universal deity, the Sun. It might seem an awful
omen that the rites which mourned the departure of
the genial deity should welcome his ardent worshipper.[y]
The outward appearance of religion must have affected
Julian with alternate hope and disappointment. From
all quarters, diviners, augurs, magicians, enchanters,
the priests of Cybele and of the other Eastern religions,
flocked to Antioch. His palace was crowded with men,
whom Chrysostom describes as branded with every crime,
as infamous for poisonings and witchcrafts. " Men who
had grown old in prisons and in the mines, and who
maintained their wretched existence by the most disgraceful trades, were suddenly advanced to places of
dignity, and invested with the priesthood and sacrificial
functions.[z] The severe Julian, as he passed through
the city, " was encircled by the profligate of every age,

---

[x] Misopogon, p. 339, 340. Amm.
xxii. 9.

[y] " Evenerat iisdem diebus annuo

cursu completo Adonica ritu veteri
celebrari." Amm. Marc. xxii. 9.

[z] Chrysostom contra Gent.

and by prostitutes with their wanton laughter and
shameless language. Among the former, the ardent,
youthful, and ascetic preacher probably included all
the Theurgists of the philosophic school; the latter
sentence describes the festal processions, which no doubt
retained much of their old voluptuous character. Julian

Temple on Mount Casius. ascended the lofty top of Mount Casius, to
solemnise, under the broad and all-embracing
cope of heaven, the rites of Jupiter Philius.[a] But in the

The Daphne. luxurious groves of Daphne, he was doomed
to a melancholy disappointment. The grove
remained with all its beautiful scenery, its shady recesses, its cool and transparent streams, in which the
Heathen inhabitants of Antioch had mingled their
religious rites with their private enjoyments. But a
serious gloom, a solemn quiet, pervaded the whole place.
The temple of Apollo, the magnificent edifice in which
the devotion of former ages had sacrificed hecatombs,
where the clouds of incense had soared above the
grove, and in which the pomp of Oriental worship had
assembled half Syria, was silent and deserted. He
expected (in his own words[b]) a magnificent procession,
victims, libations, dances, incense, boys with white and
graceful vests and with minds as pure and unspotted,
dedicated to the service of the god. He entered the
temple; he found a solitary priest, with a single goose
for sacrifice. The indignant Emperor poured out his
resentment in the bitterest language; he reproached
the impiety, the shameful parsimony of the inhabitants,
who enjoyed the large estates attached to the temple,

---

[a] The Jupiter Philius, or Casius.
This god was the tutelary deity of
Antioch, and appears on the medals of
the city. St. Martin, note to Le
Beau, iii. 6.

[b] Misopogon, 362.

and thus neglected its services; who at the same time permitted their wives to lavish their treasures on the infamous Galileans, and on their scandalous banquets, called the Maiuma.

Julian determined to restore the majesty of the temple and worship of Apollo. But it was first necessary to dispossess the Christian usurper of the sacred place. The remains of Babylas, the martyred Remains of Bishop of Antioch, who had suffered, probably Babylas. in the Decian persecution, had been removed eleven years before to Daphne; and the Christians crowded to pay their devotions near his tomb. The Christians assert, that the baffled Apollo confessed himself abashed in the presence of the saint; his oracle dared not break silence.[c] At all events, Julian determined to purify the grove from the contamination of this worship. The remains of Babylas were ordered to be transported back to Antioch. They were met by a solemn procession of a great part of the inhabitants. The relics were raised on a chariot, and conducted in triumph, with the excited multitude dancing before it, and thundering out the maledictory psalm:—" Confounded be all they that worship carved images, and delight in vain idols." Julian attempted to punish this outburst of popular feeling. But the firmness of the first victim who endured the torture, and the remonstrances of the Prefect Sallust, brought him back to his better temper of mind. The restoration of the temple was urged on with zealous haste. A splendid peristyle arose around it; when at midnight Julian received the intelligence Fire in the that the temple was on fire. The roof and all temple. the ornaments were entirely consumed, and the statue

---

[c] Chrysostom, Orat. in S. Babylam.

of the god himself, of gilded wood, yet of such as-
tonishing workmanship that it is said to have enforced
the homage of the conquering Sapor, was burned to
ashes. The Christians beheld the manifest wrath of
Heaven, and asserted that the lightning had come down
and smitten the idolatrous edifice. Julian ascribed the
conflagration to the malice of the Christians. The
most probable account is, that a devout worshipper had
lighted a number of torches before an image of the
Queen of Heaven, which had set fire to some part of
the building. Julian exacted, as it were, reprisals on
Christianity; he ordered the cathedral of Antioch to be
closed. His orders were executed with insult to the
sacred place, and the spoliation of the sacred vessels.[d]

Julian, in the mean time, was not regardless of the
advancement of the Pagan interest in other parts of
the empire. Alexandria could not be at peace
Alexandria.   while any kind of religious excitement inflamed the minds of men. The character of George,
George,   the Arian bishop of Alexandria, is loaded by
Arian Bishop   Heathen as well as by Christian writers with
of Alex-
andria.   every kind of obloquy. His low birth; the
base and sordid occupations of his youth; his servile
and intriguing meanness in manhood; his tyranny in
power, trace, as it were, his whole life with increasing
odiousness. Yet, extraordinary as it may seem, the
Arian party could find no man of better reputation to
fill this important post; and George, the impartial
tyrant of all parties, perished at last, the victim of his
zealous hostility to Paganism. A chief cause of the
unpopularity of George was the assertion of the imperial right over the fee-simple of the land on which

---

[d] Amm. Marc. xxii. 13. Theodor. iii. 11. Sozomen, v. 20.

Alexandria was built. This right was gravely deduced from Alexander the Great. During the reign of Constantius, George had seized every opportunity of depressing and insulting Paganism ; he had interdicted the festivals and the sacrifices of the Heathen ; he had pillaged the gifts, the statues, and ornaments of their temple ; he had been heard, as he passed the temple either of Serapis himself, or of the Fortune of the city, to utter the contemptuous expression, "How long will this sepulchre be permitted to stand?"[e] He had discovered a cave where the Mithriac mysteries were said to have been carried on with a horrible sacrifice of human life. The heads of a number of youths were exposed (probably disinterred from some old cemetery near which these rites had been established), as of the victims of this sanguinary idolatry. The insults and outrages rankled in the hearts of the Pagans. The fate of Artemius, the Duke of Egypt, the friend and abettor of George in all his tyrannical proceedings, prepared the way for that of George. Artemius was suspected of being concerned in the death of Gallus. He was charged with enormous delinquencies by the people of Alexandria. Whether as a retribution for the former offence against the brother of Julian, or as the penalty for his abuse of his authority in his government, Artemius was condemned to death. The intelligence of his execution was the signal for a general insurrection of the Pagans in Alexandria. The palace of George was invested by a frantic mob. In an instant he was dragged forth, murdered, trampled under foot, *His death.* dragged along the streets, and at length torn limb from limb. With him perished two officers of

---

[e] Amm. Marcell. xxii. 11. Socrates, iii. 2.

the empire, Dracontius, master of the mint, and the
Count Diodorus; the one accused of having destroyed
an altar of Serapis, the other of having built a church.
The mangled remains of these miserable men were
paraded through the streets on the back of a camel,
and at length, lest they should be enshrined and
worshipped as the relics of martyrs, cast into the sea.
The Christians, however, of all parties, appear to have
looked with unconcern on the fate of this episcopal
tryant,[f] whom, the general hatred, if it did not excite
them to assist in his massacre, prevented them from
attempting to defend. Julian addressed a letter to the
people of Alexandria. While he admitted, in the
strongest terms, the guilt of George, he severely
rebuked their violence and presumption in thus taking
the law into their own hands, and the horrible inhumanity of tearing like dogs the bodies of men in
pieces, and then presuming to lift up their blood-stained
hands to the gods. He admitted that their indignation
for their outraged temples and insulted gods might
naturally madden them to just resentment; but they
should have awaited the calm and deliberate course of
justice, which would have exacted due punishment
from the offender. Julian secured to himself part of
the spoils of the murdered prelate. George had a
splendid library, rich not merely in the writings of the
Galileans, but, what Julian esteemed as infinitely more
precious, the works of the Greek orators and philosophers. The first he would willingly have destroyed,
the latter he commanded to be carefully reserved for
his own use.[g]

---

[f] "Poterantque miserandi homines
ad crudele supplicium devoti, Christianorum adjumento defendi, ni Georgii
odio omnes indiscretè flagrabant."
Amm. Marcell. xxii. 11.

[g] Julian. Epist. ix. & x.

In the place of George arose a more powerful
adversary. Julian knew and dreaded the character of
Athanasius, who, during these tumults, had
quietly resumed his authority over the ortho-   Athanasius.
dox Christians of Alexandria. The general edict of
Julian for the recall of all exiles contained no exception; and Athanasius availed himself of its protecting
authority.[h] Under his auspices, the church, even in
these disastrous times, resumed its vigour. The Arians,
terrified perhaps by the hostility of the Pagans,
hastened to reunite themselves to the church; and
Julian heard, with bitter indignation, that some Pagan
females had received baptism from Athanasius. Julian
expressed his astonishment, not that Athanasius had
returned from exile, but that he had dared to resume
his see. He ordered him into instant banishment. He
appealed, in a letter to the prefect, to the mighty
Serapis, that if Athanasius, the enemy of the gods, was
not expelled from the city before the calends of
December, he should impose a heavy fine. "By his
influence the gods were brought into contempt; it
would be better, therefore, that 'this most wicked
Athanasius' were altogether banished from Egypt."
To a supplication from the Christian inhabitants of the
city in favour of Athanasius, he returned a sarcastic
and contemptuous reply, reminding the people of
Alexandria of their descent from Pagan ancestors, and
of the greatness of the gods they worshipped, and
expressing his astonishment that they should prefer the
worship of Jesus, the Word of God, to that of the Sun,
the glorious and visible and eternal emblem of the
Deity.[i]

---

[h] Julian. Epist. xxvi. p. 398.   [i] Julian. Epist. xi. p. 378.

In other parts, justified perhaps in their former
excèsses, or encouraged to future acts of violence, by
the impunity of the Alexandrians, Paganism awoke, if
not to make reprisals by conversion, at least to take a
bloody revenge on its Christian adversaries.[j] The
atrocious persecutions of the fanatic populace, in some of
the cities of Syria, have already been noticed. The
aged Mark of Arethusa was, if not the most blameless,
at least the victim of these cruelties whose life ought
to have been sanctified even by the rumour which
ascribed the preservation of Julian, when an infant, to
Death of the pious bishop. Mark was accused of having
Mark of
Arethusa. destroyed a temple; he was summoned to
rebuild it at his own expense. But Mark, with the
virtues, inherited the primitive poverty of the Apostles;
and, even if he had had the power, no doubt, would
have resisted this demand.[k] But the furious populace,
(according to Sozomen, men, women, and schoolboys),
seized on the old man, and inflicted every torment
which their inventive barbarity could suggest. The
patience and calm temperament of the old man resisted
and survived the cruelties.[m] Julian is said to have
expressed no indignation, and ordered no punishment.
The prefect Sallust reminded him of the disgrace to
which Paganism was exposed, by being thus put to
shame by a feeble old man.

The policy of Julian induced him to seek out every
alliance which could strengthen the cause of Paganism
against Christianity. Polytheism courted an unnatural

---

[j] Julian. Epist. x. p. 377.

[k] According to Theodoret, 'O δὲ,
ἴσον εἰς ἀσέβειαν ἔφη, τὸ ὀβολὸν
γοῦν ἕνα δοῦναι, τῷ πάντα δοῦναι.
E. H. iii. 7.

[m] Sozomen gives the most detailed
account of this cruel scene, clearly a
popular tumult, which the authorities
in no way interfered to repress. E.
H. v. 10.

union with Judaism; their bond of connection was their
common hatred to Christianity. It is not *Julian courts*
clear whether Julian was sufficiently ac- *the Jews.*
quainted with the writings of the Christians, distinctly
to apprehend that they considered the final destruction
of the Jewish temple to be one of the great prophecies
on which their religion rested. The rebuilding of that
temple was bringing, as it were, this question to direct
issue; it was an appeal to God, whether he had or had
not finally rejected the people of Israel, and admitted
the Christians to all their great and exclusive privileges.
At all events, the elevation of Judaism was the depression of Christianity. It set the Old Testament, to
which the Christians appealed, in direct and hostile
opposition to the New.

The profound interest awakened in the Jewish mind
showed that the race of Israel embraced, with eager
fervour, this solemn appeal to Heaven. With the joy
which animated the Jew, at this unexpected summons
to return to his native land and to rebuild his fallen
temple, mingled, no doubt, some natural feeling of
triumph and of gratified animosity over the Christian.
In every part of the empire the Jews awoke from their
slumber of abasement and of despondency. It was not
for them to repudiate the overtures of Paganism. The
Emperor acknowledged their God by the *Determines*
permission to build again the temple to his *to rebuild*
the temple
glory; and, if not as the sole and supreme God, *at Jerusalem.*
yet Julian's language affected a monotheistic tone, and
they might indulge the fond hope that the re-establishment of the temple upon Mount Moriah might be
preparatory to the final triumph of their faith, in the
awe-struck veneration of the whole world; the commencement of the Messiah's kingdom; the dawn of

their long-delayed, but, at length, approaching millennium of empire and of religious supremacy. Those who could not contribute their personal labour devoted their wealth to the national work. The extent of their sacrifices, the eagerness of their hopes, rather belong to the province of Jewish history. But every precaution was taken to secure the uninterrupted progress of the work. It was not an affair of the Jewish nation, but of the imperial government. It was entrusted to the ruler of the province, as the delegate of the Emperor. Funds were advanced from the public treasury ; and, if the Jews themselves, of each sex and of every age, took pride in hallowing their own hands by assisting in heaping up the holy earth, or hewing the stone to be employed in this sacred design ; if they wrought their wealth into tools of the precious metals, shovels and spades of silver, which were to become valued heirlooms as consecrated by this pious service, the Emperor seemed to take a deep personal interest in the design, which was at once to immortalize his magnificence, and to assist his other glorious undertakings. The Jews, who acknowledged that it was not lawful to offer sacrifice except on that holy place, were to propitiate their God, during his expedition into Persia; and on his triumphant return from that region, he promised to unite with them in adoration in the restored city and in the reconstructed fane of the great God of the Jews.[n]

Judaism and Paganism had joined in this solemn adjuration, as it were, of the Deity. Their vows were met with discomfiture and disappointment. The simple fact of the interruption of their labours,

Interrupted.

---

[n] In his letter to the Jews, he calls the God of the Jews, κρείττων ; in his Theologic Fragment (p. 295), μέγας Θεός.

by an event, which the mass of mankind could not but consider præternatural, even as recorded by the Pagan historians, appeared, in the more excited and imaginative minds of the Christians, a miracle of the most terrific and appalling nature. Few, if any, of the Christians could have been eye-witnesses of the scene. The Christian world would have averted its face in horror from the impious design. The relation must, in the first instance, have come from the fears of the discomfited and affrighted workmen. The main fact is indisputable, that, as they dug down to the foundations, terrific explosions took place; what seemed balls of fire burst forth; the works were shattered to pieces; clouds of smoke and dust enveloped the whole in darkness, broke only by the wild and fitful glare of the flames. Again the work was renewed by the obstinate zeal of the Jews; again they were repelled by this unseen and irresistible power, till they cast away their implements, and abandoned the work in humiliation and despair. How far natural causes—the ignition of the foul vapours, confined in the deeply excavated recesses of the hill of the temple, according to the recent theory—will account for the facts, as they are related in the simpler narrative of Marcellinus, may admit of some question; but the philosophy of the age, whether Heathen or Christian, was as unable as it was unwilling to trace such appalling events to the unvarying operations of nature.[o]

---

[o] See M. Guizot's note on Gibbon, with my additional observations. There seems a strong distinction in point of credibility between miracles addressed to the terror and those which appeal to the calmer emotions of the mind, such as most of those recorded in the Gospel. The former, in the first place, are usually momentary, or, if prolonged, endure but a short time. But the passion of fear so completely unhinges and disorders the mind, as to deprive it of all trustworthy power of observation or discrimination. In

Christianity may have embellished this wonderful
event, but Judaism and Paganism confessed by their
terrors the prostration of their hopes. The work was
abandoned; and the Christians of later ages could
appeal to the remains of the shattered works and
unfinished excavations, as the unanswerable sign of the
divine wrath against their adversaries, as the public
and miraculous declaration of God in favour of their
insulted religion.

But it was not as Emperor alone that the indefatigable Julian laboured to overthrow the Christian
religion. It was not by the public edict, the more
partial favour shown to the adherents of Paganism, the
insidious disparagement of Christianity by the depression of its ministers and apostles, and the earnest
elevation of Heathenism, to a moral code and an
harmonious religion, with all the pomp of a sumptuous
ritual; it was not in the council, or the camp, or the
temple alone, that Julian stood forth as the avowed
Writings of antagonist of Christianity. He was ambitious,
Julian. as a writer, of confuting its principles and
disproving its veracity: he passed in his closet the long
nights of the winter, and continued, during his Persian
campaign, his elaborate work against the faith of Christ.
He seemed, as it were, possessed with an equal hatred
of those whom he considered the two most dangerous
enemies of the Roman empire, the Persians and the
Christians. While oppressed by all the serious cares of

themselves, therefore, I should venture
to conclude that terrific miracles,
resting on human testimony, are less
credible than those of a less appalling
nature. Though the other class of
emotions, those of joy or gratitude, or
religious veneration, likewise disturb
the equable and dispassionate state of
mind requisite for cool reasoning, yet
such miracles are in general both more
calmly surveyed, and more permanent
in their effects.

organising and moving such an army as might bring
back the glorious days of Germanicus or of Trajan;
while his ambition contemplated nothing less than the
permanent humiliation of the great Eastern rival of the
empire; his literary vanity found time for its exercise,
and in all his visions of military glory and conquest,
Julian never lost sight of his fame as an author.[p]   It is
difficult to judge from the fragments of this   Work against
work, selected for confutation after his death   Christianity.
by Cyril of Alexandria, of the power, or even of the
candour, shown by the imperial controversialist.   But
it appears to have been composed in a purely polemic
spirit; with no lofty or comprehensive views of the real
nature of the Christian religion, no fine and philosophic
perception of that which in the new faith had so
powerfully and irresistibly occupied the whole soul of
man; with no consciousness of the utter inefficiency
of the cold and incoherent Pagan mysticism, which he
endeavoured to substitute for the Gospel.

But, at least, this was a grave and serious employment.   Whatever might be thought of his success as a
religious disputant, there was no loss of dignity in the
Emperor condescending to enlighten his subjects on
such momentous questions.   But, when he   Misopogon.
stooped to be the satirist of the inhabitants
of a city which had ridiculed his philosophy and rejected his religion, the finest and most elegant irony,
the keenest and most delicate wit, would scarcely have
justified this compromise of the imperial majesty.   But
in the Misopogon—the apology for his philosophic
beard—Julian mingled the coarseness of the Cynic with

---

[p] "Julianus Augustus septem li-
bros in expeditione Parthicâ adversus   Christum evomuit." Hieronym. Oper.
Epist. lxx.

the bitterness of personal indignity. The vulgar ostentation of his own filthiness, the description of the ver-
min which peopled his thick beard, ill accord with the
philosophic superiority with which Julian rallies the
love of amusement and gaiety among his subjects of
Antioch. Their follies were at least more graceful
and humane than this rude pedantry. There is certainly much felicity of sarcasm, doubtless much justice,
in his animadversions on the dissolute manners of the
Antiochenes, their ingratitude for his liberality, their dis-
like of his severe justice, the insolence of their contempt
for his ruder manners, throughout the Misopogon; but
it lowers Julian from a follower of Plato, to a coarse
imitator of Diogenes; it exhibits him as borrowing the
worst part of the Christian monkish character, the dis-
regard of the decencies and civilities of life, without the
high and visionary enthusiasm, or the straining after
superiority to the low cares and pursuits of the world.
It was singular to hear a Grecian sophist, for such was
undoubtedly the character of Julian's writings, extolling
the barbarians, the Celts and Germans, above the
polished inhabitants of Greece and Syria.

Paganism followed with faithful steps, and with eager
hopes, the career of Julian on the brilliant
outset of his Persian campaign. Some of the
Syrian cities through which he passed, Batne
and Hierapolis, and Carrhæ, seemed to enter into his
views, and endeavoured, with incense and sacrifice, to
propitiate the gods of Julian.[q] For the last time the
Etruscan haruspices accompanied a Roman Emperor;
but by a singular fatality, their adverse interpretation
of the signs of heaven was disdained, and Julian fol-

Julian sets
forth on his
Persian ex-
pedition.

---

[q] Julian. Epist. xxvii. p. 399.   Amm. Marc. xxii. 2.

lowed the advice of the philosophers, who coloured their predictions with the bright hues of the Emperor's ambition.[r]

The death of Julian did greater honour to his philosophy. We may reject as in itself improbable, and as resting on insufficient authority, the bitter sentence ascribed to him when he received his fatal wound. " Thou hast conquered, O Galilean."[s] He comforted his weeping friends; he expressed his readiness to pay the debt of nature, and his joy that the purer and better part of his being was so soon to be released from the gross and material body. " The gods of heaven sometimes bestow an early death as the best reward of the most pious." His conscience uttered no reproach; he had administered the empire with moderation, firmness and clemency; he had repressed the licence of public manners; he had met danger with firmness. His prescient spirit had long informed him that he should fall by the sword. And he thanked the everlasting deity that he thus escaped the secret assassination, the slow and wasting disease, the ignominious death; and departed from the world in the midst of his glory and prosperity. "It is equal cowardice to seek death before our time, and to attempt to avoid it when our time is come." His calmness was only disturbed by the intelligence of the loss of a friend. He who despised his own death lamented that of another. He reproved the distress of his attendants, declaring that it was humiliating to mourn over a prince already reconciled to the heavens and to the stars; and thus calmly discoursing with the philosophers Priscus and Maximus

Death of Julian.

---

[r] Amm. Marc. xxiii. 5.
[s] Νενίκηκας, Γάλιλαιε. Theodoret, Hist. Eccl. iii., 25.

on the metaphysics of the soul, expired Julian, the philosopher and Emperor.[t]

Julian died, perhaps happily for his fame. Perilous as his situation was, he might still have extricated himself by his military skill and courage, and eventually succeeded in his conflict with the Persian empire; he might have dictated terms to Sapor, far different from those which the awe of his name and the vigorous organisation of his army, even after his death, extorted from the prudent Persian. But in his other, his in-

Probable results of Julian's conflict with Christianity. ternal conflict, Julian could have obtained no victory, even at the price of rivers of blood shed in persecution, and perhaps civil wars throughout the empire. He might have arrested the fall of the empire, but that of Paganism was beyond the power of man.[u] The invasion of arms may be resisted or repelled, the silent and profound encroachments of opinion and religious sentiment will not retrograde. Already there had been ominous indications that the temper of Julian would hardly maintain its more moderate policy; nor would Christianity in that age have been content with opposing him with passive courage. The insulting fanaticism of the violent, no less than the stubborn contumacy of the disobedient, would have goaded him by degrees to severer measures.

Amm. Marc. *ibid.* Even the Christians, at a somewhat later period, did justice to the great qualities of Julian. The character drawn by the Pagan, Aurelius Victor, is adopted by Prudentius, who kindles into unusual vigour. " Cupido laudis immodicæ; cultus numinum superstitiosus: audax plus, quam imperatorem decet, cui salus propria cum semper ad securita-

tem omnium, maximè in bello, conservanda est." Epit. p. 228.
      Ductor fortissimus armis;
Conditor et legum celeberrimus; ore manuque
Consultor patriæ, sed non consultor habendæ
Religionis; amans ter centum millia Divûm;
Perfidus ille Deo, sed non et perfidus orbi.
                  Apoth. 430.

[u] Julian's attempt to restore Paganism was like that of Rienzi to restore the liberties of Rome.

The whole empire would have been rent by civil dissensions. The bold adventurer would scarcely have been wanting, who, either from ambition or enthusiasm, would have embraced the Christian cause; and the pacific spirit of genuine Christianity, its high notions of submission to civil authority, would scarcely, generally or constantly, have resisted the temptation of resuming its seat upon the throne. Julian could not have subdued Christianity, without depopulating the empire; nor contested with it the sovereignty of the world, without danger to himself and to the civil authority; nor yielded, without the disgrace and bitterness of failure.. He who stands across the peaceful stream of progressive opinion, by his resistance maddens it to an irresistible torrent, and is either swept away by it at once, or diverts it over the whole region in one devastating deluge.[x]

---

[x] Theodoret describes the rejoicings at Antioch on the news of the death of Julian. There were not only festal dancings in the churches and cemeteries of the martyrs, but in the theatres they celebrated the triumph of the cross, and mocked at his vaticinations. 'Η δὲ 'Αντιόχου πόλις τὴν ἐκείνου μεμαθηκυῖα σφαγὴν, δημοθοινίας ἐπετέλει καὶ πανηγύρεις καὶ οὐ μόνον ἐν ταῖς ἐκκλησίαις ἐχόρευον καὶ τοῖς μαρτύρων σηκοῖς, ἀλλὰ καὶ ἐν τοῖς θεάτροις τοῦ σταυροῦ τὴν νίκην ἐκήρυττον, καὶ τοῖς ἐκείνου μαντεύμασιν ἐπετώθαζον. E. H. iii. 27.

CHAPTER VII.

Valentinian and Valens.

It is singular to hear the Pagans taking up, in their
altered position, the arguments of the Christians. The extinction of the family of Constantine was a manifest indication of the divine
displeasure at the abandonment of Paganism.[a]
But this was the calmer conclusion of less recent
sorrow and disappointment.   The immediate expression of Pagan regret was a bitter and reproachful complaint against the ingratitude of the gods, who made
so bad a return for the zealous services of Julian.
" Was this the reward for so many victims, so many
prayers, so much incense, so much blood, shed on the
altar by night as well as by day? Julian, in his profuse
and indiscriminate piety, had neglected no deity ; he
had worshipped all who lived in the tradition of the
poets,—fathers and children, gods and goddesses, superior and subordinate deities; and they, instead of
hurling their thunderbolts and lightnings, and all the
armoury of Heaven, against the hostile Persians, had
thus basely abandoned their sacred charge.   The new
Salmoneus, the more impious Lycurgus, the senseless
image of a man (such were the appellations with
which the indignant rhetorician alluded to Constantius),
who had waged implacable warfare with the gods,
quenched the sacred fires, trampled on the altars,

Marginal note: Lamentations of the Pagans at the death of Julian.

---

[a] Liban. pro Templis, ii. 184.

closed or demolished or profaned the temples, or
alienated them to loose companions,—this man had
been permitted to pollute the earth for fifty years,
and then departed by the ordinary course of nature;
while Julian, with all his piety and all his glory, had
only given to the world a hasty glimpse of his greatness, and suddenly departed from their unsatisfied
sight."[b] On the other hand the Christians raised a shout
of undissembled triumph; Antioch was in a tumult
of joy.[c] Gregory of Nazianzum poured forth from the
pulpit his bitter eloquence on the head of the apostate.[d]
Christian legend is full of predictions of the death of
Julian. The most striking is the answer attributed
to a grammarian of Antioch, whom Libanius accosted
with a sneer, "What is the carpenter's son doing
now?" "He is making a coffin." [e] But, without regarding the vain lamentations of Paganism, Christianity
calmly resumed its ascendancy. The short reign of
Jovian sufficed for its re-establishment; and,   Reign of
as yet, it exacted no revenge for its sufferings   Jovian.
and degradation under Julian.[f] There may have been

---

[b] Libanius insults, in this passage,
the worship of the dead man, whose
sarcophagus (he seems to allude to the
pix or consecrated box in which the
sacramental symbol of our Saviour's
body was enclosed) is introduced into
the κλῆρος of the gods. Monod. in
Julian. i. p. 509.

[c] Theodoret iii. 38.

[d] Greg. Orat. iv. c. 124.

[e] Theodoret iii. 23.

[f] Themistius praises highly the
toleration of Jovian. "Thy law, and
that of God, is eternal and unchange-
able; that which leaves the soul of

every man free to follow that form of
religion which seems best to him."
Ad Jovian. p. 81., ed. Dindorf. He
proceeds to assert, that the general
piety will be increased by the rivalry
of different religions. "The Deity
does not demand uniformity of faith."
He touches on the evils which had
arisen out of religious factions, and
urges Jovian to permit supplications
to ascend to Heaven from all parts of
the empire for his prosperous reign.
He praises him, however, for suppress-
ing magic and Goetic sacrifices.

policy as well as moderation in the toleration of Jovian,
The empire had been first offered to the Prefect Sallust,
a Pagan. It was Procopius, probably another Pagan,
who laid the diadem at the feet of Jovian. Sacrifices
to the gods were still performed at Constantinople,[g] the
entrails of victims were consulted by the haruspices
on the fate of the army.[h] Yet during his eight months'
reign Jovian had time to declare himself not only a
Christian but an orthodox emperor.[i] He received
Athanasius, who had emerged from his concealment,
with distinguished favour, and repelled the Arian bishop
with scorn.[k] The character of the two brothers who
Valentinian succeeded to the empire, Valentinian and
and Valens. Valens, and their religious policy, were widely
at variance. Valentinian ascended the throne with
the fame of having rejected the favour of Julian and
the prospects of military distinction, for the sake of
his religion. He had withdrawn from the army rather
than offer even questionable adoration to standards
decorated with the symbols of idolatry. But Valentinian was content to respect those rights of conscience
which he had so courageously asserted.

The Emperor of the West maintained a calm and
A.D. 364. uninterrupted toleration, which incurred the
Toleration of
Valentinian. reproach of indifference from the Christian
party, but has received the respectful homage of the
Pagan historian.[m] The immunities and the privileges
of the Pagan priesthood were confirmed ;[n] the rites of

---

g La Bleterie, Vie de Jovien, p.
118.
  h Amm. Marcell. xxv. 6.
  i Julian died June 26, A.C. 363.
Jovian, Feb. 17, A.C. 364.
  k Athanasius ii. 622.
  m Ammianus Marcellinus, l. xxx. c. 9.

" Testes sunt leges a me in exordio
imperii mei datæ; quibus unicuique
quod animo imbibisset, colendi libera
facultas tributa est." Cod. Theod. l.
ix. tit. 16, l. 9.
  n Cod. Theod. xii. 1, 60, 75.

divination were permitted, if performed without malicious intent.[o] The prohibition of midnight sacrifices,
which seemed to be required by the public morals,
threatened to deprive the Greeks of their cherished
mysteries. Prætextatus, then proconsul of Achaia, the
head of the Pagan party, a man of high and unblemished character, represented to the Emperor that these
rites were necessary to the existence of the Greeks.
The law was relaxed in their favour, on the condition of
strict adherence to ancient usage. In Rome, the vestal
virgins maintained their sanctity ; the altar of Victory,
restored by Julian, preserved its place ; a military guard
protected the temples from insult, but a tolerant as
well as prudent provision, forbade the employment of
Christian soldiers on this service.[p] On the other hand,
Valentinian appears to have revoked some of Laws of
the lavish endowments conferred by Julian Valentinian.
on the Heathen temples. These estates were re-incor-
porated with the private treasure of the sovereign.[q] At
a later period of his reign, there must have been some
general prohibition of animal sacrifice ; the Pagan worship was restricted to the offering of incense to the
gods.[r] But, according to the expression of Libanius,
they dared not execute this law in Rome, so fatal would
it have been considered to the welfare of the empire.[s]

Valens, in the East, as Valentinian, in the West,
allowed perfect freedom to the public ritual Prosecutions
of Paganism. But both in the East, and in for magic.
the West, the persecution against magic and unlawful

---

o God. Theod. ix. 16, 9.
p Cod. Theod. xvi. 1, 1.
q Cod. Theod. x. 1, 8. The law
reads as if it were a more general and
indiscriminate confiscation.

r Lib. pro Templis, vii. p. 163, ed.
Reiske. This arose out of some recent
and peculiar circumstances.
s Liban. vol. ii. p. 180.

divination told with tremendous force against the Pagan cause. It was the more fatal, because it was not openly directed against the religion, but against practices denounced as criminal, and believed to be real, by the general sentiment of mankind, and prosecuted by that fierce animosity which is engendered by fear. Some compassion might be felt for innocent victims, supposed to be unjustly implicated in such charges; the practice of extorting evidence or confession by torture, might be revolting, to those especially who looked back with pride and with envy to the boasted immunity of all Roman citizens from such cruelties; but where strong suspicion of guilt prevailed, the public feeling would ratify the stern sentence of the law against such delinquents; the magician or the witch would pass to execution amid the universal abhorrence. The notorious connexion of any particular religious party with such dreaded and abominated proceedings, especially if proved by the conviction of a considerable majority of the condemned from their ranks, would tend to depress the religion itself. This sentiment was not altogether unjust. Paganism had, as it were, in its desperation, thrown itself upon the inextinguishable superstition of the human mind. The more the Pagans were depressed, the hope of regaining their lost superiority, the desire of vengeance, would induce them to seize on every method of awing or commanding the minds of their wavering votaries. Nor were those who condescended to these arts, or those who in many cases claimed the honours annexed to such fearful powers, only the bigoted priesthood, or mere itinerant traders in human credulity; the high philosophic party, which had gained such predominant influence during the reign of Julian, now wielded the terrors and incurred the penalties, of these dark and forbidden practices. It is impossible to read their writings without remarking a boastful display of intercourse with supernatural agents, which to the Christian would appear an illicit communion with malignant spirits. This was not indeed magic, but it was the groundwork of it. The theurgy, or mysterious dealings of the Platonic philosopher with the dæmons or still higher powers, was separated by a thin and imperceptible distinction from Goetic or unlawful enchantment. Divination, indeed, or the foreknowledge of futurity by different arts, was an essential part of the Greek and Roman religion. But divination had, in Greece at least, withdrawn from its public office. It had retired from the silenced oracles of Delphi or Dodona. The gods, rebuked according to the Christian, offended according to the Pagan, had withdrawn their presence. In Rome the Etruscan soothsayers, as part of the great national ceremonial, maintained their place, and to a late period preserved their influence over the public mind. But, in general, it was only in secret, and to its peculiar favourites, that the summoned or spontaneous deity revealed the secrets of futurity; it was by the dream, or the private omen, the sign in the heavens, vouchsafed only to the initiate; or the direct inspiration; or, if risked, it was by the secret, mysterious, usually the nocturnal rite, that the reluctant god was compelled to disclose the course of fate.

The persecutions of Valentinian in Rome were directed against magical ceremonies. The Pagans, who Cruelty of remembered the somewhat ostentatious lenity Valentinian. and patience of Julian on the public tribunal, might contrast the more than inexorable, the inquisitorial and sanguinary, justice of the Christian Valentinian, even in ordinary cases, with the benignant precepts of his religion. But justice with Valentinian, in all cases, more particularly in these persecutions, degenerated into savage tyranny. The Emperor kept two fierce bears by his own chamber, to which the miserable criminals were thrown in his presence, while the unrelenting Valentinian listened with ferocious delight to their groans. One of these animals, as a reward for his faithful service to the state, received his freedom, and was let loose into his native forest.[t]

Maximin, the representative of Valentinian at Rome.

Trials in Rome before Maximin. administered the laws with all the vindictive ferocity, but without the severe dignity, of his imperial master. Maximin was of an obscure and barbarian family, settled in Pannonia. He had attained the government of Corsica and Sardinia, and subsequently of Tuscany. He was promoted in Rome to the important office of superintendent of the markets of the city. During the illness of Olybius, the prefect of Rome, the supreme judicial authority had been delegated to Maximin. Maximin was himself rumoured to have dabbled in necromantic arts; and lived in constant terror of accusation till released by the death of his accomplice. This rumour may create a suspicion that Maximin was, at least at the time at which the accusation pointed, a Pagan. The Paganism of a large proportion of his victims is more evident. The first trial over which Maximin presided was a charge made by Chilon, vicar of the prefects, and his wife, Maximia, against three

---

[t] The Christians did not escape these legal murders, constantly perpetrated by the orders of Valentinian. In Milan the place where three obscure victims were buried was called ad Innocentes. When he had condemned the decurions of three towns to be put to death, in a remonstrance against their execution, it was stated that they would be worshipped as martyrs by the Christians. Amm. Marc. xxvii. 7.

obscure persons for attempting their lives by magical arts: of these, one was a soothsayer.[u] Cruel tortures extorted from these miserable men a wild string of charges at once against persons of the highest rank and of the basest degree. All had tampered with unlawful arts, and had mingled with them the crimes of murder, poisoning, and adultery. A general charge of magic hung over the whole city. Maximin poured these dark rumours into the greedy ear of Valentinian, and obtained the authority which he coveted, for making a strict inquisition into these offences, for exacting evidence by torture from men of every rank and station, and for condemning them to a barbarous and ignominious death. The crime of magic was declared of equal enormity with treason; the rights of Roman citizenship, and the special privileges granted by the imperial edicts, were suspended;[v] neither the person of senator or dignitary was sacred against the scourge or the rack. The powers of this extraordinary commission were exercised with the utmost latitude and most implacable severity. Anonymous accusations were received; Maximin was understood to have declared that no one should be esteemed innocent whom he chose to find guilty.

But the details of this persecution belong to our history only as far as they relate to religion. On general grounds, it may be inferred, that the chief brunt of this sanguinary persecution fell on the Pagan party. Magic— although, at that time, perhaps, the insatiate curiosity about the future, the indelible passion for supernatural excitement, and even more criminal designs, might betray

---

[u] Haruspex.
[v] Juris prisci justitia et divorum arbitria. Amm. Marc.

some few professed Christians into this direct treason
against their religion—was an offence which, in general,
would have been held in dread and abhorrence by the
members of the church. In the laws it is* invariably
denounced as a Pagan crime. The aristocracy of Rome
were the chief victims of Maximin's cruelty, and in
this class, till its final extinction, was the stronghold of
Paganism. It is not assuming too much influence for the
Connexion of these crimes with Paganism. Christianity of that age, to consider the immora-
lities and crimes, the adulteries and the poison-
ings, which were mingled up with these charges
of magic, as the vestiges of the old unpurified Roman
manners. The Christianity of that period ran into the
excess of monastic asceticism, for which the enthusiasm,
to judge from the works of St. Jerome, was at its height;
and this violation of nature had not yet produced its
remote but apparently inevitable consequence—disso-
luteness of morals. In almost every case recorded by
the historian may be traced indications of Pagan religious usages. A soothsayer, as it has appeared, was
involved in the first criminal charge. While his meaner
accomplices were beaten to death by straps loaded with
lead, the judge having bound himself by an oath that
they should neither die by fire nor steel, the soothsayer,
to whom he had made no such pledge, was burned alive.
The affair of Hymettius betrays the same connexion
with the ancient religion. Hymettius had been accused, seemingly without justice, of malversation in his
office of proconsul of Africa, in the supplies of corn to
the metropolis. A celebrated soothsayer (haruspex),
named Amantius, was charged with offering sacrifices,
by the command of Hymettius, with some unlawful or
treasonable design. Amantius resisted the torture with
unbroken courage; but among his papers was found a

writing of Hymettius, of which one part contained bitter
invectives against the avaricious and cruel Valentinian;
the other implored Amantius, by sacrifices, to induce
the gods to mitigate the anger of both the Emperors.
Amantius suffered capital punishment. A youth named
Lollianus, convicted of inconsiderately copying a book of
magical incantations and condemned to exile, had the
rashness to appeal to the Emperor, and suffered death.
Lollianus was the son of Lampadius, formerly prefect of
Rome,[x] and, for his zeal for the restoration of the
ancient buildings, and his vanity in causing his own name
to be inscribed on them, was called the Lichen. Lampadius, was probably a Pagan. The leader of that party,
Prætextatus, whose unimpeachable character maintained
the universal respect of all parties, was the head of a
deputation to the Emperor,[y] entreating him that the
punishment might be proportionate to the offences, and
claiming for the senatorial order their immemorial exemption from the unusual and illegal application of
torture. On the whole, this relentless and sanguinary
inquisition into the crime of magic, enveloping in one
dreadful proscription a large proportion of the higher
orders of Rome and of the West, even if not directly,
must, incidentally, have weakened the cause of Paganism; connected it in many minds with dark and
hateful practices; and altogether increased the deepening animosity against it.

In the East, the fate of Paganism was still more
adverse. There is strong ground for sup- In the East,
posing that the rebellion of Procopius was rebellion of
Procopius.
connected with the revival of Julian's party. A.D. 365.
It was assiduously rumoured abroad that Procopius had

---

[x] Tillemont thinks Lampadius to | are to me inconclusive.
have been a Christian; but his reasons | [y] Amm. Marc. xxvii. 1, &c.

been designated as his successor by the expiring Julian.
Procopius, before the soldiery, proclaimed himself the
relative and heir of Julian.[z] The astrologers had
predicted the elevation of Procopius to the greatest
height—of empire, as his partisans fondly hoped,—of
misery, as the ingenious seers expounded the meaning
of their oracle after his death.[a] The Pagan and
philosophic party were more directly and exclusively
implicated in the fatal event, which was disclosed to
the trembling Valens at Antioch, and brought as wide
and relentless desolation on the East as the
cruelty of Maximin on the West. It was
mingled up with treasonable designs against the throne
and the life of the Emperor. The magical ceremony
of divination, which was denounced before Valens, was
Pagan throughout all its dark and mysterious circumstances.[b] The tripod on which the conspirators performed their ill-omened rites was modelled after that at
Delphi; it was consecrated by magic songs and frequent
and daily ceremonies, according to the established
ritual. The house where the rite was held was purified
by incense: a kind of charger made of mixed metals
was placed upon the altar, around the rim of which
were letters at certain intervals. The officiating diviner
wore the habit of a Heathen priest, the linen garments,
sandals, and a fillet wreathed round his head, and held

A.D. 368.

---

[z] Amm. Marc. xxvi. 6.

[a] See Le Beau, iii. p. 250.

*Ὥστε αὐτὸν τῶν ἐπὶ ταῖς μεγίσ-
ταις ἀρχαῖς γνωρισθέντων, ἐν τῷ
μεγέθει τῆς συμφορᾶς γενέσθαι δια-
σημότερον. He was deceived by the
Genethliaci. Greg. Nyss. de Fato.

[b] Philostorgius describes it as a pre-
diction of the Gentile oracles. Τῶν

Ἑλληνικῶν χρηστηρίων. Lib. viii.
c. 15.

I cannot but suspect that the prohibition of sacrifice mentioned by Libanius, which seems contrary to the
general policy of the brothers, and
was but partially carried into execution, may have been connected with
these transactions.

9. sprig of an auspicious plant in his hand ; he chanted the accustomed hymn to Apollo, the god of prophecy. The divination was performed by a ring running round on a slender thread and pointing to certain letters, which formed an oracle in heroic verse, like those of Delphi. The fatal prophecy then pointed to the three first and the last letters of a name, like *Theo*dorus, as the fated successor of Valens.

Among the innumerable victims to the fears and the vengeance of Valens, whom the ordinary prisons were not capacious enough to contain, those who either were, or were suspected of having been entrusted with the fatal secret, were almost all the chiefs of the philosophic party. Hilarius of Phrygia, with whom are associated, by one historian, Patricius of Lydia, and Andronicus of Caria, all men of the most profound learning,[c] and skilled in divination, were those who had been consulted on that unpardoned and unpardonable offence, the enquiring the name of the successor to the reigning sovereign. They were, in fact, the conductors of the magic ceremony ; and in their confession betrayed the secret circumstances of the incantation. Some, among whom appears the name of Iamblichus, escaped by miracle from torture and execution.[d] Libanius himself (this may be observed as evidence how closely magic and philosophy were mingled up together in the popular opinion) had already escaped with difficulty two charges of unlawful practices ;[e] on this occasion, to the general surprise, he had the same good fortune : either the favour or the clemency of the Emperor, or some interest with the general accusers of his friends, exempted him from the common peril. Of those whose

---

² Zosimus, iv. 15.   ᵈ See Zonaras, 13, 2.   ᵉ Vit. i. 114.

sufferings are recorded, Pasiphilus resisted the extremity
of torture rather than give evidence against an innocent
man : that man was Eutropius, who held the rank of
proconsul of Asia. Simonides, though but a youth,
was one of the most austere disciples of philosophy.
He boldly admitted that he was cognisant of the
dangerous secret, but he kept it undivulged. Simonides
was judged worthy of a more barbarous death than
the rest ; he was condemned to be burned alive ; and
the martyr of philosophy calmly ascended the funeral
pile.

The fate of Maximus, since the death of Julian, had
been marked with strange vicissitude. With Priscus,
on the accession of Valentinian, he was summoned
before the imperial tribunal ; the blameless Priscus was
dismissed, but Maximus, who, according to his own
friends, had displayed, during the life of Julian, a pomp
and luxuriousness unseemly in a philosopher, was sent
back to Ephesus and amerced in a heavy fine, utterly
disproportioned to philosophic poverty. The fine was
mitigated, but, in its diminished amount, exacted by
cruel tortures. Maximus, in his agony, entreated his
wife to purchase poison to rid him of his miserable life.
The wife obeyed, but insisted on taking the first
draught :—she drank, expired, and Maximus—declined
to drink. He was so fortunate as to attract the notice
of Clearchus, proconsul of Asia ; he was released from
his bonds ; rose in wealth and influence, returned to
Constantinople ; and resumed his former state. The
fatal secret had been communicated to Maximus. He
had the wisdom, his partisans declared the prophetic
foresight, to discern the perilous consequences of the
treason. He predicted the speedy death of himself and
of all who were in possession of the secret. He added,

it is said, a more wonderful oracle; that the Emperor himself would soon perish by a strange death, and not even find burial. Maximus was apprehended and carried to Antioch. After a hasty trial, in which he confessed his knowledge of the oracle, but declared that he esteemed it unworthy of a philosopher to divulge a secret entrusted to him by his friends, he was taken back to Ephesus, and there executed with all the rest of his party who were implicated in the conspiracy. Festus, it is said, who presided over the execution, was haunted in after life by a vision of Maximus dragging him to judgement before the infernal deities.[f] Though a despiser of the gods, a Christian, Festus was compelled by his terrors to sacrifice to the Eumenides, the avengers of blood; and having so done, he fell down dead. So completely did the cause of the Pagan deities appear involved with that of the persecuted philosophers.

Nor was this persecution without considerable influence on the literature of Greece. So severe an inquisition was instituted into the possession of magical books, that, in order to justify their sanguinary proceedings, vast heaps of manuscripts relating to law and general literature were publicly burned, as if they contained unlawful matter. Many men of letters throughout the East in their terror destroyed their whole libraries, lest some innocent or unsuspected work should be seized by the ignorant or malicious informer, and bring them unknowingly within the relentless penalties of the law.[g] From this period, philosophy is

---

[f] Eunap. Vit. Maxim. Amm. Marc. xxix. 1.

[g] Amm. Marcell. xxix. 1. Inde factum est per Orientales provincias, ut omnes metu similium exurerent libraria omnia: tantus universos invaserat terror, xxix. 2. Compare Heyne, note on Zosimus.

almost extinct, and Paganism, in the East, drags on its
silent and inglorious existence, deprived of its literary
aristocracy, and opposing only the inert resistance of
habit to the triumphant energy of Christianity.

Arianism, under the influence of Valens, maintained
State of its ascendancy in the East. Throughout the
Christianity
in the East. whole of that division of the empire, the two
forms of Christianity still subsisted in irreconcileable
hostility. Almost every city had two prelates, each at
the head of his separate communion; the one, according
to the powers or the numbers of his party, assuming
the rank and title of the legitimate bishop, and looking
down, though with jealous animosity, on his factious
rival. During the life of Athanasius the see of
Alexandria remained faithful to the Trinitarian doctrines.
For a short period, indeed, the prelate was obliged to
retire, during what is called his fifth exile, to the tomb
of his father; but he was speedily welcomed back by
the acclamations of his followers, and the baffled
imperial authority acquiesced in his peaceful rule till
his decease. But at his death, five years afterwards,
were renewed the old scenes of discord and bloodshed.

A.D. 373. Palladius, the prefect of Egypt, received the
imperial commission to install the Arian
prelate, Lucius, on the throne of Alexandria. Palladius
was a Pagan, and the Catholic writers bitterly reproach
their rivals with this monstrous alliance. It was
rumoured that the Pagan population welcomed the
Arian prelate with hymns of gratulation as the friend of
the god Serapis, as the restorer of his worship.

In Constantinople, Valens had received baptism from
A.D. 370. Eudoxus, the aged Arian prelate of that see.
Sacerdotal influence once obtained over the
feeble mind of Valens, was likely to carry him to any

extreme; yet, on the other hand, he might be restrained and overawed by calm and dignified resistance. In general, therefore, he might yield himself up as an instrument to the passions, jealousies, and persecuting violence of his own party; while he might have recourse to violence to place Demophilus on the episcopal throne of Constantinople, he might be awed into a more tolerant and equitable tone by the eloquence and commanding character of Basil. It is unjust to load the memory of Valens with the most atrocious crime which has been charged upon him by the vindictive exaggeration of his triumphant religious adversaries. As a deputation of eighty Catholic ecclesiastics of Constantinople were returning from Nicomedia, the vessel was burned, the crew took to the boat, the ecclesiastics perished to a man. As no one escaped to tell the tale, and the crew, if accomplices, were not likely to accuse themselves, we may fairly doubt the assertion that orders had been secretly issued by Valens to perpetrate this wanton barbarity.

The memorable interview with Saint Basil, as it is related by the Catholic party, displays, if the weakness, certainly the patience and toleration, of the sovereign—if the uncompromising firmness of the prelate, some of that leaven of pride with which he is taunted by Jerome. Interview with Basil.

During his circuit through the Asiatic provinces, the Emperor approached the city of Cæsarea in Cappadocia. Modestus, the violent and unscrupulous favourite of Valens, was sent before, to persuade the bishop to submit to the religion of the Emperor. Basil was inflexible. "Know you not," said the offended officer, "that I have power to strip you of all your possessions, to banish you, to deprive you of life?" A.D. 371.

" He," answered Basil, " who possesses nothing can lose
nothing; all you can take from me is the wretched
garments I wear, and the few books, which are my only
wealth. As to exile, the earth is the Lord's; everywhere it will be my country, or rather my place of
pilgrimage. Death will be a mercy; it will but admit
me into life: long have I been dead to this world."
Modestus expressed his surprise at this unusual tone of
intrepid address. "You have never, then," replied the
prelate, "before conversed with a bishop?" Modestus
returned to his master. "Violence will be the only
course with this man, who is neither to be appalled by
menaces nor won by blandishments." But the Emperor
shrunk from such harsh measures. His humbler supplication confined itself to the admission of Arians into
the communion of Basil; but he implored in vain.
The Emperor mingled with the crowd of undistinguished
worshippers; but he was so impressed by the solemnity
of the Catholic service, the deep and full chanting of
the psalms, the silent adoration of the people, the order
and the majesty, as well as by the calm dignity of the
bishop and of his attendant clergy, which appeared
more like the serenity of angels than the busy scene of
mortal men, that, awe-struck and overpowered, he
scarcely ventured to approach to make his offering.
The clergy stood irresolute, whether they were to
receive it from the infectious hand of an Arian; Basil,
at length, while the trembling Emperor leaned for
support on an attendant priest, condescended to advance
and accept the oblation. But neither supplications, nor
bribes, nor threats, could induce the bishop to admit
the sovereign to the communion. In a personal interview, instead of convincing the bishop, Valens was so
overpowered by the eloquence of Basil, as to bestow an

endowment on the church for the use of the poor. A
scene of mingled intrigue and asserted miracle ensued.
The exile of Basil was determined, but the mind of
Valens was alarmed by the dangerous illness of his
son. The prayers of Basil were said to have restored
the youth to life; but a short time after, having been
baptized by Arian hands, he relapsed and died. Basil,
however, maintained his place and dignity to the end.[h]

But the fate of Valens drew on; it was followed by
the first permanent establishment of the bar- Effect of
barians within the frontiers of the Roman Christianity
in mitigating
empire. Christianity now began to assume a the evils of
barbarian
new and important function, that assimilation invasion.
and union between the conquerors and the conquered,
which prevented the total extinction of the Roman
civilisation, and the oppression of Europe by complete
and almost hopeless barbarism. However Christianity
might have disturbed the peace, and therefore, in some
degree, the stability of the empire by the religious factions which distracted the principal cities; however
that foreign principle of celibacy, which had now become
completely identified with it, by withdrawing so many
active and powerful minds into the cloister or the hermitage, may have diminished the civil energies, and
even have impaired the military forces of the empire,[i]
yet the enterprising and victorious religion amply repaid
those injuries by its influence in remodelling the new

---

[h] Greg. Naz. Orat. xx.; Greg.
Nyss. contra Eunom.; and the ecclesiastical historians in loco.

[i] Valens, perceiving the actual
operation of this unwarlike dedication
of so many able-bodied men to useless
inactivity, attempted to correct the
evil by law, and by the strong inter-

ference of the government. He invaded the monasteries and solitary
hermitages of Egypt, and swept the
monks by thousands into the ranks of
his army. But a reluctant Egyptian
monk would, in general, make but an
indifferent soldier.

state of society. If treacherous to the interests of
the Roman empire, it was true to those of mankind.
Throughout the whole process of the resettling of
Europe and the other provinces of the empire, by the
migratory tribes from the north and east, and the vast
system of colonisation and conquest, which introduced
one or more new races into every province, Christianity
was the one common bond, the harmonising principle,
which subdued to something like unity the adverse and
conflicting elements of society. Christianity, no doubt,
while. it discharged this lofty mission, could not but
undergo a great and desecrating change. It might
repress, but could not altogether subdue, the advance
of barbarism; it was constrained to accommodate itself
to the spirit of the times; while struggling to counteract barbarism, itself became barbarised. It lost at
once much of its purity and its gentleness ; it became
splendid and imaginative, warlike, and at length
chivalvous.

When a country in a comparatively high state of
civilisation is overrun by a foreign and martial horde,
in numbers too great to be absorbed by the local population, the conquerors usually establish themselves as a
kind of armed aristocracy, while the conquered are
depressed into a race of slaves. Where there is no connecting, no intermediate power, the two races co-exist
in stern and implacable hostility. The difference in
privilege, and often in the territorial possession of the
land, is increased and rendered more strongly marked
by the total want of communion in blood. Intermar-
riages, if not, as commonly, prohibited by law, are
almost entirely discountenanced by general opinion.
Such was, in fact, the ordinary process in the formation
of the society which arose out of the ruins of the Roman

empire. The conquerors became usually a military aristocracy; assumed the property in the conquered lands, or, at least, a considerable share in the landed estates, and laid the groundwork for that feudal system which was afterwards developed with more or less completeness in different countries of Europe.

One thing alone in some cases, tempered, during the process of conquest, the irreclaimable hostility; Influence of in all, after the final settlement, moulded up the clergy. together in some degree the adverse powers. Where, as in the Gothic invasion, it had made some previous impression on the invading race, Christianity was constantly present, silently mitigating the horrors of the war, and afterwards blending together, at least to a certain extent, the rival races. At all times, it became the connecting link, the intermediate power, which gave some community of interest, some similarity of feeling, to the master and the slave. They worshipped at least the same God, in the same church; and the care of the same clergy embraced both with something of an harmonising and equalising superintendence. The Christian clergy occupied a singular position in this new state of society. At the earlier period, they were, in general, Roman; later, though sometimes barbarian by birth, they were Roman in education. When the prostration of the conquered people was complete, there was still an order of people, not strictly belonging to either race, which maintained a commanding attitude, and possessed certain authority. The Christian bishop confronted the barbarian sovereign or took his rank among the leading nobles. During the invasion, the Christian clergy, though their possessions were ravaged in the indiscriminate warfare; though their persons were not always secure from insult, or from slavery;

yet, on the whole, retained, or very soon resumed, a
certain sanctity, and hastened, before long, to wind
their chains around the minds of the conquerors. Before
a new invasion, Christianity had, in general, mingled
the invaders with the invaded; till at length Europe,
instead of being a number of disconnected kingdoms,
hostile in race, in civil polity, in religion, was united in
a kind of federal Christian republic, on a principle of
unity, acknowledging the supremacy of the Pope.

The overweening authority claimed and exercised by
the clergy; their existence as a separate and
exclusive caste, at this particular period in the
progress of civilisation, became of the highest
utility. A religion without a powerful and separate
sacerdotal order, even, perhaps, if that order had not in
general been bound to celibacy and so prevented from
degenerating into an hereditary caste, would have been
absorbed and lost in the conflict and confusion of the
times. Religion, unless invested by general opinion in
high authority, and that authority asserted by an active
and incorporated class, would scarcely have struggled
through this complete disorganisation of all the existing
relations of society. The respect which the clergy
maintained was increased by their being almost the exclusive possessors of that learning which commands the
reverence even of barbarians, when not actually engaged
in war. A religion which rests on a written record,
however that record may be but rarely studied, and by
a few only of its professed interpreters, enforces general
respect to literary attainment. Though the tra-
ditional commentary may overload or supersede the
original book, the commentary itself is necessarily
committed to writing, and becomes another subject of
honoured and laborious study. All other kinds of litera-

ture, as far as they survive, gladly rank themselves under the protection of that which commands reve- Influence of rence for its religious authority. The cloister on literature, or the religious foundation thus became the place of refuge to all that remained of letters or of arts. Knowledge brooded in secret, though almost with unproductive, yet with life-sustaining warmth, over these secluded treasures. But it was not merely an inert and quiescent resistance which was thus offered to barbarism ; it was perpetually extending its encroachments, as well as maintaining its place. Perhaps the degree to which the Roman language modified the Teutonic tongues may be a fair example of the extent to which the Roman civilisation generally leavened the manners and the laws of the Northern nations.

The language of the conquered people lived in the religious ritual. Throughout the rapid suc- on language, cession of invaders who passed over Europe, seeking their final settlement, some in the remotest province of Africa, before the formation of other dialects, the Latin was kept alive as the language of Western Christianity. The clergy were its conservators, the Vulgate Bible and the offices of the church its depositaries, unviolated by any barbarous interruption, respected as the oracles of divine truth. But the constant repetition of this language in the ears of the mingled people can scarcely have been without influence in increasing and strengthening the Roman element in the common language, which gradually grew up from mutual intercourse, intermarriage, and all the other bonds of community which blended together the various races.

The old municipal institutions of the empire probably owed their permanence, in no inconsiderable degree, to

Christianity. It has been observed in what manner
on the mu-
nicipal in-
stitutions, the decurionate, the municipal authorities of
each town, through the extraordinary and
oppressive system of taxation, from guardians of the
liberties of the people, became mere passive and unwilling agents of the Government. Responsible for
payments which they could not exact, men of opulence,
men of humanity, shrunk from the public offices. From
objects of honourable ambition, these functions had
become burdens, loaded with unrepaid unpopularity,
assumed by compulsion, and exercised with reluctance.
The *defensors*, instituted by Valentinian and Valens,
however they might afford temporary protection and
relief to the lower orders, scarcely exercised any long
or lasting influence on the state of society. Yet the
municipal authorities at least retained the power of
administering the laws; and, as the law became more
and more impregnated with Christian sentiment, it
assumed something of a religious as well as civil
authority. The magistrate became, as it were, an ally
of the Christian bishop; the institutions had a sacred
character, besides that of their general utility. Whatever remained of commerce and of art subsisted chiefly
among the old Roman population of the cities, which
was already Christian; and hence, perhaps, the guilds
and fraternities of the trades, which may be traced up
to an early period, gradually assumed a sort of religious
bond of union. In all points, the Roman civilisation
and Christianity, when the latter had completely
pervaded the various orders of men, began to make
common cause; and during all the time that this
disorganisation of conquest and new settlement was
taking place in this groundwork of the Roman social
system, and the loose elements of society were severing

by gradual disunion, a new confederative principle arose in these smaller aggregations, as well as in the general population of the empire. The church became another centre of union. Men incorporated themselves together, not only, nor so much, as fellow-citizens, as fellow-Christians. They submitted to an authority co-ordinate with the civil power, and united as members of the same religious fraternity.

Christianity, to a certain degree, changed the general habits of men. For a time, at least, they _{on general} were less public, more private and domestic _{habits.} men. The tendency of Christianity, while the Christians composed a separate and distinct community, to withdraw men from public affairs ; their less frequent attendance on the courts of law, which were superseded by their own peculiar arbitration; their repugnance to the ordinary amusements, which soon, however, in the large cities, such as Antioch and Constantinople, wore off—all these principles of disunion ceased to operate when Christianity became the dominant, and at length the exclusive, religion. The Christian community became the people ; the shows, the pomps, the ceremonial of the religion, replaced the former seasons of periodical popular excitement ; the amusements,—which were not extirpated by the change of sentiment, some theatrical exhibitions, and the chariot race,—were crowded with Christian spectators ; Christians ascended the tribunals of law: not only the spirit and language of the New Testament, but likewise of the Old, entered both into the Roman jurisprudence and into the various barbarian codes, in which the Roman law was mingled with the old Teutonic usages. Thus Christianity was perpetually discharging the double office of conservator, with regard to the social institutions with which she had entered

into alliance; and of mediator between the conflicting
races which she was gathering together under her own
wing. Where the relation between the foreign conqueror
and the conquered inhabitant of the empire was that of
master and slave, the Roman ecclesiastic still maintained his independence, and speedily regained his
authority; he only admitted the barbarian into his order
on the condition that he became to a certain degree
Romanised; and there can be no doubt that the gentle
influence of Christian charity and humanity was not
without its effect in mitigating the lot, or at least in
consoling the misery of the change from independence
or superiority, to humiliation and servitude. Where the
two races mingled, as seems to have been the case in
some of the towns and cities, on more equal terms, by
strengthening the municipal institutions with something
of a religious character, and by its own powerful fede-
rative principle, it condensed them much more speedily
into one people, and assimilated their manners, habits,
and usages.

Christianity had early, as it were, prepared the way
for this amalgamation of the Goths with the
Roman empire. In their first inroads during
the reign of Gallienus, when the Goths ravaged
a large part of the Roman empire, they carried away
numbers of slaves, especially from Asia Minor and Cappadocia. Among these were many Christians. The
slaves subdued the conquerors; the gentle doctrines of
Christianity made their way to the hearts of the barbarous warriors. The families of the slaves continued
to supply the priesthood to this growing community.
A Gothic bishop,[k] with a Greek name, Theophilus,

Early Christianity among the Goths.

---

[k] Philostorgius, ii. 5.

attended at the council of Nicæa ; Ulphilas, at the time
of the invasion in the reign of Valens, conse- Ulphilas's
crated bishop of the Goths during an embassy version of the Scriptures.
to Constantinople, was of Cappadocian descent.[m] Among
the Goths, Christianity first assumed its new office, the
advancement of general civilisation, as well as of purer
religion. It is difficult to suppose that the art of writing
was altogether unknown to the Goths before the time of
Ulphilas. The language seems to have attained a high
degree of artificial perfection before it was employed by
that prelate in the translation of the Scriptures.[n] Still
the Mæso-Gothic alphabet, of which the Greek is by far
the principal element, was generally adopted by the
Goths.[o] It was universally disseminated ; it was per-
petuated, until the extinction or absorption of the Gothic
race in other tribes, by the translation of the sacred
writings. This was the work of Ulphilas, who, in his
version of the Scriptures,[p] is reported to have omitted,

---

[m] Socrates, ii. 41.

[n] The Gothic of Ulphilas is the link
between the East and Europe, the
transition state from the Sanscrit to
the modern Teutonic languages. It is
possible that the Goths, after their
migration from the East to the north
of Germany, may have lost the art of
writing, partly from the want of
materials. The German forests would
afford no substitute for the palm-leaves
of the East; they may have been
reduced to the barbarous runes of the
other Heathen tribes. Compare Bopp.,
Conjugations System.

[o] The Mæso-Gothic alphabet has
twenty-five letters, of which fifteen are
evidently Greek, eight Latin. The
two, th and hw, to which the Greek
and Latin have no corresponding
sound, are derived from some other
quarter. They are most likely ancient
characters. The th resembles closely
the runic letter, which expresses the
same sound. See St. Martin, note on
Le Beau, iii. p. 120.

[p] The greater part of the fragments
of Ulphilas's version of the Scriptures
now extant is contained in the celebrated Codex Argenteus, now at
Upsala. This splendid MS., written
in silver letters, on parchment of a
purple ground, contains almost the
whole four Gospels. Knittel, in 1762,
discovered five chapters of St. Paul's
Epistle to the Romans, in a Palimpsest
MS. at Wolfenbuttel. The best edition
of the whole of this is by J. Christ.

with a Christian, but vain, precaution, the books of
Kings, lest, being too congenial to the spirit of his
countrymen, they should inflame their warlike enthusiasm. Whether the genuine mildness of Christianity, or some patriotic reverence for the Roman
empire, from which he drew his descent, influenced
the pious bishop, the martial ardour of the Goths was
not the less fatal to the stability of the Roman empire.
Christianity did not even mitigate the violence of the
shock with which, for the first time, a whole host of
Northern barbarians was thrown upon the empire, never
again to be shaken off. This Gothic invasion, which
first established a Teutonic nation within the frontier
of the empire, was conducted with all the ferocity—
provoked indeed on the part of the Romans by
the basest treachery—of hostile races with no bond of
connection.[q]

The pacificatory effect of the general conversion of
the Goths to Christianity was impeded by the form
of faith which they embraced. The Gothic prelates,
Arianism of Ulphilas among the rest, who visited the court
the Goths. of Constantinople, found the Arian bishops in
possession of the chief authority; they were the recognised prelates of the empire. Whether their less

Zahn. Weissenfels, 1805. Since that
time, M. Mai has published, from
Milan Palimpsests, several other fragments, chiefly of the other Epistles of
St. Paul. Milan, 1819. St. Martin,
notes to Le Beau, iii. 100. On the
Gothic translation of the Scriptures.
See Socrat. iv. 33. Sozom. vi. 37.
Philostorgius, ii. 5. Compare Theodoret, v. 30-31. A complete edition
of the remains of the Bible of Ulphilas
was published by Dr. Gabelentz and
Dr. Löbe, 1838, but the most useful
edition is that of Massmann. Stutt-
gart, 1857.

[q] It is remarkable to find a Christian priest employed as an ambassador
between the Goths and the Romans,
and either the willing or undesigning
instrument of that stratagem of the
Gothic general which was so fatal to
Valens. Amm. Marc. xxxi. 12.

cultivated minds were unable to comprehend, or their
language to express, the fine and subtle distinctions of the
Trinitarian faith, or they were persuaded, as it was said,
by the Arian bishops that it was mere verbal dispute,
these doctrines were introduced among the Goths before
their passage of the Danube, or their settlement within
the empire. The whole nation received this form of
Christianity; from them it appears' to have spread
first embracing the other branch of the nation, the Os-
trogoths, among the Gepidæ, the Vandals, and the
Burgundians.[r] Among the barbaric conquerors was the
stronghold of Arianism; while it was gradually repudiated by the Romans both in the East and in the
West, it raised its head, and obtained a superiority
which it had never before attained, in Italy and Spain.
Whether more congenial to the simplicity of the barbaric mind, or in some respects cherished on one side
by the conqueror as a proud distinction, and more
cordially detested by the Roman population, as the
creed of their barbarous masters, Arianism appeared
almost to make common cause with the Teutonic invaders, and only fell with the Gothic monarchies in
Italy and in Spain. While Gratian and Valentinian
the Second espoused the cause of Trinitarianism in
the West (we shall hereafter resume the Christian
history of that division of the empire), by measures
which show that their sacerdotal advisers were men of
greater energy and decision than their civil ministers,

---

[r] " Sic quoque Visigothi a Valente
Imperatore Ariani potius quam Christiani effecti. De cætero tam Ostro-
gothis, quam Gepidis parentibus suis
per affectionis gratiam evangelizantes,
hujus perfidiæ culturam edocentes
omnem ubique linguæ hujus nationem
ad culturam hujus sectæ incitavere."
Jornand. c. 25.

Arianism subsisted almost as a foreign and barbarous
form of Christianity.[s]

---

[s] The Bible of Ulphilas was the Bible of all the Gothic races. Massmann, Die Unruhe wie die Nothdrang des äusseren Lebens, der inwohnenden Thatreich des einheitlichen nordischen Menschengeschlechtes, das die Welt erneuen und befreien sollte, führte dasselbe von den friedlichen Ufern der Ostsee über die Donau vielmals bis vor die Thore des Constantinopel, zu den blutbetränkten Gestaden des Schwarzsee wie des Mittelmeeres, bis tief nach Asien, in und über Italien und Frankreich bis nach Spanien und Africa, *überall aber trugen sie Ulfilas Bibel mit sich.*"—Einleitung X. Massmann observes, p. xxiii., that there is no trace of Arianism in the surviving remains of the Gothic translation of the New Testament. The Gothic of Philip ii. 6. has been misunderstood. The Arian Goths professed to adhere to the words of Scripture, they avoided the Homoiousios and Homoousios ; they called themselves Catholics, and were singularly tolerant of the orthodox tenets and of the Catholic clergy. Compare Latin Christianity, Book III. c. 2.

CHAPTER VIII.

Theodosius. Abolition of Paganism.

THE fate of Valens summoned to the empire a sovereign
not merely qualified to infuse a conservative vigour into
the civil and military administration of the empire, but
to compress into one uniform system the religion of
the Roman world. It was necessary that Christianity
should acquire a complete predominance, and that
it should be consolidated into one vigorous and harmonious system. The relegation, as it were, of Arianism
among the Goths and other barbarous tribes, though it
might thereby gain a temporary accession of strength,
did not permanently impede the final triumph of
Trinitarianism. While the imperial power was thus
lending its strongest aid for the complete triumph and
concentration of Christianity, from the peculiar character
of the mind of Theodosius, the sacerdotal order, on the
strength and unity of which was to rest the permanent
influence of Christianity during the approaching centuries
of darkness, assumed new energy. A religious emperor,
under certain circumstances, might have been the most
dangerous adversary of the priestly power; he would
have asserted with vigour, which could not at that time
be resisted, the supremacy of the civil authority. But
the weaknesses, the vices, of the great Theodosius,
bowed him down before the aspiring priesthood, who,
in asserting and advancing their own authority, were
asserting the cause of humanity. The passionate tyrant,

at the feet of the Christian prelate, deploring the rash
resentment which had condemned a whole city to massacre; the prelate exacting the severest penance for
the outrage on justice and on humanity, stand in extraordinary contrast with the older Cæsars, themselves
the priesthood, without remonstrance or without humiliation, glutting their lusts or their resentment with
the misery and blood of their subjects.

The accession of Theodosius was hailed with universal
enthusiasm throughout the empire. The pres-
A.D. 379. sing fears of barbaric invasion on every frontier
silenced for a time the jealousies of Christian and Pagan,
of Arian and Trinitarian. On the shore of each of the
great rivers which bounded the empire, appeared a host
of menacing invaders. The Persians, the Armenians,
the Iberians, were prepared to pass the Euphrates or the
eastern frontier; the Danube had already afforded a
passage to the Goths; behind them were the Huns
in still more formidable and multiplying swarms; the
Franks and the rest of the German nations were crowding to the Rhine. Paganism, as well as Christianity,
hastened to pay its grateful homage to the deliverer
of the empire; the eloquent Themistius addressed
Theodosius in the name of the imperial city; Libanius
ventured to call on the Christian Emperor to revenge
the death of Julian, that crime for which the gods were
exacting just retribution. Pagan poetry awoke from its
long silence; the glory of Theodosius and his family
inspired its last noble effort in the verse of Claudian.

Theodosius was a Spaniard. In that province Christianity had probably found less resistance from the
feeble provincial Paganism; nor was there, as in Gaul,
an old national religion which lingered in the minds of
the native population. Christianity was early and per-

manently established in the Peninsula. To Theodosius, who was but slightly tinged with the love of letters or the tastes of a more liberal education, the colossal temples of the East, or the more graceful and harmonious fabrics of Europe, would probably create no feeling but that of aversion from the shrines of idolatry. His Christianity was pure from any of the old Pagan associations; unsoftened, it may, perhaps, be said, by any feeling for art, and unawed by any reverence for the ancient religion of Rome: he was a soldier, a provincial, an hereditary Christian of a simple and unquestioning faith; and he added to all this the consciousness of consummate vigour and ability, and a choleric and vehement temperament.

Spain, throughout the Trinitarian controversy, perhaps from the commanding influence of Hosius, had firmly adhered to the Athanasian doctrines. The Manichean tenets, for which Priscillian and his followers suffered (the first heretics condemned to death for their opinions), were but recently introduced into the province.

Thus, by character and education, deeply impressed with Christianity, and that of a severe and uncompromising orthodoxy, Theodosius undertook the sacred obligation of extirpating Paganism, and of restoring to Christianity its severe and inviolable unity. Without tracing the succession of events throughout his reign, we may survey the Christian Emperor in his acts; first, as commencing, if not completing, the forcible extermination of Paganism; secondly, as confirming Christianity, and extending the authority of the sacerdotal order; and thirdly, as establishing the uniform orthodoxy of the Western Roman Church.

The laws of Theodosius against the Pagan sacrifices grew insensibly more and more severe. The inspection

of the entrails of victims, and magic rites, were made
capital offences. In A.D. 391, issued an edict
prohibiting sacrifices, and even the entering into
the temples. In the same year, a rescript was addressed
to the court and prefect of Egypt, fining the governors
of provinces who should enter a temple fifteen pounds
of gold, and giving a kind of authority to the subordi-
dinate officers to prevent their superiors from committing
such offences. The same year, all unlawful sacrifices
are prohibited by night or day, within or without the
temples. In 392, all immolation is prohibited under
the penalty of death, and all other acts of idolatry
under forfeiture of the house or land in which the
offence shall have been committed.[a]

The Pagan temples, left standing in all their majesty,
but desecrated, deserted, overgrown, would have been
the most splendid monument to the triumph of Christianity. If, with the disdain of conscious strength, she
had allowed them to remain without victim, without
priest, without worshipper, but uninjured and only exposed to natural decay from time and neglect, posterity
would not merely have been grateful for the preservation of such stupendous and graceful models of art, but
would have been strongly impressed with admiration of
her magnanimity. But such magnanimity was neither
to be expected from the age or the state of the religion.
The Christians believed in the existence of the Heathen
deities, with, perhaps, more undoubting faith than the
Heathens themselves. The dæmons who inhabited the
temples were spirits of malignant and pernicious power,
which it was no less the interest than the duty of
the Christian to expel from their proud and attractive

---

[a] Cod. Theod. xvi. 10, 7, 11, 12.

mansions.[b] The temples were the strongholds of the vigilant and active adversaries of Christian truth and Christian purity, of the enemies of God and man. The idols, it is true, were but wood and stone, but the beings they represented were real; they hovered, perhaps, in the air; they were still present in the consecrated spot, though rebuked and controlled by the mightier name of Christ, yet able to surprise the careless Christian in his hour of supineness or negligent adherence to his faith or his duty. When zeal inflamed the Christian populace to aggression upon any of these ancient and time-hallowed buildings, no doubt some latent awe lingered within; something of the suspense of doubtful warfare watched the issue of the strife. However they might have worked themselves up to the conviction that their ancient gods were but of this inferior and hostile nature, they would still be haunted by some apprehensions, lest they should not be secure of the protection of Christ, or of the angels and saints in the new tutelar hierarchy of Heaven. The old deities might not have been so completely rebuked and controlled as not to retain some power of injuring their rebellious votaries. It was at last, even to the faithful, a conflict between two unequal supernatural agencies; unequal indeed, particularly where the faith of the Christian was fervent and sincere, yet dependent for its event on the confidence of that faith which sometimes trembled at its own insufficiency, and feared lest it should be abandoned by the divine support in the moment of strife.

Throughout the East and West, the monks were the chief actors in this holy warfare. They are constantly

---

b " Dii enim Gentium dæmonia, ut Scriptura docet." Ambros. Epist. Resp. at Symmach. in init.

spoken of by the Heathen writers in terms of the bitterest reproach and contempt. The most particular
accounts of their proceedings relate to the East. Their
desultory attacks were chiefly confined to the country,
where the numberless shrines, images, and smaller
temples were at the same time less protected, and
more dear to the feelings of the people. In the towns,
the larger fanes, if less guarded by the reverence of
their worshippers, were under the protection of the
municipal police.[c] Christianity was long almost exclusively the religion of the towns; and the term Paganism
(notwithstanding the difficulties which embarrass this
explanation) appears to owe its origin to this general
distinction. The agricultural population, liable to frequent vicissitudes, trembled to offend the gods, on whom
depended the plenty or the failure of the harvest.
Habits are more intimately enwoven with the whole
being in the regular labours of husbandry, than in the
more various and changeable occupations of the city.
The whole Heathen ritual was bound up with the course
of agriculture: this was the oldest part both of the
Grecian and Italian worship, and had experienced less
change from the spirit of the times. In every field, in
every garden, stood a deity; shrines and lesser temples
were erected in every grove, by every fountain. The
drought, the mildew, the murrain, the locusts,—whatever was destructive to the harvest or to the herd, was
in the power of these capricious deities.[d] Even when
converted to Christianity, the peasant trembled at the
consequences of his own apostasy; and it is probable,

---

[c] Τολμᾶται μὲν οὖν κἄν ταῖς
πόλεσι, τὸ πολὺ δὲ εν τοῖς ἀγροῖς.
Liban. pro Templis.

[d] Καὶ τοῖς γεωργοῦσιν ἐν αὐτοῖς

αἱ ἐλπίδες, ὅσαι περὶ τε ἀνδρῶν καὶ
γυναικῶν, καὶ τέκνων καὶ βοῶν, καὶ
τῆς σπειρομένης γῆς καὶ πεφυτευ-
μένης. Liban pro Templ.

that until the whole of this race of tutelary deities had been gradually replaced by what we must call the inferior divinities of Paganising Christianity, saints, martyrs, and angels, Christianity was not extensively or permanently established in the rural districts.[e]

During the reign of Constantine, that first sign of a decaying religion, the alienation of the pro- Alienation of the reve- perty attached to its maintenance, began to nue of the be discerned. Some estates belonging to the temples. temples were seized by the first Christian Emperor, and appropriated to the building of Constantinople. The favourites of his successor, as we have seen, were enriched by the donation of other sacred estates, and even of the temples themselves.[f] Julian restored the greater part of these prodigal gifts; but they were once more resumed under Valentinian, and the estates escheated to the imperial revenue. Soon after the accession of Theodosius, the Pagans, particularly in the East, saw the storm gathering in the horizon. The monks, with perfect impunity, traversed the rural districts, demolishing all the unprotected edifices. In vain did the Pagans appeal to the episcopal authority; the bishops declined to repress the over-active, perhaps, but pious zeal of their adherents. Already much destruction had taken place among the smaller rural shrines; the temples in Antioch, of Fortune, of Jove, of Athene, of Dionysus, were still standing; but the demolition of one stately temple, either at Edessa or

---

[e] This difference prevailed equally in the West. Fleury gives an account of the martyrdom of three missionaries by the rural population of a district in the Tyrol, who resented the abolition of their deities and their religious ceremonies. Hist. Eccles. v. 64.

[f] They were bestowed, according to Libanius, with no more respect than a horse, a slave, a dog, or a golden cup. The position of the *slave* between the horse and the dog, as cheap gifts, is curious enough. Liban. Op. v. ii. p. 185.

Palmyra, and this under the pretext of the imperial
authority, had awakened all the fears of the Pagans.
Oration of Libanius addressed an elaborate oration to the
Libanius. Emperor, "For the Temples."[g] Like Christianity under the Antonines, Paganism is now making its
apology for its public worship. Paganism is reduced to
still lower humiliation; one of its modest arguments
against the destruction of its temples, is an appeal to
the taste and love of splendour, in favour of buildings at
least as ornamental to the cities as the imperial palaces.[h]
The orator even stoops to suggest that, if alienated from
religious uses, and let for profane purposes; they might
be a productive source of revenue. But the eloquence
and arguments of Libanius were wasted on deaf and
Syrian   unheeding ears. The war against the temples
temples
destroyed.   commenced in Syria; but it was not conducted
with complete success. In many cities the inhabitants
rose in defence of their sacred buildings, and, with the
Persian on the frontier, a religious war might have
endangered the allegiance of these provinces. The
splendid temples, of which the ruins have recently been
discovered, at Petra,[i] were defended by the zealous
worshippers; and in those, as well as at Areopolis and
Raphia, in Palestine, the Pagan ceremonial continued
without disturbance. In Gaza, the temple of the tutelar
deity, Marnas, the lord of men, was closed; but the
Christians did not venture to violate it. The form of
some of the Syrian edifices allowed their transformation
into Christian churches; they were enclosed, and made

---

[g] This oration was probably not
delivered in the presence of Theodosius.

[h] Liban. pro Templis, p. 190.

[i] Laborde's Journey. In most of

these buildings Roman architecture of
the age of the Antonines is manifest,
raised in general on the enormous sub-
structions of much earlier ages.

to admit sufficient light for the services of the church.
A temple at Damascus, and another at Heliopolis or
Baalbec,[k] were consecrated to the Christian worship.
Marcellus of Apamea was the martyr in this holy warfare. He had signalised himself by the destruction of
the temples in his own city, particularly that of Jupiter,
whose solid foundations defied the artificers and soldiery
employed in the work of demolition, and required the
aid of miracle to undermine them. But, on an expedition into the district of Apamea, called the Aulon,
the rude inhabitants rose in defence of their sacred
edifice, seized Marcellus, and burned him alive. The
synod of the province refused to revenge on his barbarous enemies a death so happy for Marcellus and so
glorious for his family.[m]

The work of demolition was not long content with
these less famous edifices, these outworks of Paganism;
it aspired to attack its strongest citadels, and, by the
public destruction of one of the most celebrated temples
in the world, to announce that Polytheism had for ever
lost its hold upon the minds of men.[n]

It was considered the highest praise of the magnificent
temple in Edessa, of which the roof was of re- Temple of
markable construction, and which contained in Serapis at
Alexandria.
its secret sanctuary certain very celebrated statues of
wrought iron, and whose fall had excited the indignant

---

[k] If this (as indeed is not likely)
was the vast Temple of the Sun, the
work of successive ages, it is probable
that a Christian church was enclosed
in some part of its precincts. The
sanctuary was usually taken for this
purpose.

[m] Sozomen, vii. 15. Theodoret,
v. 21.

[n] Compare throughout, Histoire
de la Destruction du Paganisme dans
l'Empire d'Orient, par Etienne
Chastel, Paris, 1850. This work,
crowned by the Institute, is perhaps
not quite of so high order as that of
M. Beugnot on the destruction of
Paganism in the West, but is still a
very valuable book.

F 2

eloquence of Libanius, to compare it to the Serapion
in Alexandria. The Serapion, at that time, appeared
secure in the superstition, which connected its inviolable
sanctity, and the honour of its god,[o] with the rise and
fall of the Nile, with the fertility and existence of
Egypt, and, as Egypt was the granary of the East, the
existence of Constantinople. The Pagans had little
apprehension that the Serapion itself, before many
years, would be levelled to the ground.

The temple of Serapis, next to that of Jupiter in the
A.D. 389,   Capitol, was the proudest monument of Pagan
or 391.   religious architecture.[p] Like the more celebrated structures of the East, and that of Jerusalem in
its glory, it comprehended within its precincts a vast
mass of buildings, of which the temple itself formed the
centre. It was built on an artificial hill, in the old
quarter of the city, called Rhacotis. The ascent to it
was by a hundred steps. All the substructure was
vaulted over ; and in these dark chambers, which
communicated with each other, were supposed to be
carried on the most fearful, and, to the Christian,
abominable mysteries. All around the spacious level
platform were the habitations of the priests, and of the
ascetics dedicated to the worship of the god. Within
these outworks of this city rather than temple, was a
square, surrounded on all sides with a magnificent
portico. In the centre arose the temple, on pillars of
enormous magnitude and beautiful proportion. The
work either of Alexander himself or of the first Ptolemy,
aspired to unite the colossal grandeur of Egyptian with

---

[o] Libanius expresses himself to this effect.

[p] " Post Capitolium, quo se venerabilis Roma in æternum attollit, nihil
orbis terrarum ambitiosius cernat."
Ammian. Marcell. xxii. 16.

the fine harmony of Grecian art. The god himself was the especial object of adoration throughout the whole country, and throughout every part of the empire into which the Egyptian worship had penetrated,[q] but more particularly in Alexandria; and the wise policy of the Ptolemies had blended together, under this pliant and all-embracing religion, the different races of their subjects. Egyptian and Greek met as wor- Worship of Serapis. shippers of Serapis. The Serapis of Egypt was said to have been worshipped for ages at Sinope; he was transported from that city with great pomp and splendour, to be reincorporated, as it were, and reidentified with his ancient prototype. While the Egyptians worshipped in Serapis the great vivific principle of the universe, the fecundating Nile, holding the Nilometer for his sceptre, the Lord of Amen-ti, the President of the regions beyond the grave,—the Greeks, at the same time, recognised the blended attributes of their Dionysus, Helios, Æsculapius, and Hades.[r]

The colossal statue of Serapis embodied these various attributes.[s] It filled the sanctuary: its out- Statue of Serapis. stretched and all-embracing arms touched the walls; the right the one, the left the other. It was said to have been the work of Sesostris; it was made of all the metals fused together, gold, silver, copper, iron, lead, and tin; it was inlaid with all kinds of precious stones; the whole was polished, and appeared of an

---

[q] In Egypt alone he had forty-two temples; innumerable others in every part of the Roman empire. Aristid. Orat. in Canop.

[r] This appears to me the most natural interpretation of the celebrated passage in Tacitus. Compare

De Guigniaut, Le Dieu Serapis et son Origine, originally written as a note for Bournouf's Translation of Tacitus.

[s] The statue is described by Macrobius, Saturn. i. 20.; Clemens Alexandrin. Exhortat. ad Gent. i. p. 42.; Rufinus, E. H. xii. 23.

azure colour. The measure or bushel, the emblem of productiveness or plenty, crowned its head. By its side stood the symbolic three-headed animal, one the fore-part of a lion, one of a dog, one of a wolf. In this the Greeks saw the type of their poetic Cerberus.[t] The serpent, the symbol of eternity, wound round the whole, and returned resting its head on the hand of the god.

The more completely the adoration of Serapis had absorbed the worship of the whole Egyptian pantheon, the more eagerly Christianity desired to triumph over the representative of Polytheism. However, in the time of Hadrian, the philosophic party may have endeavoured to blend and harmonise the two faiths,[u] they stood now in their old direct and irreconcileable opposition. The suppression of the internal feuds be-tween the opposite parties in Alexandria, enabled Christianity to direct all its concentered force against The first attacks on Paganism. Theophilus, the archbishop, was Paganism. a man of boldness and activity, eager to seize and skilful to avail himself of every opportunity to inflame the popular mind against the Heathens. A priest of Serapis was accused and convicted of practising those licentious designs against the virtue of the female worshippers, so frequently attributed to the priesthood of the Eastern religions. The noblest and most beauti-ful women were persuaded to submit to the embraces of the god, whose place, under the favourable darkness caused by the sudden extinction of the lamps in the temple, was filled by the priest. These inauspicious

---

[t] According to the interpretation of Macrobius, the three heads represented the past, the present, and the future; the rapacious wolf the past, the central lion the intermediate present, the fawning dog the hopeful future.

[u] See the Letter of Hadrian, Vol. II. p. 108.

rumours prepared the inevitable collision. A neglected temple of Osiris or Dionysus had been granted by Constantius to the Arians of Alexandria. Theophilus obtained from the Emperor a grant of the vacant site for a new church, to accommodate the increasing numbers of the Catholic Christians. On digging the foundation, there were discovered many of the obscene symbols, used in the Bacchic or Osirian mysteries. Theophilus, with more regard to the success of his cause than to decency, exposed these ludicrous or disgusting objects, in the public market place, to the contempt and abhorrence of the people. The Pagans, indignant at this treatment of their sacred symbols, and maddened by the scorn and ridicule of the Christians, took up arms. The streets ran with blood; and many Christians who fell in this tumultuous fray received the honours of martyrdom. A philosopher, named Olympus, placed himself at the head of the Pagan party. Olympus had foreseen and predicted the ruin of the external worship of Polytheism. He had endeavoured to implant a profound feeling in the hearts of the Pagans which might survive the destruction of their ordinary objects of worship. " The statues of the gods are but perishable and material images ; the eternal intelligences, which dwelt within them, have withdrawn to the heavens." [x] Yet Olympus hoped, and at first with his impassioned eloquence succeeded, in rousing his Pagan compatriots to a bold defiance of the public authorities in support of their religion. Faction and rivalry supplied what was wanting to faith ; and it appeared that Paganism would likewise boast its army

Olympus the philosopher.

---

[x] Ὕλην φθαρτὴν καὶ ἰνδάλματα λέγων εἶναι τὰ ἀγάλματα, καὶ διὰ τοῦτο ἀφανισμὸν ὑπομένειν· δυνάμεις δέ τινας ἐνοικῆσαι αὐτοῖς, καὶ εἰς οὐρανὸν ἀποπτῆναι. Sozom. H. E. vii. 15.

of martyrs,—martyrs, not indeed through patient submission to the persecutor, but in heroic despair perishing
with their gods.

The Pagans at first were the aggressors; they sallied
War in the from their fortress, the Serapion, seized the
city.   unhappy Christians whom they met, forced
them to sacrifice on their altar, or slew them upon it, or
threw them into the deep trench defiled with the blood
and offal of sacrifice. In vain Evagrius, the prefect of
Egypt, and Romanus, the commander of the troops,
appeared before the gates of the Temple, remonstrated
with the garrison, who appeared at the windows, against
their barbarities, and menaced them with the just
vengeance of the law. They were obliged to withdraw,
baffled and disregarded, and to await the orders of the
Emperor. Olympus exhorted his followers to the
height of religious heroism. "Having made a glorious
sacrifice of our enemies, let us immolate ourselves and
perish with our gods." But before the rescript arrived,
Flight of Olympus had disappeared: he had stolen out
Olympus. of the Temple, and embarked for Italy. The
Christian writers do honour to his sagacity or to his
prophetic powers, at the expense of his courage and
fidelity to his party. In the dead of night, when all
was slumbering around, and all the gates closed, he had
heard the Christian Alleluia pealing from a single
voice through the silent Temple. He acknowledged
the sign, or the omen, and anticipated the unfavourable
sentence of the Emperor, the fate of his faction and of
his gods.

The eastern Pagans, it should seem, were little
acquainted with the real character of Theodosius.
When the rescript arrived they laid down their arms,
and assembled in peaceful array before the Temple, as

if they expected the sentence of the Emperor in their own favour.[y] The officer began; the first Rescript of Theodosius. words of the rescript plainly intimated the abhorrence of Theodosius against idolatry. Cries of triumph from the Christians interrupted the proceedings; the panic-stricken Pagans, abandoning their temple and their god, silently dispersed; they sought out the most secret places of refuge; they fled their country. Two of the celebrated pontiffs, one of Amoun, one of " the Ape," retired to Constantinople, where the one, Ammonius, taught in a school, and continued to deplore the fall of Paganism; Helladius, the other, was known to boast the part he had taken in the sedition of Alexandria, in which, with his own hand, he had slain nine Christians.[z]

The imperial rescript at once went beyond and fell short of the fears of the Pagans. It disdained to exact vengeance for the blood of the Christian martyrs, who had been so happy as to lay down their lives for their Redeemer; but it commanded the destruction of the idolatrous temples; it confiscated all the ornaments, and ordered the statues to be melted or broken up for the benefit of the poor.

Theophilus hastened in his triumphant zeal to execute the ordinance of the Emperor. Marching, with the prefect at the head of the military, the invaders

---

[y] If the oration of Libanius, exhorting the Emperor to revenge the death of Julian, was really presented to Theodosius, it betrays something of the same ignorance. He seems to think his arguments not unlikely to meet with success; at all events, he appears not to have the least notion that Theodosius would not respect the memory of the apostate.

[z] Socrat. Eccl. Hist. v. 16. Helladius is mentioned in a law of Theodosius the younger, as a celebrated grammarian elevated to certain honours. This law is, however, dated 425; at least five and thirty years after this transaction.

ascended the steps to the temple of Serapis.   They
The temple   surveyed the vacant chambers of the priests
assailed.   and the ascetics; they paused to pillage the
library;[a] they entered the deserted sanctuary; they
stood in the presence of the god.   The sight of this
            colossal image, for centuries an object of
The statue. worship, struck awe to the hearts of the
Christians themselves.   They stood silent, inactive,
trembling.   The archbishop alone maintained his
courage: he commanded a soldier to proceed to the
assault.   The soldier struck the statue with his hatchet
on the knee.   The blow echoed through the breathless
hall, but no sound or sign of divine vengeance ensued;
the roof of the Temple fell not to crush the sacrilegious
assailant nor did the pavement heave and quake
beneath his feet.   The emboldened soldier climbed up to
the head and struck it off; it rolled upon the ground.
Serapis gave no sign of life, but a large colony of rats,
disturbed in their peaceful abode, ran about on all sides.
The passions of the multitude are always in extremes.
From breathless awe they passed at once to ungovernable mirth.   The work of destruction went on amid
peals of laughter, coarse jests, and shouts of acclamation; and as the fragments of the huge body of Serapis
were dragged through the streets, the Pagans, with
that revulsion of feeling common to the superstitious
populace, joined in the insult and mockery against
their unresisting and self-abandoned god.[b]

---

[a] "Nos vidimus armaria librorum;
quibus direptis, exinanita ea a nostris
hominibus, nostris temporibus memo-
rant." Oros. vi. 15.

[b] They were said to have discovered
several of the tricks by which the
priests of Serapis imposed on the
credulity of their worshippers.   An
aperture of the wall was so contrived,
that the light of the sun, at a particular time, fell on the face of Serapis.
The sun was then thought to visit
Serapis; and at the moment of their
meeting, the flashing light threw a

The solid walls and deep foundations of the Temple offered more unsurmountable resistance to the baffled zeal of the Christians ; the work of demolition proceeded but slowly with the massive architecture ;[c] and some time after a church was erected in the precincts, to look down upon the ruins of idolatry, which still frowned in desolate grandeur upon their conquerors.[d]

Yet the Christians, even after their complete triumph, were not without some lingering terrors; the Pagans not without hopes that a fearful vengeance would be exacted from the land for this sacrilegious extirpation of their ancient deities. Serapis was either the Nile, or the deity who presided over the periodical inundations of the river. The Nilometer, which measured the rise of the waters, was kept in the Temple. Would the indignant river refuse its fertilising moisture ; keep sullenly within its banks, and leave the ungrateful land blasted with perpetual drought and barrenness? As the time of the inundation approached, all Egypt was in a state of trembling suspense. Long beyond the accustomed day the waters remained at their usual level; there was no sign of overflowing. The people began to murmur ; the murmurs swelled into indignant remonstrances ; the usual rites and sacrifices were demanded from the reluctant prefect, who despatched a

---

smile on the lips of the Deity. There is another story of a magnet on the roof, which, as in the fable about Mohammed's coffin, raised either a small statue of the Deity, or the sun in a car with four horses, to the roof, and there held it suspended. A Christian withdrew the magnet, the car fell, and was dashed to pieces on the pavement.

[c] Compare Eunap. Vit. Ædesii, p. 44. edit. Boissonade.

[d] The Christians rejoiced in discovering the cross in various parts of the building ; they were inclined to suppose it miraculous or prophetic of their triumph. But, in fact, the crux ansata is a common hieroglyphic, a symbol of life.

hasty messenger to the Emperor for instructions.
There was every appearance of a general insurrection;
the Pagans triumphed in their turn; but before the
answer of the Emperor arrived, which replied, in
uncompromising faith, "that if the inundation of the
river could only be obtained by magic and impious
rites, let it remain dry ; the fertility of Egypt must not
be purchased by an act of infidelity to God "[e]—suddenly, the waters began to swell, an inundation more
full and extensive than usual spread over the land, and
the versatile Pagans had now no course but to join
again with the Christians in mockeries against the
impotence of their gods.

But Christianity was not content with the demolition
of the Serapion; its predominance throughout Egypt
may be estimated by the bitter complaint of the Pagan
writer : "Whoever wore a black dress (the monks are
designated by this description) was invested in tyrannical power ; philosophy and piety to the gods were
compelled to retire into secret places, and to dwell in
contented poverty and dignified meanness of appearance.
The temples were turned into tombs for the adoration
of the bones of the basest and most depraved of men
who had suffered the penalty of the law, whom they
made their gods."[f] Such was the light in which the
martyr-worship of the Christians appeared to the
Pagans.

The demolition of the Serapion was a penalty inflicted

---

[e] Improbable as it may seem, that
such an answer should be given by a
statesman like Theodosius, yet it is
strongly characteristic of the times.
The Emperor neither denies the power
of the malignant dæmons worshipped
by the idolaters, nor the efficacy of
enchantments, to obtain their favour,
and to force from them the retarded
overflow of the river.

[f] Eunap. Vit. Ædesii, loc. cit.

on the Pagans of Alexandria for their sedition and
sanguinary violence; but the example was too encouraging, the hope of impunity under the present
government too confident, not to spread through other
cities of Egypt. It moved on to Canopus, where the
principle of humidity was worshipped in the form of a
vase, with a human head. Theophilus, who considered
Canopus within his diocese, marched at the head of his
triumphant party, demolished the temples, abolished
the rites, which were distinguished for their dissolute
licence, and established monasteries in the place.
Canopus, from a city of revel and debauchery, became
a city of monks.[g]

The persecution extended throughout Egypt; but
the vast buildings which even now subsist, the successive
works of the Pharaohs, the Ptolemies, and the Roman
Emperors, having triumphed alike over time, Christianity, and Mahommedanism, show either some reverent
reluctance to deprive the country of its most magnificent
ornaments, or the inefficiency of the instruments which
they employed in the work of devastation. For once it
was less easy for men to destroy than to preserve; the
power of demolition was rebuked before the strength
and solidity of these erections of primeval art.

The war, as we have seen, raged with the same
partial and imperfect success in Syria; with less,
probably, in Asia Minor; least of all in Greece.
The demolition was nowhere general or systematic.
Wherever monastic Christianity was completely predominant, there emulous zeal excited the laity to these

---

g The Christians laughed at Canopus being called "the conqueror of
the gods." The origin of this name
was, that the principle of fire, the god
of the Chaldeans, had been extinguished by the water within the
statue of Canopus, the principle of
humidity.

aggressions on Paganism. But in Greece the noblest
buildings of antiquity, at Olympia, Eleusis, Athens,[h]
show in their decay the slower process of neglect and
time, of accident and the gradual encroachment of later
barbarism, rather than the iconoclastic destructiveness
of early religious zeal.[i]

In the West, the task of St. Martin of Tours, the
great extirpator of idolatry in Gaul, was comparatively
easy; and his achievements by no means so much to be
lamented as those of the destroyers of the purer models
of architecture in the East. The life of this saint by
Sulpicius, in which the comparatively polished and classical style singularly contrasts with the strange and legendary incidents which it relates, describes St. Martin as
making regular campaigns into all the region, destroying, wherever he could, the shrines and temples of the
Heathen, and replacing them by churches and monasteries. So completely was his excited imagination full
of his work, that he declared that Satan often assumed
the visible form of Jove, of Mercury, of Venus, or of
Minerva, to divert him, no doubt, from his holy design,
and to protect their trembling fanes.[k]

---

[h] The Parthenon, it is well known, was entire, till towards the close of the sixteenth century. Its roof was destroyed during the siege by the Venetians. See Spon. and Wheler's Travels.

[i] The council of Illiberis refused the honours of martyrdom to those who were killed while breaking idols Can. lx.

The invasion of the Goths (Eunapius accuses the black monks of having betrayed Thermopylæ to them) carried devastation into Greece and Peloponnesus. These newly-converted barbarians had no feeling for art. They burned Corinth, Amyclæ, Lacedæmon, Olympia, (from that time the games ceased) with all their glorious temples and noble statues. Zosimus asserts that Minerva preserved Athens. Her apparition appalled Alaric. But Ceres did not protect Eleusis. There was a frightful massacre of the Hierophants among the ruins of the temple. (Eunapius, in loc., Los. v. 6.) Compare Chastel, p. 215. Falmerayer, Geschichte der Morea, 136.

[k] Sulpic. Sever. Vit. B. Martini, p. 469.

But the power and the majesty of Paganism were still concentred at Rome; the deities of the ancient faith found their last refuge in the capital of the empire. Paganism at Rome. To the stranger, Rome still offered the appearance of a Pagan city: it contained one hundred and fifty-two temples, and one hundred and eighty smaller chapels or shrines, still sacred to their tutelary God, and used for public worship.[m] Christianity had neither ventured to usurp those few buildings which might be converted to her use, still less had she the power to destroy them. The religious edifices were under the protection of the prefect of the city, and the prefect was usually a Pagan; at all events, he would not permit any breach of the public peace, or violation of public property. Above all still towered the Capitol, in its unassailed and awful majesty, with its fifty temples or shrines, bearing the most sacred names in the religious and civil annals of Rome, those of Jove, of Mars, of Janus, of Romulus, of Cæsar, of Victory. Some years after the accession of Theodosius to the Eastern empire, the sacrifices were still performed as national rites at the public cost; the pontiffs made their offerings in the name of the whole human race. The Pagan orator ventures to assert that the Emperor dared not to endanger the safety of the empire by their abolition.[n] The Emperor still bore the title and insignia of the supreme Pontiff; the consuls before they entered upon their functions, ascended the Capitol;

---

[m] See the Descriptiones Urbis, which bear the names of Publicus Victor, and Sextus Rufus Festus. These works could not have been written before or long after the reign of Valentinian. Compare Beugnot, Histoire de la Destruction du Paganisme en Occident.

M. Beugnot has made out, on more or less satisfactory evidence, a list of the deities still worshipped in Italy. t. i. l. viii. c. 9. St. Augustin, when young, was present at the rites of Cybele, about A. D. 374.

[n] Liban. pro Templis.

the religious processions passed along the crowded
streets; and the people thronged to the festivals and
theatres, which still formed part of the Pagan worship.
But the edifice had begun to tremble to its foundations. The Emperor had ceased to reside at
Rome; the mind of Theodosius, as afterwards
that of Gratian, and that of the younger
Valentinian, was free from those early inculcated and daily renewed impressions of the majesty
of the ancient Paganism which still enthralled the
minds of the Roman aristocracy. Of that aristocracy,
the flower and the pride was Vettius Agorius Prætextatus.[o] In him the wisdom of Pagan philosophy
blended with the serious piety of Pagan religion: he
lived to witness the commencement of the last fatal
change which he had no power to avert; he died, and
his death was deplored as a public calamity, in time to
escape the final extinction, or rather degradation, of
Paganism. Only eight years before the fatal
accession of Gratian, and the year of his own
death, he had publicly consecrated twelve statues in
the Capitol, with all becoming splendour, to the Dii
curantes, the great guardian deities of Rome.[p] It was
not only the ancient religion of Rome which still
maintained some part of its dignity, all the other
religions of the empire, which still publicly celebrated
their rites, and retained their temples in the metropolis,
concentred all their honours on Prætextatus, and took
refuge, as it were, under the protection of his blameless

Margin notes: Gratian, Emperor, A.D. 367. Valentinian II., A.D. 375. Theodosius, A.D. 379. / A.D. 376.

---

[o] See on Prætextatus, Macrob.
Saturn. i. 2. Symmachi Epistolæ, i.
40. 43. 45., ii. 7. 34. 36. 53. 59.
Hieronym. Epistolæ, xxiii.

[p] This appears from an inscription
recently discovered (A. D. 1835), and
published in the Bulletino of the
Archæological Society of Rome. Compare Bunsen, Roms Beschreibung,
vol. iii. p. 9.

and venerable name.   His titles in an extant inscription
announce him as having attained, besides the countless
honours of Roman civil and religious dignity, the
highest rank in the Eleusinian, Phrygian, Syrian, and
Mithriac mysteries.[q] His wife boasted the same religious
titles; she was the priestess of the same mysteries, with
the addition of some peculiar to the female sex.[r]   She
celebrated the funeral, even the apotheosis, of
her noble husband with the utmost pomp: he   A.D. 384.
was the last Pagan, probably, who received the honours
of deification.[s]   All Rome crowded, in sorrow and
profound reverence, to the ceremony.   In the language
of the vehement Jerome there is a singular mixture of
enforced respect and of aversion; he describes (to
moralise at the awful change) and contrasts with his
funeral the former triumphant ascent of the Capitol by
Prætextatus amid the acclamations of the whole city;
he admits the popularity of his life, but condemns him,
without remorse, to eternal misery.[t]

---

[q] Augur, Pontifex Vestæ, Pontifex
Solis, Quindecemvir, Curialis Herculis,
sacratus Libero et Eleusiniis, Hiero-
phanta, Neocorus, Tauroboliatus,
Pater Patrum. Gruter, p. 1102.
No. 2.

[r] Sacratæ apud Eleusinam Deo
Baccho, Cereri, et Coræ, apud Lernam,
Deo Libero, et Cereri, et Coræ, sacratæ
apud Æginam Deabus; Taurobolitæ,
Isiacæ, Hierophantiæ Deæ Hecatæ,
sacratæ Deæ Cereris. Gruter, 309.

[s] Read the two beautiful poems,
one a short one addressed by Vettius
Agorius Prætextatus to his wife
Aconia Fabia Paulina, the other,
longer, by Paulina to her husband.
I subjoin some lines from that of

Paulina,—

Tu me, marite, disciplinarum bono
Puram ac pudicam sorte mortis eximens,
In templa ducis ac famulam divis dicas.
Te teste cunctis imbuor mysteriis,
Tu Dindymenes Atteosque antistitem
Teletis honoras taureis consors pius,
Hecates ministram trina secreta edoces,
Cererisque Graiæ tu sacris dignari paras.
Te propter omnes me beatam, me piam
Celebrant, quod ipse me bonam disseminas
Totum per orbem. Ignota noscor omnibus,
Nam te marito cui placere non queam.
Exempla de me Romulæ matres petunt.
Sobolemque pulchram, si tuæ similis, putant
Optant probantque nunc viri nunc fœminæ.

Apud Meyer Anthologia Latina, ii. 128.

[t] O quanta rerum mutatio! Ille
quem ante paucos dies dignitatum
omnium culmina præcedebant, qui
quasi de subjectis hostibus triumpha-
ret, Capitolinas ascendit arces; quem

Up to the accession of Gratian, the Christian Emperor
A.D. 367. had assúmed, as a matter of course, the supre-
Augustus. macy over the religion, as well as the state, of
A.D. 378. Rome. He had been formally arrayed in the
robes of the sovereign Pontiff. For the first few years of
Gratian re- his reign, Gratian maintained the inaggressive
fuses the
pontificate. policy of his father Valentinian.[u] But the masculine mind of Ambrose obtained, and indeed had deserved by his public services, the supremacy over the
feeble youth; and the influence of Ambrose began to reveal
itself in a succession of acts, which plainly showed that
the fate of Paganism drew near. When Gratian was in
Gaul, the senate of Rome remembered that he had not
been officially arrayed in the dignity of the supreme
Pontificate. A solemn deputation from Rome attended
A.D. 382. to perform the customary ceremonial. The idolatrous honour was disdainfully rejected. The
event was heard in Rome with consternation; it was
the first overt act of separation between the religioùs
and the civil power of the empire.[x] The next hostile
measure was still more unexpected. Notwithstanding
the manifest authority assumed by Christianity, and by
one of the Christian prelates, best qualified by his own
determined character to wield at his will the weak
and irresolute Gratian; notwithstanding the long ill-
suppressed murmurs, and now bold and authoritative

---

plausu quodam et tripudio populus
Romanus excepit, ad cujus intentum
urbs universa commota est,—nunc
desolatus et nudus, . . . non in lacteo
cœli palatio ut uxor mentitur infelix,
sed in sordentibus tenebris contine-
tur. Hieronym. Epist. xxiii. vol. i.
p. 135.

[u] M. Beugnot considers that Gratian

was tolerant of Paganism from his
accession, A.D. 367 to 382. He was
sixteen when he ascended the throne,
and became the first Augustus on the
death of Valens, A.D. 378.

[x] Zosimus, iv. 36. The date of
this transaction is conjectural. The
opinion of La Bastie, Mém. des Inscrip.
xv. 141, is followed.

remonstrances, against all toleration, and all connivance at Heathen idolatry, it might have been thought that any other victim would have been chosen from the synod of gods; that all other statues would have been thrown prostrate, all other worship proscribed, before that of Victory. Constantius, though he had calmly surveyed the other monuments of Roman superstition, admired their majesty, and read the inscriptions over the porticos of the temples, had nevertheless given orders for the removal of this statue, and this alone,—its removal, it may be suspected not without some superstitious reverence—to the rival capital.[y] Victory had been restored by Julian to the Senate-house at Rome, where she had so long presided over the counsels of the conquering republic and of the empire. She had maintained her place during the reign of Valentinian. The decree that the statue of Victory was to be ignominiously dragged from its pedestal in the Senate-house, that the altar was to be removed, and the act of public worship, with which the Senate had for centuries of uninterrupted prosperity and glory commenced and hallowed its proceedings, discontinued, fell, like a thunderbolt, among the partisans of the ancient worship. Surprise yielded to indignation. By the advice of Prætextatus, a solemn deputation was sent to remonstrate with the Emperor. The Christian party in the Senate were strong enough to forward, through the Bishop Damasus, a counter-petition, declaring their resolution to abstain from attendance in the Senate so long as it should be defiled

Statue of Victory.

A.D. 382.

---

[y] Constantius (the whole account of this transaction is vague and uncircumstantial), acting in the spirit of his father, who collected a great number of the best statues to adorn the new capital, perhaps intended to transplant Victory to Constantinople.

by an idolatrous ceremonial. Gratian coldly dismissed the deputation though headed by the eloquent Symmachus, as not representing the unanimous sentiments of the Senate.[z]

This first open aggression on the Paganism of Rome was followed by a law which confiscated at once all the property of the temples, and swept away the privileges and immunities of the priesthood. The fate of the Vestal virgins excited the strongest commiseration. They now passed unhonoured through the streets. The violence done to this institution, coeval with Rome itself, was aggravated by the bitter mockery of the Christians at the importance attached to those few and rare instances of chastity by the Pagans. They scoffed at the small number of the sacred virgins; at the occasional delinquencies (for it is singular that almost the last act of Pagan pontifical authority was the capital punishment of an unchaste Vestal); the privilege they possessed, and sometimes claimed, of marriage after a certain period of service, when, according to the severer Christians, such unholy desires should have been long extinct.[a] If the state is to reward virginity (said the vehement Ambrose), the claims of the Christians would exhaust the treasury.

By this confiscation of the sacerdotal property, which

---

[a] It is very singular that, even at this very time, severe laws seem to have been necessary to punish apostates from Christianity. In 381, Theodosius deprived such persons of the right of bequeathing their property. Similar laws were passed in 383 and 391, against those qui ex Christianis Pagani facti sunt; qui ad Paganos ritus cultusque migrarunt; qui venerabili religione neglectâ ad aras et templa transierint. Cod. Theodos. xvi. 7. 1, 2, 4, 5.

[a] Prudentius, though he wrote later, expresses this sentiment :—

Nubit anus veterana, sacro perfuncta labore,
Desertisque focis, quibus est famulata juventus,
Transfert invitas ad fulcra jugalia rugas,
Discit et in gelido nova nupta calescere lecto.

Adv. Symm. lib. ii.

had hitherto maintained the priesthood in opulence, the temples and the sacrificial rites in splendour, the Pagan hierarchy became stipendiaries of the state, the immediate step to their total dissolution. The public funds were still charged with a certain expenditure[b] for the maintenance of the public ceremonies. This was not abrogated till after Theodosius had again united the whole empire under his conquering sway, and shared with Christianity the subjugated world.

In the interval, Heathenism made perhaps more than one desperate though feeble struggle for the ascendancy. Gratian was murdered in the year 383. Valentinian II. succeeded to the sole empire of the West. The celebrated Symmachus became prefect of Rome. Symmachus commanded the respect, and even deserved the common attachment, of all his countrymen; he ventured (a rare example in those days) to interfere between the tyranny of the sovereign and the menaced welfare of the people. An uncorrupt magistrate, he deprecated the increasing burdens of unnecessary taxes which weighed down the people; he dared to suggest that the eager petitions for office should be at once rejected and the worthiest chosen out of the unpretending multitude. Symmachus inseparably connected, in his Pagan patriotism, the ancient religion with the welfare of Rome. He mourned in bitter humiliation over the acts of Gratian; the removal of the statue of Victory; the abrogation of the immunities of the Pagan priesthood. He hoped to obtain from the justice, or perhaps the fears, of the young Valentinian, that which had been refused by Gratian. The senate met under his authority; a petition was drawn up and presented in the

---

b This was called the Annona.

name of that venerable body to the Emperor. On this composition Symmachus lavished all his eloquence. His oration is written with vigour, with dignity, with elegance. It is in this respect, perhaps, superior to the Apology of reply of Saint Ambrose.[c] But in the feeble Symmachus. and apologetic tone, we perceive at once, that it is the artful defence of an almost hopeless cause; it is cautious to timidity; dexterous; elaborately conciliatory; moderate from fear of offending rather than from tranquil dignity. Ambrose, on the other hand, writes with all the fervid and careless energy of one confident in his cause and who knows that he is appealing to an audience already pledged by their own feelings to his side; he has not to obviate objections, to reconcile difficulties, to sue or to propitiate; his contemptuous and criminating language has only to inflame zeal, to quicken resentment and scorn. He is flowing down on the full tide of human passion, and his impulse but accelerates and strengthens the rapid current.

The personification of Rome, in the address of Symmachus, is a bold stroke of artificial rhetoric, but it is artificial; and Rome pleads instead of commanding; intreats for indulgence, rather than menaces for neglect. "Most excellent Princes, Fathers of your country, respect my years, and permit me still to practise the religion of my ancestors, in which I have grown old. Grant me but the liberty of living according to my

---

[c] Heyne has expressed himself strongly on the superiority of Symmachus. Argumentorum delectu, vi, pondere, aculeis, non minùs admirabilis illa est quam prudentiâ, cautione, ac verecundiâ; quam tanto magis sentias si verbosam et inanem, interdum calumniosam et veteratoriam declamationem Ambrosii compares. Censur. ingen. et mor. Q. A. Symmachi, in Heyne Opuscul.

The relative position of the parties influenced, no doubt, the style, and will, perhaps, the judgement, of posterity on the merit, of the compositions.

ancient usage. This religion has subdued the world to
my dominion ; these rites repelled Hannibal from my
walls, the Gauls from the Capitol. Have I lived thus
long, to be rebuked in my old age for my religion? It
is too late ; it would be discreditable to amend in my
old age. I intreat but peace for the gods of Rome, the
tutelary gods of our country." Rome condescends to
that plea, which a prosperous religion neither uses nor
admits, but to which a falling faith always clings with
desperate energy. " Heaven is above us all ; we cannot
all follow the same path ; there are many ways by
which we arrive at the great secret. But we presume
not to contend, we are humble suppliants!" The end
of the third century had witnessed the persecutions of
Diocletian ; the fourth had not elapsed when this is the
language of Paganism, uttered in her strongest hold by
the most earnest and eloquent of her partisans. Symmachus remonstrates against the miserable economy of
saving the maintenance of the vestal virgins; the disgrace of enriching the imperial treasury by such gains ;
he protests against the confiscation of all legacies be-
queathed to them by the piety of individuals. "Slaves
may inherit; the Vestal virgins alone, and the ministers
of religion, are precluded from this common privilege."
The orator concludes by appealing to the deified father
of the Emperor, who looks down with sorrow from the
starry citadel, to see that toleration violated which he
had maintained with willing justice.

But Ambrose was at hand to confront the eloquent
Pagan, and to prohibit the fatal concession. Reply of
Far different is the tone and manner of the Ambrose.
Archbishop of Milan. He asserts, in plain terms, the
unquestionable obligation of a Christian sovereign to
permit no part of the public revenue to be devoted

to the maintenance of idolatry. Their Roman ancestors
were to be treated with reverence; but in a question of
religion they were to consider God alone. He who
advises such grants as those demanded by the suppliants
is guilty of sacrifice. Gradually he rises to still more
imperious language, and unveils all the terrors of the
sacerdotal authority. "The Emperor who shall be guilty
of such concessions will find that the bishops will neither
endure nor connive at his sin. If he enters a church,
he will find no priest, or one who will defy his authority.
The church will indignantly reject the gifts of him who
has shared them with Gentile temples. The altar dis-
dains the offerings of him who has made offerings to
images. It is written, 'Man cannot serve two masters.'"
Ambrose, emboldened, as it were, by his success, ventures in his second letter to treat the venerable and
holy traditions of Roman glory with contempt. "How
long did Hannibal insult the gods of Rome? It was
the goose and not the deity that saved the Capitol.
Did Jupiter speak in the goose? Where were the gods
in all the defeats, some of them but recent, of the Pagan
emperors? Was not the altar of Victory then standing?"
He insults the number, the weaknesses, the marriages
of the vestal virgins. "If the same munificence were
shown to Christian virgins, the beggared treasury would
be exhausted by the claims." "Are not the baths, the
porticos, the streets, still crowded with images? Must
they still keep their place in the great council of the
empire? You compel to worship if you restore the altar.
And who is this deity? Victory is a gift, and not a
power; she depends on the courage of the legions, not
on the influence of the religion,—a mighty deity, who is
bestowed by the numbers of an army, or the doubtful
issue of a battle!"

Foiled in argument, Paganism vainly grasped at other arms, which she had as little power to wield. On the murder of Valentinian, Arbogastes the Gaul, whose authority over the troops was without competitor, hesitated to assume the purple which had never yet been polluted by a barbarian. He placed Eugenius, a rhetorician, on the throne. The elevation of Eugenius was an act of military violence; but the Pagans of the West hailed his accession with the most eager joy and the fondest hopes. The Christian writers denounce the apostasy of Eugenius, not without justice if Eugenius ever professed Christianity.[d] Throughout Italy the temples were re-opened; the smoke of sacrifice ascended from all quarters; the entrails of victims were explored for the signs of victory. The frontiers were guarded by all the terrors of the old religion. The statue of Jupiter the Thunderer, sanctified by magical rites of the most awful significance, and placed on the fortifications amid the Julian Alps, looked defiance on the advance of the Christian Emperor. The images of the gods were unrolled on the banners, and Hercules was borne in triumph at the head of the army. Ambrose fled from Milan, for the soldiery boasted that they would stable their horses in the churches and press the clergy to fill their legions.

In Rome, Eugenius consented, without reluctance, to the restoration of the altar of Victory, but he had the wisdom to foresee the danger which his cause might incur by the resumption of the temple estates, many of which had been granted away: he yielded with undis-

Murder of Valentinian, A.D. 392.

Accession of Eugenius.

---

[d] Compare the letter of Ambrose to Eugenius. He addresses Eugenius apparently as a Christian, but one in the hands of more powerful Pagans.

guised unwillingness to the irresistible importunities of
Arbogastes and Flavianus.

While this reaction was taking place in the West,
perhaps irritated by the intelligence of this formidable
conspiracy of Paganism, with the usurpation of the
throne, Theodosius published in the East the last and
most peremptory of those edicts which, gradually rising
in the sternness of their language, proclaimed the
ancient worship a treasonable and capital crime. In
its minute and searching phrases this statute seemed
eagerly to pursue Paganism to its most secret and
private lurking-places. Thenceforth no man of any
station, rank, or dignity, in any place in any city, was
to offer an innocent victim in sacrifice; the more harmless worship of the household gods, which lingered,
probably, more deeply in the hearts of the Pagans than
any other part of their system, was equally forbidden,
not merely the smoke of victims, but even lamps,
incense, and garlands. To sacrifice, or to consult the
entrails of victims, was constituted high treason, and
thereby a capital offence, although with no treasonable
intention of calculating the days of the Emperor. It
was a crime of the same magnitude to infringe the laws
of nature, to pry into the secrets of futurity, or to
inquire concerning the death of any one. Whoever
permitted any Heathen rite—hanging a tree with chap-
lets, or raising an altar of turf—forfeited the estate on
which the offence was committed. Any house profaned
with the smoke of incense was confiscated to the imperial exchequer. Whoever violated this prohibition,
A.D. 394. and offered sacrifice either in a public temple,
or on the estate of another, was amerced in
a fine of twenty-five pounds of gold (a thousand pounds
of our money); and whoever connived at the offence

was liable to the same fine: the magistrate who neglected to enforce it, to a still heavier penalty.[e] This
law, stern and intolerant as it was, spoke, no doubt, the
dominant sentiment of the Christian world;[f] but its
repetition by the successors of Theodosius, and the
employment of avowed Pagans in many of the high
offices of the state and army, may permit us charitably
to doubt whether the exchequer was much enriched by
the forfeitures, or the sword of the executioner deeply
stained with the blood of conscientious Pagans. Polytheism boasted no martyrs; and we may still hope that
if called upon to carry its own decrees into effect, its
native clemency—though, unhappily, Christian bigotry
had already tasted of heretical blood—would have revolted from the sanguinary deed,[g] and yet have seen
the inconsistency of these acts (which it justified in
theory, on the authority of the Old Testament) with
the vital principles of the Gospel.

The victory of Theodosius in the West dissipated
at once the vain hopes of Paganism ; the pageant van-
ished away. Rome heard of the triumph, perhaps
witnessed the presence of the great conqueror, who,
in the East, had already countenanced the most destructive attacks against the temples of the gods. The
Christian poet describes a solemn debate of the Senate

---

[e] Cod. Theod. xvi. 10. 12.

[f] Gibbon has quoted from Le Clerc
a fearful sentence of St. Augustine,
addressed to the Donatists. "Quis
nostrûm, quis vestrûm non laudat
leges ab Imperatoribus datas adversus
sacrificia Paganorum? Et certè longè
ibi pœna severior constituta est ; illius
quippe impietatis capitale supplicium
est." Epist. xciii. But passages
amiably inconsistent with this fierce
tone might be quoted on the milder
side. Compare Editor's note on
Gibbon, v. p. 114.

[g] Quis eorum comprehensus est in
sacrificio (cum his legibus ista pro-
hiberentur) et non negavit. Augustin,
in Psalm cxx., quoted by Gibbon from
Lardner.

on the claims of Jupiter and of Christ to the adoration
of the Roman people.   According to his account,
Jupiter was outvoted by a large number of suffrages;
the decision was followed by a general desertion of their
ancestral deities by the obsequious minority; the old
hereditary names, the Annii and the Probi, the Anicii
and Olybii, the Paulini and Bassi, the popular Gracchi,
six hundred families, at once passed over to the Christian cause.[h] The Pagan historian to a certain degree
confirms the fact of the deliberate discussion, but differs
as to the result.   The senate, he states, firmly, but
respectfully, adhered to their ancient deities.[i] But the
last argument of the Pagan advocates was fatal to their
cause.   Theodosius refused any longer to assign funds
from the public revenue to maintain the charge of the
idolatrous worship.   The senate remonstrated, that if
they ceased to be supported at the national cost, they
would cease to be national rites.   This argument was
more likely to confirm than to shake the determination
of the Christian Emperor.   From this time the temples
were deserted; the priests and priestesses, deprived of
their maintenance, were scattered abroad.   The public
temples still stood, nor was it forbidden to worship
within their walls, without sacrifice; the private, and
family, or Gentile, deities, still preserved their influence.

Theodosius died the year after the defeat of Eugenius.
We pursue to its close the history of Western Paganism, which was buried at last in the ruins
of the empire.   Gratian had dissevered the
supremacy of the national religion from the imperial

A.D. 395.

---

[h] Sexcentas numerare domos de sanguine
    prisco
Nobilium licet, ad Christi signacula versas,
Turpis ab idoli vasto emersisse profundo.
        Prud. ad Symmach.

Prudentius has probably amplified
some considerable desertion of the
wavering and dubious believers.
   [i] Zosim. Hist. iv. 59.

dignity ; he had confiscated the property of the temples ; Theodosius had refused to defray the expense of public sacrifices from the public funds. Still, however, the outward form of Paganism remained. Some priesthoods were still handed down in regular descent; the rites of various deities, even of Mythra and Cybele, were celebrated without sacrifice, or with sacrifice furtively performed ; the corporation of the haruspices was not abolished. There still likewise remained a special provision for certain festivals and public amusements.[k] The expense of the sacred banquets and of the games was defrayed by the state: an early law of Honorius respected the common enjoyments of the people.[m]

The. poem of Prudentius [n] acknowledges that the enactments of Theodosius had been far from altogether successful ;[o] his bold assertion of the universal adoption of Christianity by the whole senate is in some degree contradicted by his admission that the old pestilence of idolatry had again broken out in Rome.[p] It implies that the restoration of the statue of Victory had again been urged, and by the indefatigable Symmachus, on the sons of Theodosius.[q] The poem was written after

---

[k] It was called the vectigal templorum.

[m] Communis populi lætitia.

[n] The poem of Prudentius is by no means a recapitulation of the arguments of St. Ambrose ; it is original, and in some parts very vigorous.

[o] Inclitus ergo parens patriæ, moderator et orbis,
Nil egit prohibendo, vagas ne pristinus error
Crederet esse Deûm nigrante sub aere formas.

[p] Sed quoniam renovata lues turbare 'salutem
Tentat Romulidum.

[q] Armorum dominos, vernantes flore juventæ,
Inter castra patris genitos, sub imagine avitâ
Eductos, exempla domi congesta tenentes,
Orator catus instigat.   .   .
Si vobis vel parta, viri, victoria cordi est,
Vel parienda dehinc, templum Dea virgo sacratum
Obtineat, vobis regnantibus.

The orator catus, is Symmachus ; the parta victoria, that of Pollentia ; the Dea virgo, Victory.

the battle of Pollentia, as it triumphantly appeals to the glories of that day against the argument that Rome was indebted for the victories of former times to her ancient gods. It closes with an earnest admonition to the son of Theodosius to fulfil the task which was designedly left to him by the piety of his father,[r] to suppress at once the Vestal virgins, and, above all, the gladiatorial shows, which they were accustomed to countenance by their presence.

A.D. 403.

In the year 408 came forth the edict which aimed at the direct and complete abolition of Paganism throughout the Western empire. The whole of this reserved provision for festivals was swept away; it was devoted to the more useful purpose, the pay of the loyal soldiery.[s] The same edict proceeded to actual violence, to invade and take possession of the sanctuaries of religion. All images were to be thrown down; the edifices, now useless and deserted, to be occupied by the imperial officers, and appropriated to useful purposes.[t] The government, wavering between demolition and desecration, devised this plan for the preservation of these great ornaments of the cities, which thus, taken under the protection of the magistracy as public property, were secured from the destructive zeal of the more fanatical Christians. All sacrilegious rites, festivals, and ceremonies were prohibited. The bishops of the towns were invested with

Law of Honorius.

---

[r] Quam tibi supplendam Deus, et genitoris amica
Servavit pietas: solus ne præmia tantæ
Virtutis caperet "partem, tibi, nate reservo,"
Dixit, et integrum decus intactumque reliquit. Sub fin.

[s] Expensis devotissimorum militum profutura.

[t] Augustine (though not entirely consistent) disapproved of the forcible demolition of the temples. "Let us first extirpate the idolatry of the hearts of the Heathen; and they will either themselves invite us, or anticipate us in the execution of this good work." Tom. v. p. 62.

power to suppress these forbidden usages, and the civil authorities, as though the government mistrusted their zeal, were bound, under a heavy penalty, to obey the summons, and to assist the prelates in the extirpation of idolatry. Another edict excluded all enemies of the Christian faith from the great public offices in the state and in the army, and this, if fully carried into effect, would have transferred the whole power throughout the empire into the hands of the Christians. But the times were not yet ripe for this measure. Generides, a Pagan, in a high command in the army, threw up his commission. The edict was repealed.[u]

---

[u] Prudentius ventures to admire the tolerant impartiality of Theodosius, in admitting both parties alike to civil and military honours. He urges this argumentum ad hominem against Symmachus:—

Denique pro meritis terrestribus æqua re-
    pendens
Munera, sacricolis summos impertit honores
Dux bonus, et certare sinit cum laude
    suorum.
Nec pago implicitos per debita culmina
    mundi
Ire vetat.
Ipse magistratum tibi consulis, ipse tri-
    bunal
Contulit.

In the East, the Pagan Themistius had been appointed prefect of Constantinople by Theodosius. It is curious to read his flatteries of the orthodox Christian Emperor; he praises his love of philosophy in the most fervent language.

The most remarkable instance of this inconsistency, at a much later period, occurs in the person of Merobaudes, a general and a poet, who flourished in the first half of the fifth century. A statue in honour of Merobaudes was placed in the Forum of Trajan, of which the inscription is still extant. Fragments of his poems have been discovered by the industry and sagacity of Niebuhr. In one passage, Merobaudes, in the genuine Heathen spirit, attributes the ruin of the empire to the abolition of Paganism, and almost renews the old accusation of Atheism against Christianity. He impersonates some deity, probably Discord, who summons Bellona to take arms for the destruction of Rome; and, in a strain of fierce irony, recommends to her, among other fatal measures, to extirpate the gods of Rome:

Roma, ipsique tremant furialia murmura
    reges.
Jam superos terris, atque hospita numina
    pelle:
Romanos populare Deos, et nullus in aris
Vestæ exoratæ, fotus strue, palleat ignis.
His instructa dolis palatia celsa subibo,
Majorum mores, et pectora prisca fugabo
Funditus, atque simul, nullo discrimine
    rerum,
Spernantur fortes, nec sit reverentia justis.
Attica neglecto pereat facundia Phœbo,
Indignis contingat honos, et pondera rerum;
Non virtus sed casus agat, tristisque cupido;

Rome once more beheld the shadow of a Pagan Emperor, Attalus, while the Christian Emperor maintained his court at Ravenna; and both stood trembling before the victorious Alaric. When that triumphant Goth formed the siege of Rome, Paganism, as if grateful for the fidelity of the imperial city, made one last desperate effort to avert the common ruin. Pagan magic was the last refuge of conscious weakness. The Etrurian soothsayers were called forth from their obscurity, with the concurrence of the whole city (the Pope himself is said to have assented to the idolatrous ceremony), to blast the barbaric invader with the lightnings of Jupiter. The Christian historian saves the credit of his party, by asserting that they kept away from the profane rite.[x] But it may be doubted, after all, whether the ceremony really took place; both parties had more confidence in the power of a large sum of money, offered to arrest the career of the triumphant barbarian.

A.D. 409.

The impartial fury of Alaric fell alike on church and temple, on Christian and Pagan. But the capture of Rome consummated the ruin of Paganism. The temples, indeed, were for the most part left standing, but their worshippers had fled. The Roman aristocracy, in whom alone Paganism still retained its most powerful adherents, abandoned the city, and, scattered in the provinces of the empire, were absorbed in the rapidly Christianising population. The deserted buildings had now neither public authority

Capture of Rome by Alaric.

Pectoribus sævi demens furor æstuet ævi;
Omniaque hæc sine mente Jovis, sine numine summo.
     Merobaudes in Niebuhr's edit. of the Byzantines.

[x] Zosimus, v. Sozomen, ix. 6. Compare Latin Christianity, vol. i. p. 94.

nor private zeal and munificence to maintain them
against the encroachments of time or accident, to
support the tottering roof, or repair the broken
column. There was neither public fund, nor private
contribution, for their preservation, till at length the
Christians, in many instances, took possession of the
abandoned edifice, converted it to their own use,
and hallowed it by a new consecration.[y] Thus, in
many places, though marred and disfigured, the monuments of architecture survived, with no great violation of the ground plan, distribution, or general
proportions.[z]

Paganism was, in fact, left to die out by gradual dissolution.[a] The worship of the Heathen deities lingered
in many temples, till it was superseded by the new form
of Christianity, which, at least in its outward appearance, approximated to Polytheism : the Virgin gradually
supplanted many of the local deities. In Sicily, which
long remained obstinately wedded to the ancient faith,
eight celebrated temples were dedicated to the Mother
of God.[b] It was not till the seventh century, that the
Pantheon was dedicated by Pope Boniface IV. to the

---

[y] There are many churches in
Rome, which, like the Pantheon, are
ancient temples; thirty-nine built on
the foundations of temples. Four retain Pagan names. S. Maria sopra
Minerva, S. Maria Aventina, S. Lo-
renzo in Matuta, S. Stefano in Cacco.
At Sienna, the temple of Quirinus
became the church of S. Quirino.
Beugnot, ii. p. 266. See in Bingham,
book viii. s. 4., references to several
churches in the East, converted into
temples. But this passage must be
read with caution.

[z] In some cases, by a more destructive appropriation, they converted the materials to their own use,
and worked them up into their own
barbarous churches.

[a] The fifth council of Carthage
(A.D. 398), can. xv., petitioned the
most glorious Emperors to destroy
the remains of idolatry, not merely
" in simulacris," but in other places,
groves, and trees.

[b] Beugnot, ii. 271 ; from Aprile,
Chronologia Universale de Siciliâ.

Holy Virgin. Of the public festivals, the last which clung with tenacious grasp to the habits of the Roman people, was the Lupercalia. It was suppressed towards the close of the fifth century by Pope Ge-

A.D. 493.

lasius. The rural districts were not completely Christianised until the general introduction of monasticism. Heathenism was still prevalent in many parts of Italy, especially in the neighbourhood of Turin, in the middle of the fifth century.[c] Its conqueror was the missionary from the convent who wandered through the villages, or who, from his monastery, regularly discharged the duties of a village pastor. St. Benedict of Nursia destroyed the worship of Apollo on Mount Casino.[d]

Every where the superstition survived the religion, and that which was unlawful under Paganism, continued to be unlawfully practised under Christianity. The insatiable propensity of men to enquire into futurity, and to deal with secret and invisible agencies, which reason condemns, and often, while it condemns, consults, retained its old formularies, some religious, some pretending to be magical or theurgic. Divination and witchcraft have never been extinct in Italy, or, perhaps, in any part of Europe. The descendants of Canidia or Erictho, the seer and the magician, have still

---

[c] See the sermons of Maximus, bishop of Turin, quoted in Beugnot, ii. 253.

[d] Greg. M. Dialog. Lib. 2, p. 262. He converted many worshippers of idols in a village near his monastery. Ibid. ch. xix. 60. he mentions *idolorum cultores* in an epistle to the Bishop of Tyndaris in Sicily. So in Sardinea, iii. 23 and 26. The peasants belonging to the church were to be heavily taxed till they ceased to Paganise, also he names 29 worshippers of trees, &c. near Terracina, vii. 20. Idolatrous Aruspices and Sortilegi in Sardinia to be preached to; if obstinate, slaves to be scourged, free men imprisoned till they repent. vii. 2. 67.

practised their arts, to which the ignorant, including at times all mankind, have listened with unabated credulity.

We must resume our consideration of Paganising Christianity, as the parent of Christian art and poetry, and, in fact, as the ruler of the human mind for many ages.

CHAPTER IX.

Theodosius.   Triumph of Trinitarianism.   The great Prelates
of the East.

BUT the unity, no less than the triumph, of Christianity
Orthodoxy of occupied the vigorous mind of Theodosius.
Theodosius. He had been anticipated in this design in the
West by his feeble predecessors and his colleagues,
Gratian and Valentinian the younger.   The laws began
to speak the language not only of the exclusive
establishment of Christianity, but of Christianity under
one rigorous and unaccommodating creed and discipline.
Laws against   Almost the first act of Theodosius was the
heretics.   edict for the universal acceptance of the
A.D. 380.   Catholic faith.[a]   It appeared under the name,
and with the conjoint authority of the three Emperors,
Gratian, Valentinian II., and Theodosius.   It was
addressed to the inhabitants of Constantinople.   "We,
the three Emperors, *will* that all our subjects follow the
religion taught by St. Peter to the Romans, professed
by those saintly prelates, Damasus Pontiff of Rome,
and Peter Bishop of Alexandria, that we believe the
one divinity of the Father, Son, and Holy Spirit, of
majesty coequal, in the Holy Trinity.   We *will* that
those who embrace this creed be called Catholic
Christians; we brand all the senseless followers of
other religions by the infamous name of heretics, and
forbid their conventicles to assume the name of

---

[a] Codex Theodos. xvi. 1, 2.

churches; we reserve their punishment to the vengeance of heaven, and to such measures as divine inspiration shall dictate to us."[b] Thus the religion of the whole Roman world was enacted by two feeble boys, and a rude Spanish soldier.[c] The next year witnessed the condemnation of all heretics, particularly the Photinians, Arians, and Eunomians, and the expulsion of the Arians from the churches of all the cities in the East,[d] and their surrender to the only *lawful* form of Christianity. On the assembling of the council of Chalcedon, two severe laws were issued against Apostates and Manicheans, prohibiting them from making wills. During its sitting, the Emperor promulgated an edict, prohibiting the Arians from building churches either in the cities or in the country, under pain of the confiscation of the funds devoted to the purpose.[e]

The circumstances of the times happily coincided with the design of Theodosius to concentrate the whole Christian world into one vigorous and consistent system. The more legitimate influence of argument and intellectual and religious superiority concurred with the stern mandates of the civil power. All the great and commanding minds of the age were on the same side as to the momentous and strongly agitated questions of

All the more powerful ecclesiastical writers favourable to Trinitarianism.

---

[b] Post etiam motus nostri, quem ex cœlesti arbitrio sumpserimus, ultione plectendos. Godefroy supposes these words not to mean " cœleste oraculum," but, " Dei arbitrium, regulam et formulam juris divini."

[c] Baronius, and even Godefroy, call this law a golden, pious, and wholesome statute. Happily it was on the right side.

[d] On the accession of Theodosius, according to Sozomen, the Arians possessed all the churches of the East, except Jerusalem. H. E. vii. 2.

[e] Sozomen mentions these severe laws; but asserts that they were enacted merely in terrorem, and with no design of carrying them into execution. H. E. vii. 12.

the faith. The productive energies of Arianism seemed, as it were, exhausted; its great defenders had passed away, and left, apparently, no heirs to their virtues or abilities. It was distracted with schisms, and had to bear the unpopularity of the sects, which seemed to have sprung from it in the natural course, the Eunomians, Macedonians, and a still multiplying progeny of heresies. Everywhere the Trinitarian prelates rose to ascendancy, not merely from the support of the government, but from their pre-eminent character or intellectual powers. Each province seemed to have produced some man adapted to the particular period and circumstances of the time, who devoted himself to the establishment of the orthodox opinions. The intractable Egypt, more especially turbulent Alexandria, was ruled by the strong arm of the bold and unprincipled Theophilus. The dreamy mysticism of Syria found a congenial representative in St. Ephrem. A more intellectual, yet still somewhat imaginative, Orientalism animates the writings of St. Basil; in a less degree, those of Gregory of Nazianzum; still less, those of Gregory of Nyssa. The more powerful and Grecian eloquence of Chrysostom swayed the popular mind in Constantinople. Jerome, a link, as it were, between the East and the West, transplanted the monastic spirit and opinions of Syria into Rome; and brought into the East much of the severer thought, and more prosaic reasoning, of the Latin world. In Gaul, where Hilary of Poictiers had long maintained the cause of Trinitarianism, on the borders of civilisation, St. Martin of Tours acted the part of a bold and enterprising missionary; while in Milan, the court-capital of the West, the strong practical character of Ambrose, his sternly conscientious moral energy, though hardening at times into rigid intolerance, with

the masculine strength of his style, confirmed the Latin
church in that creed to which Rome had adhered with
almost unshaken fidelity. If not the greatest, the most
permanently influential of all, Augustine, united the
intense passion of the African mind with the most
comprehensive and systematic views and intrepid
dogmatism on the darkest subjects. United in one
common cause, acting in their several quarters according
to their peculiar temperaments and characters, these
strong-minded and influential ecclesiastics almost compelled the world into a temporary peace, till first
Pelagianism, and afterwards Nestorianism, unsettled
again the restless elements; the controversies, first in
the West concerning grace, free-will, and predestination,
then in the East on the Incarnation and two natures of
Christ, succeeded to the silenced and exhausted feud
concerning the Trinity of persons in the Godhead.

Theophilus of Alexandria[f] performed his part in
the complete subjection of the world by Theophilus of
his energy as a ruler, not by the slower Alexandria, bishop, from
and more legitimate influence of moral 385 to 412.
persuasion through his preaching or his writings.[g] He
suppressed Arianism by the same violent and coercive
means with which he extirpated Paganism. The tone
of this prelate's epistles is invariably harsh and crimi-
natory. He appears in the best light as opposing
the vulgar anthropomorphism of the monks in the
neighbourhood of Alexandria, and insisting on the pure
spiritual nature of the Deity. Yet he condescended to
appease these turbulent adversaries by an unmanly

---

[f] I have not placed these writers in
their strict chronological order, but
according to the countries in which
they lived.

[g] The Trinitarian doctrines had
been maintained in Alexandria by the
virtues and abilities of Didymus the
Blind.

artifice. He consented to condemn the doctrines of Origen, who, having reposed quietly in his tomb for many years, in general respect, if not in the odour of sanctity, was exhumed, as it were, by the zeal of later times, as a dangerous heresiarch. The Oriental doctrines with which Origen had impregnated his system were unpopular, and perhaps not clearly understood.[h] The notion that the reign of Christ was finite was rather an inference from his writings than a tenet of Origen. For if all bodies were to be finally annihilated (according to his anti-materialistic system), the humanity of Christ, and consequently his personal reign, must cease. The possibility that the devil might, after long purification, be saved, and the corruptibility of the body after the resurrection, grew out of the same Oriental cast of opinions. But the perfectly pure and immaterial nature of the Deity was the tenet of Origen which was the most odious to the monks; and Theophilus, by anathematising Origenism in the mass, while he himself held certainly the sublimest, but to his adversaries most objectionable part of the system, adopted a low and undignified deception. The persecution of Isidore, and the heads of the monasteries who befriended his cause (the tall brethren, as they were called), from personal motives of animosity, display the Alexandrian prelate in his ordinary character. We shall again encounter Theophilus in the lamentable intrigues against the advancement and influence of Chrysostom.

The character of Ephrem,[1] the Syrian, was the exact counterpart to that of the busy and worldly Theophilus. A native of Nisibis, or rather of its neighbourhood, Ephrem passed the greater part of

S. Ephrem, the Syrian, died 379.

---

[h] Socrates, vi. 10. Sozomen. viii. 13.

[1] See the Life of Ephrem prefixed to his works; and in Tillemont.

his life at Edessa, and in the monastic establishments
which began to abound in Mesopotamia and Syria, as in
Egypt. His genius was that of the people in whose
language he wrote his numerous compositions in prose
and verse.[k] In Ephrem something of the poetic
mysticism of the Gnostic was allied with the most rigid
orthodoxy of doctrine. But with his imaginative turn
were mingled a depth and intensity of feeling, which
gave him his peculiar influence over the kindred minds
of his countrymen. Tears were as natural to him as
perspiration ; day and night, in his devout seclusion,
he wept for the sins of mankind and for his own ;
his very writings, it was said, weep ; there is a deep
and latent sorrow even in his panegyrics or festival
homilies.[l]

Ephrem was a poet, and his hymns, poured forth
in the prodigality of his zeal, succeeded at length in
entirely disenchanting the popular ear from the heretical
strains of Bardesanes and his son Harmonius, which
lingered after the general decay of Gnosticism.[m] The
hymns of Ephrem were sung on the festivals of the
martyrs. His psalms, the constant occupation which
he enjoins upon his monkish companions, were always
of a sorrowful and contrite tone. Laughter was the
source and the indication of all wickedness, sorrow of
all virtue. During the melancholy psalm, God was present with his angels ; all more joyous strains belonged
to heathenism and idolatry.

---

[k] According to Theodoret, he was
unacquainted with Greek. Παιδείας
γὰρ οὐ γεγευμένος ἑλληνικῆς, τούς
τε πολυσχιδεῖς τῶν Ἑλλήνων διή-
λεγξε πλάνους καὶ πάσης αἱρετικῆς
κακοτεχνίας ἐγύμνωσε τὴν ἀσθέ-
νειαν. The refutation of Greek

heresy in Syriac must have been curious.
[l] See the two treatises in his
works, vol. i. 104-107. Non esse
ridendum sed lugendum potius atque
plorandum ; and, Quod ludicris rebus
abstinendum sit Christianis.
[m] Theodoret, iv. 29.

The monasticism, as well as the Trinitarianism, of Syria received a strong impulse from Ephrem; and in Syria monasticism began to run into its utmost extravagance. There was one class of ascetics who, at certain periods, forsook their cities, and retired to the mountains to browse on the herbage which they found, as their only food. The writings of Ephrem were the occupation and delight of all these gentle and irreproachable fanatics; and, as Ephrem was rigidly Trinitarian, he contributed to fix the doctrinal language of the various cœnobitic institutions and solitary hermitages. In fact, the quiescent intellect probably rejoiced in being relieved from these severe and ungrateful enquiries: and full freedom being left to the imagination and ample scope to the language in the vague and fervent expressions of divine love, the Syrian mind felt not the restriction of the rigorous creed, and passively surrendered itself to ecclesiastical authority. Absorbed in its painful and melancholy struggles with the internal passions and appetites, it desired not to provoke, but rather to repress, the dangerous activity of the reason. The orthodoxy of Ephrem himself savours perhaps of timidity and the disinclination to agitate such awful and appalling questions. He would elude and escape them, and abandon himself altogether to the more edifying emotions which it is the chief object of his writings to excite and maintain. The dreamer must awake in order to reason, and he prefers the passive tranquillity of the half-slumbering state.

Greece, properly so called, contributed none of the more distinguished names in Eastern Christianity. Even the Grecian part of Asia Minor was by no means fertile in names which survive in the annals of the Church. In Athens philosophy still lingered, and struggled to

maintain its predominance. Many of the more eminent
ecclesiastics had visited its schools in their youth, to
obtain those lessons of rhetoric and profane knowledge
which they were hereafter to dedicate to their own
sacred uses. But they were foreigners; and, in the old
language of Greece, would have been called barbarians.

The rude and uncivilised Cappadocia gave birth to
Basil and the two Gregories. The whole of the
less dreamy, and still active and commercial, Cappadocia.
part of Asia was influenced by Basil, on whose character
and writings his own age lavished the most unbounded
praise. The name of Basil is constantly united with
those of the two Gregories. One, Gregory of Nyssa,
was his brother; the other, named from his native town
of Nazianzum, of which his father was bishop, was the
intimate friend of his boyhood and of his later years.
The language, the eloquence, the opinions of these
writers retain, in different degrees, some tinge of Asiatic
colouring. Far more intelligible and practical than the
mystic strains and passionate homilies of Ephrem, they
delight in agitating, though in a more modest spirit,
the questions which had inflamed the imagination of the
Gnostics. But with them, likewise, enquiry proceeds with
cautious and reverent steps. On these subjects they are
rigorously orthodox, and assert the exclusive doctrines
of Athanasius with the most distinct and uncompromising
energy. Basil maintained the cause of Trinitarianism
with unshaken fidelity during its days of depression and
adversity. His friend Gregory of Nazianzum lived to
witness and bear a great part of its triumph. Both
Basil and Gregory were ardent admirers, and in themselves transcendent models, of the more monastic Christianity. The influence of Basil crowded that part of
Asia with cœnobitic institutions: but in his monasteries

labour and useful industry prevailed to a greater extent
than in the the Syrian deserts.

Basil was a native of the Cappadocian Cæsarea.[n] He
was an hereditary Christian. His grandfather
had retired during the Diocletian persecution
to a mountain-forest in Pontus. His father was a man
of estimation as a lawyer, possessed considerable property, and was remarkable for his personal beauty.
His mother, in person and character, was worthy of her
husband. The son of such parents received the best
education which could be bestowed on a Christian
youth. Having exhausted the instruction to be obtained
in his native city of Cæsarea, he went to Constantinople,
where he is reputed to have studied the art of rhetoric
under the celebrated Libanius. But Athens was still
the centre of liberal education, and, with other promising youths from the Eastern provinces, Basil and
his friend Gregory resided for some time in that city.
But with all his taste for letters and eloquence (and
Basil always spoke even of profane learning with generous respect, far different from the tone of contempt
and animosity expressed by some writers), Christianity
was too deeply rooted in his heart to be endangered
either by the studies or the society of Athens. On his
return to Cæsarea, he embraced the ascetic faith of the
times with more than ordinary fervour. He abandoned
his property; he practised such severe austerities as to
injure his health, and to reduce his bodily form to the
extreme of meagreness and weakness. He was "without
wife, without property, without flesh, almost without
blood." He fled into the desert; his fame collected, as
it were, a city around him; he built a monastery, and

S. Basil.

---

[n] Life of Basil, prefixed to his works : and Tillemont, Vie de S. Basile.

monasteries sprang up on every side. Yet the opinions
of Basil concerning the monastic life were far more
moderate and practical than the wilder and more dreamy
asceticism which prevailed in Egypt and in Syria. He
admired and persuaded his followers to cœnobitic, not
to eremitical, life. It was the life of the industrious
religious community, not of the indolent and solitary
anchorite, which to Basil was the perfection of Christianity. All ties of kindred were indeed to give place
to that of spiritual association. He that loves a brother
in blood more than a brother in the religious community
is still a slave to his carnal nature.[o] The indiscriminate
charity of these institutions was to receive orphans of all
classes for education and maintenance, but other children
only with the consent, or at the request of parents,
certified before witnesses; and vows of virginity were
by no means to be enforced upon these youthful pupils.[p]
Slaves who fled to the monasteries were to be admo-
nished, and sent back to their owners. There is one
reservation, that slaves were not bound to obey their
master, if he should order what is contrary to the laws
of God.[q] Industry was to be the animating principle of
these settlements. Prayer and psalmody were to have
their appointed hours; but by no means to intrude upon
those devoted to useful labour. These labours were
strictly defined, such as were of real use to the community, not those which might contribute to vice or luxury.
Agriculture was especially recommended. The life was
in no respect to be absorbed in a perpetual mystic communion with the Deity.

Basil lived in his monastic retirement during a great

---

[o] Basil. Opera, ii. 325. Sermo As-
ceticus.

[p] Basil. Opera, ii. 355.
[q] Basil. Opera, ii. 357.

part of the triumphant period of Arianism in the East;
A.D. 366. but during the reign of Valens, he was re-
See ch. vii. called to Cæsarea, to be the champion of Trini-
p. 45. tarianism against the Emperor and his Arian
A.D. 370. partisans. The firmness of Basil, as we have
seen, commanded the respect even of his adversaries.
In the midst of the raging controversy, he was raised to
the archepiscopal throne of Cæsarea. He governed the
see with activity and diligence : not only the influence
of his writings, but his actual authority (his pious ambition of usefulness induced him perhaps to overstep the
limits of his diocese) extended beyond Cappadocia, into
Armenia and parts of Asia Minor. He was the firm sup-
porter of the Nicene Trinitarianism, but did not
A.D. 379. live to behold its final triumph. His decease followed immediately upon the defeat and death of Valens.

The style of Basil did no discredit to his Athenian
education; in purity and perspicuity he surpasses most
of the Heathen as well as the Christian writers of his age.

Gregory of Nazianzum, as he shared the friendship,
Gregory of so he has constantly participated in the fame
Nazianzum. of Basil. He was born in a village, Arianza,
within the district of Nazianzum, his father was bishop
of that city.[r] With Basil he passed a part of his youth
at Athens, and predicted, according to his own account,
the apostasy of Julian, from the observation of his
His poems. character, and even of his person. Gregory
is his own biographer; one or rather two poems,
the first consisting of above two thousand iambics, the
second of hexameters, describe the whole course of his

---

[r] Tillemont is grievously embar- | attained the episcopate. Tillemont is
rassed by the time of Gregory's birth. | forced to acknowledge the laxity of
The stubborn dates insist upon his | ecclesiastical discipline on this head, at
having been born after his father had | this period of the church.

early life. But Grecian poetry was not to be awakened
from its long slumber by the voice of a Christian poet:
it was faithful to its ancient source of inspiration.
Christian thoughts and images will not blend with the
language of Homer and the tragedians. Yet the autobiographical poems of Gregory illustrate a remarkable
peculiarity which distinguishes modern and Christian
from the older, more particularly the Grecian, poetry.
In the Grecian poetry, as in Grecian life, the public
absorbed the individual character. The person of the
poet rarely appears, unless occasionally as the poet, as
the objective author or reciter, not as the subject of the
poem. The Elegiac poets of Greece, if we Characteristic
may judge from the few surviving fragments, between
and the amatory writers of Rome, speak in Greek and Christian
their proper persons, utter their individual poetry.
thoughts, and embody their peculiar feelings. In the
shrewd common-life view of Horace, and, indeed in
some of his higher lyric poetry, the poet is more prominent; and the fate of Ovid, one day basking in the
imperial favour, the next, for some mysterious offence,
banished to the bleak shores of the Euxine, seemed to
give him the privilege of dwelling upon his own sorrows;
his strange fate invested his life in peculiar interest.
These however are rare and exceptional instances in
Greek and Roman poetry. But by the Christian scheme,
the individual man has assumed a higher importance;
his actions, his opinions, the emotions of his mind, as
connected with his immortal state, have acquired a new
and commanding interest, not only to himself, but to
others. The poet profoundly scrutinises, and elaborately
reveals, the depths of his moral being. The psycholo-
gical history of the man, in all its minute particulars,
becomes the predominant matter of the poem. In

this respect, these autobiographical poems of Gregory,
Value of Gregory's. loose as they are in numbers, spun out with a wearisome and garrulous mediocrity, and wanting that depth and passion of religion which has made the Confessions of Augustine one of the most permanently popular of Christian writings, possess nevertheless some interest, as indicating the transition state in poetry, as well as illustrating the thought and feeling prevalent among the Christian youth of the period. The one great absorbing question was the comparative excellence of the secular and the monastic life, the state of marriage or of virginity. The enthusiasm of the East scarcely deigned to submit this point to discussion. In one of Gregory's poems, Marriage and Virginity each pleads his cause; but there can be no doubt, from the first, to which will be assigned the victory. The Saviour gives to Virginity the place of honour on his right hand. Gregory had never entangled himself with marriage, that fatal tie which enthralls the soul in the bonds of matter. For him silken robes, gorgeous banquets, splendid palaces, music and perfumes, had no charm. He disregarded wealth, and feasted contentedly on bread with a little salt, and water for his only drink. The desire of supporting the declining age of his parents thwarted his holy ambition of withdrawing from all worldly intercourse: but this became a snare. He was embarrassed by refractory servants, by public and private business. The death of his brother involved him still more inextricably in affairs arising out of his contested property. But the faithless friendship of Basil, which he deplores in the one touching passage of his whole poem,[a] still further endangered his peace.

---

[a] Gibbon's selection of this passage, and his happy illustration from Shake- speare, do great credit to his poetical taste:

Πόνοι

In the zeal of Basil to fill the bishoprics of his metropolitan diocese, calculating perhaps that Gregory, like himself, would generously sacrifice the luxury of religious quietude for the more useful duties of a difficult active position, he imposed upon his reluctant friend the charge of the newly created see of Sasima. Gregory, bishop of Sasima. A.D. 372. This was a small and miserable town, at the meeting of three roads, in a country at once arid, marshy, and unwholesome, noisy and dusty from the constant passage of travellers, the disputes with extortionate custom-house officers, and all the tumult and drunkenness belonging to a town inhabited by loose and passing strangers. With Basil, Gregory had passed the tranquil days of his youth, the contemplative period of his manhood ; together they had studied at Athens, together they had twice retired to monastic solitude ; and this was the return for his long and tried attachment! Gregory, in the bitterness of his remonstrance, at one time assumes the language of an Indian faquir. Instead of rejoicing in the sphere opened to his activity, he boldly asserts his supreme felicity to be total inaction.[t] He submitted with the strongest repugnance to the office, and abandoned it, almost immediately, on the first opposition. He afterwards administered the see of Nazianzum under his father, and even after his father's decease, without assuming the episcopal title.

Πόνοι κοίνοι λόγων
'Ομόστεγός τε, καὶ συνέστιος βίος,
Νοῦς εἷς ἐν ἀμφοῖν * * * *
Διεσκέδασται πάντα, κᾳρρίπται χαμαὶ,
Αὖραι φέρουσι τὰς παλαιὰς ἐλπίδας·
Is all the counsel that we two have shared,
The sisters' vows, &c.
Helena, in the Midsummer Night's Dream.
See Gibbon, c. xxvii. vol. v. p. 18.

t 'Εμοὶ δὲ μεγίστη πρᾶξις ἔστιν ἡ ἀπραξία.   Epist. xxiii. p. 797.

But Gregory was soon compelled by his own fame for
Gregory,
bishop of
Constanti-
nople.
From A.D.
339 to 379.
eloquence and for orthodoxy to move in a
more arduous and tumultuous sphere. For
forty years Arianism had been dominant in
Constantinople. The Arians mocked at the
small number which still lingered in the single religious
assemblage of the Athanasian party.[u] Gregory is constrained to admit this humiliating fact, and indignantly
inquires, whether the sands are more precious than the
stars of heaven, or the pebbles than pearls, because they
are more numerous.[x] But the accession of Theodosius
opened a new æra to the Trinitarians. The religion of
the Emperor would no longer condescend to this humble
and secondary station. Gregory was invited to take
charge of the small community which was still faithful
to the doctrines of Athanasius. Gregory was already
bowed with age and infirmity; his bald head stooped to
his bosom; his countenance was worn by his austerities
and his inward spiritual conflicts, when he reluctantly
sacrificed his peace for this great purpose.[y] The
Catholics had no church; they met in a small house,
on the site of which afterwards arose the celebrated
church of St. Anastasia. The eloquence of Gregory
wrought wonders in the busy and versatile capital. The
Arians themselves crowded to hear him. His adversaries were reduced to violence; the Anastasia was
attacked; the Arian monks, and even the virgins,
mingled in the furious fray: many lives were lost, and
Gregory was accused as the cause of the tumult. His
innocence, and the known favour of the Emperor, secured his acquittal; his eloquence was seconded by the
imperial edicts. The law had been promulgated which

---

[u] In the reign of Valentinian, they met ἐν μικρῷ οἰκίσκῳ. Socrates, iv. 1.

[x] Orat. xxv. p. 431.

[y] Tillemont, art. xlvi.

denounced as heretics all who rejected the Nicene Creed.

The influence of Gregory was thwarted and his peace disturbed, by the strange intrigues of one Maximus to possess himself of the episcopal throne of Constantinople. Maximus was called the Cynic, from his attempt to blend the rude manners, the coarse white dress, his enemies added, the vices, of that sect, with the profession of Christianity. His memory is loaded with every kind of infamy; yet by dexterous flattery and assiduous attendance on the sermons of Gregory, he had stolen into his unsuspecting confidence, and received his public commendations in a studied oration.[z] Constantinople and Gregory himself were suddenly amazed with the intelligence that Maximus had been consecrated the Catholic bishop of the city. This extraordinary measure had been taken by seven Alexandrians of low birth and character,[a] with some bishops deputed by Peter the orthodox Archbishop of Alexandria.[b] A number of mariners, probably belonging to the corn fleet, had assisted at the ceremony and raised the customary acclamations. A great tumult of all orders arose; all rushed to the church, from which Maximus and his party withdrew, and hastily completed a kind of tonsure (for the cynic prided himself on his long hair) in the private dwelling of a flute-player. Maximus seems to have been rejected with indignation by the Athanasians

---

[z] The panegyric on the philosopher Heron.

[a] Some of their names were whimsically connected with the Egyptian mythology, Ammon, Anubis, and Hermanubis.

[b] The interference of the Egyptians is altogether remarkable. Could there be a design to establish the primacy of Alexandria over Constantinople, and so over the East? It is observable that in his law, Theodosius names as the examples of doctrine, the Bishop of Rome in the West, of Alexandria in the East. The intrigues of Theophilus against Chrysostom rather confirm this notion of an attempt to erect an Eastern papacy.

I 2

of Constantinople, who adhered with unshaken fidelity
to Gregory; he fled to the court of Theodosius, but the
earliest measure adopted by the Emperor to restore
strength to the orthodox party, was the rejection of the
intrusive prelate.

The first act of Theodosius on his arrival at Constantinople, was to issue an edict, expelling the
Arians from the churches, and summoning
Demophilus, the Arian bishop, to conform to the Nicene
doctrine. Demophilus refused. The Emperor commanded that those who would not unite to establish
Christian peace should retire from the houses of Christian prayer. Demophilus assembled his followers, and
quoting the words of the Gospel, " If you are persecuted
in one city, flee unto another," retired before the irresistible authority of the Emperor. The next step was
the appointment of the reluctant Gregory to the see,
and his enthronisation in the principal church of the
metropolis. Environed by the armed legionaries, in
military pomp, accompanied by the Emperor himself,
Gregory, amazed and bewildered, and perhaps sensible of
the incongruity of the scene with the true Christian character, headed the triumphal procession. All around he
saw the sullen and menacing faces of the Arian multitude, and his ear might catch their suppressed murmurs;
even the heavens, for the morning was bleak and
cloudy, seemed to look down with cold indifference on
the scene. No sooner, however, had Gregory, with the
Emperor, passed the rails which divided the sanctuary
from the nave of the church, than the sun burst forth in
his splendour, the clouds were dissipated, and the glorious
light came streaming in upon the applauding congregation. At once a shout of acclamation demanded the
enthronisation of Gregory.

24th Nov.
A.D. 380.

But Gregory, commanding only in his eloquence
from the pulpit, seems to have wanted the firmness and
vigour necessary for the prelate of a great metropolis.
Theodosius summoned the council of Constantinople;
and Gregory, embarrassed by the multiplicity of affairs;
harassed by objections to the validity of his own election; entangled in the feuds which arose out of the
contested election to the see of Antioch, entreated, and
obtained, apparently the unreluctant, assent of the
bishops and the Emperor to abdicate his dignity and to
retire to his beloved privacy. His retreat, in some
degree disturbed by the interest which he still took in
the see of Nazianzum, gradually became more complete, till, at length, he withdrew into solitude, and
ended his days in that peace, which perhaps was not
less sincerely enjoyed from his experience of the cares
and vexations of worldly dignity. Arianza, his native
village, was the place of his seclusion; the gardens, the
trees, the fountain, familiar to his youth, welcomed his
old age. But Gregory had not exhausted the fears, the
dangers, or the passions of life. The desires of youth
still burned in his withered body and demanded the
severest macerations. The sight or even the neighbourhood of females afflicted his sensitive conscience;
and instead of allowing ease or repose to his aged
frame, his bed was a hard mat, his coverlid sackcloth,
his dress one thin tunic; his feet were bare; he allowed
himself no fire, and here, in the company of the wild
beasts, he prayed with bitter tears, he fasted, and devoted his hours to the composition of poetry, which,
from its extreme difficulty, he considered as an act of
penitence. His painful existence was protracted to the
age of ninety.

The complete restoration of Constantinople to the

orthodox communion demanded even more powerful eloquence, and far more vigorous anthority, than that of Gregory. If it was not finally achieved, its success was secured, by the most splendid orator who had ever adorned the Eastern church. Sixteen years after the retirement of Gregory, the fame of Chrysostom designated him as the successor to that important dignity.

Chrysostom was the model of a preacher for a great capital.[c] Clear rather than profound, his dogmatic is essentially moulded up with his moral teaching. He is the champion, not so exclusively of any system of doctrines, as of Christian holiness against the vices, the dissolute manners, the engrossing love of amusement, which prevailed in the new Rome of the East. His doctrines flow naturally from his subject or from the passage of Scripture under discussion; his illustrations are copious and happy; his style free and fluent; while he is an unrivalled master in that rapid and forcible application of incidental occurrences, which gives such life and reality to eloquence. He is, at times, in the highest sense, dramatic in his manner.

Chrysostom, like all the more ardent spirits of his age, was enamoured in his early youth of monasticism. But this he had gradually thrown off, even while he remained at Antioch. Though by no means formally abandoning these principles, or lowering his admiration of this imaginary perfection of religion, in his later works he is more free, popular, and practical. His ambition is not so much to elevate a few enthusiastic spirits to a high-toned and mystic piety, as to impregnate

---

c Compare the several lives of Chrysostom by Palladius, that in the Benedictine edition of his works, and in Tillemont. I have only the first volume of Neander's Joannes Chrysostomus. The second has since appeared.

the whole population of a great capital with Christian virtue and self-denial.

John, who obtained the name of Chrysostom, the golden-mouthed, was born at Antioch, about the year 347. He was brought up by his mother in the Christian faith; he studied rhetoric under the celebrated Libanius, who used his utmost arts, and displayed all that is captivating in Grecian poetry and philosophy, to enthral the imagination of his promising pupil. Libanius, in an extant epistle, rejoices at the success of Chrysostom at the bar in Antioch. He is said to have lamented on his death-bed the sacrilegious seduction of the young orator by the Christians; for to Chrysostom, he had intended to bequeath his school and the office of maintaining the dignity of Paganism.

But the eloquence of Chrysostom was not to waste itself in the barren litigations of the courts of justice in Antioch, or in the vain attempt to infuse new life into the dead philosophy and religion of Greece. He felt himself summoned to a nobler field. At the age of eighteen, Chrysostom began to study that one source of eloquence to which the human heart responded, the sacred writings of the Christians. The church was not slow in recognising the value of such a proselyte. He received the strongest encouragement from Meletius, Bishop of Antioch; he was appointed a reader in the church. But the soul of Chrysostom was not likely to embrace these stirring tenets with coolness or moderation. A zealous friend inflamed, by precept and emulation, the fervour of his piety: they proposed to retire to one of the most remote hermitages in Syria; and the great Christian orator was almost self-doomed to silence, or to exhaust his power of language in prayers and ejaculations heard by no human ear. The mother of Chrysostom saved the Christian church from this fatal loss. There is something exquisitely touching in the traits of domestic affection which sometimes gleam through the busy pages of history. His mother had become a widow at the age of twenty; to the general admiration, she had remained faithful to the memory of her husband and to her maternal duties. As soon as she heard the determination of her son to retire to a distant region (Chrysostom himself relates the incident), she took him by the hand, she led him to her chamber, she made him sit by her on the bed in which she had borne him, and burst out into tears and into language more sad than tears. She spoke of the cares and troubles of widowhood; grievous as they had been, she had ever one consolation, the gazing on his face, and beholding in him the image of his departed father. Before he could speak, he had thus been her comfort and her joy. She reminded him of the fidelity with which she had administered the paternal property. " Think not that I would reproach you with these things. I have but one favour to entreat—make me not a second time a widow; awaken not again my slumbering sorrows. Wait, at least, for my death; perhaps I shall depart before long. When you have laid me in the earth, and reunited my bones to those of your father, then travel wherever thou wilt, even beyond the sea; but, as long as I live, endure to dwell in my house, and offend not God by afflicting your mother, who is at least blameless towards thee." [d]

Whether released by the death of his mother, or hurried away by the irresistible impulse which would

---

[d] M. Villemain, in his Essai sur l'Eloquence Chrétienne dans le Quatrième Siècle, has pointed out the exquisite simplicity and tenderness of this passage. De Sacerdotio, i.

not allow him to withhold himself from what he calls
"the true philosophy," Chrysostom, some years afterwards, entered into one of the monasteries in the
neighbourhood of Antioch. He had hardly escaped the
episcopal dignity, which was almost forced upon him by
the admirers of his early piety. Whether he considered this gentle violence lawful to compel devout
Christians to assume awful dignity, he did not hesitate
to practise a pious fraud on his friend Basilius, with
whom he promised to submit to consecration. Basilius
found himself a bishop, but looked in vain for his
treacherous friend who had deceived him into this
momentous step, but deserted him at the appointed
hour.

But the voice of Chrysostom was not doomed to
silence even in his seclusion. The secession of so many
of the leading youths from the duties of civil life, from
the municipal offices and the service of the army, had
awakened the jealousy of the government. Valens
issued his edict against those "followers of idleness." [e]
The monks were, in some instances, assailed by popular
outrage ; parents, against whose approbation their
children had deserted their homes and retired into the
desert, appealed to the imperial authority to maintain
their own. Chrysostom came forward as the zealous,
the vehement, advocate of the "true philosophy." [f] He
threatened misery in this life, and all the pains of hell
(of which he is prodigal in his early writings) against
the unnatural, the soul-slaying fathers, who forced their
sons to expose themselves to the guilt and danger of
the world, and forbade them to enter into the earthly
society of angels ; by this phrase he describes the

---

[e] Ignaviæ sectatores.   [f] Adversus Oppugnatores Vitæ Monasticæ.

monasteries near Antioch. He relates, with triumph, the clandestine conversion of a noble youth, through the connivance of his mother, whom the father, himself a soldier, had destined to serve in the armies of the empire.

But Chrysostom himself, whether he considered that the deep devotion of the monastery for some years had braced his soul to encounter the more perilous duties of the priesthood, appeared again in Antioch. His return was hailed by Flavianus, the bishop, who had succeeded to Meletius. He was ordained deacon, and then presbyter, and at once took his station in that office, which was sometimes reserved for the Bishop, as the principal preacher in that voluptuous and effeminate city.

The fervid imagination and glowing eloquence of Chrysostom, which had been lavished on the angelic immunity of the cœnobite or the hermit from the passions, ambition, and avarice inseparable from a secular life, now arrayed his new office in a dignity and saintly perfection, which might awake the purest ambition of the Christian. Chrysostom has the most exalted notion of the majesty, at the same time of the severity, of the sacerdotal character. His views of the office, of its mission and authority, are the most sublime; his demands upon their purity, blamelessness, and superiority to the rest of mankind, proportionably rigorous.[g]

Nor, in the loftiness of his tone as a preacher or his sanctity as a man, did he fall below his own standard of the Christian priesthood. His preaching already took its peculiar character. It was not so much addressed to

---

g The treatise de Sacerdotio passim.

the opinions as to the conscience of man. He threw aside the subtleties of speculative theology and repudiated, in general, the fine-drawn allegory in which the interpreters of Scripture had displayed their ingenuity, and amazed and fruitlessly wearied their unimproved audience. His scope was plain, severe, practical. Rigidly orthodox in his doctrine, he seemed to dwell more on the fruits of a pure theology (though at times he could not keep aloof from controversy) than on theology itself.

If, in her ordinary course of voluptuous amusement, of constant theatrical excitement, Antioch could not but listen to the commanding voice of the Christian orator, it is no wonder that in her hour of danger, possibly of impending ruin, the whole city stood trembling and awestruck beneath his pulpit. Soon after he had assumed the sacerdotal office, Chrysostom was placed in an extraordinary position as the representative of the bishop.

In one of those sudden tumultuous insurrections which take place among the populace of large cities, Antioch had resisted the exorbitant A.D. 387. demands of a new taxation, maltreated the imperial officers, and thrown down and dragged about, with every kind of insult, the statues of Theodosius, his empress, and their two sons.[h] The stupor of fear succeeded to this momentary outbreak of mutiny,

---

[h] It is curious to observe the similarity between the Pagan and Christian accounts of this incident which we have the good fortune to possess. Both ascribe the guilt to a few strangers, under the instigation of diabolic agency. Τοιούτοις ὑπηρέταις ὁ κακὸς χρώμενος δαίμων, ἔπραξεν, ἃ σιωπᾶν ἐβουλόμην. This is a sentence of Libanius (ad Theodos. iv. p. 638), not of Chrysostom. Flavianus exhorts Theodosius to pardon Antioch, in order that he may disappoint the malice of the devils, to whom he ascribes the guilt. Chrys. Hom. xvi. ad Antioch.

which had been quelled by a single troop of archers.
For days the whole people awaited in shuddering
agitation the sentence of the Emperor. The anger
of Theodosius was terrible; he had not yet, it is true,
ordered the massacre of the whole population of
Thessalonica, but his stern and relentless character was
too well known. Dark rumours spread abroad that he
had threatened to burn Antioch, to exterminate its
inhabitants, and to pass the ploughshare over its ruins.
Multitudes fled destitute from the city; others remained
shut up in their houses, for fear of being seized.
Instead of the forum crowded with thousands, one or
two persons were seen timidly wandering about. The
gay and busy Antioch had the appearance of a captured
and depopulated city. The theatres, the circus, were
closed; no marriage-song was heard; even the schools
were shut up.[1] In the mean time the government
resumed its unlimited and unresisted authority, which
it administered with the sternest severity and rigorous
inquisition into the guilt of individuals. The prisons
were thronged with criminals of every rank and station;
confiscation swept away their wealth, punishments of
every degree were inflicted on their persons. Citizens
of the highest rank were ignominiously scourged; those
who confessed their guilt were put to the sword, burned
alive, or thrown to the wild beasts.[k] Chrysostom's
description of the agony of those days is in the highest
style of dramatic oratory. Women of the highest rank,
brought up with the utmost delicacy and accustomed to
every luxury, were seen crowding around the gates, or

---

[1] Liban. ad Theod. in fin.

[k] Chrysostom asserts this in a fine
passage, in which he reminds his
hearers of their greater offences against
God. Καὶ οἱ μὲν σιδήρῳ, οἱ δὲ πυρὶ,
οἱ δε θηρίοις παραδοθέντες ἀπώλοντο.
Hom. iii. 6, p. 45.

in the outer judgement hall, unattended, repelled by
the rude soldiery, but still clinging to the doors or
prostrate on the ground, listening to the clash of the
scourges, the shrieks of the tortured victims, and the
shouts of the executioners ; one minute supposing that
they recognised the familiar voices of fathers, husbands,
or brothers ; or trembling lest those who were undergoing torture should denounce their relatives and
friends. Chrysostom passes from this scene, by a bold
but natural transition, to the terrors of the final Judgement, and the greater agony of that day.

Now was the time to put to the test the power of
Christianity, and to ascertain whether the orthodox
opinions of Theodosius were altogether independent
of that humanity which is the essence of the Gospel.
Would the Christian Emperor listen to the persuasive
supplications of the Christian prelate — that prelate
for whose character he had expressed the highest
respect ?

While Flavianus, the aged and feeble bishop, quitting
the bedside of his dying sister, set forth on his Flavianus
pious mission to the West, on Chrysostom sets forth to
intercede for
devolved the duty of assuaging the fears, of mercy.
administering consolation, and of profiting by this state
of stupor and dejection to correct the vices and enforce
serious thoughts upon the light and dissolute people.
Day after day he ascended the pulpit ; the whole
population, deserting the forum, forgetting the theatre
and the circus, thronged the churches. There was even
an attendance (an unusual circumstance) after the hour
of dinner. The whole city became a church. There is
wonderful skill and judgement in the art with which
the orator employs the circumstances of the time for
his purpose ; in the manner in which he allays the

terror, without too highly encouraging the hopes, of the people : "The clemency of the Emperor *may* forgive their guilt, but the Christians ought to be superior to the fear of death; they cannot be secure of pardon in this world, but they may be secure of immortality in the world to come."

Long before the success of the bishop's intercession could be known, the delegates of the Emperor, Hellabichus and Cæsarius, arrived with the sentence of Theodosius, which was merciful, if compared with what they had feared,—the destruction of the city, and the massacre of its inhabitants. But it was fatal to the pleasures, the comforts, the pride of Antioch. The theatres and the circus were to be closed; Antioch was no longer to enjoy theatrical representations of any kind; the baths, in an Eastern city not objects of luxury alone, but of cleanliness and health, were to be shut; and Antioch was degraded from the rank of a metropolitan city, to a town under the jurisdiction of Laodicea.

Sentence of Theodosius.

The city was in the deepest depression, but Chrysostom maintained his lofty tone of consolation. Antioch ought to rejoice at the prohibition of those scenes of vice and dissipation which disgraced the theatres : the baths tended to effeminacy and luxury, they were disdained by true philosophy—the monastic system ; the dignity of the city did not depend on its rank in the empire, but on the virtue of its citizens ; it might be a heavenly, if no longer an earthly, metropolis.

The inquisition into the guilt of those who had actually assisted, or had looked on in treasonable indifference, while the statues of the Emperor and his family were treated with such unseemly contumely, had commenced under the regular authorities; it was now carried on with stern and indiscriminate impartiality. The prisoners were crowded together in a great open enclosure, in one close and agonising troop, which comprehended the whole senate of the city. The third day of the inquiry was to witness the execution of the guilty, and no one, not the relatives or kindred of the wealthiest, the noblest, or the highest in station, knew whether the doom had not fallen on their fathers or husbands.

But Hellabichus and Cæsarius were men of humanity, and ventured to suspend the execution of the sentence. They listened to the supplications of the people. One mother, especially, seized and clung to the reins of the horse of Hellabichus. The monks who, while the philosophers, as Chrysostom asserts, had fled the city, had poured down from their mountain solitudes, and during the whole time had endeavoured to assuage the fear of the people, and to awaken the compassion of the government, renewed, not without effect, their pious exertions.[m] They crowded round the tribunal, and one, named Macedonius, was so courageous as boldly to remonstrate against the crime of avenging the destruction of a few images of brass by the destruction of the image of God in so many human beings. Cæsarius himself undertook a journey to Constantinople for farther instructions.

At length Chrysostom had the satisfaction to announce to the people the return of the bishop with an act of unlimited amnesty. He described the interview of Flavianus with the Emperor; his silence, his shame, his tears, when Theodosius gently reminded him of his benefactions

Issue of the interview of Flavianus with the Emperor.

---

[m] Chrysostom, Hom. xvii. vol. ii. p. 172.

to the city which enhanced their heinous ingratitude.
The reply of Flavianus, though the orator professes to
relate it on the authority of one present at the interview,
is no doubt coloured by the eloquence of Chrysostom.
The Bishop acknowledged the guilt of the city in the
most humiliating language. But he urged, that the
greater that guilt, the greater would be the magnanimity of the Emperor if he should pardon it. He
would raise statues, not of perishable materials, in the
hearts of all mankind. It is not the glory of Theodosius, he proceeded, but Christianity itself, which is
put to the test before the world. The Jews and
Greeks, even the most remote barbarians, are anxiously
watching whether this sentence will be that of Christian
clemency. How will they, all glorify the Christian's
God if he shall restrain the wrath of the master of the
world, and subdue him to that humanity which would
be magnanimous even in a private man. Inexorable
punishment might awe other cities into obedience, but
mercy would attach mankind by the stronger bonds
of love. It would be an imperishable example of
clemency, and all future acts of other sovereigns would
be but the fruit of this, and would reflect their glory on
Theodosius. What glory to concede that to a single
aged priest, from the fear of God, which he had refused
to all other suppliants. For himself, Flavianus could
never bear to return to his native city; he would
remain an exile, until that city was reconciled with the
Emperor. Theodosius, it is said, called to mind the
prayer of the Saviour for his enemies, and satisfied his
wounded pride that in his mercy he imitated his
Redeemer. He was even anxious that Flavianus should
return to announce the full pardon before the festival
of Easter. "Let the Gentiles," exclaims the ardent

preacher, " be confounded, or rather, let them be instructed by this unexampled instance of imperial clemency and episcopal influence." [n]

Theodosius had ceased to reign many years before Chrysostom was summoned to the pontifical throne of Constantinople. The East was now governed by women and eunuchs. In assum-ing the episcopal throne of the metropolis, to which he is said to have been transported almost by force, Chrysostom, who could not but be conscious of his power over the minds of men, might entertain visions of the noblest and purest ambition. His views of the dignity of the sacerdotal character were as lofty as those of his contemporaries in the West; while he asserted their authority, which set them apart and far above the rest of mankind, he demanded a moral superiority and entire devotion to their calling, which could not but rivet their authority upon the minds of men. The clergy, such as his glowing imagination conceived them, would unite the strongest corporate spirit with the highest individual zeal and purity. The influence of the bishop in Antioch, the deference which Theodosius had shown to the intercession of Flavianus, might encourage Chrysostom in the fallacious hope of restoring peace, virtue, and piety, as well as orthodoxy, in the imperial city.

A.D. 398. Chrysostom bishop of Constantinople.

But in the East, more particularly in the metropolis, the sacerdotal character never assumed the unassailable sanctity, the awful inviolability, which it attained in the West. The religion of Constantinople was that of the Emperor. Instead of growing up, like the Bishop of Rome, first to

Difference of the sacerdotal power in Rome and Constantinople.

---

[n] Chrysostom had ventured to assert—Ἅπερ οὐδενὶ ἑτέρῳ, ταῦτα χαριεῖται τοῖς ἱερεῦσι. Hom. xxi. 3.

independence, afterwards to sovereignty, the religious
supremacy was overawed and obscured by the presence
of the Imperial Government. In Rome, the Pope was
subject at times to the rebellious control of the aristocracy, or exposed to the irreverent fury of the populace;
but he constantly emerged from his transient obscurity
and resumed his power. In Constantinople, a voluptuous court, a savage populace, at this period multitudes
of concealed Arians, and heretics of countless shades
and hues at all periods, thwarted the plans, debased the
dignity, and desecrated the person of the Patriarch of
Constantinople.

In some respects, Chrysostom's character wanted
the peculiar, and perhaps inconsistent qualifications
requisite for his position. He was the preacher, but
not the man of the world. A great capital is apt to
demand that magnificence in its prelate at which it
murmurs. It will not respect less than splendid state
and the show of authority, while at the same time it
would have the severest austerity and the strongest
display of humility,—the pomp of the Pontiff with the
poverty and lowliness of the Apostle. Chrysostom
carried the asceticism of the monk not merely into his
private chamber but into his palace and his hall. The
great prelates of the West, when it was expedient,
could throw off the monk and appear as statesmen or as
nobles in their public transactions; though this, indeed,
was much less necessary than in Constantinople. But
Chrysostom cherished all these habits with zealous,
perhaps with ostentatious, fidelity. Instead of munificent
hospitality, he took his scanty meal in his solitary
chamber. His rigid economy endured none of that
episcopal sumptuousness with which his predecessor
Nectarius had dazzled the public eye: he proscribed

all the carpets, all the silken dresses; he sold the costly furniture and the rich vessels of his residence; he was said even to have retrenched from the church some of its gorgeous plate, and to have sold some rich marbles and furniture designed for the Anastasia. He was lavish, on the other hand, in his expenditure on the hospitals and charitable institutions. But even the uses to which they were applied, did not justify to the general feeling the alienation of those ornaments from the service of the church. The populace, who, no doubt, in their hours of discontent, had contrasted the magnificence of Nectarius with apostolical poverty, were now offended by the apostolical poverty of Chrysostom, which seemed unworthy of his lofty station.

But the Bishop of Constantinople had even a more difficult task in prescribing to himself the limits of his interference with secular affairs. It is easy to imagine, in the clergy, a high and serene indifference to the political tumults of society. This is perpetually demanded by those who find the sacerdotal influence adverse to their own views; but to the calm inquirer, this simple question becomes the most difficult and intricate problem in religious history. If religion consisted solely in the intercourse between man and his Creator; if the Christian minister were merely the officiating functionary in the ceremonial of the church, —the human mediator between the devotion of man and the providence of God,—the voice which expresses the common adoration,—the herald who announces the gracious message of revelation to mankind,—nothing could be more clear than the line which might exclude him from all political, or even all worldly affairs. But Christianity is likewise a moral power; and as that

Political difficulties of Chrysostom.

Interference of the clergy in secular affairs.

K 2

moral power or guide, religion, and the minister of
religion, cannot refrain from interposing in all questions
of human conduct; as the interpreter of the divine law
to the perplexed and doubting conscience, it cannot but
spread its dominion over the whole field of human
action. In this character religion embraced the whole
life of man, public as well as private. How was the
minister of that religion to pause and discriminate as to
the extent of his powers, particularly since the public
acts of the most eminent in station possessed such
unlimited influence over the happiness of society and
even the eternal welfare of the whole community?
What public misconduct was not at the same time an
unchristian act? Were the clergy, by connivance, to
become accomplices in vices which they did not
endeavour to counteract? Christianity on the throne
as in the cottage, was equally bound to submit on every
point in which religious motive or principle ought to
operate, in every act, therefore, of life, to the admitted
restraints of the Gospel; and the general feeling of
Christianity at this period had invested the clergy with
the right, or rather the duty, of enforcing the precepts
of the Gospel on every professed believer. How, then,
were the clergy to distinguish between the individual
and political capacity of the man; to respect the
prince, yet to advise the Christian; to look with indifference on one set of actions as secular, to admonish
on the danger of another as affairs of conscience?

Nor at this early period of its still aggressive, still
consciously beneficial influence, could the hierarchy be
expected to anticipate with coldly prophetic prudence
the fatal consequence of some of its own encroachments
on worldly authority. The bishop of a great capital
was the conductor, the representative, of the moral

power of the Gospel, which was perpetually striving to obtain its ascendancy over brute force, violence, and vice ; and of necessity, perhaps, was not always cautious or discreet in the means to which it resorted. It became contaminated in the incessant strife, and forgot its end, or rather sought for the mastery as its end, rather than as the legitimate means of promoting its beneficial objects. Under the full, and no doubt, at first, warrantable persuasion, that it was advancing the happiness and virtue of mankind, where should it arrest its own course, or set limits to its own humanising and improving interpositions? Thus, under the constant temptation of assuming, as far as possible, the management of affairs which were notoriously mismanaged through the vices of public men, the administration even of public matters by the clergy might seem, to them at least, to insure justice, disinterestedness, and clemency. Till tried by the possession of power, they would be the last to discern the danger of being invested in that power.

The first signal interposition of Chrysostom in the political affairs of Constantinople was an act Eutropius not merely of humanity but of gratitude. the eunuch. Eutropius the eunuch, minister of the feeble Arcadius, is condemned to immortal infamy by the vigorous satire of Claudian. Among his few good deeds,· had been the advancement of Chrysostom to the see of Constantinople. Eutropius had found it necessary to restrict the right of asylum, which began to be generally claimed by all the Christian churches, little foreseeing that to the bold assertion of that right he would owe his life.

There is something sublime in the first notion of the right of asylum. It is one of those institutions based in the universal religious sentiment of man; it is found Right of asylum. in almost all religions. In the Greek, as in the Jewish, man took refuge from the vengeance, often from the injustice, of his fellow-men, in the presence of the gods. Not merely private revenge, but the retributive severity of the law, stands rebuked before the dignity of the divine court, in which the criminal has lodged his appeal. The lustrations in the older religions, the rites of expiation and reconciliation performed in many of the temples, the appellations of certain deities, as the reconcilers or pacifiers of man,[o] were enwoven with their mythology, and embodied in their poetry. But Christianity, in a still higher and more universal sense, might assume to take under its protection, in order to amend and purify, the outcast of society, whom human justice followed with relentless vengeance. As the representative of the God of mercy it excluded no human being from the pale of repentance, and would protect the worst, when disposed to that salutary change, if it could possibly be made consistent with the public peace and safety. The merciful intervention of the clergy between the criminal and his sentence, at a period when the laws were so implacable and sanguinary, was at once consistent with Christian charity and tended to some mitigation of the ferocious manners of the age. It gave time at least for exasperated justice to reconsider its sentence, and checked that vindictive impulse, which if it did not outrun the law, hurried it to instantaneous and irrevocable execution.[p] But that which commenced in pure

---

[o] The ἀποτρόπαιοι, or averruncatores.

[p] In a law which is extant in Greek, there is an elaborate argument, that if the right of asylum had been granted by the Heathen to their altars, and to the statues of the Emperors, it ought to belong to the temples of God.

See

benevolence had already, it should seem, begun to degenerate into a source of power. The course of justice was impeded, but not by a wise discrimination between the more or less heinous delinquents, or a salutary penitential system, which might reclaim the guilty and safely restore him to society.

Like other favourites of arbitrary sovereigns, Eutropius was suddenly precipitated from the height of power. The army forced the sentence of his dismissal from the timid Emperor ; and the furious populace, as usual, thirsted for the blood of him to whose unbounded sway they had so long submitted in humble obedience. Eutropius fled in haste to that asylum, the sanctity of which had been limited by his own decree ; and the courage and influence of Chrysostom protected that most forlorn of human beings, the discarded favourite of a despot. The armed soldiery and the raging populace were met at the door of the church by the defenceless ecclesiastic. His demeanour and the sanctity of the place arrested the blind fury of the assailants. Chrysostom before the Emperor pleaded the cause of Eutropius with the same fearless freedom ; and for once the life of a fallen minister was spared, his sentence was commuted for banishment. His fate indeed was only delayed ; he was afterwards brought back from Cyprus, his place of exile, and beheaded at Chalcedon.

A.D. 399.

Chrysostom saves the life of Eutropius.

See the laws which defined the right of asylum, Cod. Theodos. ix. 45. 3. *et seqq.* The sacred space extended to the outer gates of the church. But those who took refuge in the church were on no account to be permitted to profane the holy building itself by eating or sleeping within it. " Quibus si perfuga non adnuit, neque consentit, præferenda humanitati religio est." There was a strong prohibition against introducing arms into the churches ; a prohibition which the Emperors themselves did not scruple to violate on more than one occasion.

But with all his courage, his eloquence, his moral dignity, Chrysostom, instead of establishing a firm and permanent authority over Constantinople, became himself the victim of intrigue and jealousy. Besides his personal habits and manners, the character of Chrysostom, firm on great occasions and eminently persuasive when making a general address to the multitude, was less commanding and authoritative in his constant daily intercourse with the various orders: Calm and self-possessed as an orator, he was accused of being passionate and overbearing in ordinary business : the irritability of feeble health may have caused some part of this infirmity. Men, whose minds, like that of Chrysostom, are centered on one engrossing object, are apt to abandon the details of business to others, who thus become necessary to them, and at length, if artful and dextrous, rule them with inextricable sway: they have much knowledge of mankind, little practical acquaintance with individual men. Thus, Chrysostom was completely governed by his deacon Serapion who managed his affairs, and like all men of address in such stations, while he exercised all the power, and secured the solid advantages, left the odium and responsibility upon his master. On the whole, the character of Chrysostom retained something of the unworldly monastic enthusiasm, and wanted decisive practical wisdom, when compared, for instance, with Ambrose in the West; and thus his character powerfully contributed to his fall.[q]

But the circumstances of his situation might have

Chrysostom governed by his deacon Serapion.

---

[q] The unfavourable view of Chrysostom's character is brought out perhaps with more than impartiality by the ecclesiastical historian Sozomen, who wrote at Constantinople, and may have preserved much of the hostile tradition relating to him.

embarrassed even Ambrose himself. All orders and interests conspired against him. The court would not endure the grave and severe censor ; the clergy rebelled against the rigour of the prelate's discipline; the populace, though when under the spell of his eloquence, fondly attached to his person, no doubt, in general resented his implacable condemnation of their amusements. The Arians, to whom, in his uncompromising zeal, he had persuaded the Emperor to refuse a single church, though demanded by the most powerful subject of the empire, Gainas the Goth, were still no doubt secretly powerful. A Pagan prefect, Optatus, seized the opportunity of wreaking his animosity towards Christianity itself upon its powerful advocate. Some wealthy females are named as resenting the severe condemnation of their dress and manners.[r]

Of all these adversaries, the most dangerous, the most persevering, and the most implacable, were those of his own order and his own rank.[s] The sacerdotal authority in the East was undermined by its own divisions. The imperial power, which, in the hands of a violent, and not irreproachable woman, the Empress Eudoxia, might, perhaps, have quailed before the energy of a blameless and courageous prelate, allied itself with one section of the church, and so secured its triumph over the whole. The more Chrysostom endeavoured to carry out by episcopal authority those exalted notions of the sacerdotal character which he had developed in his work upon the priesthood, the more he estranged many of his natural supporters. He visited the whole of Asia Minor ; degraded bishops ; exposed with unsparing indignation the vices and venality of the clergy ; and involved them

---

[r] Tillemont, p. 180.

[s] The good Tillemont confesses this humiliating truth with shame and reluctance. Vie de Chrysostome, p. 181.

all in one indiscriminate charge of simony and licentiousness. The assumption of this authority was somewhat questionable; the severity with which it was exercised did not reconcile the reluctant province to submission. Among the malcontent clergy, four bishops took the lead; but the head of this unrelenting faction was Theophilus, the violent and unscrupulous Prelate of Alexandria. The apparently trivial causes which inflamed the hostility of Theophilus confirm a suspicion, previously suggested, that the rivalry of the two principal sees in the East mingled with the personal animosity of Theophilus against the Bishop of Constantinople. Chrysostom had been accused of extending his jurisdiction beyond its legitimate bounds. Certain monks of Nitria had fled from the persecutions of Theophilus, and taken refuge in Constantinople; and Chrysostom had extended his countenance, if not his protection, to these revolted subjects of the Alexandrian prelate. But he had declined to take legal cognisance of the dispute as a superior prelate, or as the head of a council; partly, he states,[t] out of respect for Theophilus, partly because he was unwilling to interfere in the affairs of another province. But Theophilus was not so scrupulous; he revenged himself for the supposed invasion of his own province by a most daring inroad on that of his rival. He assumed for the Patriarch of Alexandria the right of presiding over the Eastern bishops, and of summoning the Bishop of Constantinople before this irregular tribunal. Theophilus, with the sanction, if not by the invitation, of the Empress, landed at Constantinople. He was accompanied by a band of Alexandrian

Marginal note: Theophilus of Alexandria.

---

[t] Epist. ad Innocentium Papam, vol. iii. p. 516.

mariners as a protection against the populace of the city:

The council was held, not in Constantinople, but at a place called the Oak, in the suburb of Chalcedon. It consisted for the most part of Egyptian bishops, under the direct influence of Theophilus, and of Asiatic prelates, the personal enemies of Chrysostom.[u] For fourteen days it held its sessions, and received informations, which gradually grew into twenty-nine grave and specific charges. Four times was Chrysostom summoned to appear before this self-appointed tribunal, of which it was impossible for him to recognise the legal authority. In the mean time, he was not inactive in his peculiar sphere—the pulpit. Unfortunately, the authenticity of the sermon ascribed to him at this period is not altogether certain, nor the time at which some extant discourses, if genuine, were delivered, conclusively settled. One, however, bears strong indications of the manner and sentiments of Chrysostom; and it is generally acknowledged that he either did boldly use, or was accused of using, language full of contumelious allusion to the Empress. This sermon, therefore, if not an accurate report of his expressions, may convey the sense of what he actually uttered, or which was attributed to him by his adversaries.[x] "The billows," said the energetic prelate, "are

Council of the Oak.

---

[u] It is contested whether there were thirty or forty-six bishops.

[x] It is singularly characteristic of the Christianity of the times to observe the charges against which Chrysostom protests with the greatest vehemence; and this part of the oration in question is confirmed by one of his letters to Cyriacus. Against that of personal impurity with a female, he calmly offers the most unquestionable evidence. But he was likewise accused of having administered baptism after he had eaten. On this he breaks out :—" If I have done this, Anathema upon me; may I be no longer counted among bishops, nor be admitted among the angels accepted

mighty, and the storm furious; but we fear not to be wrecked, for we are founded on a rock. What can I fear? Death? *To me to live is Christ, and to die is gain.* Exile? *The earth is the Lord's and the fulness thereof.* Confiscation? *We brought nothing into this world, and it is certain we can carry nothing out of it.* I scorn the terrors, and smile at the advantages of life. I fear not death. I desire to live only for your profit. The church against which you strive, dashes away your assaults into idle foam. It is fixed by God, who shall revoke it? The church is stronger than Heaven itself! *Heaven and earth shall pass away, but my words shall not pass away.* * * * But you know, my brethren, the true cause of my ruin. Because I have not strewn rich carpets on my floors, nor clothed myself in silken robes; because I have discountenanced the sensuality of certain persons. The seed of the serpent is still alive, but grace is still on the side of Elijah." Then follows in obscure and embarrassed language, as though, if genuine, the preacher were startled at his own boldness, an allusion to the fate of John the Baptist, and to the hostility of Herodias:—"It is a time of wailing—lo, all things tend to "*disgrace;* but time judgeth all things." The fatal word, "*disgrace,*" (ἀδοξία) was supposed to be an allusion to Eudoxia, the Empress.

There was a secret understanding between the court and the council. The court urged the proceedings of the council, and the council pronounced the sentence of deposition, but left to the

Condemna-
tion of Chry-
sostom,

---

of God." He was said to have administered the sacrament to those who had in like manner broken their fast. " If I have done so, may I be rejected of Christ." He then justifies himself, even if guilty, by the example of Paul, and even of Christ himself, but still seems to look on this breach of discipline with the utmost horror.

court to take cognisance of the darker charge of high
treason, of which they asserted Chrysostom to be guilty,
but which was beyond their jurisdiction. The alleged
treason was the personal insult to the Empress Eudoxia,
which was construed into exciting the people to rebellion.
But the execution of this sentence embarrassed the
council and the irresolute government. Chrysostom now
again ruled the popular mind with unbounded sway.
It would have been dangerous to have seizèd him in
the church, environed, as he constantly was, by crowds
of admiring hearers, whom a few fervent words might
have maddened into insurrection.

Chrysostom, however, shrunk, whether from timidity
or Christian peacefulness of disposition, from
being the cause, even innocently, of tumult
and bloodshed. He had neither the ambition, the
desperate recklessness, nor perhaps the resolution, of
a demagogue. He would not be the Christian tribune
of the people. He seized the first opportunity of the
absence of his hearers quietly to surrender himself
to the imperial officers. He was cautiously transported by night, though the jealous populace crowded
the streets in order to release their prelate from
the hands of his enemies, to the opposite side of
the Bosphorus and confined in a villa on the Bithynian
shore.

The triumph of Chrysostom's enemies was complete.
Theophilus entered the city, and proceeded to wreak
his vengeance on the partisans of his adversary; the
Empress rejoiced in the conscious assurance of her
power; the people were overawed into gloomy and
sullen silence.

The night of the following day, strange and awful
sounds were heard throughout the city. The palace,

the whole of Constantinople, shook with an earthquake.
The Empress, as superstitious as she was

Earthquake.

violent, when she felt her chamber rock
beneath her, shuddering at the manifest wrath of
Heaven, fell on her knees, and entreated the Emperor
to revoke the fatal sentence. She wrote a hasty letter,
disclaiming all hostility to the banished prelate, and
protesting that she was " innocent of his blood." The
next day, the palace was surrounded by clamorous
multitudes, impatiently demanding his recall. The
voice of the people and the voice of God seemed to join

Return of
Chrysostom.

in the vindication of Chrysostom. The edict
of recall was issued; the Bosphorus swarmed
with barks, eager to communicate the first intelligence,
and to obtain the honour of bringing back the guardian
and the pride of the city. He was met on his arrival
by the whole population, men, women, and children ;
all who could, bore torches in their hands, and hymns
of thanksgiving, composed for the occasion, were
chanted before him, as he proceeded to the great
church. His enemies fled on all sides. Soon after,
Theophilus, on the demand of a free council, left
Constantinople, at the dead of the night, and embarked
for Alexandria.

There is again some doubt as to the authenticity of
the first discourse delivered by Chrysostom on this
occasion,—none of the second. But the first was an
extemporaneous address, to which the extant speech
appears to correspond. " What shall I say ? Blessed
be God ! These were my last words on my departure,
these the first on my return. Blessed be God ! because
he permitted the storm to rage; Blessed be God !
because he has allayed it. Let my enemies behold
how their conspiracy has advanced my peace, and

redounded to my glory. Before, the church alone was crowded, now, the whole forum is become a church. The games are celebrating in the circus, but the whole people pour like a torrent to the church. Your prayers in my behalf are more glorious than a diadem,—the prayers both of men and women; for in *Christ there is neither male nor female.*"

In the second oration he draws an elaborate comparison between the situation of Abraham in Egypt and his own. The barbarous Egyptian (this struck, no doubt, at Theophilus) had endeavoured to defile his Sarah, the church of Constantinople; but the faithful church had remained, by the power of God, uncontaminated by this rebuked Abimelech. He dwelt with pardonable pride on the faithful attachment of his followers. They had conquered; but how? by prayer and submission. The enemy had brought arms into the sanctuary, they had prayed; like a spider's web the enemy had been scattered, the faithful remained firm as a rock. The Empress herself had joined the triumphal procession, when the sea became, as the city, covered with all ranks, all ages, and both sexes.[y]

But the peace and triumph of Chrysostom were not lasting. As the fears of the Empress were allayed, the old feeling of hatred to the Bishop, embittered by the shame of defeat, and the constant suspicion that either the preacher or his audience pointed at her his most · vigorous declamation, rankled in the mind of Eudoxia. It had become a strife for ascendancy, and neither could recede with safety and honour. Opportunities could not but occur to enrage and exasperate; nor

---

[y] Chrysostom, in both these discourses, states a curious circumstance, that the Jews of Constantinople took great interest in his cause.

would ill-disposed persons be wanting to inflame the
passions of the Empress, by misrepresenting and
personally applying the bold and indignant language
of the prelate.

A statue of the Empress was about to be erected;
Statue of the and on these occasions of public festival the
Empress. people were wont to be indulged in dances,
pantomimes, and every kind of theatrical amusement.
The zeal of Chrysostom was always especially directed
against these idolatrous amusements, which often, he
confesses, drained the church of his hearers. This,
now ill-timed, zeal was especially awakened, because
the statue was to be erected, and the rejoicings to take
place, in front of the entrance to the great church, the
St. Sophia. His denunciations were construed into
personal insults to the Empress; she threatened a new
council. The prelate threw off the remaining restraints
of prudence; repeated more explicitly the allusion
which he had before but covertly hinted. He
thundered out a homily, with the memorable exordium,
" Herodias is maddening, Herodias is dancing, Herodias
demands the head of John." If Chrysostom could
even be suspected of such daring outrage against
the temporal sovereign; if he ventured on language
approaching to such unmeasured hostility; it was
manifest that either the imperial authority must
quail and submit to the sacerdotal domination, or
employ, without scruple, its power to crush the bold
usurpation.

An edict of the Emperor suspended the prelate from
Second con- his functions. Though forty-two bishops
demnation of
Chrysostom. adhered, with inflexible fidelity, to his cause,
he was condemned by a second hostile council, not on
any new charge, but for contumacy in resisting the

decrees of the former assembly, and for a breach of the ecclesiastical laws, in resuming his authority while under the condemnation of a council.

The soldiers of the Emperor were more dangerous enemies than the prelates. In the midst of A.D. 404. the solemn celebration of Good Friday, in the Tumults in the church. great church of Santa Sophia, the military forced their way, not merely into the nave, but up to the altar, on which were placed the consecrated elements. Many worshippers were trodden under foot; many wounded by the swords of the soldiers; the clergy were dragged to prison; some females, who were about to be baptized, were obliged to fly with their disordered apparel : the waters of the font were stained with blood; the soldiers pressed up to the altar ; seized the sacred vessels as their plunder : the sacred elements were scattered about ; their garments were bedewed with the blood of the Redeemer.[z] Constantinople for several days had the appearance of a city which had been stormed. Wherever the partisans of Chrysostom were assembled, they were assaulted and dispersed by the soldiery ; females were exposed to insult, and one frantic attempt was made to assassinate the prelate.[a]

Chrysostom at length withdrew from the contest; he escaped from the friendly custody of his Chrysostom adherents, and surrendered himself to the surrenders. imperial officers. He was immediately conveyed by night to the Asiatic shore. At the instant of his departure, another fearful calamity agitated the public

---

[z] Chrysostom, Epist. ad Innocentium, c. iii. v. iii. p. 519. Chrysostom exempts the Emperor from all share in this outrage; but attributes it to the hostile bishops.

[a] See Letter to Olympias, p. 548.

mind. The church which he left burst into flames,
and the conflagration, said to have first broken out in
the episcopal throne, reached the roof of the building,
and spread from thence to the senate-house. These
two magnificent edifices, the latter of which contained
some noble specimens of ancient art, became in a few
hours a mass of ruins. The partisans of Chrysostom,
and Chrysostom himself, were, of course, accused of this
act, the author of which was never discovered, and in
which no life was lost. But the bishop was charged
with the horrible design of destroying his enemies in
the church; his followers were charged with the guilt
of incendiarism with a less atrocious object, that no
bishop after Chrysostom might be seated in his
pontifical throne.[b]

The prelate was not permitted to choose his place
of exile. The peaceful spots which might have been
found in the more genial climate of Bithynia, or in the
adjacent provinces, would have been too near the
capital. He was transported to Cucusus, a small town
in the mountainous and savage district of Armenia.
On his journey thither of several days, he suffered much
from fever and disquiet of mind, and from the cruelty
of the officer who commanded the guard.[c]

Yet his influence was not extinguished by his

---

[b] There are three laws in the
Theodosian Code against unlawful
and seditious meetings (conventicula),
directed against the followers of
Chrysostom,—the Joannitæ, as they
were called, "qui sacrilego animo
auctoritatem nostri numinis ausi
fuerint expugnare." The *deity* is the
usual term, but the deity of the feeble
Arcadius, and of the passionate
Eudoxia, reads strangely.

[c] The zeal of Chrysostom did not
slumber even in this remote retreat.
In his power he had caused to be
destroyed all the temples of Cybele
in Phrygia. He now urged the tardy
monks to the destruction of all the
Heathen Temples in the neighbouring
districts. Epist. 129. 126. Compare
Chastel, p. 220.

absence. The Eastern Church was almost governed from the solitary cell of Chrysostom. He corre- His retreat. sponded in all quarters ; women of rank and opulence sought his solitude in disguise. The bishops of many distant sees sent him assistance, and coveted his advice. The Bishop of Rome received his letters with respect, and wrote back ardent commendations of his patience. The exile of Cucusus exercised perhaps more extensive authority than the Patriarch of Constantinople.[d]

He was not, however, permitted to remain in peace in this miserable seclusion : sometimes his life was endangered by the invasions of the Isaurian marauders ; and he was obliged to take refuge in a neighbouring fortress, named Ardissa. He encouraged his ardent disciples with the hope, the assurance, of his speedy return ; but he miscalculated the obstinate and implacable resentment of his persecutors. At length an order came to remove him to Pityus, on the Euxine, a still more savage place on the verge of the empire. He died on the journey, near Comana, in Pontus.

Some years afterwards, the remains of Chrysostom were transported to Constantinople with His remains transported to Constantinople. the utmost reverence, and received with solemn pomp. Constantinople, and the imperial family, submitted with eager zeal to worship

---

[d] Among his letters may be remarked those written to the celebrated Olympias. This wealthy widow, who had refused the solicitations or commands of Theodosius to marry one of his favourites, had almost washed away, by her austerities and virtues, the stain of her nuptials, and might rank in Christian estimation with those unsullied virgins who had never been contaminated by marriage. She was the friend of all the distinguished and orthodox clergy,—of Gregory of Nazianzum, and of Chrysostom. Chrysostom records to her *praise*, that by her austerities, she had brought on painful diseases, which baffled the art of medicine. Chrysost. Epist. viii. p. 540.

as a saint him whom they would not endure as a prelate.

The remarkable part in the whole of this persecution of Chrysostom is that it arose not out of difference of doctrine or polemic hostility. No charge of heresy darkened the pure fame of the great Christian orator. His persecution had not the dignity of conscientious bigotry; it was a struggle for power between the temporal and ecclesiastical supremacy; but the passions and the personal animosities of ecclesiastics, the ambition, and perhaps the jealousy of the Alexandrian Patriarch as to jurisdiction, lent themselves to the degradation of the episcopal authority in Constantinople, from which it never rose. No doubt the choleric temper, the overstrained severity, the monastic habits, the ambition to extend his authority, perhaps beyond its legitimate bounds, and the indiscreet zeal of Chrysostom, laid him open to his adversaries; but in any other station, in the episcopate of any other city, these infirmities would have been lost in the splendour of his talents and his virtues. Though he might not have weaned the general mass of the people from their vices or their amusements, which he proscribed with equal severity, yet he would have commanded general respect; and nothing less than a schism, arising out of religious difference, would have shaken or impaired his authority.

At all events, the fall of Chrysostom was an inauspicious omen, and a warning which might repress the energy of future prelates; and, doubtless, the issue of this conflict materially tended to degrade the office of the chief bishop in the Eastern empire. It may be questioned whether the proximity of the court, and such a ccurt as that of the East, would, under any circumstances, have allowed the episcopate to assume its legitimate power, far less to have encroached on the temporal sovereignty. But after this time, the Bishop of Constantinople almost sank into a high officer of state ; appointed by the influence, if not directly nominated by the Emperor, his gratitude was bound to reverence, or his prudence to dread, that arbitrary power which had raised him from nothing, and might dismiss him to his former insignificance. Except on some rare occasions, he bowed with the rest of the empire before the capricious will of the sovereign or the ruling favourite ; he was content if the Emperor respected the outward ceremonial of the church, and did not openly espouse any heretical doctrine.

Christianity thus remained, in some respects, an antagonist principle, counteracting by its perpetual remonstrance, and rivalling by its attractive ceremonial, the vices and licentious diversions of the capital ; but its moral authority was not allied with power ; it quailed under the universal despotism, and was entirely inefficient as a corrective of imperial tyranny. It thus escaped the evils inseparable from the undue elevation of the sacerdotal character, and the temptations to encroach beyond its proper limits on the civil power; but it likewise gradually sank far below that uncompromising independence, that venerable majesty, which might impose some restraint on the worst excesses of violence, and infuse justice and humanity into the manners of the court and of the people.

CHAPTER X.

The great Prelates of the West.

THE character and the fate of Ambrose offer the
Ambrose
Archbishop
of Milan. strongest contrast with that of Chrysostom.
Ambrose was no dreaming solitary brought
up in the seclusion of the desert or among a fraternity
of religious husbandmen. He had been versed in civil
business from his youth; he had already obtained a
high station in the Imperial service. His ˉeloquence
had little of the richness, imaginative variety, or
dramatic power of the Grecian orator; hard but
vigorous, it was Roman, forensic, practical—I mean
where it related to affairs of business, or addressed men
in general; it has, as we shall hereafter observe, a very
different character in some of his theological writings.

In Ambrose the sacerdotal character assumed a
dignity and an influence as yet unknown; it first began
to confront the throne not only on terms of equality,
but of superior authority, and to exercise a spiritual
dictatorship over the supreme magistrate. The resistance of Athanasius to the Imperial authority had
been firm but deferential, passive rather than aggressive.
In his *public* addresses he had respected the majesty of
the empire; at all events, the hierarchy of that period
only questioned the authority of the sovereign in
matters of faith. But in Ambrose the episcopal power
acknowledged no limits to its moral dominion, and
admitted no distinction of persons. While the bishops
of Rome were comparatively without authority, and

still partially obscured by the concentration of Paganism
in the aristocracy of the Capitol, the Archbishop of
Milan began to develop papal power and papal im-
periousness. Ambrose was the spiritual ancestor of the
Hildebrands and the Innocents. Like Chrysostom,
Ambrose had to strive against the passionate animosity
of an empress, not merely exasperated against him by
his suspected disrespect and disobedience, but by the
bitterness of religious difference. Yet how opposite
the result! And Ambrose had to assert his religious
authority, not against the feeble Arcadius, but against
his father, the great Theodosius. We cannot, indeed,
but recognise something of the undegraded Roman or
the West in Ambrose; Chrysostom has something of
the feebleness and degeneracy of the Byzantine.

The father of Ambrose, who bore the same name,
had administered the province of Gaul as   Youth of
prætorian prefect. The younger Ambrose,   Ambrose.
while pursuing his studies at Rome, had attracted the
notice of Probus, prætorian prefect of Italy. Ambrose,
through his influence, was appointed to the administration of the provinces of Æmilia and Liguria.[a] Probus
was a Christian, and his parting admonition to the
young civilian was couched in these prophetic words—
"Rule the province, not as a judge, but as a bishop."[b]
Milan was within the department assigned to Ambrose.
This city had now begun almost to rival or eclipse
Rome as the capital of the Occidental empire, and from
the celebrity of its schools it was called the Athens of
the West. The Church of Milan was rent with

---

[a] Chiefly from the life of Ambrose
affixed to the Benedictine edition of
his works; the Life by Paulinus; and

Tillemont.
[b] Paul. Vit. Ambros. 8.

divisions. On a vacancy caused by the death of Auxentius, the celebrated Arian, the two parties, the Arian and the Athanasian, violently contested the appointment of the bishop.

Ambrose appeared in his civil character to allay the tumult, by the awe of his presence and by the persuasive force of his eloquence. He spoke so wisely, and in such a Christian spirit, that a general acclamation suddenly broke forth, "Ambrose, be bishop—Ambrose, be bishop." Ambrose was yet only a catechumen; he attempted in every way, by assuming a severe character as a magistrate, and by flight, to elude the unexpected honour.[c] The ardour of the people, and the approbation of the Emperor,[d] compelled him to assume the office. Ambrose cast off at once the pomp and majesty of his civil state; but that which was in some degree disadvantageous to Chrysostom, his severe simplicity of life, only increased the admiration and attachment of the less luxurious, or at least less effeminate, West, to their pious prelate; for Ambrose assumed only the austerity, nothing of the inactive and contemplative seclusion of the monastic system. The only Eastern influence which fettered his strong mind was his earnest admiration of celibacy; in all other respects he was a Roman statesman, not a meditative Oriental, or rhetorical Greek. The strong contrast of this doctrine with the dissolute manners of Rome, which no doubt extended to Milan, made it the more impressive: it was received with all the ardour of novelty, and the impetuosity of the Italian character; it captivated all ranks and all

Ambrose Bishop. A.D. 374.

Ambrose advocate of celibacy.

---

[c] De Offic.; Vita S. Ambros. p. xxxiv.; Epist. xxi. p. 865; Epist. lxiii.

[d] Compare the account of Valentinian's conduct in Theodoret, iv. 7.

orders. Mothers shut up their daughters, lest they
should be exposed to the chaste seduction of the
bishop's eloquence; and, binding themselves by rash
vows of virginity, forfeit the hope of becoming Roman
matrons. Ambrose, immediately on his appointment,
under Valentinian I., asserted that ecclesiastical power
which he confirmed under the feeble reign of Gratian
and Valentinian II.;[e] he maintained it when he was
confronted by a nobler antagonist, the great Theodosius.
He assumed the office of director of the royal conscience,
and he administered that office with all the uncompromising moral dignity which had no indulgence for
unchristian vices, for injustice, or cruelty, even in an
emperor; and with all the stern and conscientious
intolerance of one, with whom hatred of paganism and
of heresy was a prime article of his creed. The Old
and the New Testament met in the person of Ambrose
—the implacable hostility to idolatry, the abhorrence
of every deviation from the established formulary of
belief; the wise and courageous benevolence, the
generous and unselfish devotion to the great interests of
humanity.

If Christianity assumed a haughtier and more rigid
tone in the conduct and writings of Ambrose, it was by
no means forgetful of its gentler duties, in allaying
human misery and extending its beneficent care to the
utmost bounds of society. With Ambrose it began its
high office of mitigating the horrors of slavery, which
now that war raged in turn on every frontier, might
seem to threaten individually the whole free population
of the empire. Rome, who had drawn new supplies of
slaves from almost every frontier of her dominions, now

---

e Theodoret, iv. 7.

suffered fearful reprisals; her free citizens were sent
into captivity and sold in the markets by the barbarians,
whose ancestors had been bought and bartered by her
Redemption
of captives
by Ambrose. insatiable slave trade. The splendid offerings
of piety, the ornaments, even the consecrated
vessels of the churches, were prodigally expended by
the Bishop of Milan, in the redemption of captives.[f]
" The church possesses gold, not to treasure up, but to
distribute it for the welfare and happiness of men.
We are ransoming the souls of men from eternal
perdition. It is not merely the lives of men and the
honour of women, which are endangered in captivity,
but the faith of their children. The blood of redemption which has gleamed in those golden cups has
sanctified them, not for the service alone, but for the
redemption of man."[g] These arguments may be
considered as a generous repudiation of the ecclesiastical
spirit for the nobler ends of beneficence ; and, no doubt,
in that mediation of the church between mankind and
the miseries of slavery, which was one of her most
constant and useful ministrations during the darker
period of human society, the example and authority of
Ambrose perpetually encouraged the generosity of the
more liberal, and repressed the narrow view of those
who considered the consecrated treasures of the church
inviolable, even for these more sacred objects.[h]

The ecclesiastical zeal of Ambrose, like that of
Chrysostom, scorned the limits of his own diocese.
The see of Sirmium was vacant ; Ambrose appeared

[f] Numerent quos redemerint templa
captivos. So Ambrose appeals, in
excusable pride, to the heathen
orator. Ambros. Epist. ii. in Symmachum.

[g] Offic. c. 15. c. 28.. Compare
Greg. M. Epist. vi. 35. vii. 2. 14.
[h] Even Fleury argues that these
could not be *consecrated* vessels.

in that city to prevent the election of an Arian, and to secure the appointment of an orthodox bishop. The strength of the opposite party lay in the zeal and influence of the Empress Justina. Am- A.D. 379. brose defied both, and made himself a powerful and implacable enemy.

But, for a time, Justina was constrained to suppress her resentment. In a few years, Ambrose appears in a new position for a Christian A.D. 383. bishop, as the mediator between rival competitors for the empire. The ambassador sent to Maximus (who had assumed the purple in Gaul, and, after the murder of Gratian, might be reasonably suspected of hostile designs on Italy), was no distinguished warrior, or influential civilian ; the difficult negociation was forced upon the bishop of Milan. The character and weight of Ambrose appeared the best protection of the young Valentinian. Ambrose is said to have refused to communicate with Maximus, the murderer A.D. 375. of his sovereign. The interests of his earthly monarch or of the empire would not induce him to sacrifice for an instant those of his heavenly Master ; he would have no fellowship with the man of blood.[i] Yet so completely, either by his ability as a negociator or by his dignity and sanctity as a prelate, did he overawe the usurper, as to avert the evils of war, and to arrest the hostile invasion of his diocese and of Italy. He succeeded in establishing peace.

But the gratitude of Justina for this essential service could not avert the collision of hostile religious Dispute with the Empress creeds. The Empress demanded one of the Justina. churches in Milan for the celebration of the Arian

---

[i] The seventeenth Epistle of Ambrose relates the whole transaction, p. 852.

service. The first and more modest request named the Porcian Basilica without the gates, but these demands rose to the now and largest edifice within the walls.[k] The answer of Ambrose was firm and distinct; it asserted the inviolability of all property in the possession of the church—" A bishop cannot alienate that which is dedicated to God." After some fruitless negociation, the officers of the Emperor proceeded to take possession of the Porcian Basilica. Where these buildings had belonged to the state, the Emperor might still, perhaps, assert the right of property. Tumults arose: an Arian priest was severely handled and only rescued from the hands of the populace by the influence of Ambrose. Many wealthy persons were thrown into prison by the government, and heavy fines exacted on account of these seditions. But the inflexible Ambrose persisted in his refusal to acknowledge the imperial authority over things dedicated to God. When he was commanded to allay the populace, "it is in my power," he answered, " to refrain from exciting their violence, but it is for God to appease it when excited.[m] The soldiers surrounded the building; they threatened to violate the sanctity of the church in which Ambrose was performing the usual solemnities. The bishop calmly continued his functions, and his undisturbed countenance seemed as if his whole mind was absorbed in its devotion. The soldiers entered the church; the affrighted females began to fly; but the rude and armed men fell on their knees and assured Ambrose that they came to pray and not to fight.[n] Ambrose ascended the pulpit; his

---

[k] Paul. Vit. Ambrose. Ambros. Epist. xx.

[m] Referebam in meo jure esse, ut non excitarem, in Dei manu, uti mitigaret.

[n] It would be curious if we could ascertain the different constitution of the troops employed in the irreverent

sermon was on the Book of Job; he enlarged on the conduct of the wife of the patriarch, who commanded him to blaspheme God; he compared the Empress with this example of impiety; he went on to compare her with Eve, with Jezebel, with Herodias. "The Emperor demands a church—what has the Emperor to do with the adulteress, the church of the heretics?" Intelligence arrived that the populace were tearing down the hangings of the church on which was the sacred image of the sovereign, and which had been suspended in the Porcian Basilica, as a sign that the church had been taken into the possession of the Emperor. Ambrose sent some of his priests to allay the tumult, but went not himself. He looked triumphantly around on his armed devotees: "The Gentiles have entered into the inheritance of the Lord; but the armed Gentiles have become Christians and co-heirs of God. My enemies are now my defenders."

A confidential secretary of the Emperor appeared, not to expel or degrade the refractory prelate, but to deprecate his *tyranny*. "Why do ye hesitate to strike down *the tyrant*," replied Ambrose, "my only defence is in my power of exposing my life for the honour of God." He proceeded with proud humility, "Under the ancient law, priests have bestowed, they have not condescended to assume empire; kings have desired the priesthood rather than priests the royal power." He appealed to his influence over Maximus, The Emperor which had averted the invasion of Italy. The yields to Ambrose. imperial authority quailed before the resolute prelate;

---

scenes in the churches of Alexandria and Constantinople, and here at Milan. Were the former raised from the vicious population of the Eastern cities, the latter partly composed of barbarians? How much is justly to be attributed to the character of the prelate?

the soldiers were withdrawn, the prisoners released, and the fines annulled.° When the Emperor himself was urged to confront Ambrose in the church, the timid or prudent youth replied, "His eloquence would compel yourselves to lay me bound hand and foot before his throne." To such a height had the sacerdotal power attained in the West, when wielded by a man of the energy and determination of Ambrose.ᵖ

But the pertinacious animosity of the Empress was not yet exhausted. A law was passed authorising the assemblies of the Arians. A second struggle took place; a new triumph for Ambrose; a new defeat for the Imperial power. From his inviolable citadel, his church, Ambrose uttered in courageous security his defiance. An emphatic sentence expressed the prelate's notion of the relation of the civil and religious power, and proclaimed the subordination of the Emperor within the mysterious circle of sacerdotal authority— "The Emperor is of the church, and in the church, but not above the church."

Was it to be supposed that the remonstrances of expiring Paganism would make any impression upon a court thus under subjection to one, who, by exercising the office of protector in the time of peril, assumed the right to dictate on subjects which appeared more completely within his sphere of jurisdiction? If

---

° Certatim hoc nuntiare milites, irruentes in altaria, osculis significare pacis insigne. Ambrose perceived that God had stricken Lucifer, the great Dragon (vermem antelucanum).

ᵖ Ambrose relates that one of the officers of the court, more daring than the rest, presumed to resent this outrage, as he considered it, on the Emperor. "While I live, dost thou thus treat Valentinian with contempt? I will strike off thy head." Ambrose replied, "God grant that thou mayest fulfil thy menace. I shall suffer the fate of a bishop, thou wilt do the act of an eunuch" (tu facies, quod spadones).

Arianism in the person of the Empress was compelled to bow, Paganism could scarcely hope to obtain even a patient hearing.

We have already related the contest between expiring Polytheism and ascendant Christianity in the persons of Symmachus and of Ambrose. The more polished periods and the gentle dignity of Symmachus might delight the old aristocracy of Rome. But the full flow of the more vehement eloquence of Ambrose, falling into the current of popular opinion at Milan, swept all before it.[q] By this time the Old Testament language and sentiment with regard to idolatry were completely incorporated with the Christian feeling; and when Ambrose enforced on a Christian Emperor the sacred duty of intolerance against opinions and practices which scarcely a century before had been the established religion of the Empire, his zeal was supported by almost the unanimous applause of the Christian world.

Ambrose did not rely on his eloquence alone, or on the awfulness of his sacerdotal character, to control the public mind. The champion of the Church was invested by popular belief, perhaps by his own ardent faith, with

---

[q] The most curious fact relating to Ambrose, is the extraordinary contrast between his vigorous, practical, and statesmanlike character as a man, as well as that of such among his writings as may be called public and popular, and the mystic subtlety which fills most of his theological works. He treats the Scripture as one vast allegory, and propounds his own fanciful interpretation, or corollaries, with as much authority as if they were the plain sense of the sacred writer. No retired schoolman follows out the phantastic analogies and recondite significations which he perceives in almost every word, with more vain ingenuity than Ambrose. Every word or number reminds him of every other place in the Scripture in which the same word or number occurs; and stringing them together with this loose connexion, he works out some latent mystic signification, which he would suppose to have been within the intention of the inspired writer. See particularly the Hexaemeron.

miraculous power, and the high state of religious excitement was maintained in Milan by the increasing dignity
and splendour of the ceremonial, and by the pompous
installation of the reliques of saints within the principal
church.

It cannot escape the observation of a calm inquirer
into the history of man, or be disguised by an admirer
of a rational, pious, and instructive Christian ministry,
that whenever, from this period, the clergy possessed a
full and dominant power, the claim to supernatural
power is more frequently and ostentatiously made, while
where they possess a less complete ascendency, miracles
cease. While Ambrose was at least availing himself of,
if not encouraging, this religious credulity, Chrysostom,
partly, no doubt, from his own good sense, partly from
respect for the colder and more inquisitive character of
his audience, not merely distinctly disavows miraculous
powers in his own person, but asserts that long ago
they had come to an end.[r] But in Milan the arch-

---

[r] Διὰ τοῦτο παρὰ μὲν τὴν ἀρχὴν
καὶ ἀναξίοις χαρίσματα ἐδίδοτο· χρεί-
αν γὰρ εἶχε το παλαιόν, τῆς πίστεως
ἕνεκα, ταύτης τῆς βοηθείας· νῦν δὲ
οὐδὲ ἀξίοις δίδοται. In Act. vol. iii.
65. Μὴ τοίνυν τὸ μὴ γένεσθαι νῦν
σημεῖα, τεκμήριον ποιοῦ τοῦ μὴ γε-
γενῆσθαι τοτε, καὶ γὰρ δὴ τότε χρησίμως ἐγίνετο, καὶ νῦν χρησίμως οὐ
γίνεται. See the whole passage in
Cor. Hom. vi. xi. 45. On Psalm cx.,
indeed, vol. v. p. 271, he seems to
assert the continuance of miracles,
particularly during the reign of Julian
and of Maximin. But he gives the
death of Julian as one of those miracles. Καὶ γὰρ καὶ διὰ τοῦτο, καὶ
δἰ ἕτερον τὰ σημεῖα ἔπαυσεν ὁ Θεός,
in Matt. vii. 375. Compare also vol.

i. p. 411; xi. 397, in Coloss.; on
Psalm cxlii. vol. v. p. 455. Mid-
dleton has dwelt at length on this
subject. Works, vol. i. p. 103.

Augustine denies the continuance of
miracles with equal distinctness.
Cum enim Ecclesia Catholica per
totum orbem diffusa atque fundata
sit, nec miracula illa in nostra tempora durare permissa sunt, ne animus
semper visibilia quæreret, et eorum
consuetudine frigesceret genus humanum, quorum novitate flagravit. De
Verâ Relig. c. 47. Oper. i. 765.
Yet Fleury appeals, and not without
ground, to the repeated testimony
of St. Augustine, as eye-witness of
this miracle ; and the reader of St.
Augustine's works, even his noblest

bishop asserts his belief in, and the eager enthusiasm of the people did not hesitate to embrace as unquestionable truth, the public display of preternatural power in the streets of the city. A dream revealed to the pious prelate the spot, where rested the reliques of the martyrs, SS. Gervaise and Protadius. As they approached the place, a man possessed by a demon was seized with a paroxysm which betrayed his trembling consciousness of the presence of the holy remains. The bones of two men of great stature were found, with much blood.[s] The bodies were disinterred, and conveyed in solemn pomp to the Ambrosian Church. They were reinterred under the altar ; they became the tutelary Saints of the spot.[t] A blind butcher, named Severus, recovered his eyesight by the application of a handkerchief, which had touched the reliques, and this was but one of the many wonders which were universally supposed to have been wrought by the smallest article of dress, which had imbibed the miraculous virtue of these sacred bones.

The awe-struck mind was never permitted to repose ; more legitimate means were employed to maintain the

---

see lib. xx. c. 8.), the City of God, cannot but call to mind perpetual instances of miraculous occurrences related with unhesitating faith. It is singular how often we hear at one time the strong intellect of Augustine, at another the age of Augustine, speaking in his works.

[s] The Arians denied this miracle, Ambrose, Epist. xxii. Invenimus miræ magnitudinis viros duos, ut *prisca ætas ferebat.* Did Ambrose suppose that the race of men had degenerated in the last two or three centuries ? or that the heroes of the

faith had been gifted with heroic stature ? The sermon of Ambrose is a strange rhapsody, which would only suit an highly excited audience. He acknowledges that these martyrs were unknown, and that the church of Milan was before barren of reliques.

[t] " Succedunt victimæ triumphales in locum ubi Christus natus est ; sed ille super altare qui pro omnibus passus est ; isti sub altari qui illius reveriti sunt passionem ; " but Ambrose calls them the guardians and defenders of the Church.

ardent belief, thus enforced upon the multitude. The whole ceremonial of the church was conducted by Ambrose with unrivalled solemnity and magnificence. Music was cultivated with the utmost care, some of the noblest hymns of the Latin Church are attributed to Ambrose himself, and the Ambrosian service for a long period distinguished the Church of Milan by the grave dignity and simple fullness of its harmony.[a]

But the sacerdotal dignity of Ambrose might command a feeble boy : he had now to confront the imperial majesty in the person of one of the greatest men who had ever worn the Roman purple. Even in the midst of his irreconcileable feud with the heretical Empress, Ambrose had been again entreated to spread the shield of his protection over the youthful Emperor. He had Second em- undertaken a second embassy to the usurper bassy to Maximus. Maximus. Maximus, as if he feared the awful influence of Ambrose over his mind, refused to admit the priestly ambassador, except to a public audience. Ambrose was considered as condescending from his dignity, in approaching the throne of the Emperor. The usurper reproached the prelate for his former interference, by which he had been arrested in his invasion of Italy, and had lost the opportunity of becoming master of the unresisting province. Ambrose answered with pardonable pride, that he accepted the honourable accusation of having saved the orphan Emperor. He then arrayed himself, as it were, in his priestly inviolability, reproached Maximus with the murder of Gratian, and demanded his remains. He again refused all spiritual communion with one guilty of innocent blood, for which as yet he had submitted

---

[a] This subject will recur at a later part of this volume.

to no ecclesiastical penance. Maximus, as might have
been expected, drove from his court the daring prelate,
who had thus stretched to the utmost the sanctity
of person attributed to an ambassador and a bishop.
Ambrose, however, returned not merely safe, but without insult or outrage, to his Italian diocese.[x]

The arms of Theodosius decided the contest, and
secured the trembling throne of Valentinian Accession of
the younger. But the accession of Theodosius, A.D. 388.
instead of obscuring the rival pretensions of the Church
to power and influence, seemed to confirm and strengthen
them. That such a mind as that of Theodosius should
submit with humility to ecclesiastical remonstrance and
discipline tended no doubt, beyond all other events, to
overawe mankind. Everywhere else throughout the
Roman world, the state, and even the Church, bowed
at the foot of Theodosius; in Milan alone, in the height
of his power, he was confronted and subdued by
the more commanding mind and religious majesty of
Ambrose. His justice as well as his dignity quailed
beneath the ascendancy of the prelate. A synagogue of
the Jews at Callinicum, in Osroene, had been Jewish
burned by the Christians, it was said, at the synagogue destroyed.
instigation, if not under the actual sanction of the
Bishop. The church of the Valentinian Gnostics had
likewise been destroyed and plundered by the zeal of
some monks. Theodosius commanded the restoration
of the synagogue at the expense of the Christians, and
fair compensation to the heretical Valentinians for their
losses.

The pious indignation of Ambrose was not restrained
either by the remoteness of these transactions from the

---

[x] Epist. xxiv.

M 2

scene of his own labours or by the undeniable violence
Conduct of
Ambrose. of the Christian party. He stood forward,
designated, it might seem, by his situation and
character, as the acknowledged champion of the whole
of Christianity; the sacerdotal power was embodied in
his person. In a letter to the Emperor, he boldly
vindicated the Bishop; he declared himself, as far as
his approbation could make him so, an accomplice in
the glorious and holy crime. If martyrdom was the
consequence, he claimed the honour of that martyrdom;
he declared it to be utterly irreconcileable with Christianity, that it should in any way contribute to the
restoration of Jewish or heretical worship.[y] If the
Bishop should comply with the mandate, he would be
an apostate, and the Emperor would be answerable for
his apostasy. This act was but a slight and insufficient
retaliation for the deeds of plunder and destruction
perpetrated by the Jews and heretics against orthodox
Christians. The letter of Ambrose did not produce the
desired effect; but the Bishop renewed his address in
public in the church, and at length extorted from the
Emperor the impunity of the offenders. Then, and not
till then, he condescended to approach the altar, and to
proceed with the service of God.

Ambrose felt his strength; he feared not to assert
that superiority of the altar over the throne which was

[y] Hac propositâ conditione, puto dicturum episcopum, quòd ipse ignes sparserit, turbas compulerit, populos concluserit, ne amittat occasionem martyrii, ut pro invalidis subjiciat validiorem. O beatum mendacium quo adquiritur sibi aliorum absolutio, sui gratia. Hoc est, Imperator, quod poposci et ego, ut in me magis vindicares, et hoc si crimen putares mihi adscriberes. Quid mandas in absentes judicium? Habes præsentem, habes confitentem reum. Proclamo, quod ego synagogam incenderim, certè quod ego illis mandaverim, ne esset locus, in quo Christus negaretur. Si objiciatur mihi, cur hic non incenderim? Divino jam cœpit cremari judicio; meum cessavit opus. Epist. xxiv. p. 561.

a fundamental maxim of his Christianity. There is no
reason to ascribe to ostentation, or to sacerdotal ambition, rather than to the profound conviction of his mind,
the dignity which he vindicated for the priesthood, the
authority supreme and without appeal in all things
which related to the ceremonial of religion. Theodosius
endured, and the people applauded, the public exclusion
of the Emperor from within the impassable rails, which
fenced off the officiating priesthood from the profane
laity. An exemption had usually been made for the
sacred person of the Emperor, and, according to this
usage, Theodosius ventured within the forbidden precincts. Ambrose, with lofty courtesy, pointed to the
seat or throne reserved for the Emperor, at the head of
the laity. Theodosius submitted to the rebuke, and
withdrew to the lowlier station.

But if these acts of Ambrose might to some appear
unwise or unwarrantable aggressions on the dignity of
the civil magistrate ; or if to the prophetic sagacity of
others they might foreshow the growth of an enormous
and irresponsible authority, and awaken well-grounded
apprehension or jealousy, the Roman world could not
withhold its admiration from another act of the Milanese
prelate. It could not but hail the appearance of a new
moral power, enlisted on the side of humanity and
justice; a power which could bow the loftiest, as well
as the meanest, under its dominion. For the first time
since the establishment of the imperial despotism, the
voice of a subject was heard in deliberate, public, and
authoritative condemnation of a deed of atrocious
tyranny and sanguinary vengeance; for the first time,
an Emperor of Rome trembled before public opinion,
and humbled himself to a contrite confession of guilt and
cruelty.

With all his wisdom and virtue Theodosius was liable
Massacre of to paroxysms of furious and ungovernable
Thessalonica. anger. A dispute had arisen in Thessalonica
A.D. 390. about a favourite charioteer in the circus; out
of the dispute a sedition, in which some lives were lost.
The imperial officers, who interfered to suppress the
fray, were wounded or slain, and Botheric, the representative of the Emperor, treated with indignity. Notwithstanding every attempt on the part of the clergy to
allay the furious resentment of Theodosius, the counsels
of the more violent advisers prevailed. Secret orders
were issued; the circus, filled with the whole population
of the city, was surrounded by troops, and a general
and indiscriminate massacre of all ages and sexes, the
guilty and the innocent, revenged the insult on the imperial dignity. Seven thousand lives were sacrificed in
this remorseless carnage.

On the first intelligence of this atrocity, Ambrose,
with prudent self-command, kept aloof from the exasperated Emperor. He retired into the country, and
a letter from his own hand was delivered to the
sovereign. The letter expressed the horror of Ambrose
and his brother bishops at this inhuman deed, in which
he should consider himself an accomplice if he could
refrain from expressing his detestation of its guilt; if
he should not refuse to communicate with a man stained
with the innocent blood, not of one, but of thousands.
He exhorts Theodosius to penitence; he promises to
offer prayers in his behalf. He acted up to his
declaration; the Emperor of the world found the doors
of the church closed against him. For eight months
he endured this ignominious exclusion. Even on the
sacred day of the Nativity, Theodosius implored in vain
to be admitted within those precincts which were open

to the slave and to the beggar; those precincts which were the vestibule to heaven, for through the church alone was heaven to be approached. Submission and remonstrance were alike in vain; to an urgent minister of the sovereign, Ambrose calmly replied, that the Emperor might kill him and pass over his body into the sanctuary.

At length Ambrose consented to admit the Emperor to an audience; with difficulty he was persuaded to permit him to enter, not into the church itself, but into the outer porch, the place of the public penitents. At length the interdict was removed on two conditions; that the Emperor should issue an edict prohibiting the execution of capital punishments for thirty days after conviction, and that he should submit to public penance. Stripped of his imperial ornaments, prostrate on the pavement, beating his breast, tearing his hair, watering the ground with his tears, the master of the Roman empire, the conqueror in so many victories, the legislator of the world, at length received the hard-wrung absolution.

This was the culminating point of pure Christian influence. Christianity appeared before the world as the champion and vindicator of outraged humanity; as having founded a tribunal of justice, which extended its protective authority over the meanest, and suspended its retributive penalties over the mightiest of mankind.

Nearly at the same time (about four years before) had been revealed the latent danger from this new unlimited sovereignty over the human mind. *The first blood was judicially shed for religious opinion.* Far, however, from apprehending the fatal consequences which might arise out of their own _{First capital punishment for religion. A.D. 385.}

exclusive and intolerant sentiments, or foreseeing that
the sacerdotal authority, which they fondly and sincerely
supposed they were strengthening for the unalloyed
welfare of mankind, would seize and wield the sword of
persecution with such remorseless and unscrupulous
severity—this first fatal libation of Christian blood,
which was the act of an usurping Emperor, and of a
few foreign bishops—was solemnly disclaimed by all the
more . influential dignitaries of the Western Church.
Priscillian and his followers. Priscillian, a noble and eloquent Spaniard,
had embraced some Manichean or rather
Gnostic opinions. The same contradictory accusations
of the severest asceticism and of licentious habits,
which were so perpetually adduced against the Manicheans, formed the chief charge against Priscillian and
his followers. The leaders of the sect had taken refuge,
from the persecutions of their countrymen, in Gaul, and
propagated their opinions to some extent in Aquitaine.
They were pursued with unwearied animosity by the
Spanish Bishops Ithacius and Idacius. Maximus, the
usurping Emperor of Gaul, who then resided at Treves,
Martin of Tours. took cognisance of the case. In vain the
celebrated Martin of Tours, whose life was
almost an unwearied campaign against idolatry, and
whose unrelenting hand had demolished every religious
edifice within his reach—a prelate whose dread of
heresy was almost as sensitive as of Paganism, urged
his protest against these proceedings with all the
vehemence of his character. During his absence, a
capital sentence was extorted from the Emperor;
Priscillian and some of his followers were put to death
by the civil authority for the crime of religious error.
The fatal precedent was disowned by the general voice
of Christianity. It required another considerable

period of ignorance and bigotry to deaden the fine moral sense of Christianity to the total abandonment of its spirit of love.   When Ambrose reproached Conduct of the usurper with the murder of his sovereign Ambrose. Gratian, he reminded him likewise of the unjust execution of the Priscillianists; he refused to communicate with the bishops who had any concern in that sanguinary and unchristian transaction.[z]

Ambrose witnessed and lamented the death of the young Valentinian, over whom he pronounced A.D. 392. a funeral oration.   On the usurpation of the Death of
Valentinian. Pagan Eugenius, he fled from Milan; but A.D. 393. returned to behold and to applaud the triumph of Theodosius.   The conquering Emperor gave a new proof of his homage to Christianity and to its representative.   Under the influence of Ambrose, he refrained for a time from communicating in the Christian mysteries, because his hands were stained with blood, though that blood had been shed in a just and necessary war.[a] To Ambrose the dying Emperor commended Death of
Theodosius. his sons, and the Bishop of Milan pronounced A.D. 395. the funeral oration over the last great Emperor of the world.

He did not long survive his imperial friend.   It is related that, when Ambrose was on his death- Death of bed, Stilicho, apprehending the loss of such a Ambrose.
A.D. 397. man to Italy and to Christendom, urged the principal inhabitants of Milan to entreat the effective prayers of the bishop for his own recovery.   "I have not so lived among you," replied Ambrose, "as to be ashamed to live; I have so good a Master, that I am

---

[z] Ambros. Epist. xxiv.   The whole transaction in Sulpicius Sever. E. H. | and Life of St. Martin.
[a] Oratio de Obitu Theodos. 34.

not afraid to die." Ambrose expired in the attitude
and in the act of prayer.

While Ambrose was thus assuming an unprecedented
supremacy over his own age, and deepening and
strengthening the foundation of the ecclesiastical power,
Augustine was beginning gradually to consummate that
total change in human opinion which was to influence
the Christianity of the remotest ages.

Of all Christian writers since the Apostles, Augustine
has maintained the most permanent and
extensive influence. That influence, indeed,
was unfelt, or scarcely felt, in the East; but as the
East gradually became more estranged, till it was little
more than a blank in Christian history, the dominion
of Augustine over the opinions of the Western world
was eventually over the whole of Christendom. Basil
and Chrysostom spoke a language foreign or dead to
the greater part of the Christian world. The Greek
empire, after the reign of Justinian, gradually contracting its limits and sinking into abject superstition, forgot
its own great writers on the more momentous subjects
of religion and morality, for new controversialists on
frivolous and insignificant points of difference. The
more important feuds, as of Nestorianism, made little
progress in the West; the West repudiated almost with
one voice the iconoclastic opinions; and at length
Mohammedanism swept away its fairest provinces, and
limited the Greek church to a still narrowing circle.
The Latin language thus became almost that of
Christianity; Latin writers the sole authority to which
men appealed, or from which they imperceptibly
imbibed the tone of religious doctrine or sentiment.
Of these, Augustine was the most universal, the most
commanding, the most influential.

Augustine.

The earliest Christian writers had not been able or
willing altogether to decline some of the more obvious
and prominent points of the Augustinian theology; but
in his works they were first wrought up into a regular
system. Abstruse topics, which had been but slightly
touched, or dimly hinted in the Apostolic writings, and
of which the older creeds had been entirely silent,
became the prominent and unavoidable tenets of
Christian doctrine. Augustinianism has constantly revived, in all its strongest and most peremptory statements, in every period of religious excitement. In
later days, it formed much of the doctrinal system of
Luther; it was worked up into a still more rigid and
uncompromising system by the severe intellect of
Calvin; it was remoulded into the Roman Catholic
doctrine by Jansenius; the popular theology of most of
the Protestant sects is but a modified Augustinianism.

Christianity had now accomplished its divine mission,
so far as impregnating the Roman world with $_{Augustinian}$
its first principles, the unity of God, the $^{theology.}$
immortality of the soul, and future retribution. These
vital questions between the old Paganism and the new
religion had been decided by their almost general
adoption into the common sentiments of mankind.
And now questions naturally and necessarily arising out
of the providential government of that Supreme Deity,
out of that conscious immortality, and out of that
acknowledged retribution, had begun profoundly to
agitate the human heart. The nature of man had been
stirred in its inmost depths. The hopes and fears, now
centered on another state of being, were ever restlessly
hovering over the abyss into which they were forced to
gaze. As men were not merely convinced, but deeply
penetrated, with the belief that they had souls to be

saved, the means, the process, the degree of attainable
assurance concerning salvation, became subjects of
anxious inquiry. Every kind of information on these
momentous topics was demanded with importunity and
hailed with eagerness. With the ancient philosophy,
the moral condition of man was a much simpler and
calmer subject of consideration. It could coldly analyse
every emotion, trace the workings of every passion, and
present its results ; if in eloquent language, kindling
the mind of the hearer, rather by that language, than
by the excitement of the inquiry. It was the attractive
form of the philosophy, the adventitious emotion
produced by bold paradox, happy invention, acute
dialectics, which amused and partially enlightened the
inquisitive mind. But now mingled up with religion,
every sensation, every feeling, every propensity, every
thought, had become not merely a symptom of the
moral condition, but an element in that state of
spiritual advancement or deterioration which was to be
weighed and examined in the day of Judgement. The
ultimate and avowed object of philosophy, the *summum
bonum*, the greatest attainable happiness, shrunk into
an unimportant consideration. These were questions of
spiritual life and death, and the solution was therefore
embraced rather by the will and the passions, than by
the cool and sober reason. This solution in all these
difficulties was the more acceptable in proportion as it
was peremptory and dogmatic. Any thing could be
endured rather than uncertainty, and Augustine himself
was, doubtless, urged more by the desire of peace to his
own anxious spirit than by the ambition of dictating to
Christianity on these abstruse topics. The influence of
Augustine thus concentered the Christian mind on
subjects to which Christianity led, but did not answer

with fulness or precision. The Gospels and Apostolic
writings paused within the border of attainable human
knowledge; Augustine fearlessly rushed forward, or
was driven by his antagonists; and partly from the
reasonings of a new religious philosophy, partly by
general inferences from limited and particular phrases
in the sacred writings, framed a complete, it must be
acknowledged, and as far as its own consistency, an
harmonious system; but of which it was the inevitable
tendency to give an overpowering importance to
problems on which Christianity, wisely measuring, it
should seem, the capacity of the human mind, had
declined to utter any final or authoritative decrees.
Almost up to this period in Christian history,[b] on these
mysterious topics, all was unquestioned and undefined ;
and though they could not but cross the path of
Christian reasoning, and could not but be incidentally
noticed, they had, as yet, undergone no full or direct
investigation. Nothing but the calmest and firmest
philosophy could have avoided or eluded these points,
on which, though the human mind could not attain to
knowledge, it was impatient of ignorance. The immediate or more remote, the direct or indirect, the
sensible or the imperceptible, influence of the divine
agency (grace) on the human soul, with the inseparable
consequences of necessity and free-will, thus became
the absorbing and agitating points of Christian doctrine.
From many causes, these inevitable questions had
forced themselves, at this period, on the general
attention. Manicheism on one hand, Pelagianism on

---

[b] In the Historia Pelagiana of
Vossius may be found quotations
expressive of the sentiments of the
earlier Fathers on many of these
points.

the other, stirred up their darkest depths. The
Christian mind demanded on all these topics at once
excitement and rest. Nothing could be more acceptable than the unhesitating and peremptory decisions
of Augustine. His profound piety ministered perpetual
emotion; his glowing and perspicuous language, his
confident dogmatism, and the apparent completeness of
his system, offered repose.

But the primary principle of the Augustinian theology
was already deeply rooted in the awe-struck piety of
the Christian world. In this state of the general mind,
that which brought the Deity more directly and more
perpetually in contact with the soul, at once enlisted all
minds which were under the shadow of religious fears,
or softened by any milder religious feeling. It was not
a remote supremacy, a government through unseen and
untraceable influences, a general reverential trust in
the divine protection, which gave satisfaction to the
agitated spirit; but an actually felt and immediate
presence, operating on each particular and most minute
part of the creation; not a regular and unvarying
emanation of the divine will, but a special and peculiar
intervention in each separate case. The whole course
of human events, and the moral condition of each
individual, were alike under the acknowledged, or
conscious and direct, operation of the Deity. But the
more distinct and unquestioned this principle, the more
the problem which in a different form had agitated the
Eastern world,—the origin of evil,—forced itself on the
consideration. In the East it had taken a kind of
speculative or theogonical turn, and allied itself with
physical notions; in the West it became a moral and
practical, and almost every-day question, involving the
prescience of God and the freedom of the human soul.

Augustine had rejected Manicheism; the antagonistic and equally conflicting powers of that system had offended his high conception of the supremacy of God. Still his earlier Manicheism lent an unconscious colouring to his maturer opinions. In another form, he divided the world into regions of cloudless light and total darkness. But he did not mingle the Deity in any way in the darkness which enveloped the whole of mankind, a chosen portion of which alone were rescued, by the gracious intervention of the Redeemer and the Holy Spirit. The rest were separated by an insuperable barrier, that of hereditary evil; they bore within, the fatal and inevitable proscription. Within the pale of Election was the world of Light, without, the world of Perdition; and the human soul was so reduced to a subordinate agent before the mysterious and inscrutable power, which, by the infusion of faith, rescued it from its inveterate hereditary propensity, as to become entirely passive, altogether annihilated, in overleaping the profound though narrow gulph, which divided the two kingdoms of Grace and of Perdition.

Thus that system which assigned the most unbounded and universal influence to the Deity was seized upon by devout piety as the truth which it would be an impious limitation of Omnipotence to question. Man offered his free agency on the altar of his religion, and forgot that he thereby degraded the most wonderful work of Omnipotence, a being endowed with free agency. While the internal consciousness was not received as sufficient evidence of the freedom of the will, it was considered as unquestionable testimony to the operations of divine grace.

At all events, these questions now became unavoid-

able articles of the Christian faith. From this time
the simpler Apostolic Creed, and the splendid ampli-
fications of the divine attributes of the Trinity, were
enlarged, if not by stern definitions, by dictatorial
axioms on original sin, on grace, predestination, the
total depravity of mankind, election to everlasting life,
and final reprobation. To the appellations which
awoke what was considered righteous and legitimate
hatred in all true believers, Arianism and Manicheism, was now added as a term of equal obloquy,—
Pelagianism.[e]

---

[e] The doctrines of Pelagius have
been represented as arising out of the
monastic spirit, or at least out of one
form of its influence. The high ideal
of moral perfection (it has been said)
which the monk set before himself,
the conscious strength of will which
was necessary to aspire to that height,
the proud impatience and disdain of
the ordinary excuse for infirmity, the
inherited weakness and depravity of
human nature, induced the colder and
more severe Pelagius to embrace his
peculiar tenets ; the rejection of original sin ; the assertion of the entire
freedom of the will ; the denial or
limitation of the influence of divine
grace. Of the personal history of
Pelagius little is known, except that
he was a British or French monk
(his name is said, in one tradition, to
have been Morgan), but neither he
nor his colleague Cælestius appears to
have been a secluded ascetic ; they
dwelt in Rome for some time, where
they propagated their doctrines. Of
his character perhaps still less is
known, unless from his tenets, and
some fragments of his writings, preserved by his adversaries ; excepting

that the blamelessness of his manners
is admitted by his adversaries (the
term egregiè Christianus is the expression of St. Augustine) : and even
the violent Jerome bears testimony to
his innocence of life.

But the tenets of Augustine appear
to flow more directly from the monastic system. His doctrines (in his
controversy with Pelagius, for in his
other writings he holds another tone)
are tinged with the Encratite or
Manichean notion, that there was a
physical transmission of sin in the
propagation of children, even in lawful
marriage. (See, among other writers.
Jer. Taylor's Vindication of his Deus
Justificatus.) Even this concupis-
centia carnis peccatum est, quia inest
illi inobedientia contra dominatum
mentis. De Pecc. Remis. i. 3. This
is the old doctrine of the inherent evil
of matter. We are astonished that
Augustine, who had been a father
and a fond father, though of an illegitimate son, could be driven by the
stern logic of polemics to the damnation of unbaptized infants, a *milder*
damnation, it is true, to eternal fire.
This was the more genuine doctrine of

Augustine, by the extraordinary adaptation of his
genius to his own age, the comprehensive grandeur of
his views, the intense earnestness of his character, his
inexhaustible activity, the vigour, warmth, and perspicuity of his style, had a right to command the
homage of Western Christendom. He was at once the
first universal, and the purest and most powerful of the
Latin Christian writers. It is singular that almost all
the earlier Christian authors in the West were provincials, chiefly of Africa. But the works of Tertullian
were, in general, brief treatises on temporary subjects of
controversy; if enlivened by the natural vehemence
and strength of the man, disfigured by the worst
barbarisms of style. The writings of Cyprian were
chiefly short epistles or treatises on subjects of immediate or local interest. Augustine retained the
fervour and energy of the African style with much

men in whose hearts all the sweet
charities of life had been long seared
up by monastic discipline; men like
Fulgentius, to whose name the title of
saint is prefixed, and who lays down
this benignant and Christian axiom:
"Firmissimè tene et nullatenus dubites,
parvulos, sive in uteris matrum vivere
incipiunt, et ibi moriuntur, sive cum
de matribus nati, sine sacramento
sancto baptismatis de hoc seculo
transeunt, *ignis æterni sempiterno
supplicio puniendos.*" Fulgentius
de Fide, quoted in Vossius, Hist.
Pelag. p. 257.

The assertion of the entire freedom
of the will, and the restricted sense in
which Pelagius appears to have received the doctrine of divine grace,
confining it to the influences of the
divine revelation, appear to arise out
of philosophical reasonings rather than
out of the monastic spirit. The
severe monastic discipline was more
likely to infuse the sense of the slavery
of the will; and the brooding over
bodily and mental emotions, the general
cause and result of the monastic spirit,
would tend to exaggerate rather than
to question or limit the actual, and
even sensible workings of the divine
spirit within the soul. The calmer
temperament, indeed, and probably
more peaceful religious developement
of Pelagius, may have disposed him to
his system; as the more vehement
character, and agitated religious life of
Augustine, to his vindication, founded
on his internal experience, of the constant divine agency upon the heart
and the soul.

purer and more perspicuous Latinity. His ardent
imagination was tempered by reasoning powers which
boldly grappled with every subject. He possessed and
was unembarrassed by the possession of all the knowledge which had been accumulated in the Roman world.
He commanded the whole range of Latin literature, and
perhaps his influence over his own hemisphere was not
diminished by his ignorance, or at best imperfect and
late-acquired acquaintance with Greek.[d] But all his
knowledge and all his acquirements fell into the train
of his absorbing religious sentiments or passions. On
the subjects with which he was conversant, a calm and
dispassionate philosophy would have been indignantly
repudiated by the Christian mind, and Augustine's
temperament was too much in harmony with that of
the time to offend by deficiency in fervour. It was
profound religious agitation, not cold and abstract
truth, which the age required; the emotions of piety,
rather than the convictions of severe logical inquiry;
and in Augustine, the depth or abstruseness of the
matter never extinguished or allayed the passion, or in
one sense, the popularity, of his style. At different
periods of his life, Augustine aspired to and succeeded
in enthralling all the various powers and faculties of
the human mind. That life was the type of his
theology; and as it passed through its various changes
of age, of circumstance, and of opinion, it left its own
impressions strongly and permanently stamped upon
the whole of Latin Christianity. The gentleness of his
childhood, the passions of his youth, the studies of his
adolescence, the wilder dreams of his immature Chris-

---

[d] On St. Augustine's knowledge
of Greek, compare Tillemont, in his
Life, p. 7. Punic was still spoken by
the common people in the neighbourhood of Carthage.

tianity, the Manicheism, the intermediate stage of
Platonism, through which he passed into orthodoxy,
the fervour with which he embraced, the vigour with
which he developed, the unhesitating confidence with
which he enforced his final creed—all affected more or
less the general mind. His Confessions became the
manual of all those who were forced by their temperament or inclined by their disposition to brood over
the inward sensations of their own minds; to trace
within themselves all the trepidations, the misgivings,
the agonies, the exultations, of the religious conscience;
the gradual formation of opinions till they harden into
dogmas, or warm into objects of ardent passion. Since
Augustine, this internal autobiography of the soul has
always had the deepest interest for those of strong
religious convictions; it was what multitudes had felt,
but no one had yet embodied in words; it was the
appalling yet attractive manner in which men beheld
all the conflicts and adventures of their own spiritual
life reflected with bold and speaking truth. Men
shrunk from the divine and unapproachable image
of Christian perfection in the life of the Redeemer,
to the more earthly, more familiar picture of the
developement of the Christian character, crossed with
the light and shade of human weakness and human
passion.

The religious was more eventful than the civil life of
St. Augustine. He was born A.D. 354, in Tagasta, an
episcopal city of Numidia. His parents were Christians
of respectable rank. In his childhood, he was attacked
by a dangerous illness; he entreated to be baptized.
His mother Monica took the alarm; all was prepared
for that solemn ceremony; but on his recovery, it was
deferred, and Augustine remained for some years in the

N 2

humbler rank of catechumen. He received the best education, in grammar and rhetoric, which the neigh-
A.D. 371. bouring city of Madaura could afford. At seventeen, he was sent to Carthage to finish his studies. Augustine has, perhaps, highly coloured both the idleness of his period of study in Madaura, and the licentious habits to which he abandoned himself in the dissolute city of Carthage. His ardent mind plunged into the intoxicating enjoyments of the theatre, and his excited passions demanded every kind of gratification. He had a natural son, called by the somewhat inappropriate name A-deo-datus. He was first arrested in his sensual course, not by the solemn voice of religion, but by the gentler remonstrances of Pagan literature. He learned from Cicero, not from the Gospel, the higher dignity of intellectual attainments. From his brilliant success in his studies, it is clear that his life, if yielding at times to the temptations of youth, was not a course of indolence or total abandonment to pleasure. It was the Hortensius of Cicero which awoke his mind to nobler aspirations and to the contempt of worldly enjoyments.

But philosophy could not satisfy the lofty desires which it had awakened : Augustine panted for some better hopes, and more satisfactory objects of study. He turned to the religion of his parents, but his mind was not subdued to a feeling for the inimitable beauty of the New Testament. Its simplicity of style appeared rude, after the stately march of Tully's eloquence. But Manicheism seized at once upon his kindled imagination. For nine years, from the age of nineteen to twenty-eight, the mind of Augustine wandered among the vague and fantastic reveries of Oriental theology.

The virtuous and holy Monica, with the anxious apprehensions and prescient hopes of a mother's heart,
watched over the irregular development of his powerful
faculties. Her distress at his Manichean errors was
consoled by an aged bishop, who had himself been
involved in the same opinions. "Be of good cheer,
the child of so many tears cannot perish." The step
against which she remonstrated most strongly, led
to that result which she scarcely dared to hope.
Augustine grew discontented with the wild Manichean
doctrines, which neither satisfied the religious yearnings
of his heart nor the philosophical demands of his
understanding. He was in danger of falling into a
desperate Pyrrhonism, or at best the proud indifference
of an Academic. He determined to seek a more
distinguished sphere for his talents as a teacher of
rhetoric; and, notwithstanding his mother's tears, he
left Carthage for Rome. The fame of his   A.D. 383.
abilities obtained him an invitation to teach   Ætat. 29.
at Milan. He was there within the magic circle of the
great ecclesiastic of the West. But we cannot
pause to trace the throes and pangs of his   A.D. 385.
final conversion. The writings of St. Paul accomplished what the eloquence of Ambrose had begun.
In one of the paroxysms of his religious agony, he
seemed to hear a voice from heaven,—"Take and read,
take and read." Till now he had rejected the writings
of the Apostle; he opened on the passage which contains the awful denunciations of Paul against the
dissolute morals of the Heathen. The conscience of
Augustine recognised "in the chambering and wanton-
ness" the fearful picture of his own life; for though
he had abandoned the looser indulgences of his youth
(he had lived in strict fidelity, not to a lawful wife

indeed, but to a concubine) even his mother was
anxious to disengage him, by an honourable marriage,
from the bonds of a less legitimate connexion.   But
he burst at once his thraldom ; shook his old nature
from his heart ; renounced for ever all, even lawful
indulgences, of the carnal desires ; forswore the world,
and withdrew himself, though without exciting any
unnecessary astonishment among his hearers, from his
Baptism of   profaner function as teacher of rhetoric.   His
Augustine.
A.D. 387.   mother, who had followed him to Milan, lived
to witness his baptism as a Catholic Christian by the
hands of Ambrose ; and in all the serene happiness of her
accomplished hopes and prayers, expired in his arms
before his return to Africa.   His son, Adeodatus, who
died a few years afterwards, was baptized at the same time.

To return to the writings of St. Augustine, or rather
Controversial   to his life in his writings.   In his controversial
writings.   treatises against the Manicheans and against
Pelagius, Augustine had the power of seemingly at
least, bringing down those abstruse subjects to popular
comprehension.   His vehement and intrepid dogmatism
hurried along the unresisting mind, which was allowed
no pause for the sober examination of difficulties, or was
awed into acquiescence by the still suspended charge
of impiety.   The imagination was at the same time
kept awake by a rich vein of allegoric interpretation,
dictated by the same bold decision, and enforced as
necessary conclusions from the sacred writings, or as
latent truths intentionally wrapped up in those mysterious phrases.

The City of God was unquestionably the noblest
            work, both in its original design, and in the
City of God.   fulness of its elaborate execution, which the
genius of man had as yet contributed to the support of

Christianity. Hitherto the Apologies had been framed to meet particular exigences : they were either brief and pregnant statements of the Christian doctrines; refutations of prevalent calumnies; invectives against the follies and crimes of Paganism ; or confutations of anti-Christian works like those of Celsus, Porphyry, or Julian, closely following their course of argument, and rarely expanding into general and comprehensive views of the great conflict. The City of God, in the first place, indeed, was designed to decide for ever the one great question, which alone kept in suspense the balance between Paganism and Christianity, the connection between the fall of the empire and the miseries under which the whole Roman society was groaning, with the desertion of the ancient religion of Rome. Even this part of his theme led Augustine into a full, and, if not impartial, yet far more comprehensive survey of the whole religion and philosophy of antiquity than had been yet displayed in any Christian work. It has preserved more on some branches of these subjects than the whole surviving Latin literature. The City of God was not merely a defence, it was likewise an exposition of Christian doctrine. The last twelve books developed the whole system with a regularity and copiousness, as far as we know, never before attempted by any Christian writer. It was the first complete Christian theology.

The immediate occasion of this important work of Augustine was worthy of this powerful concentration of his talents and knowledge. The capture of Rome by the Goths had appalled the whole empire. So long as the barbarians only broke through the frontiers, or severed province after province from the dominion of the Emperor, men

A.D. 410.

Occasion of its composition.

could close their eyes to the gradual declension and
decay of the Roman supremacy; and in the rapid
alternations of power, the empire, under some new
Cæsar or Constantine, might again throw back the
barbaric inroads; or where the barbarians were settled
within the frontiers, awe them into peaceful subjects,
or array them as valiant defenders of their dominions.
As long as both Romes, more especially the ancient
city of the West, remained inviolate, so long the fabric
of the Roman greatness seemed unbroken, and she
might still assert her title as Mistress of the World.
The capture of Rome dissipated for ever these proud
illusions; it struck the Roman world to the heart;
and in the mortal agony of the old social system, men
wildly grasped at every cause which could account
for this unexpected, this inexplicable, phenomenon.
They were as much overwhelmed with dread and
wonder as if there had been no previous omens of
decay, no slow and progressive approach to the sacred
walls; as if the fate of the city had not been already
twice suspended by the venality, the mercy, or the
prudence of the conqueror. Murmurs were again heard
impeaching the new religion as the cause of this disastrous consummation: the deserted gods had deserted
in their turn the apostate city.[e]

There seems no doubt that Pagan ceremonies took
place in the hour of peril, to avert, if possible, the
imminent ruin. The respect paid by the barbarians

---

[e] Orosius attempted the same
theme: the Pagans, he asserts, "præ-
sentia tantum tempora, veluti malis
extra solitum infestissima, ob hoc
solum, quod creditur Christus, et
colitur, idola autem minus coluntur,
infamant." Heyne has well observed
on this work of Orosius,—Excitaverat
Augustini vibrantis arma exemplum
Orosium, discipulum, ut et ipse arma
sumeret, etsi imbellibus manibus.
Opuscula, vi. p. 130.

to the churches might, in the zealous or even the
wavering votaries of Paganism, strengthen the feeling
of some remote connexion between the destroyer of
the civil power and the destroyer of the ancient
religions. The Roman aristocracy, which fled to
different parts of the world, more particularly to the
yet peaceful and uninvaded province of Africa ; and
among whom the feelings of attachment to the institutions and to the gods of Rome were still the strongest,
were not likely to suppress the language of indignation
and sorrow, or to refrain from the extenuation of their
own cowardice and effeminacy, by ascribing the fate of
the city to the irresistible power of the alienated deities.

Augustine dedicated thirteen years to the completion
of this work, which was for ever to determine A.D. 413 to
this solemn question, and to silence the last   426.
murmurs of expiring Paganism. The City of God is at
once the funeral oration of the ancient society and the
gratulatory panegyric on the birth of the new. It
acknowledged, it triumphed in the irrevocable fall of
the Babylon of the West, the shrine of idolatry ; it
hailed at the same time the universal dominion which
awaited the new theocratic policy. The earthly city
had undergone its predestined fate ; it had passed
away with all its vices and superstitions, with all its
virtues and its glories (for the soul of Augustine
was not dead to the noble reminiscences of Roman
greatness), with its false gods and its Heathen sacrifices. Its doom was sealed, and for ever. But in
its place had arisen the City of God, the Church of
Christ; a new social system had emerged from the
ashes of the old ; that system was founded by God,
was ruled by divine laws, and had the divine promise
of perpetuity.

The first ten books of the City of God are devoted
to the question of the connection between the prosperity
and the religion of Rome; five of them to the influence
of Paganism in this world; five to that in the world
to come. Augustine appeals in the five first to the
mercy shown by the conqueror as the triumph of
Christianity. Had the *Pagan* Radagaisus taken Rome,
not a life would have been spared, no place would have
been sacred. The *Christian* Alaric had been checked
and overawed by the sanctity of the Christian character
and his respect for his Christian brethren. He denies
that worldly prosperity is an unerring sign of the divine
favour; he denies the exemption of the older Romans
from disgrace and distress, and recapitulates the crimes
and the calamities of their history during their worship
of their ancient gods. He ascribes their former glory
to their valour, their frugality, their contempt of wealth,
their fortitude, and their domestic virtues; he assigns
their vices, their frightful profligacy of manners, their
pride, their luxury, their effeminacy, as the proximate
causes of their ruin. Even in their ruin they could not
forget their dissolute amusements; the theatres of
Carthage were crowded with the fugitives from Rome.
In the five following books he examines the pretensions
of Heathenism to secure felicity in the world to come;
he dismisses with contempt the old popular religion,
but seems to consider the philosophic Theism, the
mystic Platonism of the later period, a worthier antagonist. He puts forth all his subtlety and power in
refutation of these tenets.

The last twelve books place in contrast the origin,
the pretensions, the fate, of the new city, that of God.
He enters at large into the evidences of Christianity;
he describes the sanctifying effects of the faith; but

pours forth all the riches of his imagination and
eloquence on the destinies of the church at the
Resurrection. Augustine had no vision of the worldly
power of the new city; he foresaw not the spiritual
empire of Rome which would replace the new fallen
Rome of Heathenism. With him the triumph of
Christianity is not complete till the world itself,—not
merely its outward framework of society and the constitution of its kingdoms,—has experienced a total
change. In the description of the final kingdom of
Christ, he treads his way with great dexterity and
address between the grosser notions of the Millenarians
with their kingdom of earthly wealth, and power, and
luxury (this he repudiates with devout abhorrence);
and that finer and subtler spiritualism, which is ever
approaching to Pantheism, and by the rejection of the
bodily resurrection, renders the existence of the disembodied spirit too fine and impalpable for the general
apprehension.

The uneventful personal life of St. Augustine, at
least, till towards its close, contrasts with that Life of
of Ambrose and that of Chrysostom. After Augustine.
the first throes and travail of his religious life, described
with such dramatic fidelity in his Confessions, he
subsided into a peaceful bishop in a remote and rather
inconsiderable town.[f] He had not, like Ambrose, to
interpose between rival Emperors, or to rule the
conscience of the universal sovereign. He had not, like
Chrysostom, to enter into a perilous conflict with the
vices of a capital and the intrigues of a court. Forced
by the devout admiration of the people to assume the

---

[f] He was thirty-five before he was | was chosen coadjutor to the Bishop of
ordained presbyter, A.D. 389 : he | Hippo, A.D. 395.

episcopate in the city of Hippo, he was faithful to his
first bride, his earliest, though humble, see. Not that
his life was that of contemplative inactivity, or tranquil
literary exertion; his personal conferences with the
leaders of the Donatists, the Manicheans, the Arians,
and Pelagians, and his presence in the councils of
Carthage, displayed his power of dealing with men.
His letter to Count Boniface showed that he was not
unconcerned with the public affairs, and his former
connection with Boniface, who at one time had expressed
his determination to embrace the monastic life, might
warrant his remonstrance against the fatal revolt which
involved Boniface and Africa in ruin.

At the close of his comparatively peaceful life,
Augustine was exposed to the trial of his severe and
lofty principles. His faith and his superiority to the
world were brought to the test in the fearful calamities
which desolated the whole African province. No part
of the empire had so long escaped; no part was so
fearfully visited, as Africa by the invasion of the
Vandals. The once prosperous and fruitful region
presented to the view only ruined cities, burning
villages, a population thinned by the sword, bowed to
slavery, and exposed to every kind of torture and
mutilation. With these fierce barbarians, the awful
presence of Christianity imposed no respect. The
churches were not exempt from the general ruin, nor
the bishops and clergy from cruelty and death, nor the
dedicated virgins from worse than death. In many
places the services of religion entirely ceased from the
extermination of the worshippers or the flight of the
priests. To Augustine, as the supreme authority in
matters of faith or conduct, was submitted the grave
question of the course to be pursued by the clergy;

whether they were to seek their own security or to confront the sword of the ravager. The advice of Augustine was at once lofty and discreet. Where the flock remained it was cowardice, it was impiety, in the clergy to desert them and to deprive them in those disastrous times of the consolatory offices of religion, their childern of baptism, themselves of the holy Eucharist. But where the priest was an especial object of persecution and his place might be supplied by another; where the flock was massacred or dispersed or had abandoned their homes, the clergy might follow them, and if possible, provide for their own security.

Augustine did not fall below his own high notions of Christian, of episcopal duty. When the Vandal army gathered around Hippo, one of the few cities which still afforded a refuge for the persecuted provincials, he refused, though more than seventy years old, to abandon his post. In the third month of the siege he was released by death, and escaped the horrors of the capture, the cruelties of the conqueror, and the desolation of his church.[g]

A.D. 430.

---

[g] In the life of Augustine, I have chiefly consulted that prefixed to his works, and Tillemont, with the passages in his Confessions and Epistles.

CHAPTER XI.

Jerome.—The Monastic System.

THOUGH not so directly or magisterially dominant over
                    the Christianity of the West, the influence of
Jerome.   Jerome has been of scarcely less importance
than that of Augustine. Jerome was the connecting
link between the East and the West; through him,
as it were, passed over into the Latin hemisphere of
Christendom that which was still necessary for its
permanence and independence during the succeeding
ages. The time of separation approached, when the
Eastern and Western empires, the Latin and the Greek
languages, were to divide the world. Western Christianity was to form an entirely separate system. The
different nations and kingdoms which were to arise out
of the wreck of the Roman empire were to maintain,
each its national church, but there was to be a permanent centre of unity in that of Rome, considered as the
common parent and federal head of Western Christendom. But before this vast and silent revolution took
place, certain preparatives, in which Jerome was chiefly
instrumental, gave strength, and harmony, and vitality
to the religion of the West, from which the precious
inheritance has been secured to modern Europe.

The two leading transactions in which Jerome took
the effective part, were—1st, the introduction, or at
least the general reception, of Monachism in the West;
2nd, the establishment of an authoritative and universally recognised version of the sacred writings into the

Latin language. For both these important services, Jerome qualified himself by his visits to the East. He was probably the first occidental (though born in Dalmatia, he may be almost considered a Roman, having passed all his youth in that city) who became completely naturalised and domiciliated in Judæa: and his example, though it did not originate, strengthened to an extraordinary degree the passion for pilgrimages to the Holy Land; a sentiment in later times productive of such vast and unexpected results. In the earlier period, the repeated devastations of that devoted country, and still more its occupation by the Jews, had overpowered the natural veneration of the Christians for the scene of the life and sufferings of the Redeemer. It was an accursed rather than a holy region, desecrated by the presence of the murderers of the Lord, rather than endeared by the reminiscences of his personal ministry and expiatory death. The total ruin of the Jews, and their expulsion from Jerusalem by Hadrian; their dispersion into other lands, with the simultaneous progress of Christianity in Palestine, and their settlement in Ælia, the Roman Jerusalem, notwithstanding the profanation of that city by idolatrous emblems, allowed those more gentle and sacred feelings to grow up in strength and silence.[a] Already, before the time of Jerome, pilgrims had flowed from all quarters of the

---

[a] Augustine asserts that the *whole world* flocked to Bethlehem to see the place of Christ's nativity. t. i. p. 561. Pilgrimages, according to him, were undertaken to Arabia, to see the dung-heap on which Job sat. t. ii. p. 59. For 180 years, according to Jerome, from Hadrian to Constantine, the statue of Jupiter occupied the place of the resurrection, and a statue of Venus was worshipped on the *rock* of Calvary. But as the object of Hadrian was to insult the Jewish, not the Christian, religion, it seems not very credible that these two sites should be chosen for the Heathen temples. Hieronym. Oper. Epist. xlix. p. 505.

world; and during his life, whoever had attained to any proficiency in religion, in Gaul, or in the secluded island of Britain, was eager to obtain a personal knowledge of these hallowed places. They were met by strangers from Armenia, Persia, India (the Southern Arabia), Æthiopia, the countless monks of Egypt, and from the whole of Western Asia.[b] Yet Jerome was, no doubt, the most influential pilgrim to the Holy Land; the increasing and general desire to visit the soil printed, as it were, with the footsteps, and moist with the redeeming blood of the Saviour, may be traced to his writings, which opened as it were a constant and easy communication, and established an intercourse, more or less regularly maintained, between Western Europe and Palestine.[c]

---

[b] Quicunque in Galliâ fuerat primus huc properat. Divisus ab orbe nostro Britannus, si in religione processerit, occiduo sole dimisso, quærit locum famâ sibi tantum, et Scripturarum relatione cognitum. Quid referamus Armenios, quid Persas, quid Indiæ, quid Æthiopiæ populos, ipsamque juxta Ægyptum, fertilem monachorum, Pontum et Cappadociam, Syriam, Cretam, et Mesopotamiam cunctaque orientis examina. This is the letter of a Roman female, Paula. Hieronym. Oper. Epist. xliv. p. 551.

[c] See the glowing description of all the religious wonders in the Holy Land in the Epitaphium Paulæ. An epistle, however, of Gregory of Nyssa strongly remonstrates against pilgrimages to the Holy Land, even from Cappadocia. He urges the dangers and suspicions to which pious recluses, especially women, would be subject with male attendants, either strangers or friends, on a lonely road; the dissolute words and sights which may be unavoidable in the inns; the dangers of robbery and violence in the Holy Land itself, of the moral state of which he draws a fearful picture. He asserts the religious superiority of Cappadocia, which had more churches than any part of the world; and inquires, in plain terms, whether a man will believe the virgin birth of Christ the more by seeing Bethlehem, or his resurrection by visiting his tomb, or his ascension by standing on the Mount of Olives. Greg. Nyss. de eunt. Hieros.

The authenticity of this epistle is indeed contested by Roman Catholic writers; but I can see no internal evidence against its genuineness. Jerome's more sober letter to Paulinus, Epist. xxix. vol. iv. p. 563., should also be compared.

But besides this subordinate, if indeed subordinate, effect of Jerome's peculiar position between the East and West, he was thence both incited and enabled to accomplish his more immediately influential undertakings. In Palestine and in Egypt, Jerome became himself deeply imbued with the spirit of Monachism, and laboured with all his zeal to awaken the more tardy West to rival Egypt and Syria in displaying this sublime perfection of Christianity. By his letters, descriptive of the purity, the sancity, the total estrangement from the deceitful world in these blessed retirements, he kindled the holy emulation, especially of the females, in Rome. Matrons and virgins of patrician families embraced with contagious fervour the monastic life; and though the populous districts in the neighbourhood of the metropolis were not equally favourable for retreat, yet they attempted to practise the rigid observances of the desert in the midst of the busy metropolis.

For the second of his great achievements, the version of the sacred Scriptures, Jerome derived inestimable advantages, and acquired unprecedented authority, by his intercourse with the East. His residence in Palestine familiarised him with the language and peculiar habits of the sacred writers. He was the first Christian writer of note who thought it worth while to study Hebrew. Nor was it the language alone; the customs, the topography, the traditions, of Palestine were carefully collected, and applied by Jerome, if not always with the soundest judgement, yet occasionally with great felicity and success to the illustration of the sacred writings.

The influence of Monachism upon the manners, opinions, and general character of Christianity, as well as that of the Vulgate translation of the Bible, not only

O

on the religion, but on the literature of Europe, appear
to demand a more extensive investigation; and
as Jerome, if not the representative, was the
great propagator of Monachism in the West, and as
about this time this form of Christianity overshadowed
and dominated throughout the whole of Christendom, it
will be a fit occasion, although I have in former parts
of this work not been able altogether to avoid it, to
develope more fully its origin and principles.

Monachism.

It is singular to see this oriental influence succes-
sively enslaving two religions in their origin and in
their genius so totally opposite to Monachism as Christianity and the religion of Mohammed. Both gradually
and unreluctantly yield to the slow and inevitable
change. Christianity, with very slight authority from
the precepts, and none from the practice of the Author
and first teachers of the faith, admitted this without
inquiry as the perfection and consummation of its own
theory. Its advocates and their willing auditors equally
forgot that if Christ and his apostles had retired into
the desert, Christianity would never have spread beyond
the wilderness of Judæa. The transformation which
afterwards took place of the fierce Arab marauder, or
the proselyte to the martial creed of the Koran, into a
dreamy dervish, was hardly more violent and complete,
than that of the disciple of the great example of Christian virtue, or of the active and popular Paul, into a
solitary anchorite.

Still that which might appear most adverse to the
universal dissemination of Christianity eventually tended to its entire and permanent incorporation with the whole of society. When Eremitism
gave place to Cœnobitism; when the hermitage grew
up into a convent, the establishment of these religious

Cœnobitism.

fraternities in the wildest solitudes gathered round them a Christian community, or spread, as it were, a gradually increasing belt of Christian worship, which was maintained by the spiritual services of the monks. The monks, though not generally ordained as ecclesiastics, furnished a constant supply for ordination. In this manner, the rural districts, which, in most parts, long after Christianity had gained the predominance in the towns, remained attached by undisturbed habit to the ancient superstition, were slowly brought within the pale of the religion. The monastic communities commenced, in the more remote and less populous districts of the Roman world, that ameliorating change which, at later times, they carried on beyond the frontiers. As afterwards they introduced civilisation and Christianity among the barbarous tribes of North Germany or Poland, so now they continued in all parts a quiet but successful aggression on the lurking Paganism.

Monachism was the natural result of the incorporation of Christianity with the prevalent opinions of mankind, and in part of the state of profound Origin of Monachism. excitement into which it had thrown the human mind. We have traced the universal predominance of the great principle, the inherent evil of matter. This primary tenet, as well of the Eastern religions as of the Platonism of the West, coincided with the somewhat ambiguous use of the term "world" in the sacred writings. Both were alike the irreclaimable domain of the Adversary of good. The importance assumed by the soul, now through Christianity become profoundly conscious of its immortality, tended to the same end. The deep and serious solicitude for the fate of that everlasting part of our being, the concentration of all its energies on its own individual welfare, withdrew it entirely

o 2

within itself. A kind of sublime selfishness excluded
all subordinate considerations.[d] The only security
against the corruption which environed it on all sides
seemed entire alienation from the contagion of matter;
the constant mortification, the extinction, if possible, of
those senses which were necessarily keeping up a dangerous and treasonable correspondence with the external
universe. On the other hand, entire estrangement from
the rest of mankind, included in the proscribed and infectious *world*, appeared no less indispensable. Communion with God alone was at once the sole refuge
and perfection of the abstracted spirit; prayer the sole
unendangered occupation, alternating only with that
coarse industry which might give employment to the
refractory members, and provide that scanty sustenance
required by the inalienable infirmity of corporeal existence. The fears and the hopes were equally wrought
upon—the fear of defilement and consequently of eternal
perdition; the hope of attaining the serene enjoyment
of the divine presence in the life to come. If any
thought of love to mankind, as an unquestionable duty
entailed by Christian brotherhood, intruded on the iso-
lated being, thus labouring on the single object, his own
spiritual perfection, it found a vent in prayer for their
happiness, which excused all more active or effective
benevolence.

---

[d] It is remarkable how rarely, if ever (I cannot call to mind an in-stance), in the discussions on the comparative merits of marriage and celibacy, the social advantages appear to have occurred to the mind; the benefit to mankind of raising up a race born from Christian parents and brought up in Christian principles. It is always argued with relation to the interests and the perfection of the individual soul; and even with regard to that, the writers seem almost un-conscious of the softening and human-ising effect of the natural affections, the beauty of parental tenderness and filial love.

On both principles, of course, marriage was inexorably condemned.[e] Some expressions in the writings of St. Paul,[f] and emulation of the Gnostic sects, combining with these general sentiments, had very early raised celibacy into the highest of Christian virtues: marriage was a necessary evil, an inevitable infirmity of the weaker brethren. With the more rational and earlier writers, Cyprian, Athanasius, and even in occasional passages in Ambrose or Augustine, it had its own high and peculiar excellence; but even with them, virginity, the absolute estrangement from all sensual indulgence, was the transcendant virtue, the pre-assumption of the angelic state, the approximation to the beatified existence.[g]

Celibacy.

---

[e] There is a sensible and judicious book, entitled "Die Einführung der erzwungenen Ehelosigkeit bei den Christlichen Geistlichen und ihre Folge," von J. A. und Aug. Theiner, Altenburg, 1828, which enters fully into the origin and consequences of celibacy in the whole church. This is an early work of Theiner, now become a Roman Catholic, and labouring in the library of the Vatican, as the Continuator of Baronius.

[f] I agree with Theiner (p. 24) in considering these precepts local and temporary, relating to the especial circumstances of those whom St. Paul addressed.

[g] The general tone was that of the vehement Jerome. There must not only be vessels of gold and silver, but of wood and earthenware. This contemptuous admission of the necessity of the married life distinguished the orthodox from the Manichean, the

Montanist, and the Encratite. Jerom. adv. Jovin. p. 146.

The sentiments of the Fathers on marriage and virginity may be thus briefly stated. I am not speaking with reference to the marriage of the clergy, which will be considered hereafter.

The earlier writers, when they are contending with the Gnostics, though they elevate virginity above marriage, speak very strongly on the folly, and even the impiety, of prohibiting or disparaging lawful wedlock. They acknowledge and urge the admitted fact that several of the Apostles were married. This is the tone of Ignatius (Cotel. Pat. Apost. ii. 77), of Tertullian (licebat et Apostolis nubere et uxores circumducere. De Exhort. Castit.), above all, of Clement of Alexandria.

In the time of Cyprian, vows of virginity were not irrevocable. Si

Every thing conspired to promote, nothing remained
Causes which to counteract, this powerful impulse. In the
tended to East this seclusion from the world was by no
promote
Monachism. means uncommon. Even among the busy and
restless Greeks some of the philosophers had asserted
the privilege of wisdom to stand aloof from the rest of
mankind; the question of the superior excellence of the
active or the contemplative life had been agitated on
equal terms. But in some regions of the East, the
sultry and oppressive heats, the general relaxation of
the physical system, dispose constitutions of a certain
temperament to a dreamy inertness. The indolence
and prostration of the body produce a kind of activity
in the mind, if that may properly be called activity
which is merely giving loose to the imagination and the

---

autem perseverare nolunt, vel non
possunt, melius est ut nubant, quam
in ignem delictis suis cadant. Epist.
62. And his general language, more
particularly his tract de Habitu Virginum, implies that strong discipline
was necessary to restrain the dedicated
virgins from the vanities of the world.

But in the fourth century the
eloquent Fathers vie with each other
in exalting the transcendant, holy,
angelic virtue of virginity. Every
one of the more distinguished writers,
—Basil, the two Gregories, Ambrose,
Augustine, Chrysostom, has a treatise
or treatises upon virginity, on which
he expands with all the glowing language which he can command. It
became a common doctrine that sexual
intercourse was the sign and the consequence of the Fall ; they forgot that
the command to " increase and mul-

tiply " is placed in the Book of Genesis
(i. 28) before the Fall.

We have before (p. 199) quoted
passages from Greg. of Nazianzum.
Gregory of Nyssa says,—ἡδονὴ δὲ
ἀπάτης ἐγγινόμενη τῆς ἐκπτώσεως
ἥρξατο—ἐν ἀνομίαις ἐστὶν ἡ σύλλη-
ψις, ἐν ἁμαρτίαις ἡ κύησις. Greg.
Nyss. de Virgin. c. 12, c. 13. But
Jerome is the most vehement of all :—
Nuptiæ terram replent, virginitas
Paradisum. The unclean beasts went
by pairs into the ark, the clean by
seven. Though there is another mystery in the pairs, even the unclean
beasts were not to be allowed a second
marriage :—Ne in bestiis quidem et
immundis avibus digamia comprobata
sit. Adv. Jovin. vol. iv. p. 160.
Laudo nuptias, laudo conjugium, sed
quia mihi virgines generat. Ad
Eustoch. p. 36.

emotions, as they follow out a wild train of incoherent
thought, or are agitated by impulses of spontaneous and
ungoverned feeling. Ascetic Christianity ministered
new aliment to this common propensity; it gave an
object both vague and determinate enough to stimulate,
yet never to satisfy or exhaust. The regularity of
stated hours of prayer, and of a kind of idle industry,
weaving mats, or plaiting baskets, alternated with
periods of morbid reflection on the moral state of the
soul, and of mystic communion with the Deity.[h] It
cannot, indeed, be wondered that the new revelation, as
it were, of the Deity; this profound and rational cer-
tainty of his existence; this infelt consciousness of his
perpetual presence; these yet unknown impressions of
his infinity, his power, and his love, should give a higher
character to this eremitical enthusiasm, and attract men
of loftier and more vigorous minds within its sphere.
It was not merely the pusillanimous dread of encoun-
tering the trials of life which urged the humbler spirits
to seek the safe retirement, or the natural love of peace
and the weariness and satiety of life, which commended
this seclusion to those who were too gentle to mingle
in, or who were exhausted with, the unprofitable turmoil
of the world. Nor was it always the anxiety to mortify
the rebellious and refractory body with more advantage.
The one absorbing idea of the majesty of the Godhead
almost seemed to swallow up all other considerations;
the transcendant nature of the Triune Deity, the rela-

---

[h] Nam pariter exercentes corporis
animæque virtutes, exterioris hominis
stipendia cum emolumentis interioris
exæquant, lubricis motibus cordis, et
fluctuationi cogitationum instabili,
operum pondera, velut quandam
tenacem atque immobilem anchoram
præfigentes, cui volubilitas ac perva-
gatio cordis innexa intra cellæ claustra,
velut in portu fidissimo valeat con-
tineri. Cassian. Instit. ii. 13.

tion of the different persons in the Godhead to each other, seemed the only worthy objects of man's contemplative faculties. If the soul never aspired to that Pantheistic union with the spiritual essence of being which is the supreme ambition of the higher Indian mysticism, their theory seemed to promise a sublime estrangement from all sublunary things, an occupation for the spirit, already, as it were, disembodied and immaterialised by its complete concentration on the Deity.

In Syria and in Egypt, as well as in the remoter East, the example had already been set both of solitary retirement and of religious communities. The Jews had both their hermitages and their cœnobitic institutions. Anchorites swarmed in the deserts near the Dead Sea; [1] and the Essenes, in the same district, and the Egyptian Therapeutæ, were strictly analogous to the Christian monastic establishments. In the neighbourhood of many of the Eastern cities were dreary and dismal wastes, incapable of, or unimproved by, cultivation, which seemed to allure the enthusiast to abandon the haunts of men and the vices of society. Egypt especially, where everything excessive and extravagant found its birth or ripened with unexampled vigour, seemed formed for the encouragement of the wildest anchoritism. It is a long narrow valley, closed in on each side by craggy or by sandy deserts. The rocks were pierced either with natural caverns, or hollowed out by the hand of man into long subterranean cells and galleries for various uses, either of life, or of superstition, or of sepulture. The Christian, sometimes driven out by persecution (for persecution no doubt

---

[1] Josephi Vita.

greatly contributed to people these solitudes),[k] or
prompted by religious feelings to fly from the face of
man, found himself, with no violent effort, in a dead and
voiceless wilderness, under a climate which required no
other shelter than the ceiling of the rock-hewn cave,
and where actual sustenance might be obtained with
little difficulty.

St. Antony is sometimes described as the founder of
the monastic life; it is clear, however, that he
only imitated and excelled the example of less   Antony.
famous anchorites. But he may fairly be considered as
its representative.

Antony[m] was born of Christian parents, bred up in
the faith, and before he was twenty years old, found
himself master of considerable wealth, and charged with
the care of a younger sister. He was a youth of ardent
imagination, vehement impulses, and so imperfectly
educated as to be acquainted with no language but his
native Egyptian.[n] A constant attendant on Christian
worship, he had long looked back with admiration on
those primitive times when the Christians laid all their
worldly goods at the feet of the Apostles. One day he
heard the sentence, " Go, sell all thou hast, and give to
the poor, ... and come, and follow me." It seemed
personally addressed to himself by the voice of God.
He returned home, distributed his lands among his

---

[k] Paul, the first Christian hermit,
fled from persecution. Hieronym. Vit.
Paul, p. 69.

[m] The fact that the great Athanasius paused in his polemic warfare
to write the life of Antony, may show
the general admiration towards the
monastic life.

[n] Jerome claims the honour of

being the first hermit for Paul, in
the time of Decius or Valerian, (Vit.
Paul. p. 68); but the whole life of
Paul, and the visit of Antony to him,
read like religious romance ; and, it
appears from the preface of Jerome to
the Life of Hilarion, did not find
implicit credit in his own day.

neighbours, sold his furniture and other effects, except a
small sum reserved for his sister, whom he placed under
the care of some pious Christian virgins.   Another text,
" Take no thought for the morrow," transpierced his
heart, and sent him forth for ever from the society of
men.   He found an aged solitary, who dwelt without
the city.   He was seized with pious emulation, and from
that time devoted himself to the severest asceticism.
There was still, however, something gentle and humane
about the asceticism of Antony.   His retreat (if we may
trust the romantic life of St. Hilarion, in the works of
St. Jerome), was by no means of the horrid and savage
character affected by some other recluses: it was at the
foot of a high and rocky mountain, from which welled
forth a stream of limpid water, bordered by palms,
which afforded an agreeable shade.   Antony had
planted this pleasant spot with vines and shrubs; there
was an enclosure for fruit trees and vegetables, and a
tank from which the labour of Anthony irrigated his
garden.   His conduct and character seemed to partake
of this less stern and gloomy tendency.[o]   He visited
the most distinguished anchorites, but only to observe,
that he might imitate, the peculiar virtue of each; the
gentle disposition of one; the constancy of prayer in
another; the kindness, the patience, the industry, the
vigils, the macerations, the love of study, the passionate
contemplation of the Deity, the charity towards mankind.   It was his devout ambition to equal or transcend
each in his particular austerity or distinctive excellence.

But man does not violate nature with impunity; the
solitary state had its passions, its infirmities, its perils.
The hermit could fly from his fellow men, but not from

---

[o] Vita St. Hilarion. p. 85.

himself.   The vehement and fervid temperament which
drove him into the desert was not subdued; Dæmonology.
it found new ways of giving loose to its suppressed impulses.   The self-centred imagination began
to people the desert with worse enemies than mankind.
Dæmonology, in all its multiplied forms, was now an
established part of the Christian creed, and embraced
with the greatest ardour by men in such a state of religious excitement as to turn hermits.   The trials, the
temptations, the agonies, were felt and described as personal conflicts with hosts of impure, malignant, furious,
fiends.   In the desert, these beings took visible form
and substance; in the day-dreams of profound religious
meditation, in the visions of the agitated and exhausted
spirit, they were undiscernible from reality.[p]   It is impossible, in the wild legends which became an essential
part of Christian literature, to decide how much is the
disordered imagination of the saint, the self-deception
of the credulous, or the fiction of the zealous writer.
The very effort to suppress certain feelings has a natural
tendency to awaken and strengthen them.   The horror
of carnal indulgence would not permit the sensual
desires to die away into apathy.   Men are apt to find
what they seek in their own hearts, and by anxiously
searching for the guilt of lurking lust, or desire of
worldly wealth or enjoyment, the conscience, as it were,
struck forcibly upon the chord which it wished to deaden,
and made it vibrate with a kind of morbid, but more
than ordinary, energy.   Nothing was so licentious or so
terrible as not to find its way to the cell of the recluse.
Beautiful women danced around him; wild beasts of
every shape, and monsters with no shape at all, howled

---

[p] Compare Jerome's Life of St. Hilarion, p. 76.

and yelled and shrieked about him, while he knelt in
prayer, or snatched his broken slumbers. " Oh how
often in the desert," says Jerome, " in that vast solitude,
which, parched by the sultry sun, affords a dwelling to
the monks, did I fancy myself in the midst of the
luxuries of Rome. I sat alone; for I was full of bitterness. My misshapen limbs were rough with sackcloth;
and my skin was so squalid that I might have been
taken for a negro. Tears and groans were my occupation every day, and all day; if sleep surprised me
unawares, my naked bones, which scarcely held together, clashed on the earth. I will say nothing of my
food or beverage: even the rich have nothing but cold
water; any warm drink is a luxury. Yet even I, who
for the fear of hell had condemned myself to this dun-
geon, the companion only of scorpions and wild beasts
was in the midst of girls dancing. My face was pale
with fasting, but the mind in my cold body burned with
desires; the fires of lust boiled up in the body, which
was already dead. Destitute of all succour, I cast
myself at the feet of Jesus, washed them with my tears,
dried them with my hair, and subdued the rebellious
flesh by a whole week's fasting." After describing the
wild scenes into which he fled, the deep glens and shaggy
precipices,—" The Lord is my witness," he concludes;
" sometimes I appeared to be present among the angelic
hosts, and sang, ' We will haste after thee for the sweet
savour of thy ointments.' "[q] For at times, on the other
hand, gentle and more than human voices were heard
consoling the constant and devout recluse; and sometimes the baffled dæmon would humbly acknowledge
himself to be rebuked before the hermit. But this was

---

[i] Song of Solomon. Hieronym. Epist. xxii.

in general after a fearful struggle. Desperate diseases require desperate remedies. The severest pain could alone subdue or distract the refractory desires or the preoccupied mind. Human invention _{Self-torture.} was exhausted in self-inflicted torments. The Indian faquir was rivalled in the variety of distorted postures and of agonising exercises. Some lived in clefts and caves; some in huts, into which the light of day could not penetrate; some hung huge weights to their arms, necks, or loins; some confined themselves in cages; some on the tops of mountains, exposed to the sun and weather. The most celebrated hermit at length for life condemned himself to stand in a fiery climate, on the narrow top of a pillar.[r] Nor were these always rude or uneducated fanatics. St. Arsenius had filled, and with universal respect, the dignified post of tutor to the Emperor Arcadius. But Arsenius became an hermit; and, among other things, it is related of him, that, employing himself in the common occupation of the Egyptian monks, weaving baskets of palm-leaves, he changed only once a year the water in which the leaves were moistened. The smell of the fœtid water was a just penalty for the perfumes which he had inhaled during his worldly life. Even sleep was a sin; an hour's un-

---

[r] The language of Evagrius (H. E. i. 13) about Simeon vividly expresses the effect which he made on his own age. " Rivalling, while yet in the flesh, the conversation of angels, he withdrew himself from all earthly things, and doing violence to nature, which always has a downward tendency, he aspired after that which is on high; and standing midway between earth and heaven, he had communion with God, and glorified God with the angels; from the earth offering supplications (πρεσβείας προάγων) as an ambassador to God; bringing down from heaven to men the divine blessing." The influence of the most holy martyr in the air (παναγίου καὶ ἀερίου μάρτυρος) on political affairs, lies beyond the range of the present history.

broken slumber was sufficient for a monk. On Saturday evening, Arsenius lay down with his back to the setting sun, and continued awake, in fervent prayer, till the rising sun shone on his eyes;[s] so far had Christianity departed from its humane and benevolent and social simplicity.

It may be a curious question how far enthusiasm repays its votaries as far as the individual is concerned; in what degree these self-inflicted tortures added to or diminished the real happiness of man; how far these privations and bodily sufferings, which to the cool and unexcited reason appear intolerable, either themselves produced a callous insensibility, or were met by apathy arising out of the strong counter-excitement of the mind; to what extent, if still felt in unmitigated anguish, they were compensated by inward complacency from the conscious fulfilment of religious duty; the stern satisfaction of the will at its triumph over nature; the elevation of mind from the consciousness of the great object in view, or the ecstatic pre-enjoyment of certain reward. In some instances, they might derive some recompense from the respect, veneration, almost adoration, of men. Emperors visited the cells of these ignorant, perhaps superstitious, fanatics, revered them as oracles, and conducted the affairs of empire by their advice. The great Theodosius is said to have consulted John the Solitary on the issue of the war with Eugenius.[t] His feeble successors followed faithfully the example of his superstition.

Antony appeared at the juncture most favourable for the acceptance of his monastic tenets.[u] His fame and

---

[s] Compare Fleury, xx. 1, 2.

[t] Evagr. Vit. St. Paul, c. 1. Theodoret, v 24. See Flechier, Vie de

Theodose, iv. 43.

[u] Hujus vitæ auctor Paulus, illustrator Antonius. Jerom. p. 46.

his example tended still further to disseminate the
spreading contagion. In every part the desert Influence of
began to swarm with anchorites, who found it Antony.
difficult to remain alone. Some sought out the most
retired chambers of the ancient cemeteries; some those
narrow spots which remained above water during the
inundations, and saw with pleasure the tide arise which
was to render them unapproachable to their fellow-
creatures. But in all parts the determined solitary
found himself constantly obliged to recede farther and
farther; he could scarcely find a retreat so dismal, a
cavern so profound, a rock so inaccessible, but that he
would be pressed upon by some zealous competitor or
invaded by the humble veneration of some disciple.

It is extraordinary to observe this infringement on
the social system of Christianity, this disconnecting
principle, which, pushed to excess, might appear fatal
to that organisation in which so much of the strength of
Christianity consisted, gradually self-expanding into a
new source of power and energy, so wonderfully adapted
to the age. The desire of the anchorite to isolate himself in unendangered seclusion was constantly balanced
and corrected by the holy zeal or involuntary tendency
to proselytism. The farther the saint retired from the
habitations of men, the brighter and more attractive
became the light of his sanctity; the more he concealed
himself, the more was he sought out by a multitude of
admiring and emulous followers. Each built or occupied
his cell in the hallowed neighbourhood. A monastery
was thus imperceptibly formed around the hermitage;
and nothing was requisite to the incorporation of a
regular community, but the formation of rules for common intercourse, stated meetings for worship, and
something of uniformity in dress, food, and daily occu-

pations. Some monastic establishments were no doubt formed at once, in imitation of the Jewish Therapeutæ; but many of the more celebrated Egyptian establishments gathered, as it were, around the central cell of an Antony or a Pachomius.[x]

Something like an uniformity of usage appears to have Cœnobitic prevailed in the Egyptian monasteries. The establishments. brothers were dressed, after the fashion of the country, in long linen tunics, with a woollen girdle, a cloak, and over it a sheep-skin. They usually went barefooted, but at certain very cold or very parching seasons, they wore a kind of sandal. They did not wear the hair-cloth.[y] Their food was bread and water; their luxuries, occasionally a little oil or salt, a few olives, peas, or a single fig: they ate in perfect silence, each decury by itself. They were bound to strict obedience to their superiors; they were divided into decuries and centenaries, over whom the decurions and centurions presided: each had his separate cell.[z] The furniture of their cells was a mat of palm-leaves and a bundle of the papyrus, which served for a pillow by night and a seat by day. Every evening and every night they were summoned to prayer by the sound of a horn. At each meeting were sung twelve psalms, pointed out, it was believed, by an angel. On certain occasions, lessons

---

[x] Pachomius was, strictly speaking, the founder of the cœnobitic establishments in Egypt; Eustathius in Armenia; Basil in Asia. Pachomius had 1400 monks in his establishment; 7000 acknowledged his jurisdiction.

[y] Jerome speaks of the cilicium as common among the Syrian monks, with whom he lived. Epist. i. Horrent sacco membra deformi. Even women assumed it. Epitaph. Paulæ, p. 678. Cassian is inclined to think it often a sign of pride. Instit. i. 3.

[z] The accounts of Jerome (in Eustochium, p. 45) and of Cassian are blended. There is some difference as to the hours of meeting for prayers, but probably the cœnobitic institutes differed as to that and on some points of diet.

were read from the Old or New Testament. The
assembly preserved total silence; nothing was heard
but the voice of the chanter or reader. No one dared
even to look at another. The tears of the audience
alone, or if he spoke of the joys of eternal beatitude, a
gentle murmur of hope, was the only sound which broke
the stillness of the auditory. At the close of each psalm,
the whole assembly prostrated itself in mute adoration.[a]
In every part of Egypt, from the Cataracts to the Delta,
the whole land was bordered by these communities;
there were 5000 cœnobites in the desert of Nitria
alone;[b] the total number of male anchorites and monks
was estimated at 76,000; the females at 27,700. Parts
of Syria were, perhaps, scarcely less densely peopled
with ascetics. Cappadocia and the provinces bordering
on Persia boasted of numerous communities, as well as
Asia Minor and the eastern parts of Europe. Though
the monastic spirit was in its full power, the establishment of regular communities in Italy must be reserved
for Benedict of Nursia, and lies beyond the bounds of
our present history. The enthusiasm pervaded all
orders. Men of rank, of family, of wealth, of education,
suddenly changed the luxurious palace for the howling
wilderness, the flatteries of men for the total silence of
the desert. They voluntarily abandoned their estates,

---

[a] Tantum a cunctis præbetur silen-
tium, ut cum in unum tam numerosa
fratrum multitudo conveniat, præter
illum, qui consurgens psalmum decantat
in medio, nullus hominum penitus
adesse credatur. No one was heard
to spit, to sneeze, to cough, or to
yawn—there was not even a sigh or
a groan—nisi fortè hæc quæ per ex-
cessum mentis claustra oris effugerit,
quæque insensibiliter cordi obrepserit,
immoderato scilicet atque intolerabili
spiritûs fervore succenso, dum ea quæ
ignita mens in semetipsâ non prævalet
continere, per ineffabilem quendam
gemitum pectoris sui conclavibus eva-
porare conatur. Cassian. Instit. ii.
10.

[b] Jerom. ad Eustoch. p. 44.

their connections, their worldly prospects. The desire of fame, of power, of influence, which might now swell the ranks of the ecclesiastics, had no concern in their sacrifice. Multitudes must have perished without the least knowledge of their virtues or their fate transpiring in the world. Few could obtain or hope to obtain the honour of canonisation, or that celebrity which Jerome promises to his friend Blesilla, to live not merely in heaven, but in the memory of man; to be consecrated to immortality by his writings.[c]

But the cœnobitic establishments had their dangers no less than the cell of the solitary hermit.

Dangers of cœnobitism. Besides those consequences of seclusion from the world, the natural results of confinement in this close separation from mankind and this austere discharge of stated duties, were too often found to be the proscription of human knowledge and the extinction of human sympathies. Christian wisdom and Christian humanity could find no place in their unsocial system. A morose, and sullen, and contemptuous ignorance could not but grow up where there was no communication with the rest of mankind, and the human understanding was rigidly confined to certain topics. The want of objects of natural affection could not but harden the heart; and those who, in their stern religious austerity are

Bigotry. merciless to themselves, are apt to be merciless to others:[d] their callous and insensible hearts have no sense of the exquisitely delicate and

---

[c] Quæ cum Christo vivit in cœlis, in hominum quoque ore victura est. . . . . Nunquam in meis moritura est libris. Epist. xxiii. p. 60.

[d] There is a cruel history of an abbot, Mucius, in Cassian. Mucius en-

treated admission into a monastery. He had one little boy with him of eight years old. They were placed in separate cells, lest the father's heart should be softened and indisposed to total renunciation of all earthly joys,

poignant feelings which arise out of the domestic affections. Bigotry has always found its readiest and sternest executioners among those who have never known the charities of life.

These fatal effects seem inherent consequences of Monasticism ; its votaries could not but degenerate from their lofty and sanctifying purposes. That which in one generation was sublime enthusiasm, in the next became sullen bigotry, or sometimes wrought the same individual into a stern forgetfulness not only of the vices and follies but of all the more generous and sacred feelings of humanity. In the cœnobitic insti-   Fanaticism.
tutes was added a strong corporate spirit, and a blind attachment to their own opinions, which were identified with religion and the glory of God.   The monks of Nitria, from simple and harmless enthusiasts, became ferocious bands of partisans ; instead of remaining aloof in jealous seclusion from the factions of the rest of the world, they rushed down armed into Alexandria : what they considered a sacred cause inflamed and warranted a ferocity not surpassed by the turbulent and blood-thirsty rabble of that city.   In support of a favourite doctrine or in defence of a popular prelate,

---

by the sight of his child. That he might still farther prove his Christian obedience!! and self-denial, the child was systematically neglected, dressed in rags, and so dirty, as to be disgusting to the father ; he was frequently beaten, to try whether it would force tears down the parent's squalid cheeks. "*Nevertheless, for the love of Christ!!!* and from the *virtue* of obedience, the heart of the father remained hard and unmoved ;" he thought little of his child's tears, only of his own humility and perfection. He at length was urged to show the last mark of his submission by throwing the child into the river. As if this was a *commandment of God*, he seized the child, and " the work of faith and obedience " would have been accomplished, if the brethren had not interposed, " and, as it were, rescued the child from the waters." And Cassian relates this as an act of the highest religious heroism ! Lib. iv. 27.

they did not consider that they were violating their own
first principles, in yielding to all the savage passions,
and mingling in the bloody strife of that world which
they had abandoned.

Total seclusion from mankind is as dangerous to
enlightened religion as to Christian charity. We might
have expected to find among those who separated themselves from the world, to contemplate, undisturbed, the nature and perfections of the Deity,
in general, the purest and most spiritual notions of the
Godhead. Those whose primary principle was dread of
the corruption of matter would be the last coarsely to
materialise their divinity. But those who could elevate
their thoughts or could maintain them at this height,
were but a small part of the vast numbers, whom the
many-mingled motives of zeal, superstition, piety, pride,
emulation, or distaste for the world, led into the desert.
They required something more gross and palpable than
the fine and subtle conception of a spiritual being.
Superstition, not content with crowding the brain with
imaginary figments, spread its darkening mists over the
Deity himself.

It was among the monks of Egypt that anthropomorphism assumed its most vulgar and obstinate form.
They would not be persuaded that the expressions in
the sacred writings which ascribe human acts, and
faculties, and passions to the Deity were to be understood as a condescension to the weakness of our nature;
they seemed disposed to compensate to themselves for
the loss of human society by degrading the Deity, whom
they professed to be their sole companion, to the likeness of man. Imagination could not maintain its flight,
and they could not summon reason, which they surrendered with the rest of their dangerous freedom, to supply

Ignorance.

its place; and generally superstition demanded and received the same implicit and resolute obedience as religion itself. Once having humanised the Deity, they could not be weaned from the object of their worship. The great cause of quarrel between Theophilus, the Archbishop of Alexandria, and the monks of the adjacent establishments, was his vain attempt to enlighten them on those points to which they obstinately adhered, as the vital and essential part of their faith.

Pride, moreover, is almost the necessary result of such distinctions as the monks drew between themselves and the rest of mankind; and prejudice and obstinacy are the natural fruits of pride. Once having embraced opinions, however, as in this instance, contrary to their primary principles, small communities are with the utmost difficulty induced to surrender those tenets in which they support and strengthen each other by the general concurrence. The anthropomorphism of the Egyptian monks resisted alike argument and authority. The bitter and desperate remonstrance of the aged Serapion, when he was forced to surrender his anthropomorphic notions of the Deity,—" You have deprived me of my God," [e] shows not merely the degraded intellectual state of the monks of Egypt, but the incapacity of the mass of mankind to keep up such high-wrought and imaginative conceptions. Enthusiasm of any particular kind wastes itself as soon as its votaries become numerous. It may hand down its lamp from individual to individual for many generations; but when it would include a whole section of society, it substitutes some new incentive, strong party or corporate feeling habit,

[e] Cassian Collat. x. 1.

advantage, or the pride of exclusiveness, for its original
disinterested zeal; and can never for a long period
adhere to its original principles.

The effect of Monachism on Christianity, and on
General society at large, was of a very mingled cha-
effects of Mo-
nachism on racter. Its actual influence on the population
Christianity. of the empire was probably not considerable,
and would scarcely counterbalance the increase arising
out of the superior morality, as regards sexual intercourse, introduced by the Christian religion.[f] Some
apprehensions, indeed, were betrayed on this point, and
when the opponents of Monachism urged, that if such
principles were universally admitted, the human race
would come to an end, its resolute advocates' replied,
that the Almighty, if necessary, would appoint new
means for the propagation of mankind.

The withdrawal of so much ardour, talent, and virtue
On political into seclusion, which, however elevating to the
affairs. individual, became altogether unprofitable to
society, might be considered a more serious objection.
The barren world could ill spare any active or inventive

---

[f] There is a curious passage of St.
Ambrose on this point. "Si quis
igitur putat, conservatione virginum
minui genus humanum, consideret,
quia, ubi paucæ virgines, ibi etiam
pauciores homines: ubi virginitatis
studia crebriora, ibi numerum quoque
hominum esse majorem. Dicite, quan-
tas Alexandrina, totiusque Orientis, et
Africana ecclesia, quotannis sacrare
consueverint. Pauciores hîc homines
prodeunt, quam illic virgines conse-
crantur." We should wish to know
whether there was any statistical
ground for this singular assertion,
that, in those regions in which celibacy
was most practised, the population
increased—or whether Egypt, the East,
and Africa, were generally more prolific than Italy. The assertion that
the vows of virginity in those countries exceeded the births in the latter
is, most probably, to be set down to
antithesis. Compare a good Essay of
Zumpt, in the Transactions of the
Berlin Academy, 1840, on this subject.
He concludes that Christianity generally tended to diminish the population
of the Empire. (1863.)

mind. Public affairs, at this disastrous period, demanded the best energies which could be combined from
the whole Roman empire for their administration. This
dereliction of their social duties by so many, could not
but leave the competition more open to the base and
unworthy; particularly as the actual abandonment of
the world, and the capability of ardent enthusiasm, in
men of high station, or of commanding intellect, displayed a force and independence of character which
might, it should seem, have rendered important active
service to mankind. If barbarians were admitted by a
perilous, yet inevitable policy, into the chief military
commands, was not this measure at least hastened, not
merely by the general influence of Christianity, which
reluctantly permitted its votaries to enter into the
army, but still more by Monachism, which withdrew
them altogether into religious inactivity? The civil
and fiscal departments, and especially that of public
education conducted by salaried professors, might also
be deprived of some of the most eligible and useful
candidates for employment. At a time of such acknowledged deficiency, it may have appeared little less than
treasonable indifference to the public welfare, to break
all connection with mankind, and to dwell in unsocial
seclusion entirely on individual interests. Such might
have been the remonstrance of a sober and dispassionate
Pagan,[g] and in part of those few more rational Christians,
who could not consider the rigid monastic Christianity
as the original religion of its divine founder.

If, indeed, this peaceful enthusiasm had counteracted
any general outburst of patriotism, or left vacant or
abandoned to worthless candidates posts in the public

---

[g] Compare the law of Valens, de Monachis, quoted above.

service which could be commanded by great talents and honourable integrity, Monachism might fairly be charged with weakening the energies and deadening the resistance of the Roman empire to its gathering and multiplying adversaries. But the state of public affairs probably tended more to the growth of Monachism than Monachism to the disorder and disorganisation of public affairs. The partial and unjust distribution of the rewards of public service; the uncertainty of distinction in any career, in which success entirely depended on the favouritism and intrigue within the narrow circle of the court; the difficulty of emerging to eminence under a despotism by fair and honourable means; disgust and disappointment at slighted pretensions and baffled hopes; the general and apparently hopeless oppression which weighed down all mankind; the total extinction of the generous feelings of freedom; the conscious decrepitude of the human mind; the inevitable conviction that its productive energies in knowledge, literature, and arts, were extinct and effete, and that every path was preoccupied,—all these concurrent motives might naturally, in a large proportion of the most vigorous and useful minds, generate a distaste and weariness of the world. Religion, then almost universally dominant, would seize on this feeling, and enlist it in her service : it would avail itself of, not produce, the despondent determination to abandon an ungrateful world; it would ennoble and exalt the preconceived motives for seclusion; give a kind of conscious grandeur to inactivity, and substitute a dreamy but elevating love for the Deity for contemptuous misanthropy, as the justification for the total desertion of social duty. Monachism, in short, instead of precipitating the fall of the Roman empire, by enfeebling in any great degree its powers of resist-

ance, enabled some portion of mankind to escape from
the feeling of shame and misery. Amid the irreme-
diable evils and the wretchedness that could not be
averted, it was almost a social benefit to raise some part
of mankind to a state of serene indifference, to render
some at least superior to the general calamities.

Monachism, indeed, directly secured many in their
isolation from all domestic ties, from that worst suffering
inflicted by barbarous warfare, the sight of beloved
females outraged, and innocent children butchered. In
those times, the man was happiest who had least to lose,
and who exposed the fewest vulnerable points of feeling
or sympathy. The natural affections, in which, in ordinary times, consists the best happiness of man, were in
those days such perilous indulgences, that he who was
entirely detached from them embraced, perhaps, considering temporal views alone, the most prudent course.
The solitary could but suffer in his own person ; and
though by no means secure in his sanctity from insult,
or even death, his self-inflicted privations hardened him
against the former, his high-wrought enthusiasm enabled
him to meet the latter with calm resignation : he had
none to leave whom he had to lament, none to lament
him after his departure. The spoiler who found his
way to his secret cell was baffled by his poverty ; and
the sword which cut short his days but shortened his
painful pilgrimage on earth, and removed him at once
to an anticipated heaven. With what different feelings
would he behold, in his poor, and naked, and solitary
cell, the approach of the blood-thirsty barbarians, from
the father of a family, in his splendid palace, or his
more modest and comfortable private dwelling, with a
wife in his arms, whose death he would desire to see
rather than that worse than death to which she might

first be doomed in his presence; with helpless children
clinging around his knees: the blessings which he had
enjoyed, the wealth or comfort of his house, the beauty
of his wife, of his daughters, or even of his sons, being
the strongest attraction to the spoiler, and irritating
more violently that spoiler's merciless and unsparing
passions. If to some the monastic state offered a refuge
for the sad remainder of their bereaved life, others may
have taken warning in time, and with deliberate forethought refused to implicate themselves in tender connections, which were threatened with such deplorable
end. Those, who secluded themselves from domestic
relations, from other motives, at all events, were secured
from such miseries, and might be envied by those who
had played the game of life for a higher stake and ventured on its purest pleasures, with the danger of incurring
all its bitterest reverses.

Monachism tended powerfully to keep up the vital
enthusiasm of Christianity. Allusion has been
made to its close connection with the conversion both of the Roman and the Barbarian;
and to the manner in which, from its settlement in some
retired Pagan district, it gradually disseminated the faith,
and sometimes the industrious, always the moral, influence of Christianity through the neighbourhood in a
gradually expanding circle. Its peaceful colonies, within
the frontier of Barbarism, slowly but uninterruptedly
subdued the fierce or indolent savages to the religion of
Christ and the manners and habits of civilisation. But
its internal influence was not less visible, immediate,
and inexhaustible. The more extensive dissemination
of Christianity naturally weakened its authority. When
the small primitive assembly of the Christians grew into
an universal church; when the village, the town, the

Effect on the maintenance of Christianity.

city, the province, the empire, became in outward form
and profession Christian, the practical Heathenism only
retired to work more silently and imperceptibly into the
Christian system. The wider the circle, the fainter
the line of distinction from the surrounding waters.
Small societies have a kind of self-acting principle of con-
servation within. Mutual inspection generates mutual
awe ; the generous rivalry in religious attainment keeps
up regularity in attendance on the sacred institutions,
and at least propriety of demeanour. Such small communities may be disturbed by religious faction, but are
long before they degenerate into unchristian licentiousness or languish into religious apathy. But when a
large proportion of Christians received the faith as an
inheritance from their fathers rather than from personal
conviction ; when hosts of deserters from Paganism
passed over into the opposite camp, not because it was
the best, but because it was the most flourishing cause ;
it became inexpedient, as well as impossible, to maintain
the severer discipline of former times. But Monachism
was constantly reorganising small societies, in which the
bond of aggregation was the common religious fervour,
in which emulation continually kept up the excitement,
and mutual vigilance exercised unresisted authority.
The exaggeration of their religious sentiments was at
once the tenure of their existence and the guarantee for
their perpetuity. Men would never be wanting to enrol
themselves in their ranks, and their constitution prevented them from growing to an unmanageable size.
When one establishment or institution wore out, another
was sure to spring up. The republics of Monachism
were constantly reverting to their first principles, and
undergoing a vigorous and thorough reformation. Thus,
throughout the whole of Christian history, until, or even

after, the Reformation, within the church of Rome, we
find either new monastic orders rising, or the old re-
modelled and regulated by the zeal of some ardent
enthusiast. The associatory principle, that great political
and religious engine which is either the conservative or
the destructive power in every period of society, was
constantly embracing a certain number of persons
devoted to a common end ; and the new sect, distinguished by some peculiar badge of dress, of habit, or
of monastic rule, re-embodied some of the fervour of
primitive Christianity, and awakened the growing
lethargy, by the example of unusual austerities or rare
and exemplary activity in the dissemination of the
faith.

The beneficial tendency of this constant formation of
young and vigorous societies in the bosom of Christianity
was of more importance in the times of desolation and
confusion which impended over the Roman empire. In
this respect, likewise, their lofty pretensions insured
their utility. Where reason itself was about to be in
abeyance, rational religion would have had but little
chance : it would have commanded no respect. Christianity, in its primitive simple and unassuming form,
might have imparted its holiness, and peace, and happiness, to retired families, whether in the city or the
province, but its modest and retiring dignity would have
made no impression on the general tone and character
of society. There was something in the seclusion
of religious men from mankind, in their standing aloof
from the rest of the world, calculated to impress barbarous minds with a feeling of their peculiar sanctity.
The less they were like to ordinary men, the more, in
the ordinary estimation, they were approximated to the
divinity. At all events, this apparently broad and

manifest evidence of their religious sincerity would be more impressive to unreasoning minds than the habits of the clergy, which approached more nearly to those of the common laity.[h]

The influence of this continual rivalry of another sacred, though not decidedly sacerdotal class, upon the secular clergy, led to important results. Influence on the clergy.

We may perhaps ascribe to the constant presence of Monachism the continuance and the final recognition of the celibacy of the clergy, the vital principle of the ecclesiastical power in the middle ages. Without the powerful direct support which they received from the monastic orders; without the indirect authority over the minds of men which flowed from their example, and inseparably connected, in the popular mind, superior sanctity with the renunciation of marriage, the ambitious Popes would never have been able, particularly in the north, to part the clergy by this strong line of demarcation from the profane laity.   As it was, it required the most vigorous and continued effort to establish, by ecclesiastical regulation and papal power, that which was no longer in accordance with the In promoting celibacy. religious sentiments of the clergy themselves.   The general practice of marriage, or of a kind of legalised concubinage, among the northern clergy, showed the tendency, if it had not been thus counteracted by the rival order, and by the dominant *ecclesiastical* policy of

---

[h] The monks were originally laymen (Cassian, v. 26); gradually churches were attached to the monasteries, but these were served by regularly ordained clergy.—(Pallad. Hist. Lausiaca.): but their reputation for sanctity constantly exposed them to be seized and consecrated by the ardent admiration of their followers. Theiner has collected with considerable labour a long list of the more celebrated prelates of the church who had been monks, p. 106. Ita ergo age et vive in monasterio, ut clericus esse merearis. Hieron. Epist. ad Rustic. 95.

the Church.[1] But it is impossible to calculate the effect
of that complete blending up of the clergy with the rest
of the community which would probably have ensued
from the gradual abrogation of this single distinction at
this juncture. The interests of their order, in men connected with the community by the ordinary social ties,
would have been secondary to their own personal advancement, or that of their families. They would have
ceased to be a peculiar and separate caste, and sunk
down into the common penury, rudeness, and ignorance.
Their influence would be closely connected with their
wealth and dignity, which, of course, on the other hand,
would tend to augment their influence; but that corporate ambition which induced them to consider the cause
of their order as their own; that desire of riches, which
wore the honorable appearance of personal disinterestedness, and zeal for the splendour of religion, could not
have existed but in a class completely insulated from
the common feelings and interests of the community.
Individual members of the clergy might have become
wealthy, and obtained authority over the ignorant
herd, but there would have been no opulent and
powerful Church, acting with vigorous unity, and arranged in simultaneous hostility against Barbarism and
Paganism.

Our history must hereafter trace the connection of
the independence and separate existence of the clergy
with the maintenance and the authority of Christianity.
But even as conservators of the lingering remains of
science, arts, and letters, as the sole order to which

---

[1] The general question of the
celibacy of the clergy will be subsequently examined. Compare Latin
Christianity, especially the great
struggle at Milan. Book vi. c. iii.

some kind of intellectual education was necessary, when knowledge was a distinction which alone commanded respect, the clergy were, not without advantage, secured by their celibacy from the cares and toils of social life. In this respect, Monachism acted in two ways; as itself the most efficient guardian of what was most worth preserving in the older civilisation, and as preventing, partly by emulation, partly by this enforcement of celibacy, the secular clergy from degenerating universally into that state of total ignorance which prevailed among them in some quarters.

It is impossible to survey Monachism in its general influence, from the earliest period of its interworking into Christianity, without being astonished and perplexed with its diametrically opposite effects. Here, it is the undoubted parent of the blindest ignorance and the most ferocious bigotry, sometimes of the most debasing licentiousness; there, the guardian of learning, the author of civilisation, the propagator of humble and peaceful religion. To the dominant spirit of Monachism may be ascribed some part at least of the gross superstition and moral inefficiency of the church in the Byzantine empire; to the same spirit much of the salutary authority of Western Christianity, its constant aggressions on barbarism, and its connection with the Latin literature. Yet neither will the different genius of the East and West account for this contradictory operation of the monastic spirit in the two divisions of the Roman empire. If human nature was degraded by the filth and fanatic self-torture, the callous apathy, and the occasional sanguinary violence, of the Egyptian or Syrian monk, yet the monastic retreat sent forth its Basils and Chrysostoms, who seemed to have braced their strong

intellects by the air of the desert. Their intrepid and
disinterested devotion to their great cause, the complete
concentration of their whole faculties on the advancement of Christianity, seemed strengthened by this entire
detachment from mankind.

Nothing can be conceived more apparently opposed
to the designs of the God of nature, and to the mild
and beneficent spirit of Christianity; nothing more
hostile to the dignity, the interests, the happiness, and
the intellectual and moral perfection of man, than the
monk afflicting himself with unnecessary pain, and
thrilling his soul with causeless fears; confined to a dull
routine of religious duties, jealously watching, and pro-
scribing every emotion of pleasure as a sin against the
benevolent Deity; dreading knowledge as an impious
departure from the becoming humility of man.

On the other hand, what generous or lofty mind can
refuse to acknowledge the grandeur of that superiority
to all the cares and passions of mortality; the felicity of
that state which is removed far above the fears or the
necessities of life; that sole passion of admiration and
love of the Deity, which no doubt was attained by some
of the purer and more imaginative enthusiasts of the
cell or the cloister? Who still more will dare to depre-
ciate that heroism of Christian benevolence, which
underwent this self-denial of the lawful enjoyments and
domestic charities of which it had neither extinguished
the desire, nor subdued the regret—not from the slavish
fear of displeasing the Deity, or the selfish ambition
of personal perfection—but from the genuine desire of
advancing the temporal and eternal improvement of
mankind; of imparting the moral amelioration and
spiritual hopes of Christianity to the wretched and the

barbarous ; of being the messengers of Christian faith,
and the ministers of Christian charity, to the Heathen,
whether in creed or in character ?

We return from this long, but not unnecessary, digres-
sion, to the life of Jerome, the great advocate Life of
of Monachism in the West. Jerome began Jerome.
and closed his career as a monk of Palestine : he attained, he aspired to, no dignity in the church. Though
ordained a presbyter against his will, he escaped the
episcopal dignity which was forced upon his distinguished contemporaries. He left to Ambrose, to Chrysostom, and to Augustine, the authority of office, and
was content with the lower, but not less extensive influence of personal communication, or the effect of his
writings. After having passed his youth in literary
studies in Rome, and in travelling throughout the West,
he visited Palestine. During his voyage to the East,
he surveyed some great cities, and consulted their
libraries ; he was received in Cyprus by the Bishop
Epiphanius. In Syria, he plunged at once into the
severest austerities of asceticism. I have already in-
serted the lively description of the inward struggles and
agonies which tried him during his first retreat in the
Arabian desert.

But Jerome had other trials peculiar to himself. It
was not so much the indulgence of the coarser Trials of
passions, the lusts, and ambition of the world, Jerome in
his retreat.
which distressed his religious sensibilities,[k] it was the
nobler and more intellectual part of his being which
was endangered by the fond reminiscences of his former

---

[k] Jerome says,—"Prima est virginitas à nativitate ; secunda virginitas à secundâ nativitate ;" he
ingenuously confesses that he could
only boast of the second. Epist. xxv.
iv. p. 242; Oper. iv. p. 459.

days. He began to question the lawfulness of those
literary studies which had been the delight of his
youth. He had brought with him, his sole companions,
besides the sacred books of his religion, the great masters
of poetry and philosophy, of Greek and Latin style; and
the magic of Plato's and Cicero's language, to his refined
and fastidious ear, made the sacred writings of Christianity, on which he was intently fixed, appear rude and
His classical barbarous. In his retreat in Bethlehem he
studies. had undertaken the study of Hebrew,[m] as a
severe occupation to withdraw him from those impure
and worldly thoughts which his austerities had not
entirely subdued; and in the weary hours when he was
disgusted with his difficult task, he could not refrain
from recurring, as a solace, to his favourite authors.
But even this indulgence alarmed his jealous conscience;
though he fasted before he opened his Cicero, his mind
dwelt with too intense delight on the language of the
orator; and the distaste with which he passed from the
musical periods of Plato to the verses of the Prophets,
of which his ear had not yet perceived the harmony,
and his Roman taste had not perhaps imbibed the full
sublimity, appeared to him as an impious offence against
his religion.[n] The inward struggles of his mind threw
him into a fever, he was thought to be dead, and in the
lethargic dream of his distempered imagination, he
thought that he beheld himself before the throne of the

---

[m] His description of Hebrew, as
compared with Latin, is curious:—
"Ad quam edomandam, cuidem fratri,
qui ex Hebræis crediderat, me in dis-
ciplinam dedi ut post Quintiliani
acumina, gravitatemque Frontonis, et
levitatem Plinii, alphabetum discerem
et *stridentia anhelaque verba* medi-
tarer—quid ibi laboris insumserim?"
Epist. xcv. ad Rusticum, p. 774.

[n] Si quando in memet reversus,
Prophetas legere cœpissem, sermo
horrebat incultus. Epist. xviii. ad
Eustoch. iv. p. 42.

great Judge, before the brightness of which he dared
not lift up his eyes. " Who art thou?" demanded the
awful voice.—" A Christian," answered the trembling
Jerome.[o] " 'Tis false," sternly replied the voice, "thou
art no Christian, thou art a Ciceronian. Where the
treasure is, there is the heart also." Yet, however
the scrupulous conscience of Jerome might tremble at
this profane admixture of sacred and heathen studies,
he was probably qualified in a high degree by this very
discordant collision of opposite tastes for one of the
great services which he was to render to Christianity.
No writer, without that complete mastery over the
Latin language, which could only be attained by constant familiarity with its best models, could so have
harmonised its genius with the foreign elements which
were to be mingled with it, as to produce the vivid and
glowing style of the Vulgate Bible. That this is far
removed from the purity of Tully, no one will question:
I shall hereafter consider more at length its genius and
its influence; but we may conjecture what would have
been the harsh, jarring, and inharmonious discord of
the opposing elements, if the translator had only been
conversant with the African Latinity of Tertullian,
or the elaborate obscurity of writers like Ammianus
Marcellinus.

Jerome could not, in the depths of his retreat, or in
the absorbing occupation of his studies, escape being

---

[o] Interim parantur exequiæ, et
vitalis animæ calor, toto frigescente
jam corpore, in solo tantum tepente
pulvisculo, palpitabat; quum subitò
raptus in spiritu, ad tribunal judicis
pertrahor; ubi tantum luminis, et
tantum erat ex circumstantium claritate
fulgoris, ut projectus in terram, sur- sùm aspicere non auderem. Inter-
rogatus de conditione, Christianum
me esse respondi. Et ille qui præ-
sidebat mortuis ait, Ciceronianus es,
non Christianus; *ubi enim thesaurus
tuus, ibi et cor tuum.* Ad Eustoch.
Epist. xviii. iv. p. 42.

involved in those controversies which distracted the
Return to Rome. Eastern churches, and penetrated to the cell of
the remotest anchorite. He returned to the
West to avoid the restless polemics of his brother monks.
On his return to Rome, the fame of his piety and
talents commended him to the confidence of the Pope
Damasus,[p] by whom he was employed in the most important affairs of the Roman see. But either the
Morality of the Roman clergy. influence or the opinions of Jerome excited
the jealousy of the Roman clergy, whose vices
Jerome paints in no softened colours. We almost, in
this contest, behold a kind of prophetic prelude to the
perpetual strife, which has existed in almost all ages,
between the secular and regular clergy, the hierarchical
and monastic spirit. Though the monastic opinions and
practices were by no means unprecedented in Italy
(they had been first introduced by Athanasius in his
flight from Egypt); though they were maintained by
Ambrose, and practised by some recluses; yet the
pomp, the wealth, and the authority of the Roman
ecclesiastics, which is described by the concurrent testimony of the Heathen historian[q] and the Christian
Jerome, would not humbly brook the greater popularity
of these severer doctrines, nor patiently submit to the
estrangement of some of their more opulent and distinguished proselytes, particularly among the females.
Jerome admits, indeed, with specious, but doubtful
humility, the inferiority of the unordained monk to the
ordained priest. The clergy were the successors of
the Apostles; their lips could make the body of Christ;
they had the keys of heaven, until the day of judgement;

---

[p] Epist. xii. p. 744. Tillemont,
Vie de Jerome.

[q] Ammianus Marcellinus. See
postea.

they were the shepherds, the monks only part of the flock. Yet the clergy, no doubt, had the sagacity to foresee the dangerous rival, as to influence and authority, which was rising up in Christian society. The great object of contention now was the command over the high-born and wealthy females of Rome. Jerome, in his advice to the clergy, cautiously warns them against the danger of female intimacy.[r] He, however, either considered himself secure, or under some peculiar privilege, or justified by the prospect of greater utility, to suspend his laws on his own behalf. He became a kind of confessor, he directed the sacred studies, he overlooked the religious conduct of more than one of these pious ladies. The ardour and vehemence with which his ascetic opinions were embraced, and the more than usually familiar intercourse with matrons and virgins of rank, may perhaps have offended the pride, if not the propriety, of Roman manners. The more temperate and rational of the clergy, in their turn, may have thought the zeal with which these female converts of Jerome were prepared to follow their teacher to the Holy Land, by no means a safe precedent; they may have taken alarm at the unusual fervour of language with which female ascetics were celebrated as united, by the nuptial tie, to Christ,[s] and exhorted, in

Influence over females of Rome.

---

[r] Epist. ad Heliodorum, p. 10.

[s] See the Epistle ad Eustochium. The whole of this letter is a singular union of religious earnestness and what, to modern feeling, would seem strange indelicacy if not immodesty, and still stranger liberty with the language of Scripture. He seems to say that Eustochium was the first noble Roman maiden who embraced virginity:—"Quæ ... prima Romanæ urbis virgo nobilis esse cœpisti." He says, however, of Marcella,—"Nulla eo tempore nobilium fœminarum noverat Romæ propositum monacharum, nec audebat propter rei novitatem, ignominiosum, ut tunc putabatur, et vile in populis, nomen assumere." Marcellæ Epitaph, p. 780.

the glowing imagery of the Song of Solomon, to devote
themselves to their spiritual spouse. They were the
brides of Christ;—Christ, worshipped by angels in
heaven, ought to have angels to worship him on earth.[t]
With regard to Jerome and his high-born friends, their
suspicions were, doubtless, unjust.

It is singular, indeed, to contrast the different descriptions of the female aristocracy of Rome
at the various periods of her history; the
secluded and dignified matrons, the Volumnias or Cor-
nelias, employed in household duties, and educating with
severe discipline, for the military and civil service of
the state, her future consuls and dictators; the gorgeous
luxury, the almost incredible profligacy, of the later
days of the republic and of the empire, the Julias and
Messalinas, so darkly coloured by the satirists of the
times; the active charity and the stern austerities of
the Paulas and Eustochiums of the present period. It
was not, in general, the severe and lofty Roman matron
of the age of Roman virtue whom Christianity induced
to abandon her domestic duties, and that highest of all
duties to her country, the bringing up of noble and
virtuous citizens; it was the soft, and at the same time,
the savage female, who united the incongruous, but too
frequently reconciled, vices of sensuality and cruelty;
the female, whom the facility of divorce, if she abstained
from less lawful indulgence, enabled to gratify in a
more decent manner her inconstant passions; who had
been inured from her most tender age, not merely to
theatrical shows of questionable modesty, but to the

Marginal note: Character of Roman females.

[t] In Jerome's larger interpretation
of Solomon's Song (adv. Jovin. p. 171)
is a very curious and whimsical passage, alluding to the Saviour as the
spouse. There is one sentence, however, in the letter to Eustochium, so
blasphemously indecent that it must
not be quoted even in Latin. p. 38.

bloody scenes of the arena, giving the signal perhaps with her own delicate hand for the mortal blow to the exhausted gladiator. We behold with wonder, not unmixed with admiration, women of the same race and city either forswearing from their earliest youth all intercourse with men, or preserving the state of widowhood with irreproachable dignity ; devoting their wealth to the foundation of hospitals, and their time to religious duties and active benevolence. These monastic sentiments were carried to that excess which seemed inseparable from the Roman character. At twelve years old, the young Asella devoted herself to God ; from that time she had never conversed with a man ; her knees were as hard as a camel's, by constant genuflexion and prayer.[u] Paula, the fervent disciple of Jerome, after devoting the wealth of Paula. an ancient and opulent house to charitable uses,[x] to the impoverishment of her own children, deserted her family. Her infant son and her marriageable daughter watched, with entreating looks, her departure ; she did not even turn her head away to hide her maternal tears, but lifted up her unmoistened eyes to heaven, and continued her pilgrimage to the Holy Land. Jerome celebrates

---

[u] Hieronym. Epist. xxi.

[x] Jerome thus describes the charity of Paula :—Quid ego referam, amplæ et nobilis domus, et quondam opulentissimæ, omnes pæne divitias in pauperes erogatas. Quid in cunctos clementissimum animum, et bonitatem etiam in eos quos nunquam viderat, evagantem. Quis inopum moriens, non illius vestimentis obvolutus est? Quis clinicorum non ejus facultatibus sustentatus . est? Quos curiosissimè totâ urbe perquirens, damnum putabat, si quis debilis et esuriens cibo sustentaretur alterius. *Spoliabat filios,* et inter objurgantes propinquos, majorem se eis hæreditatem, Christi misericordiam dimittere loquebatur. Epitaph. Paulæ, p. 671. At her death, Jerome relates, with great pride, that she did not leave a penny to her daughter, but a load of debts (magnum æs alienum).

this sacrifice of the holiest charities of life as the height of female religious heroism.[y]

The vehement and haughty temper of Jerome was *Controversies* not softened by his monastic austerities, nor *of Jerome.* humbled by the severe proscription of the gentler affections. His life, in the capital and in the desert, was one long warfare. After the death of his friend and protector, Damasus, the growing hostility of the clergy, notwithstanding the attachment of his disciples, rendered his residence in Rome disagreeable. Nor was the peace of the monastic life his reward for *Retreat to* his zealous exertions in its cause. He retired *Palestine.* to Palestine, where he passed the rest of his days in religious studies, and in polemic disputes. Wherever any dissentient from the doctrine or the practice of the dominant Christianity ventured to express his opinions, Jerome launched the thunders of his interdict from his cell at Bethlehem. No one was more perpetually involved in controversy, or opposed with greater rancour of personal hostility, than this earnest advocate of unworldly religious seclusion. He was engaged in a vehement dispute with St. Augustine on

---

[y] It is a passage of considerable beauty:—Descendit ad portum, fratre, cognatis, affinibus, et (quod his majus est) liberis prosequentibus, et clementissimam matrem pietate vincere cupientibus. Jam carbasa tendebantur, et remorum ductu navis in altum protrahebatur. Parvus Toxotius supplices manus tendebat in littora. Rufina, jam nubilis, ut suas expectaret nuptias, tacens fletibus obsecrabat, et tamen illa siccos ad cœlum oculos, pietatem in filios, pietate in Deum superans, nesciebat se matrem ut

Christi probaret ancillam. . . . . Hoc contra jura naturæ plena fides pat·ebatur, imo gaudens animus appetebat. Epitaph. Paulæ 672.

This was her epitaph:—

Aspicis angustum precisâ rupe sepulcrum?
Hospitium Paulæ est, cœlestia regna tenentis.
Fratrem, cognatos, Romam, patriamque relinquens,
Divitias, sobolem, Bethlehemite conditur antro.
Hic præsepe tuum, Christe, atque hic mystica Magi
Munera portantes, hominique, Deoque dedere.

the difference between St. Peter and St. Paul. But his repose was most embittered by the acrimonious and obstinate contest with Rufinus, which was rather a personal than a polemic strife.

In one controversy, Christendom acknowledged and hailed him as her champion. Jovinian and Vigilantius are involved in the dark list of _{Jovinian and Vigilantius.} heretics; but their error appears to have been that of unwisely attempting to stem the current of popular Christian opinion, rather than any departure from the important doctrines of Christianity. They were premature Protestants; they endeavoured, with vain and ill-timed efforts, to arrest the encroaching spirit of Monachism, which had now enslaved the whole of Christianity; [z] they questioned the superior merit of celibacy; they protested against the growing worship of relics.[a] Their effect upon the dominant sentiment of the times may be estimated by the language of wrath, bitterness, contempt, and abhorrence, with which Jerome assails these bold men, who thus presumed to encounter the spirit of their age. The four points of Jovinian's heresy, were,—1st, that virgins had no higher merit, unless superior in their good works, than widows and married women; 2nd, that there was no distinction of meats; 3rd, that those who had been baptized in full faith,

---

[z] Hieronym. adv. Vigilantium, p. 281.

[a] The observation of Fleury shows how mistimed was the attempt of Vigilantius to return to the simpler Christianity of former days :—" On ne voit pas que l'hérésie (de Vigilance), ait eu de suite; ni qu'on ait eu besoin d'aucun concile pour la condamner tant elle étoit contraire à la tradition de l'Eglise Universelle." Tom. v. p. 278.

I have purposely, lest I should overstrain the *Protestantism* of these remarkable men, taken this view of their tenets from Fleury, perhaps the fairest and most dispassionate writer of his church. Tom. iv. p. 602 ; tom. v. p. 275.

would not be overcome by the Devil; and 4th, that
those who had preserved the grace of baptism would
meet with an equal reward in heaven. This last clause
was perhaps a corollary from the first, as the panegyrists
of virginity uniformly claimed a higher place in heaven
for the immaculate than for those who had been polluted
by marriage. To those doctrines Vigilantius added, if
possible, more hated tenets. He condemned the respect
paid to the martyrs and their relics; he questioned the
miracles performed at their tombs; he condemned the
lighting lamps before them as a Pagan superstition;
he rejected the intercession of the saints; he blamed
the custom of sending alms to Jerusalem, and the selling
all property to give it to the poor; he asserted that it
was better to keep it and distribute its revenues in
charity; he protested against the whole monastic life,
as interfering with the duty of a Christian to his neigh-
bour. These doctrines were not without their followers;
the resentment of Jerome was embittered by their effect
on some of the noble ladies of Rome, who began to fall
off to marriage. Even some bishops embraced the doctrines of Vigilantius, and, asserting that the high professions of continence led the way to debauchery, refused
to ordain unmarried deacons.

The tone of Jerome's indignant writings against those
new heretics is that of a man suddenly arrested in his
triumphant career by some utterly unexpected opposition; his resentment at being thus crossed is mingled
with a kind of wonder that men should exist who could
entertain such strange and daring tenets. The length,
it might be said the prolixity, to which he draws out
his answer to Jovinian, seems rather the outpouring of
his wrath and his learning, than as if he considered it
necessary to refute such obvious errors. Throughout it

is the master condescending to teach, not the adversary
to argue.   He fairly overwhelms him with a mass of
scripture, and of classical learning : at one time he pours
out a flood of allegorical interpretations of the scripture ; he then confounds him with a clever passage
from Theophrastus on the miseries of marriage.   Even
the friends of Jerome, the zealous Pammachius himself,
were offended by the fierceness of his first invective
against Jovinian,[b] and his contemptuous disparagement
of marriage.   The injustice of his personal charges is
shewn and the charges refuted by the more temperate
statements of Augustine and by his own admissions.[c]
He was obliged, in his apology, to mitigate his vehemence, and reluctantly to fall into a milder strain ; but
even the Apology has something of the severe and contemptuous tone of an orator who is speaking on the
popular side, with his audience already in his favour.

But his language to Jovinian is sober, dispassionate,
and argumentative, in comparison with that to Vigilantius.   He describes all the monsters ever invented

---

[b] Indignamini mihi, quod Jovi-
nianum non docuerim, sed vicerim.
Imo indignantur mihi qui illum
anathematizatum dolent. Apolog. p.
236.

[c] Jerome admits that Jovinian did
not assert the privilege which he vindicated ; he remained a monk, though
Jerome highly colours his luxurious
habits. After his coarse tunic and
bare feet, and food of bread and water,
he has betaken himself to white garments, sweetened wine, and highly
dressed meats : to the sauces of an
Apicius or a Paxamus, to baths, and
shampooings (fricticulæ,—the Bene-
dictines translate this fritter shops),

and cooks' shops, it is manifest that
he prefers earth to heaven, vice to
virtue, his belly to Christ, and thinks
his rubicund colour (purpuram coloris ejus) the kingdom of heaven.
Yet this handsome, this corpulent,
smooth monk, always goes in white
like a bridegroom : let him marry a
wife to prove the equal value of virginity and marriage ; but if he will
not take a wife, though he is against
us in his words, his actions are for us.
He afterwards says,—Ille Romanæ
ecclesiæ auctoritate damnatus inter
fluviales aves, et carnes suillas, non
tam emisit animam quam eructavit.
p. 183.

by poetic imagination, the centaurs, the leviathan,
the Nemean lion, Cacus, Geryon. Gaul, by
Vigilantius. her one monster, Vigilantius,[d] had surpassed
all the pernicious and portentous horrors of other regions. " Why do I fly to the desert?—That I may
not see or hear thee; that I may no longer be
moved by thy madness, nor be provoked to war by thee;
lest the eye of a harlot should captivate me, and a
beautiful form seduce me to unlawful love." But his
great and conclusive argument in favour of reverence
for the dust of martyrs (that little dust which, covered
with a precious veil, Vigilantius presumed to think but
dust) is universal authority. " Was the Emperor Constantine sacrilegious, who transported the relics of
Andrew, Luke, and Timothy to Constantinople, at whose
presence the devils (such devils as inhabit the wretched
Vigilantius) roar, and are confounded? or the Emperor
Arcadius, who translated the bones of the holy Samuel
to Thrace? Are all the bishops sacrilegious who enshrined these precious remains in silk, as a vessel of
gold; and all the people who met them, and received
them as it were the living prophet? Is the Bishop of
Rome, who offers sacrifice on the altar under which are
the venerable bones (the vile dust, would Vigilantius
say?) of Peter and Paul; and not the bishop of one city
alone, but the bishops of all the cities in the world who
reverence these relics, around which the souls of the
martyrs are constantly hovering to hear the prayers of
the supplicant?"

---

[d] His brief sketch of the enor-
mities of Vigilantius is as follows :—
Qui immundo spiritu pugnat contra
Christi spiritum, et martyrum negat
sepulcra esse veneranda; damnandas
dicit esse vigilias; nunquam nisi in
Pascha Alleluia cantandum : conti-
nentiam hæresim, pudicitiam libidinis
seminarium.

The great work of Jerome, the authoritative Latin version of the scriptures, will demand our attention, as one of the primary elements of Christian literature, a subject which must form one most important branch of our inquiry into the extent and nature of the general revolution in the history of mankind, brought about by the complete establishment of Christianity.[e]

---

[e] Compare Latin Christianity, book i. ch. 2. Note on Jerome. Especially the passages about the destruction of Rome by Alaric, vol. i. p. 101.

BOOK IV.

—•◆•—

CHAPTER I.

The Roman empire under Christianity.

THE period is now arrived when we may survey the
General survey of the change effected by Christianity. total change in the habits and manners, as
well as in the sentiments and opinions, of
mankind, effected by the dominance of the
new faith. Christianity is now the mistress of the
Roman world; on every side the struggles of Paganism
become more feeble; it seems resigned to its fate, or
rather only hopes, by a feigned allegiance, and a simu-
lation of the forms and language of Christianity, to be
permitted to drag on a precarious and inglorious existence. The Christians are now no longer a separate
people, founding and maintaining their small independent republics, fenced in by marked peculiarities of
habits and manners from the rest of society; they have
become to all outward appearance *the people;* the
general manners of the world may be contemplated as
the manners of Christendom. The monks, and in some
respects the clergy, have, as it were, taken the place of
the Christians as a separate and distinct body of men;
the latter in a great degree, the former altogether, differing from the prevalent usages in their modes of life,
and abstaining from the common pursuits and avoca-
tions of society. The Christian writers, therefore, be-

come our leading, almost our only, authorities for the general habits and manners of mankind (for the notice of such matters in the Heathen writers are few Sources of information. and casual), except the Theodosian code. This indeed is of great value as a record of manners Theodosian code. as well as a history of legislation ; for that which demands the prohibition of the law, or is in any way of sufficient importance to require the notice of the legislature, may be considered as a prevalent custom : particularly as the Theodosian code is not a system of abstract and general law, but the register of the successive edicts of the Emperors, who were continually supplying, by their arbitrary acts, the deficiencies of the existing statutes, or as new cases arose, adapting those statutes to temporary exigences.

But the Christian preachers are the great painters of Roman manners ; Chrysostom of the East, Christian writers. more particularly of Constantinople ; Jerome, and though much less copiously, Ambrose and Augustine, of Roman Christendom. Considerable allowance must, of course, be made in all these statements for oratorical vehemence ; much more for the ascetic habits of the writers, particularly of Chrysostom, who maintained, and would have exacted, the rigid austerity of the desert in the midst of a luxurious capital. Nor must the general morality of the times be estimated from their writings without considerable discretion. It is the office of the preacher, though with a different design yet with something of the manner of the satirist, to select the vices of mankind for his animadversion, and to dwell with far less force on the silent and unpretending virtues. There might be, and probably was, an under-current of quiet Christian piety and gentleness

and domestic happiness, which would not arrest the
notice of the preacher who was denouncing the common
pride and luxury, or, if kindling into accents of praise,
was enlarging on the austere self-denial of the anchorite,.
or the more shining virtues of the saint.

Christianity disturbed not the actual relations of
society, it interfered in no way with the existing gradations of rank. Though, as we shall see, it introduced a
new order of functionaries,—what may be considered
from the estimation in which they were held, a new
aristocracy,—it left all the old official dignitaries in possession of their distinctions. With the great
vital distinction between the freeman and the
slave, as yet it made no difference.[a] It broke down
none of the barriers which separated this race of men
from the common rights of human kind ; and in no
degree legally brought up this Pariah caste of antiquity
to the common level of the human race.

Slavery.

In the new relation established between mankind and
the Supreme Being, the slave was fully participant ; he
shared in the redemption through Christ, he might
receive all the spiritual blessings, and enjoy all the im-
mortalising hopes of the believer ; he might be dismissed from his death-bed to heaven by the absolving
voice of the priest ; and besides this inestimable consolation in misery and degradation, this religious
equality, at least with the religious part of the community, could not fail to elevate his condition, and to
strengthen that claim to the sympathies of mankind
which was enforced by Christian humanity. The axiom
of Clement of Alexandria that by the common law of

---

[a] The laws of Justinian, it must be remembered, are beyond this period.

Christian charity, we were to act to them as we would
be acted by, because they were men,[b] though perhaps
it might have been uttered with equal strength of language by some of the better philosophers, spoke with
far more general acceptance to the human heart. The
manumission, which was permitted by Constantine to
take place in the Church, must likewise have tended
indirectly to connect freedom with Christianity.[c]

Still, down to the time of Justinian, the inexorable
law, which, as to their treatment, had already been
wisely tempered by the Heathen Emperors, as to their
rights, pronounced the same harsh and imperious sentence. It beheld them as an inferior class of human
beings; their life was placed but partially under the
protection of the law. If they died under a punishment
of extraordinary cruelty, the master was guilty of homicide; if under more moderate application of the scourge,
or any other infliction, the master was not accountable
for their death.[d] While it refused to protect, the law
inflicted on the slave punishments disproportionate to
those of the freeman. If he accused his master for any
crime, except high treason, he was to be burned;[e] if
free women married slaves, they sank to the abject state
of their husbands, and forfeited their rights as free
women;[f] if a free woman intrigued with a slave, she
was capitally punished, the slave was burned.[g]

The possession of slaves was in no degree limited by
law. It was condemned as a mark of inordinate luxury,

---

[b] Clemens Alex. Pædagog. iii. 12.
[e] See Blair on Slavery, p. 288.
[d] Cod. Theodos. ix. 12, 1.
[e] Ibid. ix. 6, 2.
[f] Ibid. iv. 9, 1, 2, 3.

[g] Ibid. ix. 11, 1. Since the publication of this book has appeared the
best and most comprehensive work on
that subject—Wallon's 'Histoire de
l'Esclavage dans l'Antiquité.'

but by no means as in itself contrary to Christian justice
or equity.[h]

On the pomp and magnificence of the court, Chris-
Manners of   tianity either did not aspire, or despaired of
the court.   enforcing moderation or respect for the common
dignity of mankind. The manners of the East, as the
Emperor took up his residence in Constantinople, were
too strong for the religion. With the first Christian
Emperor commenced that Oriental ceremonial, which it
might almost seem, that, rebuked by the old liberties of
Rome, the imperial despot would not assume till he
had founded another capital; or at least, if the first
groundwork of this Eastern pomp was laid by Diocletian, Rome had already been deserted, and was
not insulted by the open degradation of the first men
in the empire to the language, attitudes, and titles of
servitude.

The eunuchs, who, however admitted in solitary in-
Government   stances to the confidence or favour of the
of the
eunuchs.   earlier Emperors, had never formed a party or
handed down to each other the successive administra-
tions, now ruled in almost uncontested sovereignty, and
except in some rare instances, seemed determined not
to incur, without deserving, the antipathy and contempt
of mankind. The luxury and prodigality of the court
equalled its pomp and its servility. The parsimonious
reformation introduced by Julian may exaggerate in its
contemptuous expressions, the thousand cooks, the thousand barbers, and more than thousand cupbearers, with
the host of eunuchs and drones of every description who

---

[h] Clemens Alex. Pædagog. iii. 12.
It is curious to compare this passage
of Clement with the beautiful essay of

Seneca. See likewise Chrysostom almost *passim*. Some had 2000 or 3000,
t. vii. p. 633.

lived at the charge of the Emperor Constantius.[i] The
character of Theodosius gave an imposing dignity to his
resumption of that magnificence, of which Julian, not
without affectation, had displayed his disdain. The
Heathen writers, perhaps with the design of contrasting
Theodosius with the severer Julian, who are the representatives, or at least, each the pride of the opposing
parties, describe the Christian as immoderately in-
dulging in the pleasures of the table, and of The Em-
re-enlisting in the imperial service a countless peror.
multitude of cooks and other attendants on the splendour and indulgence of the court.[k]

That which in Theodosius was the relaxation or the
reward for military services, and the cares and agitations
of an active administration, degenerated with his feeble
sons into indolent and effeminate luxury. The head of
the empire became a secluded Asiatic despot. When,
on rare occasions, Arcadius condescended to reveal to
the public the majesty of the sovereign, he was preceded by a vast multitude of attendants, dukes, tribunes,
civil and military officers, their horses glittering with
golden ornaments, with shields of gold, set with precious
stones, and golden lances. They proclaimed the coming
of the Emperor, and commanded the ignoble crowd to
clear the streets before him.[m] The Emperor stood or
reclined on a gorgeous chariot surrounded by his immediate attendants distinguished by shields with golden
bosses set round with golden eyes, and drawn by white

---

[i] Libanius, Epitaph. Julian. p. 565.
[k] Zosimus, iv. 28.
[m] Montfaucon, in an essay in the
last volume of the works of Chrysostom, and in the twelfth vol. of the
Memoirs of the Academy of Inscriptions; and Müller, in his treatise de
Genio, Moribus, et Luxu Ævi Theodo-
siani, have collected the principal features of this picture, chiefly from
Chrysostom.

mules with gilded trappings; the chariot was set with precious stones, and golden fans vibrated with the movement, and cooled the air. The multitude contemplated at a distance the snow-white cushions, the silken carpets with dragons enwoven upon them in rich colours. Those who were fortunate enough to catch a glimpse of the Emperor beheld his ears loaded with golden rings, his arms with golden chains, his diadem set with gems of all hues, his purple robes, which with the diadem were reserved for the Emperor, in all their sutures embroidered with precious stones. The wondering people, on their return to their homes, could talk of nothing but the splendour of the spectacle, the robes, the mules, the carpets, the size and splendour of the jewels. On his return to the palace, the Emperor walked on gold; ships were employed with the express purpose of bringing gold dust[n] from remote provinces, which was strewn by the officious care of a host of attendants, so that the Emperor rarely set his foot on the bare pavement.

The official aristocracy, which had succeeded to the The aristo- hereditary patriciate of Rome, reflected in cracy. more moderate splendour, and less unapproachable seclusion, the manners of the court. The chief civil offices were filled by men of ignoble birth, often eunuchs. These, by the prodigal display of their ill-acquired wealth, insulted the people, who admired, envied, and hated their arrogant state. The military officers, in the splendour of their trappings and accoutrements, vied with the gorgeousness of the court-favourites; and even the barbarians, who began to force their way by their valour to these posts, in the capital caught the infection of luxury and pomp. As in all

---

[n] Χρύσιτιν. See Müller, p. 10.

despotisms, especially in the East, there was a rapid rise and fall of unworthy favourites, whose vices, exactions, and oppressions, were unsparingly laid open by hostile writers, directly they had lost the protecting favour of the court. Men then found out that the enormous wealth, the splendour, the voluptuousness, in which an Eutropius or a Rufinus had indulged, had been obtained by the sale of appointments, by vast bribes from provincial governors, by confiscations, and every abuse of inordinate power.[o]

Christianity had not the power to elevate despotism into a wise and beneficent rule, or to dignify its inseparable consequence, court favouritism. Yet after all, feeble and contemptible as are many of the Christian Emperors, pusillanimous even in their vices; odious as was the tyranny of their ministers; they may bear no unfavourable comparison with the Heathen Emperors of Rome. Human nature is not so outraged; our belief in the possible depravity of man is not so severely tried, as by the monstrous vices and cruelties of a Tiberius, a Caligula, or a Nero. Theodora, even, if we credit the malignant satire of Procopius, maintained some decency upon the throne. The superstitions of the Emperors debased Christianity; the Christian bishop was degraded by being obliged at times to owe his promotion to an eunuch or a favourite; yet even the most servile and intriguing of the hierarchy could not be entirely for-

---

o " Hic Asiam villâ pactus regit; ille redemit
Conjugis ornatu Syriam; dolet ille paternâ
Bithynos mutâsse domo. Suffixa patenti
Vestibulo pretiis distinguit regula gentes."—*Claud. in Eutrop.* i. 199.

" . . . . . clientes
Fallit, et ambitos à principe vendit honores.
   *   *   *   *
Congestæ cumulantur opes, orbisque rapinas
Accipit una domus. Populi servire coacti
Plenaque privato succumbunt oppida regno."—*In Rufin.* i. 179-193.

getful of their high mission; there was still a kind of moral repugnance, inseparable from the character they bore, which kept them above the general debasement.

The aristocratical life, at this period, seems to have been characterised by gorgeous magnificence without grandeur, inordinate luxury without refinement, the pomp and prodigality of a high state of civilisation with none of its ennobling or humanising effects. The walls of the palaces were lined with marbles of all colours, crowded with statues of inferior workmanship, mosaics, of which the merit consisted in the arrangement of the stones; the cost, rather than the beauty or elegance, was the test of excellence, and the object of admiration. The nobles were surrounded with hosts of parasites or servants. " You reckon up," Chrysostom thus addresses a patrician, " so many acres of land, ten or twenty palaces, as many baths, a thousand or two thousand slaves, chariots plated with silver or overlaid with gold." [p]

Their banquets were merely sumptuous, without social grace or elegance. The dress of the females, the fondness for false hair, sometimes wrought up to an enormous height, and especially affecting the golden dye, and for paint, from which irresistible propensities they were not to be estranged even by religion, excite the stern animadversion of the ascetic Christian teacher. " What business have rouge and paint on a Christian cheek ? Who can weep for her sins when her tears wash her face bare and mark furrows on her skin ? With what trust can faces be lifted up towards heaven, which the Maker cannot recognise as his own workman-

Manners of the aristocracy.

Females.

---

[p] T. vii. p. 533.

ship ?" [q] Their necks, heads, arms, and fingers, were
loaded with golden chains and rings; their persons
breathed precious odours, their dresses were of gold
stuff and silk; and in this attire they ventured to enter
the church. Some of the wealthier Christian matrons
gave a religious air to their vanity; while the more profane wore their thin silken dresses embroidered with
hunting-pieces, wild beasts, or any other fanciful device,
the more pious had the miracles of Christ, the marriage
in Cana of Galilee, or the paralytic carrying his bed.
In vain the preachers urged that it would be better to
emulate these acts of charity and love, than to wear
them on their garments. [r]

It might indeed be supposed that Christianity, by the
extinction of that feeling for the beauty, grandeur, and
harmony of outward form, which was a part of the religion of Greece, and was enforced by her purer and
loftier philosophy, may have contributed to this total
depravation of the taste. Those who had lost the finer
feeling for the pure and noble in art and in social life,
would throw themselves into the gorgeous, the sumptuous, and the extravagant. But it was rather the
Roman character than the influence of Christianity
which was thus fatal to the refinements of life. The
degeneracy of taste was almost complete before the
predominance of the new religion. The manners of
ancient Rome had descended from the earlier empire, [s]

---

[q] Hieronym. Epist. 54. Compare
Epist. 19, vol. i. p. 284.

[r] Müller, p. 112. There are several
statutes prohibiting the use of gold
brocade or dresses of silk in the Theodosian Code. x. tit. 20. Other statutes regulate the dress in Rome, xiv.

10, 1.

[s] Compare the description of the
manners and habits of the Roman
nobles in Ammianus Marcellinus, so
well transferred into English in the
31st chapter of Gibbon, vol. v. p. 258-
268.

and the manners of Constantinople were in most respects
an elaborate imitation of those of Rome.

The provincial cities, according to the national character, imitated the old and new Rome ; and in all, no
doubt, the nobility, or the higher order, were of the
same character and habits.

On the appointment to the provincial governments,
and the high civil offices of the empire, Christianity at
this time exercised by no means a commanding, certainly no exclusive, influence. Either superior merit,
or court intrigue, or favour, bestowed civil offices with
impartial hand on Christian and Pagan. The Rufinus
or the Eutropius cared little whether the bribe was
offered by a worshipper in the church or in the temple.
The Heathen Themistius was appointed prefect of Constantinople by the intolerant Theodosius; Prætextatus
and Symmachus held the highest civil functions in
Rome. The prefect who was so obstinate an enemy to
Chrysostom was Optatus, a Pagan. At a later period,
as I have observed, a statue was raised to the Heathen
poet Merobaudes.

But, besides the officers of the imperial government,
of the provinces and the municipalities, there now
appeared a new order of functionaries, with recognised,
if undefined powers, the religious magistrates of the
religious community. In this magisterial character, the
new hierarchy differed from the ancient priesthoods, at
least of Greece and Rome. In Greece, these were
merely the officiating dignitaries in the religious ceremonial; in Rome, the pontifical was attached to, and in
effect merged in, the important civil function. But
Christianity had its own distinct and separate aristocracy, which not merely officiated in the church, but
ruled the public mind, and mingled itself with the

various affairs of life, far beyond this narrow sphere of
religious ministration.

The Christian hierarchy was completely organised
and established in the minds of men before the great
revolutions which, under Constantine, legalised Christianity, and, under Theodosius and his successors, identified the Church and State. The strength of the
sacerdotal power was consolidated before it came into
inevitable collision, or had to dispute its indefinable
limits with the civil authority. Mankind was now submitted to a double dominion, the civil supremacy of the
Emperor and his subordinate magistrates, and that of
the Bishop with his inferior priesthood.

Up to the establishment of Christianity as the religion of the State, the clerical order had been Gradual
the sole magistracy of the new communities. ment of the
But it is not alone from the scantiness of power. hierarchical
authentic documents concerning the earliest Christian
history, but from the inevitable nature of things, that
the developement of the hierarchical power, as has
already been partially shown,[t] was gradual and untraceable. In the infant Christian community, we have seen
that the chief teacher and the ruler, almost immediately.
if not immediately, became the same person. It was
not so much that he was formally invested in authority,
as that his advice, his guidance, his control, were sought
on all occasions with timid diffidence, and obeyed with
unhesitating submission. In the Christian, if it may be
so said, the civil was merged in the religious being; he
abandoned willingly his rights as a citizen, almost as a
man, his independence of thought and action, in order
to be taught conformity to the new doctrines which he

---

[t] Book ii. ch. 4.

had embraced, and the new rule of life to which he had submitted himself. Community of sentiment, rather than any strict federal compact, was the primary bond of the Christian republic ; and this general sentiment, even prior, perhaps, to any formal nomination or ordination, designated the heads and the subordinate rulers, the Bishops, the Presbyters, and the Deacons; and therefore, where all agreed, there was no question in whom resided the right of conferring the title.[u]

The simple ceremonial of "laying on of hands," which dedicated the individual for his especial function, ratified and gave its religious character to this popular election which took place by a kind of silent acclamation; and without this sacred commission by the bishop, no one, from the earliest times of which we have any record, presumed, it should seem, to invest himself in the sacred office.[x] The civil and religious power of the hierarchy grew up side by side, or intertwined with each other, by the same spontaneous vital energy. Every thing in the primary formation of the communities tended to increase the power of their ecclesiastical superiors. The investiture of the blended teacher and ruler in a sacred, and at

---

[u] The growth of the Christian hierarchy, and the general constitution of the Church, are developed with learning, candour, and moderation, by Planck, in his Geschichte der Christlich-Kirchlichen Verfassung. Hanover, 1803.

[x] Gradually the admission to orders became a subject not merely of ecclesiastical, but of civil regulation. It has been observed that the decurion was prohibited from taking orders in order to obtain exemption from the duties of his station. Cod. Theod. xii.

1, 49. No slave, curialis, officer of the court, public debtor, procurator, or collector of the purple dye (murilegulus), or one involved in business, might be ordained, or, if ordained, might be reclaimed to his former state. Cod. Theod. ix. 45, 3. This was a law of the close of the fourth century, A.D. 398. The Council of Illiberis had made a restriction that no freedman, whose patron was a Gentile, could be ordained; he was still too much under control. Can. lxxx.

length in a sacerdotal character, the rigid separation of this sacred order from the mass of the believers, could not but arise out of the unavoidable developement of the religion. It was not their pride or ambition that withdrew them, but the reverence of the people which enshrined them in a separate sphere: they did not usurp or even assume their power and authority; it was heaped upon them by the undoubting and prodigal confidence of the community. The hopes and fears of men would have forced this honour upon them, had they been humbly reluctant to accept it. Man, in his state of religious excitement, imperiously required some authorised interpreters of those mysterious revelations from heaven which he could read himself but imperfectly and obscurely; he felt the pressing necessity of a spiritual guide. The privileges and distinctions of the clergy, so far from being aggressions on his religious independence, were solemn responsibilities undertaken for the general benefit. The Christian commonalty, according to the general sentiment, could not have existed without them, nor could such necessary but grave functions be entrusted to casual or common hands. No individual felt himself safe, except under their superintendence. Their sole right of entering the sanctuary arose as much out of the awe of the people as out of their own self-invested holiness of character. The trembling veneration for the mysteries of the sacrament must by no means be considered as an artifice to exalt themselves as the sole guardians and depositaries of these blessings; it was the genuine expression of their own profoundest feelings. If the clergy had not assumed the keys of heaven and hell; if they had not appeared legitimately to possess the power of pronouncing the eternal destiny of man, of suspending or

excommunicating from those Christian privileges which
were inseparably connected in Christian belief with the
eternal sentence, or of absolving and readmitting into the
pale of the Church and of salvation,—among the mass of
believers, the uncertainty, the terror, the agony of minds
fully impressed with the conviction of their immortality,
and yearning by every means to obtain the assurance
of pardon and peace, with heaven and hell constantly
before their eyes, and agitating their inmost being,
would have been almost insupportable. However the
clergy might exaggerate their powers, they could not extend them beyond the ready acquiescence of the people
They could not possess the power of absolving without
that of condemning; and men were content to brave the
terrors of the gloomier award, for the indescribable
consolations of confidence in their brighter and more
ennobling promises.

The change in the relative position of Christianity to
the rest of the world tended to the advancement of the
hierarchy. At first there was no necessity to guard
the admission into the society with rigid or suspicious
jealousy, since the profession of Christianity in the face
of a hostile world was in itself almost a sufficient test of
sincerity. Expulsion from the society, or a temporary
exclusion from its privileges, which afterwards grew into
the awful forms of interdict or excommunication, must
have been extremely rare or unnecessary,[y] since he who

---

[y] The case in St. Paul's Epistle to
the Corinthians (1 Cor. v. 5), which
seems to have been the first of forcible
expulsion, was obviously an act of
Apostolic authority. This, it is probable, was a Jewish convert, and
these persons stood in a peculiar position; they would be ashamed, or
would not be permitted, to return into
the bosom of the Jewish community,
which they had abandoned, and, if
expelled from the Christian Church,
would be complete outcasts. Not so
the Heathen apostate, who might one
day leave, and the next return to his
old religion with all its advantages.

could not endure the discipline, or who doubted again
the doctrines of Christianity, had nothing to do but to
abandon a despised sect and revert to the freedom of
the world. The older and more numerous the community, severer regulations were requisite for the admission of members, the maintenance of order, of unity
in doctrine, and propriety of conduct, as well as for the
ejection of unworthy disciples. Men began to Expulsion or
be Christians, not from personal conviction, cation.
excommuni-
but from hereditary descent, as children of Christian
parents. The Church was filled with doubtful converts,
some from the love of novelty, others, when they incurred less danger and obloquy, from less sincere faith;
some, no doubt, of the base and profligate, from the
desire of partaking in the well-known charity of the
Christians to their poorer brethren. Many became
Christians, having just strength of mind enough to embrace its tenets, but not to act up to its duties. A
more severe investigation, therefore, became necessary
for admission into the society, a more summary authority for the expulsion of improper membe rs.[z] These
powers naturally devolved on the heads of the community, who had either originally possessed, and trans

---

[z] It is curious to find that both
ecclesiastical and civil laws against
apostasy were constantly necessary.
The Council of Elvira readmits an
apostate to communion, who has not
worshipped idols, after ten years'
penance. The laws of Gratian and
Theodosius, and even of Arcadius and
Valentinian III., speak a more menacing
language: the Christian who has become a Pagan forfeits the right of
bequeathing by will—his will is null
and void. Cod. Theod. xvi. 7. 1, 22.
A law of Valentinian II. inflicts the
same penalty (only with some limitation) on apostates to Judaism or
Manicheism. The laws of Arcadius
and Valentinian III. prove, by the
severity of their prohibitions, not only
that cases of apostasy took place, but
that sacrifices were still frequently
offered. Cod. Theodos. xvi. tit. de
Apostatis.

mitted by regularly appointed descent, or held by
general consent, the exclusive administration of the
religious rites, the sacraments, which were the federal
bonds of the community. Their strictly civil functions
became likewise more extensive and important. All
Increase in   legal disputes had, from the first, been sub-
their civil
influence.   mitted to the religious magistracy, not as
interpreters of the laws of the empire, but as best
acquainted with the higher principles of natural justice
and Christian equity. The religious heads of the communities were the supreme and universally recognised
arbiters in all the transactions of life. When the
magistrate became likewise a Christian, and the two
communities were blended into one, considerable difficulty could not but arise, as we shall hereafter see, in
the limits of their respective jurisdictions.

But the magisterial or ruling part of the ecclesiastical
function became thus more and more relatively important; government gradually became an affair of asserted
superiority on one hand, of exacted submission on the
other; but still the general voice would long be in
favour of the constituted authorities. The episcopal
power would be a mild, a constitutional, an unoppres-
sive, and therefore unquestioned and unlimited sovereignty; for, in truth, in the earlier period, what was
the bishop, and in a subordinate degree, the presbyter,
or even the deacon?—He was the religious superior,
elected by general acclamation, or at least, by general
consent, as commanding that station by his unrivalled
religious qualifications; he was solemnly invested in his
office by a religious ceremony; he was the supreme
arbiter in such civil matters as occurred among the
members of the body, and thus the conservator of
peace; he was the censor of morals, the minister in holy

rites, the instructor in the doctrines of the faith, the adviser in all scruples, the consoler in all sorrows; he was the champion of the truth; in the hour of The bishop trial the first victim of persecution, the de- community. signated martyr. Of a being so sanctified, so ennobled to the thought, what jealous suspicion would arise, what power would be withholden from one whose commission would seem ratified by the Holy Spirit of God? Power might generate ambition, distinction might be attended by pride, but the transition would not be perceived by the dazzled sight of respect, of reverence, of veneration, and of love.

Above all, diversities of religious opinion would tend to increase the influence and the power of Dissensions those who held the religious supremacy. It in the Church has been said, not without some authority, that crease of the establishment of episcopacy in the Apo- power. stolic times arose for the control of the differences with the Judaising converts.[a] The multitude of believers would take refuge under authority from the doubts and perplexities thus cast among them; they would be grateful to men who would think for them, and in whom their confidence might seem to be justified by their station; a formulary of faith for such persons would be the most acceptable boon to the Christian society. This would be more particularly the case when, as in the Asiatic communities, these were not merely slight and unimportant, but vital points of difference. The Gnosticism, which the bishops of Asia Minor and of Syria had to combat, was not a Christian sect or heresy, but

[a] No doubt this kind of constant and of natural appeal to the supreme religious functionary must have materially tended to strengthen and confirm this power. See vol. ii. page 28, and note.

another religion, although speaking in some degree Christian language. The justifiable alarm of these dangerous encroachments would induce the teachers and governors to assume a loftier and more dictatorial tone; those untainted by the new opinions would vindicate and applaud their acknowledged champions and defenders. Hence we account for the strong language in the Epistles of Ignatius, which appears to claim the extraordinary rank of actual representatives, not merely of the Apostles, but of Christ himself, for the bishops, precisely in this character, as maintainers of the true Christian doctrine.[b] In the pseudo-Apostolic Constitu-

---

[b] My own impression is decidedly in favour of the genuineness of these Epistles,—the shorter ones I mean—which are vindicated by Pearson; nor do I suspect that these passages, which are too frequent, and too much in the style and spirit of the whole, are later interpolations. Certainly the fact of the existence of two different copies of these Epistles throws doubt on the genuineness of both; but I receive them partly from an historical argument, which I have suggested, vol. ii. p. 151, partly from internal evidence. Some of their expressions, e. g., "Be ye subject to the bishop as to Jesus Christ" (ad Trall. c. 2); "Follow your bishop as Jesus Christ the Father, the presbytery as the Apostles: reverence the deacons as the ordinance of God" (ad Smyrn. c. 8); taken as detached sentences, and without regard to the figurative style and ardent manner of the writer, would seem so extraordinary a transition from the tone of the Apostles, as to throw still further doubts on the authenticity at least of these sentences. But it may be observed that in these strong expressions the object of the writer does not seem to be to raise the sacerdotal power, but rather to enforce Christian unity, with direct reference to these fatal differences of doctrine. In another passage he says, "Be ye subject to the bishop and to each other (τῷ ἐπισκόπῳ καὶ ἀλλήλοις), as Jesus Christ to the Father, and the Apostles to Christ, to the Father and to the Spirit."

I cannot indeed understand the inference that all the language or tenets of Christians who may have heard the Apostles are to be considered of Apostolic authority. Ignatius was a vehement and strongly figurative writer, very different in his tone, according to my judgement, to the Apostolic writings. His eager desire for martyrdom, his deprecating the interference of the Roman Christians in his behalf, is remarkably at variance with the sober dignity with which the Apostles did not seek, but submitted to death.

tions, which belong probably to the latter end of the
third century, this more than Apostolic authority is
sternly and unhesitatingly asserted.[c] Thus, the separation between the clergy and laity continually widened;
the teacher or ruler of the community became the
dictator of doctrine, the successor, not of the bishop
appointed by Apostolic authority,[d] or according to
Apostolic usage, but of the Apostle; and at length took
on himself a sacerdotal name and dignity. A strong
corporate spirit, which arises out of associations formed
for the noblest as well as for the most unworthy objects,
could not but actuate the hierarchical college which
was formed in each diocese or each city by the bishop
and more or less numerous presbyters and deacons.
The control on the autocracy of the bishop, which was
exercised by this senate of presbyters, without whom he

That which may have been high-
wrought metaphor in Ignatius, is repeated by the author of the Apostolic
Constitutions, without reserve or limitation. This, I think, may be fairly
taken as indicative of the language
prevalent at the end of the third or
beginning of the fourth century,—ὑμῖν
ὁ ἐπίσκοπος εἰς Θεὸν τετιμήσθω.
The bishop is to be honoured as God,
ii. 30. The language of Psalm lxxxi.
"Ye are Gods," is applied to them :—
they are as much greater than the
king as the soul is superior to the
body—στέργειν ὀφείλετε ὡς πατέρα,
—φοβεῖσθαι ὡς βασιλέα.—1st Edit.
The question of the genuineness and
authority of the Ignatian Epistles has
been placed in an entirely new light,
or perhaps has been enwrapped in a
more indistinct haze, by the valuable
publication of the Syriac Ignatius by

Dr. Cureton. With this should be
read some of the answers, especially
Dr. Hussey's, and Baron Bunsen's Dissertation. My conclusion is, that I
should be unwilling to claim historical
authority for any passage not con
tained in Dr. Cureton's Syriac reprint.
There is enough in Dr. Cureton's copy
to justify the text, which I leave un-
altered, though some of the quotations
are probably not genuine. (1863.)

[c] Οὗτος ὑμῖν ἐπίγειος Θεὸς μετὰ
Θεοῦ. Lib. ii. c. 26.

[d] The full Apostolic authority was
claimed for the bishops, I think, first
distinctly, at a later period. See the
letter from Firmilianus in Cyprian's
works, Epist. lxxv. "Potestas pecca-
torum remittendorum Apostolis data
est * * et episcopis qui eis vicariâ
ordinatione successerunt."

rarely acted, tended to strengthen, rather than to inva-
lidate, the authority of the general body, in which all
particular and adverse interests were absorbed in that
of the clerical order.[e]

Language of the Old Testament, which was re-
Language of   ceived perhaps with greater readiness, from
the Old
Testament.   the contemptuous aversion in which it was
held by the Gnostics, on this as on other subjects,
gradually found its way into the Church.[f] But the
Clergy and   strong and marked line between the minis-
laity.   terial or magisterial order (the clergy) and
the inferior Christians, the people (the laity), had been
drawn, before the bishop became a pontiff (for the
Heathen names were likewise used), the presbyters the
sacerdotal order, and the deacons, a class of men who
shared in the indelible sanctity of the new priesthood.
The common priesthood of all Christians, as distin-
guishing them by their innocent and dedicated character from the profane Heathen, asserted in the Epistle
of St. Peter, was the only notion of the sacerdotal character at first admitted into the popular sentiment.[g]
The appellation of the sacerdotal order began to be
metaphorically applied to the Christian clergy,[h] but

---

[e] Even Cyprian enforces his own
authority by that of his concurrent
College of Presbyters:—"Quando à
primordio episcopatûs mei statuerem,
nihil sine consilio vestro, et cum con-
sensu plebis, meâ privatim sententiâ
gerere." Epist. v. In other passages
he says, " Cui rei non potui me solum
judicem dare." He had acted, therefore, " cum collegis meis, et cum plebe
ipsâ universâ." Epist. xxviii.

[f] It is universally adopted in the
Apostolic Constitutions. The crime

of Korah is significantly adduced ;
tithes are mentioned, I believe, for the
first time, ii. 25. Compare vi. 2.

[g] See the well-known passage of Tertullian :—"Nonne et laici sacerdotes
sumus? * * Differentiam inter ordi-
nem et plebem constituit ecclesiæ auc-
toritas." Tertullian evidently Mon-
tanises in this treatise, de · Exhort.
Castit. c. 7, yet seems to deliver these
as maxims generally acknowledged.

[h] We find the first appearance of
this in the figurative Ignatius. Ter-

soon became real titles ; and by the close of the third century, they were invested in the names and claimed the rights of the Levitical priesthood in the Jewish theocracy.[i] The Epistle of Cyprian to Cornelius, Bishop of Rome, shows the height to which the episcopal power had aspired before the religion of Christ had become that of the Roman empire. The passages of the Old Testament, and even of the New, in which honour or deference are paid to the Hebrew pontificate, are recited in profuse detail; implicit obedience is demanded for the priest of God, who is the sole infallible judge or delegate of Christ.[k]

Even if it had been possible that, in their state of high-wrought attachment and reverence for the teachers and guardians of their religion, any mistrust could have arisen in the more sagacious and far-sighted minds of the vast system of sacerdotal domination, of which they were thus laying the deep foundations in the Roman world, there was no recollection or tradition of any priestly tyranny from which they could take warning or imbibe caution. These sacerdotal castes were obsolete or Oriental ; the only one within their sphere of knowledge was that of the Magians in the hostile kingdom

---

tullian uses the term " summi Sacerdotes."

[i] The passage in the Epistle of Clemens (ad Roman. c. 40), in which the analogy of the ministerial offices of the Church with the priestly functions of the Jewish temple is distinctly developed, is rejected as an interpolation by all judicious and impartial scholars.

[k] See his 68th Epistle, in which he draws the analogy between the legitimate bishop and the sacerdos of the law, the irregularly elected and Korah, Dathan, and Abiram :—" Neque enim aliunde hæreses obortæ sunt, aut nata sunt schismata, quam inde quod *sacerdoti Dei non obtemperatur*, nec unus in ecclesia ad tempus sacerdos, et ad tempus *Judex*, *vice Christi* cogitatur : cui si secundum magisteria divina obtemperaret fraternitas universa, nemo adversum sacerdotum collegium quicquam moveret." Ad Cornel., Epist. lv.

of Persia. In Greece, the priesthood had sunk into the neglected ministers of the deserted temples; their highest dignity was to preside over the amusements of the people. The Emperor had now at length disdainfully cast off the supreme pontificate of the Heathen world, which had long been a title, and nothing more. Even among the Jews, the rabbinical hierarchy, which had gained considerable strength, even during our Saviour's time, but after the fall of the temple, and the publication of the Talmuds, had assumed a complete despotism over the Jewish mind, was not a priesthood. The Rabbins came promiscuously from all the tribes; their claims rested on learning and on knowledge of the traditions of the Fathers, not on Levitical descent.

Nor indeed could any danger be apparent, so long as the free voice of the community, guided by fervent piety and rarely perverted by less worthy motives, summoned the wisest and the holiest to these important functions. The nomination to the sacred office experienced the same, more gradual, perhaps, but not less inevitable, change from the popular to the self-electing form. The acclamation of the united, and seldom, if ever, discordant voices of the presbyters and the people, might be trusted with the appointment to the headship of a poor and devout community, whose utmost desire was to worship God, and to fulfil their Christian duties in uninterrupted obscurity. But as the episcopate became an object of ambition or interest, the disturbing forces which operate on the justice and wisdom of popular elections could not but be called forth; and slowly the clergy, by example, by influence, by recommendation, by dictation, by usurpation, identified their acknowledged right of consecration for a particular office with that of appointment to it. This

Change in the mode of election.

was one of their last triumphs. In the days of Cyprian, and towards the close of the third century, the people had the right of electing, or at least of rejecting, candidates for the priesthood.[1] In the latter half of the fourth century, the streets of Rome ran with blood in the contest of Damasus and Ursicinus, for the bishopric of Rome ; both factions arrayed against each other the priests and the people who were their respective partisans.[m] Thus the clergy had become a distinct and recognised class in society, consecrated by a solemn ceremony, the imposition of hands, which, however, does not yet seem to have been indelible.[n] But each church was still a separate and independent community ; the bishop as its sovereign, the presbyters, and sometimes the deacons, as a kind of religious senate, conducted all its internal concerns. Great deference was paid from the first to the bishops of the more important sees : the number and wealth of the congregations would give them weight and dignity ; and in general those prelates would be men of the highest character and attainments. Yet promotion to a wealthier or more distinguished see was looked upon as betraying worldly

---

[1] " Plebs ipsa maximè habeat potestatem vel eligendi dignos sacerdotes, vel indignos recusandi." Epist. lxvii. Cornelius was " testimonio cleri, ac suffragio populi electus." Compare Apostol. Constit. viii. 4. The Council of Laodicea (at the beginning of the fourth century) ordains that bishops are to be appointed by the metropolitans, and that the multitude, of ὄχλοι, are not to designate persons for the priesthood.

[m] Ammianus Marcell. xxvii. 3. Hierom. in Chron. Compare Gibbon,

vol. iv. 259.

[n] A canon of the Council of Chalcedon (can. 7), prohibits the return of a spiritual person to the laity, and his assumption of lay offices in the state. See also Conc. Turon. i. c. 5. The laws of Justinian confiscate to the Church the property of any priest who has forsaken his orders. Cod. Just. i. tit. iii. 53 ; Nov. v. 4. 125 c. 15. This seems to imply that the practice was not uncommon even at that late period. Compare Planck, vol. i. 399.

ambition. The enemies of Eusebius, the Arian, or semi-
Arian, bishop of Constantinople, bitterly taunted him
with his elevation from the less important see of Nicomedia to the episcopate of the Eastern metropolis. This
translation was prohibited by some councils.[o]

The level of ecclesiastical or episcopal dignity gra-
Metropolitan dually broke up; some bishops emerged into
bishops. a higher rank; the single community over
which the bishop originally presided grew into the
aggregation of several communities, and formed a
diocese; the metropolitan rose above the ordinary
bishop, the patriarch assumed a rank above the metropolitan, till at length, in the regularly graduated scale,
the primacy of Rome was asserted, and submitted to
by the humble and obsequious West.

The diocese grew up in two ways,—1. In the larger
Formation of cities, the rapid increase of the Christians led
the diocese. necessarily to the formation of separate congregations, which, to a certain extent, required each its
proper organization, yet invariably remained subordinate
to the single bishop. In Rome, towards the beginning
of the fourth century, there were above forty churches,
rendering allegiance to the prelate of the metropolis.

2. Christianity was first established in the towns and
Chorepiscopi. cities, and from each centre diffused itself with
more or less success into the adjacent country.
In some of these country congregations, bishops appear
to have been established, yet these chorepiscopi, or
rural bishops, maintained some subordination to the
head of the mother church;[p] or where the converts

---

[o] Synod. Nic. can. 15 ; Conc. Sard.
c. 2; Conc. Arel. 21.
[p] See in Bingham, Ant. b. ii. c. 14,

the controversy about the chorepiscopi
or rural bishops.

were fewer, the rural Christians remained members of the mother church in the city.[q] In Africa, from the immense number of bishops, each community seems to have had its own superior ; but this was peculiar to the province. In general, the churches adjacent to the towns or cities, either originally were, or became, the diocese of the city bishop ; for as soon as Christianity became the religion of the state, the powers of the rural bishops were restricted, and the office at length was either abolished or fell into disuse.[r]

The rank of the metropolitan bishop, who presided over a certain number of inferior bishops, and the convocation of ecclesiastical or episcopal synods, grew up apparently at the same time and from the same causes. The earliest authentic synods seem to have arisen out of the disputes about the time of observing Easter ;[s] but before the middle of the third century, these occasional and extraordinary meetings of the clergy in certain districts took the form of provincial synods. These began in the Grecian provinces,[t] but extended throughout the Christian world. In some cases they seem to have been assemblies of bishops alone, in others of the whole clergy. They met once or twice in the year ; they were summoned by the metropolitan bishop, who presided in the meeting, and derived from, or confirmed his metropolitan dignity by this presidency.[u]

---

q Justin Martyr speaks of the country converts : παντῶν κατὰ πόλεις ἢ ἄγρους μενόντων, ἐπὶ τὸ αὐτὸ συνέλευσις γίνεται. Apolog. i. 67.

r Concil. Antioch. can. 10 ; Concil. Ancyr. c. 13 ; Conc. Laod. c. 57.

s See the list of earlier synods chiefly on this subject, Labbe, Concilia, vol. i. pp. 595, 650, edit. Paris, 1671.

t See the remarkable passage in Tertullian, de Jejunio, with the ingenious commentary of Mosheim, De Reb. Christ. ante Const. M. pp. 264, 268.

u " Necessario apud nos fit, ut per singulos annos seniores et præpositi in

As the metropolitans rose above the bishops, so the
Archbishops
and patri-
archs. archbishops or patriarchs rose above the
metropolitans. These ecclesiastical dignities
seem to have been formed according to the civil divisions of the empire.[x] The Patriarchs of Antioch, Jerusalem, Alexandria, Rome, and by a formal decree of
the Council of Chalcedon, Constantinople, assumed
even a higher dignity. They asserted the right, in
some cases, of appointing, in others of deposing, even
metropolitan bishops.[y]

While Antioch, Alexandria, and Constantinople contested the supremacy of the East, the two former as
more ancient and Apostolic churches, the latter as the
imperial city, Rome stood alone, as in every respect
the most eminent church in the West. While other
churches might boast their foundation by a single
apostle (and those churches were always held in peculiar respect), Rome asserted that she had been founded
by, and preserved the ashes of two, and those the most
distinguished of the Apostolic body. Before the end
of the third century, the lineal descent of her bishops
from St. Peter was unhesitatingly claimed, and obse-
quiously admitted by the Christian world.[z] The name

---

unum conveniamus, ad disponenda ea,
quæ curæ nostræ commissa sunt."
Firm. ad Cyprian. Ep. 75.

[x] Bingham names thirteen or fourteen patriarchs : Alexandria, Antioch,
Cæsarea, Jerusalem, Ephesus, Constantinople, Thessalonica, Sirmium,
Rome, Carthage, Milan, Lyons, Toledo, York. But their respective
claims do not appear to have been
equally recognised, or at the same
period.

[y] Chrysostom deposed Gerontius,
metropolitan of Nicomedia. Sozomen, viii. 6.

[z] The passage of Irenæus (lib. ii.
c. 3), as is well known, is the first
distinct assertion of any primacy in
Peter, and derived from him to the
see of Rome. This passage would be
better authority if it existed in the
original language, not in an indifferent
translation ; if it were the language of
an Eastern, not a Western, prelate,

of Rome was still imposing and majestic, particularly
in the West; the wealth of the Roman bishop
probably surpassed that of other prelates; for
Rome was still the place of general concourse and
resort; and the pious strangers who visited the capital
would not withhold their oblations to the metropolitan
church. Within the city, he presided over above forty
churches, besides the suburbicarian districts. The
whole clerical establishment at Rome amounted to
forty-six presbyters, seven deacons, seven sub-deacons,
forty-two acolyths, fifty-two exorcists, readers, and
doorkeepers. It comprehended fifteen hundred widows
and poor brethren, with a countless multitude of the
higher orders and of the people. No wonder that the
name, the importance, the wealth, the accredited Apostolic foundation of Rome, arrayed her in pre-eminent
dignity. Still, in his correspondence with the Bishop
of Rome, the general tone of Cyprian, the great advocate
of Christian unity is that of an equal; though he shows
great respect to the Church of Rome, it is to the
faithful guardian of an uninterrupted tradition, not as
invested with superior authority.[a]

who might acknowledge a supremacy
in Rome, which would not have been
admitted by the older Asiatic sees;
still more, if it did not assert what is
manifestly untrue, the *foundation* of
the Church of Rome by St. Peter and
St. Paul (see vol. ii. p. 44); and,
finally, if Irenæus could be conclusive
authority on such a subject. Planck
justly observes, that the potior princi-
palitas of the city of Rome was the
primary reason why a potior princi-
palitas was recognised in the see of
Rome.

[a] While I deliver my own conclusions, without fear or compromise, I
would avoid all controversy on this as
well as on other subjects. It is but
right, therefore, for me to give the
two apparently conflicting passages in
Cyprian on the primacy of St. Peter:—
" Nam nec Petrus quem primùm Dominus elegit, et super quem ædificavit
Ecclesiam suam * * vindicavit sibi
aliquid insolenter aut arroganter as-
sumpsit, ut diceret se primatum te-
nere, et obtemperari à novellis et pos-
teris sibi potius oportere." Epist.

As the hierarchical pyramid tended to a point, its base spread out into greater width. The greater pomp of the services, the more intricate administration of affairs, the greater variety of regulations required by the increasing and now strictly separated classes of votaries, imposed the necessity for new functionaries, besides the bishops, priests, and deacons. These were the archdeacon and the five subordinate officiating ministers, who received a kind of ordination. 1. The New sacred sub-deacon, who, in the Eastern church, col- offices. lected the alms of the laity and laid them upon the altar ; and, in the Western, acted as a messenger, or bearer of despatches. 2. The reader, who had the custody of the sacred books, and, as the name implies, read them during the service. 3. The acolyth, who was an attendant on the bishop, carried the lamp before him, or bore the Eucharist to the sick. 4. The exorcist, who read the solemn forms over those possessed by dæmons, the energoumenoi, and some-times at baptisms. 5. The ostiarius or doorkeeper, who assigned his proper place in the church to each member, and guarded against the intrusion of improper persons.

As Christianity assumed a more manifest civil existence, the closer correspondence, the more intimate sympathy between its remote and scattered members, became indispensable to its strength and consistency. Its uniformity of development in all parts of the world

lxxi. " Hoc erant utique cæteri Apo-stoli, quod fuit Petrus, pari consortio præditi et honoris et potestatis; sed exordium ab unitate proficiscitur, et primatus Petro datur, ut una Christi ecclesia, et cathedra una monstretur." De Unit. Eccles. But this last pas-sage is of more than doubtful authen-ticity; it is, no doubt, spurious. On the whole of this I have enlarged in the history of Latin Christianity.

arose out of, and tended to promote, this unity. It led
to that concentration of the governing power in a few,
which terminated at length in the West in the unre-
stricted power of one.

The internal unity of the Church, or universally
disseminated body of Christians, had been maintained
by the general similarity of doctrine, of sentiment, of
its first simple usages and institutions, and the common
dangers which it had endured in all parts of the world.
It possessed its consociating principles in the occasional correspondence between its remote members, in
those recommendatory letters with which the Christian
who travelled was furnished to his brethren Unity in the
in other parts of the empire; above all, in Church.
the common literature, which, including the sacred
writings, seems to have spread with more or less regularity through the various communities. Nothing,
however, tended so much, although they might appear
to exacerbate and perpetuate diversities of opinion, to
the maintenance of this unity, as the assemblage and
recognition of general Councils as the representatives
of universal Christendom.[b] The bold impersonation,

---

[b] The earliest councils (not Œcumenic) were those of Rome (1st and
2nd) and the seven held at Carthage,
concerning the lapsi, the schism of
Novatianus, and the re-baptizing of
heretics. The seventh in Routh, Reliquiæ Sacræ (Labbe, Concilia III.), is
the first of which we have anything
like a report ; and from this time,
either from the canons which they
issue, or the opinions delivered by the
bishops, the councils prove important
authorities, not merely for the decrees
of the Church, but for the dominant
tone of sentiment, and even of manners. Abhorrence of heresy is the
prevailing feeling in this council,
which decided the validity of heretical
baptism. "Christ," says one bishop,
"founded the Church, the Devil
heresy. How can the synagogue of
Satan administer the baptism of the
Church?" Another subjoins, "He
who yields or betrays the baptism of
the Church to heretics, what is he but
a Judas of the spouse of Christ?"
The Synod or Council of Antioch
(A.D. 269) condemned Paul of Samo-

the Church, seemed now to assume a more imposing
General Councils. visible existence. Its vital principle was no
longer that unseen and hidden harmony which
had united the Christians in all parts of the world with
their Saviour and with each other. By the assistance
of the orthodox Emperors, and the commanding
abilities of its great defenders, one dominant form of
doctrine had obtained the ascendancy; Gnosticism,
Donatism, Arianism, Manicheism, had been thrown
aside; and the Church stood, as it were, individualised,
or idealised, by the side of the other social impersonation, the State. The Emperor was the sole ruler of the
latter, and at this period the aristocracy of the superior
clergy, at a later the autocracy of the Pope, at least as

sata. The Council of Illiberis (Elvira, or Granada), A.D. 303, affords some curious notices of the state of Christianity in that remote province. Some of the Heathen flamines appear to have attempted to reconcile the performances of some of their religious duties, at least their presiding at the games, with Christianity. There are many moral regulations which do not give a high idea of Spanish virtue. The bishops and clergy were not to be itinerant traders ; they might trade within the province (can. xviii.), but were on no account to take upon usury. The Jews were settled in great numbers in Spain (compare Hist. of the Jews) : the taking food with them is interdicted, as also to permit them to reap the harvest. Gambling is forbidden. The Councils of Rome and of Arles were held to settle the Donatist controversy ; but of the latter there are twenty-two canons chiefly of ecclesiastical regula-

tions. The Council of Ancyra (A.D. 358) principally relates to the conduct of persons during the time of persecution. The Council of Laodicea (A.D. 368) has some curious general canons. The first Œcumenic council was that of Nicæa. See book iii. c. iv. It was followed by the long succession of Arian, and anti-Arian councils, at Tyre, Antioch, Rome, Milan, Sardica, Rimini, &c. The Arian Council of Antioch is very strict in its regulations for the residence of the bishops and the clergy, and their restriction of their labours to their own dioceses or cures (A.D. 341). Apud Labbe, vol. ii. 559. The first of Constantinople was the second Œcumenic council (A.D. 381). It re-established Trinitarianism as the doctrine of the East; it elevated the bishopric of Constantinople into a patriarchate, to rank after Rome. The two other Œcumenic councils are beyond the bounds of the present history.

the representative of the Western Church, became the supreme authority of the former. The hierarchical power, from exemplary, persuasive, amiable, was now authoritative, commanding, awful. When Christianity became the most powerful religion, when it became the religion of the many, of the Emperor, of the State, the convert, or the hereditary Christian had no strong Pagan party to receive him back into its bosom when outcast from the Church. If he ceased to believe, he no longer dared cease to obey. No course remained but prostrate submission, or the endurance of any penitential duty which might be enforced upon him; and on the penitential system, and the power of excommunication, to which we shall revert, rested the unshaken hierarchical authority over the human soul.

With the power of the clergy increased both those other sources of influence, pomp and wealth. Increase in Distinctions in station and in authority natu- pomp. rally lead to distinctions in manners, and those adventitious circumstances of dress and habits, which designate different ranks. Confederating upon equal terms, the superior authorities in the church began to assume an equal rank with those of the state. In the Christian city, the bishop became a personage of the highest importance; and the clergy, as a kind of subordinate religious magistracy, claimed, if a different kind, yet an equal share of reverence, with the civil authority. Where the civil magistrate had his insignia of office, the natural respect of the people, and the desire of maintaining his official dignity, would invest the religious functionary likewise with some peculiar symbol of his character. With their increased rank and estimation, the clergy could not but assume a more imposing demeanour; and that majesty in which they

were arrayed during the public ceremonial could not be
entirely thrown off when they returned to ordinary life.
The reverence of man exacts dignity from those who
are its objects. The primitive Apostolic meanness of
appearance and habit was altogether unsuited to their
altered position, as equal in rank, more than equal in
real influence and public veneration, to the civil officers
of the empire or municipality. The consciousness of
power will affect the best disciplined minds, and the
unavoidable knowledge that salutary authority is maintained over a large mass of mankind by imposing
manners, dress, and mode of living, would reconcile
many to that which otherwise might appear incongruous
to their sacred character. There was, in fact, and
always has been, among the more pious clergy, a perpetual conflict between a conscientious sense of the
importance of external dignity, and a desire, as conscientious, of retaining something of outward humility.
The monkish and ascetic waged implacable war against
that secular distinction which, if in some cases eagerly
assumed by pride and ambition, was forced upon others
by the deference, the admiration, the trembling sub-
servience of mankind. The prelate who looked the
most imperious, and spoke most sternly, on his throne,
fasted and underwent the most humiliating privations
in his chamber or his cell. Some prelates supposed,
that as ambassadors of the Most High, as supreme
governors in that which was of greater dignity than the
secular empire, the earthly kingdom of Christ, they
ought to array themselves in something of imposing
dignity. The bishops of Rome early affected state and
magnificence. Chrysostom, on the other hand, in Constantinople, differing from his predecessors, considered
poverty of dress, humility of demeanour, and the most

severe austerity of life, as more becoming a Christian
prelate, who was to set the example of the virtues which
he inculcated, and to show contempt for those worldly
distinctions which properly belonged to the civil power.
Others, among whom was Ambrose of Milan, while in
their own persons and in private they were the plainest,
simplest, and most austere of men, nevertheless threw
into the service of the Church all that was solemn and
magnificent; and as officiating functionaries, put on for
the time the majesty of manner, the state of attendance,
the splendour of attire, which seemed to be authorised
by the gorgeousness of dress and ceremonial pomp in
the Old Testament.[c]

With the greater reverence, indeed, peculiar sanctity
was exacted, and no doubt, in general, observed by the
clergy. They were imperatively required to surpass the
general body of Christians in purity of morals, and,
perhaps even more, in all religious performances. As

---

[c] The clergy were long without any
distinction of dress, except on ceremonial occasions. At the end of the
fourth century, it was the custom for
them in some churches to wear black.
Socr. H. E. vi. 22. Jerome, however,
recommends that they should neither
be distinguished by too bright nor too
sombre colours. Ad Nepot. The
proper habits were probably introduced at the end of the fifth century,
as they are recognised by councils in
the sixth. Conc. Matisc. A.D. 581,
can. l. 5; Trull. c. 27. The tonsure
began in the fourth century. " Prima
del iv. secolo i semplici preti non
avevano alcun abito distinto dagli altri
o Pagani o Cristiani, se non in quanto
la professata loro umiltà faceva una

certa pompa di abjezione e di povertà."
Cicognara, Storia di Scultura, t. i. p.
27. Count Cicognara gives a curious
account of the date and origin of the
different parts of the clerical dress.
The mitre is of the eighth century,
the tiara of the tenth.

The fourth Council of Carthage
(A.D. 398) has some restrictions on
dress. The clericus was not to wear
long hair or beard (nec comam habeat
nec barbam. Can. xliv.); he was to
approve his profession by his dress
and walk, and not to study the beauty
of his dress or sandals. He might
obtain his sustenance by working as
an artisan, or in agriculture, provided
he did not neglect his duty. Can.
li. lii.

the outward ceremonial, fasting, public prayer during
almost every part of the day, and the rest of the ritual
service, were more completely incorporated with Christianity, they were expected to maintain the public devotion by their example, and to encourage self-denial by
their more rigid austerity.

Wealth as well as pomp followed in the train of
Wealth of the power. The desire to command wealth (we
clergy.   must not yet use the ignoble term covetous-
ness) not merely stole imperceptibly into intimate connexion with religion, but appeared almost a part of
religion itself. The individual was content to be disinterested in his own person; the interest which he felt in
the opulence of the Church, or even of his own order,
appeared not merely excusable, but a sacred duty. In
the hands of the Christian clergy, wealth, which
seemed at that period to be lavished on the basest of
mankind, and squandered on the most criminal and
ignominious objects, might seem to be hallowed to the
noblest purposes. It enabled Christianity to vie with
Paganism in erecting splendid edifices for the worship
of God, to provide an imposing ceremonial, lamps for
midnight service, silver or golden vessels for the altar,
veils, hangings, and priestly dresses; it provided for the
Uses to   wants of the poor, whom misgovernment, war,
which it was
applied.   and taxation, independent of the ordinary
calamities of human life, were grinding to the earth.
To each church were attached numbers of widows and
other destitute persons; the redemption of slaves was
an object on which the riches of the Church were freely
lavished: the sick in the hospitals and prisons, and
destitute strangers were under their especial care. "How
many captives has the wealth of the Pagan establishment released from bondage?" This is among the

triumphant questions of the advocates of Christianity.[d]
The maintenance of children exposed by their parents,
and taken up and educated by the Christians, was
another source of generous expenditure. When, then,
at first the munificence of the Emperor, and afterwards
the gratitude and superstitious fears of the people,
heaped up their costly offerings at the feet of the clergy,
it would have appeared not merely ingratitude and folly,
but impiety and uncharitableness to their brethren, to
have rejected them. The clergy, as soon as they were
set apart from the ordinary business of life, were maintained by the voluntary offerings of their brethren.
The piety which embraced Christianity never failed in
liberality. The payments seem chiefly to have been
made in kind rather than in money; though on extraordinary occasions large sums were raised for some
sacred or charitable object. One of the earliest acts of
Constantine was to make munificent grants to the
despoiled and destitute Church.[e] A certain portion of
the public stores of corn and other produce, which was
received in kind by the officers of the revenue, was
assigned to the Church and clergy.[f] This was withdrawn by Julian, and when regranted by the Christian
Emperors, was diminished one-third.

The law of Constantine which empowered the clergy
of the Church to receive testamentary be- Law of Conquests, and to hold land, was a gift which stantine em-
powering the
would scarcely have been exceeded if he had Church to
receive be-
granted them two provinces of the empire.[g] quests.
It became almost a sin to die without some bequest to
pious uses; and before a century had elapsed, the mass

---

[d] Ambros. contra Symmachum. [f] Sozomen, H. E. v. 5.
[e] Euseb. H. E. x. 6. [g] This is the observation of Planck.

of property which had passed over to the Church was
so enormous, that the most pious of the Emperors were
obliged to issue a restrictive law, which the most ardent
of the Fathers were constrained to approve. Jerome
acknowledges, with the bitterness of shame, the necessity
Restrictive   of this check on ecclesiastical avarice.[h]   " I
edict of Va-
lentinian.   complain not of the law, but that we have
deserved such a law." The ascetic father and the
Pagan historian describe the pomp and avarice of the
Roman clergy in the fourth century. Ammianus, while
he describes the sanguinary feud which took place for
Pope Da-   the prelacy between Damasus and Ursicinus,
masus.   intimates that the magnificence of the prize
may account for the obstinacy and ferocity with which it
was contested. He dwells on the prodigal offerings of
the Roman matrons to their bishop; his pomp, when in
elaborate and elegant attire he was borne in his chariot
through the admiring streets; the costly luxury of his
almost imperial banquets. But the just historian contrasts this pride and luxury of the Roman pontiff with
the more temperate life and dignified humility of the
provincial bishops.[i] Jerome goes on sternly to charge
the whole Roman clergy with the old vice of the
Heathen aristocracy, hæredipety or legacy hunting, and
asserts that they used the holy and venerable name of

---

[h] Valentinian II. de Episc. "Solis
clericis et monachis hac lege prohibetur, et prohibetur non à persecutori-
bus sed à principibus Christianis; nec
de lege conqueror, sed doleo cur me-
ruerimus hanc legem." Hieronym. ad
Nepot. He speaks also of the "pro-
vida severaque legis cautio, *et tamen*
non sic refrænatur avaritia." Ambrose (l. ii. adv. Symm.) admits the
necessity of the law. Augustine,
while he loftily disclaims all participa-
tion in such abuses, acknowledges
their frequency. "Quicunque vult,
exhæredato filio hæredem facere ecclesiam, quærat alterum qui suscipiat,
non Augustinum, immo, Deo propitio,
inveniat neminem." Serm. 49.

[i] Amm. Marcellinus, xxvii. 3.

the Church to extort for their own personal emolument, the wealth of timid or expiring devotees. The law of Valentinian justly withheld from the clergy and the monks alone that privilege of receiving bequests which was permitted to the "lowest of mankind, Heathen priests, actors, charioteers and harlots."

Large parts of the ecclesiastical revenues, however, arose from more honourable sources. Some of the estates of the Heathen temples, though in general confiscated to the imperial treasury, were alienated to the Christian churches. The Church of Alexandria obtained the revenue of the Temple of Serapis.[k]

These various estates and properties belonged to the Church in its corporate capacity, not to the clergy. They were charged with the maintenance of Application of the wealth of the fabric of the church, and the various of the church. charitable purposes, including the sustenance of their own dependent poor. Strong enactments were made to prevent their alienation from those hallowed purposes,[m] the clergy were even restrained from bequeathing by will what they had obtained from the property of the Church. The estates of the Church were liable to the ordinary taxes, the land and capitation tax, but exempt from what were called sordid and extraordinary charges, and from the quartering of troops.[n]

---

[k] Sozomen, v. 7. The Church of Antioch possessed lands, houses, rents, carriages, mules, and other kinds of property. It undertook the daily sustenance of 3000 widows and virgins, besides prisoners, the sick in the hospitals, the maimed, and the diseased, who sat down, as it were before the Christian altar, and received food and raiment, besides many other accidental claims on their benevolence. Chrysostom, Oper. Montfaucon in his dissertation, gives the references.

[m] Conc. Carth. iii. 40; Antioch, 24. Constit. Apost. 40. Cod. Theodos. de Episc. et Clericis, t. 33.

[n] Planck, P. iii. c. vi. 3.

The bishops gradually obtained almost the exclusive management of this property. In some churches, a steward (œconomus) presided over this department, but he would, in general, be virtually under the control of the bishop. In most churches, the triple division began to be observed; one-third of the revenue to the bishop, one to the clergy, the other to the fabric and the poor; the Church of Rome added a fourth, a separate portion for the fabric.[o]

The clergy had become a separate community; they had their own laws of internal government, their own special regulations, or recognised proprieties of life and conduct. Their social delinquencies were not as yet withdrawn from the civil jurisdiction; but besides this, they were amenable to the severe judgments of ecclesiastical censure;[p] the lowest were liable to corporal chastisement. Flagellation, which was administered in the synagogue, and was so common in Roman society, was by no means so disgraceful as to exempt the persons at least of the inferior clergy from its infliction.[q]

---

[o] By a law of Theodosius and Valent. A.D. 434, the property of any bishop, presbyter, deacon, deaconess, sub-deacon, &c., or of any monk, who died intestate, and without legal heirs, fell, not to the treasury, as in ordinary cases, but to the church or monastery to which he belonged. The same privilege was granted to the Corporation of Decurions. Codex Theodos. v. iii. 1.

[p] Sozomen states that Constantine gave his clergy the privilege of rejecting the jurisdiction of the civil tribunal, and bringing their causes to the bishop. H. E. i. 9. But these were probably disputes between clergy-man and clergyman. All others were cases of arbitration, by mutual agreement; but the civil power was to ratify their decree. In a Novella of Valentinian II., A.D. 452, it is expressly said,—"Quoniam constat episcopos et presbyteros forum legibus non habere * * nec de aliis causis præter religionem posse cognoscere." Compare Planck, p. 300. The clericus was bound to appear, if summoned by a layman, before the ordinary judge. Justinian made the change, and that only in a limited manner.

[q] Bishops were accustomed to order flagellations. "Qui modus coercitionis, a magistris artium liberalium, et ab

But the more serious punishment was degradation into the vulgar class of worshippers. To them it was the most fearful condemnation to be ejected from the inner sanctuary and thrust down from their elevated station.[r] As yet the clergy were not entirely estranged from society, they had not become a caste by the legal enforcement or general practice of celibacy. Clement of Alexandria asserts and vindicates the marriage of some of the Apostles.[s] The discreet remonstrance of the old Egyptian bishop perhaps prevented the Council of Nicæa from imposing that heavy burden on the reluctant clergy. The aged Paphnutius, himself unmarried, boldly asserted that the conjugal union was chastity.[t] But that, which, in the third century is asserted to be free to all mankind, clergy as well as laity, in Egypt;[u] in the fourth, according to Jerome, was prohibited or limited by vows of continence. It has been asserted,[x] and without refutation, that there was no ecclesiastical law or regulation which compelled the celibacy of the clergy for the first three centuries.

Celibacy of the clergy.

---

ipsis parentibus, et sæpe in judiciis solet ab Episcopis adhiberi." Augustin. Epist. cxxxiii.—High authority for the antiquity of flogging in public schools!

[r] The decrees of the fourth council of Carthage show the strict morals and humble subordination demanded of the clergy at the close of the fourth century.

[s] *Ἦ καὶ τοὺς Ἀποστόλους ἀποδοκιμάζουσι; Πέτρος μὲν γὰρ καὶ Φίλιππος ἐπαιδοποιήσαντο. Φίλιππος δὲ καὶ τὰς θυγατέρας ἀνδράσιν ἐξέδωκεν, καὶ ὅγε Παῦλος οὐκ ὀκνεῖ ἔν τινι ἐπιστολῇ τὴν αὑτοῦ προσαγορεύειν σύζυγον, ἣν οὐ περιεκόμιζεν διὰ τὸ*

τῆς ὑπηρεσίας εὐσταλές.—Strom. l. iii. c. 6. On the question of the marriage òf the Apostles and their immediate followers, almost everything is collected in a note of Cotelerius, Patres Apostolici, ii. 241.

[t] Gelasii Histor. Conc. Nic. c. xxxii. Socrat. i. 11. Sozomen, i. 23. Baronius insists upon this being *Greek* fable.

[u] *Ναὶ μὴν καὶ τὸν τῆς μιᾶς γυναικὸς ἄνδρα πανὺ ἀποδέχεται κἂν πρεσβύτερος ᾖ, κἂν διάκονος, κἂν λαϊκὸς, ἀνεπιλήπτως γάμῳ χρωμένος. Σωθήσεται δὲ διὰ τῆς τεκνογονίας.* Strom. iii. 12, 9.

[x] By Bingham, book iv.

Clement of Alexandria, as we see, argues against enforced celibacy from the example of the Apostles.
Married bishops and presbyters frequently occur in the
history of Eusebius. The martyrdom of Numidicus was
shared and not dishonoured by the companionship of his
wife.[y] It was a sight of joy and consolation to the
husband to see her perishing in the same flames. The
wives of the clergy are recognised, not merely in the
older writings, but also in the public documents of the
Church.[z] Council after council, in the East, introduced
regulations, which, though intended to restrict, recognise
the legality of these ties.[a] Highly as they exalt the
angelic state of celibacy, neither Basil in the East, nor
Augustine in the West, positively prohibits the marriage
of the clergy.[b]

But in the fourth century, particularly in the latter
half, the concurrent influence of the higher honours
attributed to virginity by all the great Christian writers;
of the hierarchical spirit, which, even at that time, saw
how much of its corporate strength depended on this
entire detachment from worldly ties; of the monastic
system, which worked into the clerical, partly by the
frequent selection of monks for ordination and for consecration to ecclesiastical dignities, partly by the emulation of the clergy, who could not safely allow themselves

---

[y] " Numidicus presbyter uxorem
adhærentem lateri suo, concrematam
cum cæteris, vel conservatam potius
dixerim, lætus aspexit." Cyprian, p.
525. See in Basnage, Dissertatio
Septima, a list of married prelates.

[z] Conc. Gang. c. 4. Conc. Ancyr.
c. 10. This law allows any deacon to
marry.

[a] In the West, the Council of

Elvira commands the clergy to abstain
from connubial intercourse and the
procreation of children. Can. xxxiii.
This was frequently re-enacted. Among
others, Conc. Carthag. v. 2. Labbe,
ii. 1216.

[b] Basil speaks of a presbyter who
had contumaciously contracted an unlawful marriage. Can. ii. c. 27. On
Augustine, compare Theiner, p. 154.

to be outdone in austerity by these rivals for popular
estimation; all these various influences introduced restrictions and regulations on the marriage of the clergy,
which darkened at length into the solemn ecclesiastical
interdict. First, the general sentiment repudiated a
second marriage as a monstrous act of incontinence, an
infirmity or a sin which ought to prevent the Christian
from ever aspiring to any ecclesiastical office.[c] The
next offence against the general feeling was marriage
with a widow; then followed the restriction of marriage
after entering into holy orders; the married priest retained his wife, but to condescend to such carnal ties
after ordination, was revolting to the general sentiment,
and was considered to imply a total want of feeling for
the dignity of their high calling. Then was generally
introduced a demand of abstinence from sexual connexion from those who retained their wives: this was
imperatively required from the higher orders of the
clergy. It was considered to render unclean, and to
disqualify even from prayer for the people, as the
priest's life was to be a perpetual prayer.[d] Not that
there was as yet any uniform practice. The bishops
assembled at the Council of Gangra[e] condemned the

---

[c] Athenagoras laid down the general
principle, ὁ γὰρ δεύτερος (γάμος)
εὐπρεπὴς ἐστι μοιχεία. De Resurr.
Carn. Compare Orig. contr. Cels. vii.,
and Hom. vi., in Num. xviii., in Luc.
xviii., in Matt. Tertull. ad Uxor. 1-5.
This was almost an universal moral
axiom. Epiphanius said, that since
the coming of Christ no digamous
clergyman had ever been ordained.
Barbeyrac has collected the passages
of the Fathers expressive of their abhorrence of second marriages. Morale
des Pères, p. 1. 29, 34, 37, &c. The

Council of Neo-Cæsarea forbade clergymen to be present at a feast for a
second marriage — πρεσβύτερον εἰς
γάμους διγαμούντων μὴ ἐστιᾶσθαι.
Can. vii.
[d] Such is the distinct language of
Jerome. "Si laicus et quicunque fidelis
orare non potest nisi careat officio
conjugali, sacerdoti, cui semper pro
populo offerenda sunt sacrificia semper orandum est. Si semper orandum
est, semper carendum matrimonio."
Adv. Jovin. p. 175.
[e] In the Council of Gangra (about

followers of Eustathius, who refused to receive the sacraments from any but unmarried priests. The heresy of Jovinian, on the other hand, probably called forth the severe regulations of Pope Siricius.[f] This sort of encyclical letter positively prohibited all clergy of the higher orders from any intercourse with their wives. A man who lived to the age of thirty, the husband of one wife, that wife, when married, a virgin, might be an acolyth or subdeacon; after five years of strict continence, he might be promoted to a priest; after ten years more of the same severe ordeal, a bishop. A clerk, any one in holy orders, even of the lowest degree, who married a widow, or a second wife, was instantly deprived: no woman was to live in the house of a clerk.

The Council of Carthage, reciting the canon of a former council, commands the clergy to abstain from all connexion with their wives. The enactment is perpetually repeated, and in one extended to subdeacons.[g] The Council of Toledo prohibited the promotion of ecclesiastics who had children. The Council of Arles prohibited the ordination of a married priest,[h] unless he made a promise of divorce from the married state. Jerome distinctly asserts that it was the universal regulation of the East, of Egypt, and of Rome [i] to ordain

---

350) the preamble and the first canon do not appear to refer necessarily to the wives of the clergy. They anathematise certain teachers (the Eustathians) who had blamed marriage, and said that a faithful and pious woman who slept with her husband could not enter into the kingdom of heaven. A sacred virgin is prohibited from vaunting over a married woman, canon x. Women are forbidden to abandon their husbands and children.

[f] The letter of Siricius in Mansi Concil. iii. 635, A.D. 385.

[g] These councils of Carthage are dated A.D. 390, 418, and 419.

[h] "Assumi aliquem ad sacerdotium non posse in vinculo sacerdotii constitutum, nisi primum fuerit promissa conversio." A.D. 452.

[i] "Quid facient Orientis Ecclesiæ? quid Ægypti, et sedis Apostolicæ, quæ aut virgines clericos accipiunt aut continentes; aut si uxores habuerint,

only those who were unmarried, or who ceased to be
husbands. But even in the fourth, and the beginning
of the fifth centuries, the practice rebelled Married
against this severe theory. Married clergymen, clergy.
even married bishops, and with children, occur in the
ecclesiastical annals. Athanasius, in his letter to
Dracontius, admits and allows the full right of the
bishop to marriage.[k] Gregory of Nazianzum was born
after his father was bishop, and had a younger brother
named Cæsarius.[m] Gregory of Nyssa, and Hilary of
Poictiers, were married. Less distinguished names frequently occur: those of Spyridon[n] and Eustathius.[o]
Synesius, whose character enabled him to accept episcopacy on his own terms, positively repudiated these
unnatural restrictions on the freedom and holiness of
the conjugal state. " God and the law, and the holy
hand of Theophilus bestowed on me my wife. I declare,
therefore, solemnly, and call you to witness, that I will
not be plucked from her, nor lie with her in secret, like
an adulterer. But I hope and pray that we may have
many and virtuous children." [p]

The Council in Trullo only demanded this high test
of spirituality, absolute celibacy, from bishops, and left
the inferior clergy to their freedom. But the earlier
Western Council of Toledo only admitted the deacon,

---

mariti esse desistunt." Adv. Vigilantium, p. 281. Jerome appeals to
Jovinian himself:—" Certè confiteris
non posse esse episcopum qui in epi-
scopatu filios faciat, alioqui si depre-
hensus fuerit, non quasi vir tenebitur,
sed quasi adulter damnabitur." Adv.
Jovin. 175. Compare Epiphanius,
Hæres. liv. 4.

[k] Athanasii Epistola ad Dracon-
tium.

[m] Gregory makes his father thus
address him :—

Οὔπω τοσοῦτον ἐκμεμέτρηκας βίον
Ὅσος διῆλθε θυσίων ἐμοὶ χρόνος.
De Vitâ Suâ, v. 512.

[n] Sozom. i. 11. Socrat. i. 12.
[o] Socrat. ii. 43.
[p] Synesii Epist. 105.

and that under restrictions, to connubial intercourse;
the presbyter who had children after his ordination could
not be a bishop.[q]

This overstrained demand on the virtue, not of indi-

Moral conse-
quences. viduals in a high state of enthusiasm, but of a
whole class of men; this strife with nature, in
that which, in its irregular and lawless indulgence, is
the source of so many evils and of so much misery, in
its more moderate and legal form is the parent of the
purest affections, and the holiest charities; this isolation
from those social ties which, if at times they might
withdraw them from total dedication to their sacred
duties, in general, would, by their tending to soften and
humanise, be the best school for the gentle and affec-
tionate discharge of those duties—the enforcement of
the celibacy of the clergy, though not yet by law, by
dominant opinion, was not slow in producing its inevi-

Mulieres sub-
introductæ. table evils. Simultaneously with the sterner
condemnation of marriage, or at least the ex-
aggerated praises of chastity, we hear the solemn denunciations of the law, and the deepening remonstrances of
the more influential writers, against those secret evasions
by which the clergy endeavoured to obtain the fame
without the practice of celibacy, to enjoy some of the
pleasures and advantages without the crime of marriage.
From the middle of the third century, in which the
growing aversion to the marriage of the clergy begins
to appear, we find the "sub-introduced" females constantly proscribed.[r] The intimate union of the priest

---

[q] Conc. Tolet. A.D. 400, can. i.

[r] They are mentioned in the letter
of the bishops of Antioch, against Paul
of Samosata. The Council of Illiberis
(incautiously) allowed a sister, or a
virgin, dedicated to God, to reside
with a bishop or presbyter, not a
stranger.

with a young, often a beautiful female, who still passed to
the world under the name of a virgin, and was called by
the priest by the unsuspected name of sister, seems from
the strong and reiterated language of Jerome,[s] Gregory
Nazianzen, Chrysostom, and others, to have been almost
general. It was interdicted by an imperial law.[t]

Thus, in every city, in almost every town and every
village of the Roman empire, had established itself a
new permanent magistracy, in a certain sense independent of the government, with considerable inalienable
endowments, and filled by men of a peculiar and sacred
character, and recognised by the state. Their authority
extended far beyond their jurisdiction; their influence

---

[s] " Unde sine nuptiis aliud nomen
uxorum? Imo unde novum concu-
binarum genus? Plus inferam. Unde
meretrices univiræ? Eadem domo,
uno cubiculo, sæpe uno tenentur et
lectulo. Et suspiciosos nos vocant, si
aliquid existimamus. Frater sororem
virginem deserit: cælibem spernit virgo
germanum : fratrem quærit extraneum,
et cum in eodem proposito esse se
simulent quærunt alienorum spiritale
solatium, ut domi habeant carnale
commercium." Hieronym. Epist. xxii.
ad Eustochium. If the vehemence of
Jerome's language betrays his own
ardent character and his monkish hostility to the clergy, the general charge
is amply borne out by other writers.
Many quotations may be found in
Gothofred's Note on the Law of Honorius. Gregory of Nazianzum says,—
Αρσενα παντ' αλέεινε, συνείσακτον
τε μάλιστα. The language of Cyprian,
however, even in the third century, is
the strongest:—"Certè ipse concubitus,
ipse amplexus, ipsa confabulatio, et

inosculatio, et conjacentium duorum
turpis et fœda dormitio quantum dede-
coris et criminis confitetur." Cyprian
justly observes, that such intimacy
would induce a jealous husband to
take to his sword. Epist. lxii. ad
Pomponium.

But the canon of the Council of
Nicæa, which prohibits the usage, and
forbids the priest to have a subintro-
ducta mulier, unless a mother, sister,
or aunt, the only relationships beyond
suspicion, and the still stronger tone
of the law, show the frequency, as
well as the evil, of the practice. Unhappily they were blind to its real
cause.

[t] " Eum qui probabilem sæculo disci-
plinam agit decolorari consortio soro-
riæ appellationis non decet." But this
law of Honorius, A. D. 420, allowed
the clergy to retain their wives, if
they had been married before entering
into orders. See, too, the third and
fourth canons of the Council of Carthage, A. D. 348.

far beyond their authority. The internal organisation
was complete. The three great patriarchs in the East,
throughout the West the Bishop of Rome, exercised a
supreme, and, in some points, an appellant jurisdiction.
Great ecclesiastical causes could be removed to their
tribunal. Under them, the metropolitans, and in the
next rank the bishops, governed their dioceses, and
ruled the subordinate clergy, who now began to form
parishes, separate districts to which their labours were
to be confined. In the superior clergy had gradually
become vested, not the ordination only, but the appointment, of the inferior; these could not quit the diocese
without letters from the bishop, or be received or exercise
their functions in another, without permission.

On the incorporation of the Church with the State,
Union of the co-ordinate civil and religious magistracy
Church and
State. maintained each its separate powers. On one
side, as far as the actual celebration of the ecclesiastical
ceremonial, and in their own internal affairs in general;
on the other, in the administration of the military,
judicial, and fiscal affairs of the state, the bounds of
their respective authority were clear and distinct. As a
citizen and subject, the Christian, the priest, and the
bishop, were alike amenable to the laws of the empire
and to the imperial decrees, and liable to taxation, unless
specially exempted, for the service of the state.[u] The

---

[u] The law of Constantius which
appears to withdraw the bishops entirely from the civil jurisdiction, and
to give the privilege of being tried
upon all charges by a tribunal of
bishops, is justly considered by Gothofred as a local or temporary act, probably connected with the feuds concerning Arianism. Cod. Theod. xvi.
2, 12, with Gothofred's note. Valens
admitted the ecclesiastical courts to
settle religious difficulties and slight
offences, xvi. 2, 23. The same is the
scope of the more explicit law of
Honorius. xvi. 2, 201. The immunity of the clergy from the civil courts
was of very much later date.

Christian statesman, on the other hand, of the highest
rank, was amenable to the ecclesiastical censures, and
was bound to submit to the canons of the Church in
matters of faith and discipline, and was entirely dependent on their judgement for his admission or rejection
from the privileges or hopes of the Christian.

So far the theory was distinct and perfect; each had
his separate and exclusive sphere; yet there could not
but appear a debateable ground on which the two
authorities came into collision, and neither could altogether refrain from invading the territory of his ally or
antagonist.

The treaty between the contracting parties was, in
fact, formed with such haste and precipitancy, Union of the
that the rights of neither party could be de- Church and
the State.
fined or secured. Eager for immediate union, and
impatient of delay, they framed no deed of settlement,
by which, when their mutual interests should be less
identified, and jealousy and estrangement should arise,
they might assert their respective rights, and enforce
their several duties.

In ecclesiastical affairs, strictly so called, the supremacy of the Christian magistracy, it has been said, was
admitted. They were the legislators of discipline,
order, and doctrine. The festivals, the fasts, the usages
and canons of the Church, the government of the clergy,
were in their exclusive power. The decrees of particular
synods and councils possessed undisputed authority, as
far as their sphere extended. General councils were
held binding on the whole Church. But it was far
more easy to define that which did belong to the province of the Church than that which did not. Religion
asserts its authority, and endeavours to extend its
influence over the whole sphere of moral action, which

is, in fact, over the whole of human life, its habits, manners, conduct. Christianity, as the most profound moral religion, exacted the most complete and universal obedience; and as the acknowledged teachers and guardians of Christianity, the clergy continued to draw within their sphere every part of human life in which man is actuated by moral or religious motives. The moral authority, therefore, of the religion, and consequently of the clergy, might appear legitimately to extend over every transaction of life, from the legislature of the sovereign, which ought, in a Christian king, to be guided by Christian motive, to the domestic duties of the peasant, which ought to be fulfilled on the principle of Christian love.

But, on the other hand, the State was supreme over all its subjects, even over the clergy, in their character of citizens. The whole tenure of property, to what use soever dedicated (except in such cases as the State itself might legalise on its first principles, and guarantee, when bestowed, as by gift or bequest), was under its absolute control; the immunities which it conferred it might revoke; and it would assert the equal authority of the constitutional laws over every one who enjoyed the protection of those laws. Thus, though in extreme cases, these separate bounds of jurisdiction were clear, the tribunals of ecclesiastical and civil law could not but, in process of time, interfere with and obstruct each other.

But there was another prolific source of difference. The clergy, in one sense, from being the representative body, had begun to consider themselves the Church; but in another and more legitimate sense, the State, when Christian, as comprehending all the Christians of the empire, became the Church. Which was the legis-

lative body,—the whole community of Christians? or
the Christian aristocracy, who were in one sense the
admitted rulers? And who was to appoint these rulers?
It is quite clear that, from the first, though the consecration to the religious office was in the bishop and
clergy, the laity had a voice in the ratification if not in
the appointment. Did not the State fairly succeed to
all the rights of the laity, more particularly when
privileges and endowments, attached to the ecclesiastical
offices, were conferred or guaranteed by the State, and
therefore might appear in justice revocable, or liable to
be regulated by the civil power?

This vital question at this time was still farther
embarrassed by the rash eagerness with which the dominant Church called upon the State to rid it of its internal
adversaries. When once the civil power was recognised
as cognisant of ecclesiastical offences, where was that
power to end? The Emperor, who commanded his
subjects to be of one religion, might command them,
by the same title, to adopt another. The despotic head
of the State might assert his despotism as head of the
Church. It must be acknowledged that no theory, which
has satisfactorily harmonised the relations of these two,
at once, in one sense separate, in another identical, communities, has satisfied the reasoning and dispassionate
mind; while the separation of the two communities, the
total dissociation, as it were, of the Christian and the
citizen, is an experiment apparently not likely to advance
or perpetuate the influence of Christianity.

At all events, the hasty and unsettled compact of this
period left room for constant jealousy and strife. As
each was the stronger, it encroached upon and extended
its dominion into the territory of the other. In general,
though with very various fortunes, in different parts of

the world, and at different periods, the Church was in
the ascendant, and for many centuries confronted the
State, at least on equal terms.

The first aggression, as it were, which the Church
made on the State, was in assuming the cognisance over all questions and causes relating to
marriage. In sanctifying this solemn contract,
it could scarcely be considered as transgressing its proper
limits as guardian of this primary element of social
virtue and happiness. In the early Church, the benediction of the bishop or presbyter seems to have been
previously sought by the Christian at the time of marriage. The Heathen rite of marriage was so manifestly
religious, that the Christian, while he sought to avoid
that idolatrous ceremony, would wish to substitute some
more simple and congenial form. In the general sentiment that this contract should be public and sacred, he
would seek the sanction of his own community as its
witnesses. Marriage not performed in the face of his
Christian brethren was little better than an illicit
union.[x]

It was an object likewise of the early Christian community to restrict the marriage of Christians to Christ-

Marginal note: Marriage brought under ecclesiastical discipline.

---

[x] " Ideo penes nos occultæ conjunc-
tiones, id est, non prius apud ecclesiam
professæ, juxta mœchiam et fornica-
tionem judicari periclitantur." Tertull.
de Pudic. c. 4.

Though the rite was solemnised in
the presence of the Christian priest,
and the Church attempted to impose a
graver and more serious dignity, it
was not so easy to throw off the gay
and festive character which had prevailed in the Heathen times. Paganism, or rather, perhaps, human nature,
was too strong to submit. The austere
preacher of Constantinople reproved
the loose hymns to Venus, which
were heard even at Christian wed-
dings. The bride, he says, was borne
by drunken men to her husband's
house, among choirs of dancing harlots, with pipes and flutes, and songs,
full, to her chaste ear, of offensive
license.

ians—to discountenance, if not prohibit, those with
unbelievers.[y] This was gradually extended to marriages
with heretics, or members of another Christian sect.
When, therefore, the Church began to recognise five
legal impediments to marriage, this was the Ist—difference of religion as between Christians and infidels,
Jews, or heretics. The IInd was, the impediment of
crime. Persons guilty of adultery were not allowed to
marry according to the Roman law: this was recognised
by the Church. A law of Constantius had made rape,
or forcible abduction of a virgin, a capital offence; so,
even with the consent of the injured female, marriage
could not take place. III. Impediments from relationship. Here also the Church was content to follow the
Roman law, which was as severe and precise as the
Mosaic Institutes.[z] IV. The civil impediment. Children adopted by the same father could not marry. A
freeman could not marry a slave; the connection was
only concubinage. It does not appear that the Church
yet ventured to correct this vice of Roman society. V.
Spiritual relationship, between godfathers and their
spiritual children: this was afterwards carried much
farther. To these regulations for the repression of im-

---

[y] A law of Valentinian II., Theodosius and Arcadius (A. D. 388), prohibited the intermarriage of Jews and
Christians. Codex Theodos. iii. 7, 2.
It was to be considered adultery.—
" Cave, Christiane, Gentili aut Judæo
filiam tradere ; cave, inquam, Gen-
tilem aut Judæam atque alienigenam,
hoc est, hæreticam, et omnem alienam
à fide tuâ uxorem accersas tibi." Ambros. de Abraham. c. 9. "Cum cer-
tissimè noveris tradi à nobis Christi-
anam nisi Christiano non posse." Augustin. Ep. 234, ad Rusticum.

The Council of Illiberis had prohibited Christians from giving their
daughters in marriage to Gentiles
(propter copiam puellarum), also to
Jews, heretics, and especially to Heathen priests. Can. xv. xvi. xvii.

[z] See the various laws in the Cod.
Theod., lib. iii. tit. 12, De Incestis
Nuptiis.

proper connections were added some other ecclesiastical
impediments. There were holy periods in the year, in
which it was forbidden to contract marriage. No one
might marry while under ecclesiastical interdict, nor
one who had made a vow of chastity.

The facility of divorce was the primary principle of
corruption in Roman social life. Augustus had
attempted to enforce some restrictions on this
unlimited power of dissolving the matrimonial contract
from caprice or the lightest motive. Probably, the
severity of Christian morals had obtained that law of
Constantine which was so much too rigid for the state
of society, as to be entirely ineffective from the impos-
sibility of carrying it into execution.[a] It was relaxed
by Constantius, and almost abrogated by Honorius.[b]
The inveterate evil remained. A Christian writer, at
the beginning of the fifth century, complains that men
changed their wives as quickly as their clothes, and that
marriage chambers were set up as easily as booths in a
market.[c] At a later period than that to which our

Divorce.

---

[a] Codex Theodos. iii. 16, 1. See
vol. ii. p. 397.

[b] By the law of Honorius,—1. The
woman who demanded a divorce without sufficient proof forfeited her dowry,
was condemned to banishment, could
not contract a second marriage, and was
without hope of restoration to civil
rights. 2. If she made out only a
tolerable case (convicted her husband
only of mediocris culpa), she only forfeited her dowry, and could not contract a second marriage, but was
liable to be prosecuted by her husband for adultery. 3. If she made a
strong case (gravis causa), she retained
her dowry, and might marry again
after five years. The husband, in the
first case, forfeited the gifts and
dowry, and was condemned to perpetual celibacy, not having liberty to
marry again after a certain number of
years. In the second, he forfeited the
dowry but not the donation, and could
marry again after two years. In the
third, he was bound to prosecute his
guilty wife. On her conviction, he
retained the dowry, and might marry
again immediately. Cod. Theodos. iii.
xvi. 2.

[c] " Mulieres à maritis tanquam ves-
tes subinde mutari, et thalamos tam
sæpe et facile strui quam nundinarum
tabernas." Asterius Amasenus apud
Combefis. Auct. t. i.

The story has been often quoted

history extends, when Justinian attempted to prohibit all divorces except those on account of chastity, that is when the parties embraced the monastic life, he was obliged to relax the law on account of the fearful crimes, the plots and poisonings, and other evils, which it introduced into domestic life.

But though it could not correct or scarcely mitigate this evil by public law in the general body of society, Christianity, in its proper and more peculiar sphere, had invested marriage in a religious sanctity, which at least, to a limited extent, repressed this social evil. By degrees, separation from bed and board, even in the case of adultery, the only cause which could dissolve the tie, was substituted and enforced by the clergy instead of legal divorce. Over all the ceremonial forms, and all expressions which related to marriage, the Church threw the utmost solemnity ; it was said to resemble the mystic union of Christ and the Church ; till at length marriage grew up into a sacrament, indissoluble until the final separation of death, except by the highest ecclesiastical authority.[d] It is impossible to calculate the effect of this canonisation, as it were, of marriage, the only remedy which could be applied, first to the corrupt manners of Roman society, and afterwards to the consequences of the barbarian invasions, in which, notwithstanding the strong moral element in the Teutonic character, and the respect for women (which, no doubt, was one of the

from St. Jerome, of the man (of the lowest class) in Rome, who had had twenty wives, not divorced (he had buried them all) ; his wife had had twenty-two husbands. There was a great anxiety to know which would outlive the other. The man carried the day, and bore his wife to the grave in a kind of triumphal procession. Hieronym. Epist. xci. p. 745.

[d] The Eastern churches had a horror of second marriage ; a presbyter was forbidden to be present at the wedding-feast of a digamist. Can. vii. See above.

original principles of chivalry), yet the dominance of brute force, and the unlimited rights of conquest, could not but lead to the perpetual, lawless, and violent dissolution of the marriage tie.[e]

The cognisance of wills, another department in which Wills. the Church assumed a power not strictly ecclesiastical, seems to have arisen partly from an accidental cause. It was the custom among the Heathen to deposit wills in the temples, as a place of security; the Christians followed their practice, and chose their churches as the depositaries of these important documents. They thus came under the custody of the clergy, who, from guardians, became, in their courts, the judges of their authenticity or legality, and at length a general tribunal for all matters relating to testaments.

Thus religion laid its sacred control on all the material incidents of human life, and around the ministers of religion gathered all the influence thus acquired over the sentiments of mankind. The font of baptism usually received the Christian infant, and the form of baptism was uttered by the priest or bishop; the marriage was unhallowed without the priestly benediction; and at the close of life, the minister of religion was at hand to absolve and to reassure the departing spirit; at the funeral, he ratified, as it were, the solemn promises of immortality. But the great, permanent, and perpetual source of sacerdotal authority was the penitential discipline of the Church, which was universally recognised

---

[e] It is curious to trace the rapid fall of Roman pride. Valentinian made the intermarriage of a Roman provincial with a *barbarian* a capital crime (A. D. 370). Codex Theodos. iii. 14, 1. Under Theodosius, Fra-vitta, the Goth, married a Roman woman with the consent of the Emperor. Eunap. Excerpt. Legat. In another century, the daughters of emperors were the willing or the enforced brides of barbarian kings.

as belonging exclusively to the jurisdiction of the clergy. Christianity had sufficient power, in a certain degree, to engross the mind and heart, but not to keep under perpetual restraint the unruly passions or the inquisitive mind. The best were most conscious of human infirmity, and most jealous of their own slight aberrations from the catholic belief; the bad had not merely their own conscience, but public fame and the condemnatory voice of the community, to prostrate them before the visible arbiters of the All-seeing Power. Sin, from the most heinous delinquency, or the darkest heresy, to the most trivial fault or the slightest deviation from the established belief, could only be reconciled by the advice, the guidance, at length by the direct authority, of the priest. He judged of its magnitude, he prescribed the appointed penance. The hierarchy were supposed to be invested with the keys of heaven and of hell; they undoubtedly held those which unlock the human heart—fear and hope. And when once the mind was profoundly affected by Christianity — when hope had failed to excite to more generous obedience—they applied the baser and more servile instrument without scruple and without remorse.

The penitential discipline of the Church, no doubt, grew up, like other usages, by slow degrees: its regulations were framed into a system to meet the exigences of the times; but we discern, at a very early period, the awful power of condemning to the most profound humiliation, to the most agonising contrition, to the shame of public confession, to the abasing supplication before the priest, to long seclusion from the privileges and the society of the Christian community. Even then public confession was the first process in the fearful yet in-

evitable ceremonial. "Confession of sin," says Tertullian,[f] "is the proper discipline for the abasement and
humiliation of man; it enforces that mode of life which
can alone find mercy with God; it prescribes the fitting
dress and food of the penitent to be in sackcloth and
ashes, to darken the body with filth, to depress the soul
with anguish; it allows only the simplest food, enough
and no more than will maintain life. Constantly to fast
and pray, to groan, to weep, to howl day and night
before the Lord our God, to grovel at the feet of the
presbyter, to kneel at the altar of God, to implore from
all the brethren their deprecatory supplications." Subsequently, the more complete penitential system rigidly
regulated the most minute particulars; the attitude, the
garb, the language, or the more expressive silence. The
place in which the believer stood, showed to the whole
Church how far the candidate for salvation through
Christ had been thrown back in his spiritual course,
what progress he was making to pardon and peace. The
penitent was clothed in sackcloth, his head was strewn
with ashes; men shaved their heads, women left their
dishevelled hair flung over their bosoms; they wore a
peculiar veil. The severest attendance on every religious
service was exacted, all diversions were proscribed, marriage was not permitted during the time of penance, the
lawful indulgence of the marriage bed was forbidden.
Although a regular formulary, which gradually grew
into use,[g] imposed canonical penances of a certain period
for certain offences, yet that period might be rigidly
required or shortened by the authority of the bishop.
For some offences the penitent, who it was believed

---

[f] De Pœnitentiâ, c. 9.

[g] On the Penitentiaries compare Latin Christianity, Book iii. c. 5.

was abandoned to the power of Satan, was excluded from all enjoyment, all honour, and all society, to the close of life; and the doors of reconciliation were hardly opened to the departing spirit—wonderful proof how profoundly the doctrines of Christianity had sunk into the human heart, and of the enormous power (and what enormous power is not liable to abuse) in which the willing reverence of the people had invested the priesthood.

But something more fearful still remained. Over all the community hung the tremendous sentence of excommunication, tantamount to a sentence of spiritual death.[h] This sentence, though not as yet dependent on his will, was pronounced and executed by the religious magistrate. The clergy adhered to certain regular forms of process, but the ultimate decree rested with them.

Excommunication was of two kinds : first, that which excluded from the communion, and threw back the initiate Christian into the ranks of the uninitiate. This separation or suspension allowed the person under ban to enter the church, to hear the psalms and sermon, and, in short, all that was permitted to the catechumen.

But the more terrible excommunication by anathema altogether banished the delinquent from the church and the society of Christians : it annulled for ever his hopes of immortality through Christ; it drove him out as an

---

h " Interfici Deus jussit sacerdotibus non obtemperantes, judicibus à se ad tempus constitutis non obedientes; sed tunc quidem gladio occidebantur, quando adhuc et circumcisio carnis manebat. Nunc autem quia circumcisio spiritalis esse apud fideles Dei servos cœpit, spiritali gladio superbi et contumaces *necantur*, dum de ecclesiâ ejiciuntur." Cyprian. Epist. lxii.

" Nunc agit in ecclesiâ excommunicatio, quod agebat tunc in interfectis." Augustin. Q. 39, in Deuteron.

outcast to the dominion of the Evil Spirit. The Christian might not communicate with him in the ordinary intercourse of life: he was a moral leper, whom it was the solemn duty of all to avoid, lest they should partake in his contagion. The sentence of one church was rapidly promulgated throughout Christendom; and the excommunicated in Egypt or Syria found the churches in Gaul or Spain closed against him: he was an exile without a resting place. As long as Heathenism survived, at least in equal temporal power and distinction, and another society received with welcome, or at least with undiminished respect, the exile from Christianity, the excommunicated might lull his remaining terrors to rest, and forget, in the business or dissipation of the world, his forfeited hopes of immortality. But when there was but one society, that of the Christians, throughout the world, or at best but a feeble and despised minority, he stood a marked and branded man. Those who were, perhaps, not better Christians, but who had escaped the fatal censures of the Church, would perhaps seize the opportunity of showing their zeal by avoiding the outcast: if he did not lose civil privileges, he lost civil estimation; he was altogether excluded from human respect and human sympathies; he was a legitimate, almost a designated, object of scorn, distrust, and aversion.

The nature, the extent, and some of the moral and even political advantages of excommunication, are illustrated in the act of the celebrated Synesius. Synesius. The power of the Christian bishop, in his hands, appears under its noblest and most beneficial form. Synesius became a Christian bishop without renouncing the habits, the language, and, in a great degree, the opinions, of a philosopher. His writings,

more especially his Odes, blend, with a very scanty
Christianity, the mystic theology of the later Platonism;
but it is rather philosophy adopting Christian language
than Christianity moulding philosophy to its own uses.
Yet so high was the character of Synesius, that even the
worldly prelate of Alexandria, Theophilus, approved of
his elevation to the episcopate in the obscure town of
Ptolemais, near Cyrene. Synesius felt the power with
which he was invested, and employed it with a wise
vigour and daring philanthropy, which commanded the
admiration both of philosophy and of religion. The low-
born Andronicus was the prefect or rather the scourge
and tyrant of Libya; his exactions were unprecedented,
and enforced by tortures of unusual cruelty even in that
age and country. The province groaned and bled, without hope of relief, under the hateful and sanguinary
oppression. Synesius had tried in vain the milder language of persuasion upon the intractable tyrant. At
length he put forth the terrors of the Church to shield
the people; and for his rapacity, which had amounted
to sacrilege, and for his inhumanity, the president of the
whole province was openly condemned, by a sentence of
excommunication, to the public abhorrence, excluded
from the society and denied the common rights of men.
He was expelled from the church, as the Devil from
Paradise; every Christian temple, every sanctuary, was
closed against the man of blood; the priest was not
even to permit him the rites of Christian burial; every
private man and every magistrate was to exclude him
from their houses and from their tables. If the rest of
Christendom refused to ratify and execute the sentence
of the obscure Church of Ptolemais, they were guilty of
the sin of schism. The Church of Ptolemais would not
communicate or partake of the divine mysteries with

those who thus violated ecclesiastical discipline. The excommunication included the accomplices of the President's guilt, and by a less justifiable extension of power, their families. Andronicus quailed before the interdict, which he feared might find countenance in the court of Constantinople; bowed before the protector of the people, and acknowledged the justice of his sentence.[1]

The salutary thunder of sacerdotal excommunication might here and there strike some eminent delinquent;[k] but ecclesiastical discipline, which in the earlier and more fervent period of the religion, had watched with holy jealousy the whole life of the individual, was baffled by the increase of votaries, which it could no longer submit to this severe and constant superintendence. The clergy could not command, nor the laity require, the sacred duty of secession and outward penance from the multitude of sinners, when they were the Ecclesiastical larger part of the community. But heresy of censures chiefly con- opinion was more easily detected than heresy fined to heresy. of conduct. Gradually, from a moral as well as a religious power, the discipline became almost exclusively religious, or rather confined itself to the speculative, while it almost abandoned in despair the practical effects of religion. Heresy became the one great crime for which excommunication was pronounced in its most awful form; the heretic was the one being with whom it was criminal to associate, who forfeited all the privileges of religion, and all the charities of life.

---

[1] Synesii Epistolæ, lvii. lviii.

[k] There is a canon of the Council of Toledo (A.D. 408), that if any man in power shall have robbed one in holy orders, or a *poor man* (quemlibet pauperiorem), or a monk, and the bishop shall send to demand a hearing for the cause, should the man in power treat his message with contempt, letters shall be sent to all the bishops of the province, declaring him excommunicated till he has heard the cause or made restitution. Can. xi. Labbe, ii. 1225.

Nor was this all; in pursuit of the heretic, the Church was not content to rest within her own sphere, Executed to wield her own arms of moral temperament, by the State and to exclude from her own territory. She formed a fatal alliance with the State, and raised that which was strictly an ecclesiastical, an offence against the religious community, into a civil crime, amenable to temporal penalties. The Church, when she ruled the mind of a religious or superstitious emperor, could not forego the immediate advantage of his authority to further her own cause, and hailed his welcome intrusion on her own internal legislation. In fact, the autocracy of the Emperor over the Church, as well as over the State, was asserted in all those edicts which the Church, in its blind zeal, hailed with transport as the marks of his allegiance, but which confounded in inextricable, and to the present time, in deplorable confusion, the limits of the religious and the civil power. The imperial rescripts, which made heresy a civil offence, by affixing penalties which were not purely religious, trespassed as much upon the real principles of the original religious republic, as against the immutable laws of conscience and Christian charity. The tremendous laws Civil punishment for ecclesiastical offence, punishable by the civil power, are offences. said to have been enacted only as a terror to evil-believers, but they betrayed too clearly the darkening spirit of the times; the next generation would execute what the laws of the last would enact. The most distinguished bishops of the time raised a cry of horror at the first executions for religion; but it was their humanity which was startled; they did not perceive that they

---

m See ch. viii.

had sanctioned, by the smallest civil penalty, a false and
fatal principle; that though, by the legal establishment,
the Church and the State had become, in one sense, the
same body, yet the associating principle of each remained
entirely distinct, and demanded an entirely different and
independent system of legislation and administration of
the law. The Christian hierarchy bought the privilege
of persecution at the price of Christian independence.

It is difficult to decide whether the language of the
book in the Theodosian code, entitled "On Heretics,"
contrasts more strongly with the comprehensive, equitable, and parental tone of the Roman jurisprudence, or
with the gentle and benevolent spirit of the Gospel, or
even with the primary principles of the ecclesiastical
community.[n] The Emperor, of his sole and supreme
authority, without any recognition of ecclesiastical advice or sanction; the Emperor, who himself might be
an Arian or Eunomian, or Manichean—who had so
recently been an Arian—defines heresy to be the very
slightest deviation from Catholic verity; and in a succession of statutes inflicts civil penalties, and excludes
from the common rights of men, the maintainers of
certain opinions. Nothing treasonable, immoral, dangerous to the peace of society, is alleged; the crime,
the civil crime, as it now becomes, consists solely in
opinions. The law of Constantine, which granted special
immunities to certain of his subjects, might perhaps,
with some show of equity, confine those immunities to a
particular class.[o] But the gradually darkening statutes

[n] "Hæreticorum vocabulo continen-
tur, et latis adversus eos sanctionibus
debent succumbere, qui vel levi argu-
mento à judicio Catholicæ religionis et
tramite *detecti* fuerint deviare." This
is a law of Arcadius. The practice
was more lenient than the law.

[o] The first law of Constantine re-
stricts the immunities which he grants
to Catholics. Cod. Theodos. xvi.

proceed from the withholding of privileges to the prohibition of meetings,[p] then through confiscation,[q] the refusal of the common right of bequeathing property, fine,[r] exile,[s] to capital punishment.[t] The latter, indeed, was enacted only against some of the more obscure sects, and some of the Donatists, whose turbulent and seditious conduct might demand the interference of the civil power; but still they are condemned not as rebels and insurgents but as heretics.[u]

In building up this vast and majestic fabric of the hierarchy, though individuals might be actuated by personal ambition or interest, and the narrow corporate spirit might rival loftier motives in the consolidation of ecclesiastical power, yet the great object, which was steadily, if dimly seen, was the advancement of mankind in religion, and through religion to temporal and eternal happiness. Dazzled by the glorious spectacle of provinces, of nations, gradually brought within the pale of Christianity, the great men of the fourth century of Christianity were not and could not be endowed with prophetic sagacity to discern the abuses of sacerdotal domination, and the tyranny which, long centuries after, might be exercised over the human mind in the name of religion. *We* may trace the

Objects of the great defenders of the hierarchical power.

---

[p] The law of Gratian (IV.) confiscates the houses or even fields in which heretical conventicles are held. See also law of Theodosius, viii.

[q] Leges xi. xii.

[r] Ibid. xxi.

[s] Ibid. xviii. liii. lviii.

[t] The law of Theodosius enacts this not against the general body, but some small sections of Manicheans, " Summo supplicio et inexpiabili pœnâ jube-

mus affligi." ix. This law sanctions the ill-omened name of inquisitors. Compare law xxxv. The "interminata pœna " of law lx. is against Eunomians, Arians, and Macedonians.

[u] Ad Heraclianum, lvi. The imperial laws against second baptisms are still more singular invasions of the civil upon the ecclesiastical authority. xvi. tit. vi.

hierarchical principles of Cyprian or of Ambrose to what may seem their natural consequences, religious crusades and the fires of the inquisition; *we* may observe the tendency of unsocial monasticism to quench the charities of life, to harden into cruelty, grovel into licentiousness, and brood over its own ignorance; *we* may trace the predestinarian doctrines of Augustine darkening into narrow bigotry, or maddening to uncharitable fanaticism; *they* only contemplated, *they* only could contemplate, a great moral and religious power opposing civil tyranny, or at least affording a refuge from it; purifying domestic morals, elevating and softening the human heart;[x] a wholesome and benevolent force compelling men by legitimate means to seek wisdom, virtue, and salvation; the better part of mankind withdrawing, in holy prudence and wise timidity, from the corruptions of a foul and cruel age, and devoting itself to its own self-

---

[x] The laws bear some pleasing testimonies to the activity of Christian benevolence in many of the obscure scenes of human wretchedness. See the humane law regarding prisoners, that they might have proper food, and the use of the bath. "Nec deerit antistitum Christianæ religionis cura laudabilis, quæ ad observationem constituti judicis hanc ingerat monitionem." The Christian bishop was to take care that the judge did his duty. Cod. Theodos. ix. 3. 7.

As early as the reign of Valentinian and Valens, prisoners were released at Easter (ob diem paschæ, quem intimo corde celebramus), excepting those committed for the crimes of treason, poisoning, magic, adultery, rape, or homicide, ix. 36. 3. 4. These statutes were constantly renewed, with the addition of some more excepted crimes —sacrilege, robbery of tombs, and coining.

There is a very singular law of Arcadius prohibiting the clergy and the monks from interfering with the execution of the laws, and forcibly taking away condemned criminals from the hands of justice. They were allowed, at the same time, the amplest privilege of merciful intercession. This was connected with the privilege of asylum. Codex Theodos. ix. 40. 16.

There is another singular law by which corporal punishments were not to be administered in Lent, except against the Isaurian robbers, who were to be dealt with without delay. ix. 35. 5, 6, 7.

advancement to the highest spiritual perfection; and the general pious assertion of the universal and unlimited providence and supremacy of God. None but the hopeful achieve great revolutions; and what hopes could equal those which the loftier Christian minds might justly entertain of the beneficent influences of Christianity?

We cannot wonder at the growth of the ecclesiastical power, if the Church were merely considered as a new sphere in which human genius, virtue, and benevolence, might develope their unimpeded energies, and rise above the general debasement. This was almost the only way in which any man could devote great abilities or generous activity to a useful purpose with reasonable hopes of success. The civil offices were occupied by favour and intrigue, often acquired most easily and held most permanently by the worst men for the worst purposes. The utter extinction of freedom had left no course of honourable distinction, as an honest advocate or an independent jurist. Literature was worn out; rhetoric had degenerated into technical subtlety; philosophy had lost its hold upon the mind. Even the great military commands were filled by fierce and active barbarians, on whose energy Rome relied for the protection of her frontiers. In the Church alone was security, influence, independence, fame, even wealth, and the opportunity of serving mankind. The pulpit was the only rostrum from which the orator would be heard; feeble as was the voice of Christian poetry, it found an echo in the human heart. The episcopate was the only office of dignity which could be obtained without meanness, or exercised without fear. Whether he sought the peace of a contemplative, or the usefulness of an active life, this was the only sphere for

Dignity and advantage of the clerical station.

the man of conscious mental strength; and if he felt
the inward satisfaction that he was either securing his
own, or advancing the salvation of others, the lofty mind
would not hesitate what path to choose through the
darkening and degraded world.

The just way to consider the influence of the Christian
General
influence of
the clergy.
hierarchy (without which, in its complete and
vigorous organisation, it is clear that the religion could not have subsisted throughout these ages of
disaster and confusion) is to imagine, if possible, the
state of things without that influence.   Consider a
tyranny the most oppressive and debasing, without
any principles of free or hopeful resistance, or resistance
only attainable by the complete dismemberment of the
Roman empire and its severance into a number of
hostile states; the general morals at the lowest state of
depravation, with nothing but a religion totally without
influence, and a philosophy without authority, to correct
its growing cruelty and licentiousness; a very large
portion of mankind in hopeless slavery, with nothing to
mitigate it but the insufficient control of fear in the
master, or occasional gleams of humanity or political
foresight in the government, with no inward consolation
or feeling of independence whatever.   In the midst of
this, contemplate the invasion of hostile barbarians in
every quarter, and the complete wreck of civilisation;
with no commanding influence to assimilate the adverse
races, without the protection or conservative tendency of
any religious feeling to soften them, and at length to re-
organise and re-create, literature, the arts of building,
painting, and music; the Latin language itself breaking
up into as many countless dialects as there were settlements of barbarous tribes, without a guardian or sacred
depositary.   It is difficult adequately to darken the

picture of ignorance, violence, confusion, and wretchedness; but without this adequate conception of the
probable state of the world without it, it is impossible to judge with fairness or candour the obli-
gations of Europe and of civilisation to the Christian
hierarchy.

CHAPTER II.

Public Spectacles.

THE Greek and Roman inhabitants of the empire were
Public   attached with equal intensity to their favourite
spectacles.   spectacles, whether of more solemn religious
origin, or of lighter and more festive kind. These
amusements are perhaps more congenial to the southern
character, from the greater excitability of temperament,
the less variable climate, which rarely interferes with
enjoyment in the open air; and throughout the Roman
world, they had long been fostered by those republican
institutions which gave to every citizen a place and an
interest in all public ceremonials, privileges which, in this
respect, long outlived the institutions themselves. The
population of the great capitals had preserved only the
dangerous and pernicious part of freedom, the power of
subsisting either without regular industry or with but
moderate exertion. The perpetual distribution of corn,
and the various largesses at other times, emancipated
them in a great degree from the wholesome control of
their own necessities; and a vast and uneducated multitude was maintained in idle and dissolute inactivity. It
was absolutely necessary to occupy much of this vacant
time with public diversions; and the invention, the
wealth, and the personal exertions of the higher orders,
were taxed to gratify this insatiable appetite. Policy
demanded that which ambition and the love of popularity had freely supplied in the days of the republic,

and which personal vanity continued to offer, though
with less prodigal and willing munificence. The more
retired and domestic habits of Christianity might in
some degree seclude a sect from the public diversions,
but it could not change the nature or the inveterate
habits of a people : it was either swept along by, or
contented itself with giving a new direction to, the
impetuous and irresistible current; it was obliged to
substitute some new excitement for that which it
peremptorily prohibited, and reluctantly to acquiesce in
that which it was unable to suppress.

Christianity had cut off that part of the public spectacles which belonged exclusively to Paganism. Even
if all the temples at Rome were not, as Jerome asserts,
covered with dust and cobwebs,[a] yet, notwithstanding
the desperate efforts of the old aristocracy, the tide
of popular interest, no doubt, set away from the deserted
and mouldering fanes of the Heathen deities, and towards
the churches of the Christians. And if this was the
case in Rome, at Constantinople and throughout the
empire, the Pagan ceremonial was either extinct, or
gradually expiring, or lingering on in unimpressive regularity. On the other hand, the modest and unimposing
ritual of Christianity naturally, and almost necessarily,
expanded into pomp and dignity. To the deep devotion
of the early Christians the place and circumstances
of worship were indifferent : piety finds everywhere its
own temple. In the low and unfurnished chamber,
in the forest, in the desert, in the catacomb, the
Christian adored his Redeemer, prayed, chanted his
hymn, and partook of the sacred elements. Devotion

---

[a] " Fuligine et aranearum telis omnia
Romæ templa cooperta sunt : inun-
dans populus ante delubra semiruta,
currit ad martyrum tumulos." Epist.
lvii. p. 590.

wanted no accessories; faith needed no subsidiary excitement; or if it did, it found them in the peril, the
novelty, the adventurous and stirring character of the
scene, or in the very meanness and poverty, contrasted
with the gorgeous worship which it had abandoned; in
the mutual attachment, and in the fervent emulation,
which spreads throughout a small community.

But among the more numerous and hereditary Christians of this period, the temple and the solemn service
were indispensable to enforce and maintain the devotion.
Religion was not strong enough to disdain, and far too
Religious   earnest to decline, any legitimate means of ad-
ceremonial. vancing her cause. The whole ceremonial was
framed with the art which arises out of the intuitive
perception of that which is effective towards its end. That
which was felt to be awful was adopted to enforce awe;
that which drew the people to the church, and affected
their minds when there, became sanctified to the use of
the Church. The edifice itself arose more lofty with the
triumph of the faith, and enlarged itself to receive the
multiplying votaries. Christianity disdained that its
God and its Redeemer should be less magnificently
honoured than the dæmons of Paganism. In the service it delighted to transfer and to breathe, as it were, a
sublimer sense into the common appellations of the
Pagan worship, whether from the ordinary ceremonial,
or the more secret mysteries. The church became
a temple;[b] the table of the communion an altar; the
celebration of the Eucharist the appalling or the un-
bloody sacrifice.[c] The ministering functionaries multi-

---

[b] Ambrose and Lactantius, and
even Irenæus, use this term. See
Bingham, b. viii. 1. 4.

[c] The φρίκτη, or the ἀναίμακτος
θυσία.

plied with the variety of the ceremonial; each was
consecrated to his office by a lower kind of ordination;
but a host of subordinate attendants by degrees swelled
the officiating train. The incense, the garlands, the
lamps, all were gradually adopted by zealous rivalry, or
seized as the lawful spoils of vanquished Paganism and
consecrated to the service of Christ.

The Church rivalled the old Heathen mysteries in
expanding by slow degrees its higher privileges. Christianity was itself the great Mystery, unfolded gradually
and in general after a long and searching probation. It
still reserved the power of opening at once its gates to
the more distinguished proselytes, and of jealously and
tardily unclosing them to more doubtful neophytes. It
permitted its sanctuary, as it were, to be stormed at
once by eminent virtue and unquestioned zeal; but the
common mass of mankind were never allowed to consider
it less than a hard-won privilege to be received into the
Church; and this boon was not to be dispensed with
lavish or careless hands.[d] Its preparatory ceremonial of
abstinence, personal purity, ablution, secrecy, closely
resembled that of the Pagan mysteries (perhaps each
may have contributed to the other); so the theologic
dialect of Christianity spoke the same language. Yet
Christianity substituted for the feverish enthusiasm
of some of these rites, and the phantasmagoric terrors
of others, with their vague admonitions to purity, a
searching but gently administered moral discipline, and
more sober religious excitement. It retained, indeed,

---

[d] It is one of the bitterest charges
of Tertullian against the heretics, that
they did not keep up this distinction
between the catechumens and the
faithful. "Imprimis quis catechu-
menus, quis fidelis, incertum est:
pariter adeunt, pariter orant." Even
the Heathen were admitted; thus
"pearls were cast before swine." De
Præscript. Hæret. c. 41.

much of the dramatic power, though under another form.

The divisions between the different orders of worship-
pers enforced by the sacerdotal authority, and observed with humble submission by the people, could not but impress the mind with astonishment and awe. The stranger, on entering the spacious open court, which was laid out before the more splendid churches, with porticos or cloisters on each side, beheld first the fountain or tank, where the worshippers were expected to wash their hands, and purify themselves, as it were, for the divine presence. Lingering in these porticos, or approaching timidly the threshold which they dared not pass, or, at the farthest, entering only into the first porch, or vestibule,[e] and pressing around the disciples to solicit their prayers, he would observe men, pale, dejected, clad in sackcloth, oppressed with the profound consciousness of their guilt, acquiescing in the justice of the ecclesiastical censure which

Divisions of the church.

The porch.

---

[e] There is much difficulty and confusion respecting these divisions of the church. The fact probably is, that, according to the period or the local circumstances, the structure and the arrangement were more or less complicated. Tertullian says distinctly, "non modò limine verum omni ecclesiæ tecto submovemus." Where the churches were of a simpler form, and had no roofed narthex or vestibule, these penitents stood in the open court before the church; even later, the "flentes" and the "hiemantes" formed a particular class.

A canon of St. Gregory Thauma-turgus gives the clearest view of these arrangements: Ἡ πρόσκλαυσις ἔξω τῆς πύλης τοῦ εὐκτηρίου ἐστὶν, ἔνθα ἑστῶτα τὸν ἁμαρτάνοντα χρὴ τῶν εἰσιόντων δεῖσθαι πιστῶν ὑπὲρ αὐτοῦ εὔχεσθαι· ἡ ἀκρόασις ἔνδοθι τῆς πύλης ἐν τῷ νάρθηκι, ἔνθα ἑστάναι χρὴ τὸν ἡμαρτηκότα, ἕως τῶν κατηχουμένων, καὶ ἐντεῦθεν ἐξέρχεσθαι· ἀκούων γὰρ φησὶ τῶν γραφῶν καὶ τῆς διδασκαλίας, ἐκβαλέσθω, καὶ μὴ ἀξιούσθω προσευχῆς· ἡ δὲ ὑπό-πτωσις, ἵνα ἔσωθεν τῆς πύλης τοῦ ναοῦ ἱστάμενος, μετὰ τῶν κατηχουμένων ἐξέρχηται· ἡ σύστασις, ἵνα συνίσταται τοῖς πιστοῖς καὶ μὴ ἐξέρχηται μετὰ τῶν κατηχουμένων· τελευταῖον ἡ μέθεξις τῶν ἁγιασμά-των. Apud Labbe, Conc. i. p 842.

altogether excluded them from the christian community.
These were the first class of penitents, men of The
notorious guilt, whom only a long period of penitents.
this humiliating probation could admit even within the
hearing of the sacred service. As he advanced to
the gates, he must pass the scrutiny of the doorkeepers,
who guarded the admission into the church, and distributed each class of worshippers into their proper
place. The stranger, whether Heathen or Jew, might
enter into the part assigned to the catechumens or
novices and the penitents of the second order (the
hearers), that he might profit by the religious instruction.[f] He found himself in the first division of
the main body of the church, of which the walls   The narthex.
were lined by various marbles, the roof often ceiled
with mosaic, and supported by lofty columns with gilded
capitals; the doors were inlaid with ivory or silver; the
distant altar glittered with precious stones.[g] In the
midst of the nave stood the pulpit, or reading-desk (the
ambo), around which were arranged the singers, who
chanted to the most solemn music, poetry, much of it

[f] This part of the church was
usually called the narthex. But this
term, I believe, of the sixth century,
was not used with great precision, or
rather, perhaps, was applied to different parts of the church, according
to their greater or less complexity of
structure. It is sometimes used for
the porch or vestibule : in this sense
there were several nartheces (St.
Sophia had four). Mamachi (vol. i.
p. 216), insists that it was divided
from the nave by a wall. But this
cannot mean the narthex into which
the ἀκροώμενοι were admitted, as the

object of their admission was that
they might hear the service.
   "Episcopus nullum prohibeat intrare
ecclesiam, et audire verbum Dei, sive
hæreticum, sive Judæum usque ad
missam catechumenorum." Concil.
Carthag. iv. c. 84.
   [g] " Alii ædificent ecclesias, vestiant
parietes marmorum crustis, colum-
narum moles advehant, earumque
deaurent capita, pretiosum ornatum
non sentientia, ebore argentoque valvas,
et gemmis distinguant altaria. Non
reprehendo, non abnuo." Hieronym.
Epist. viii. ad Demetriad.

familiar to the Jew, as belonging to his own sacred writings, to the Heathen full of the noblest images, expressive of the divine power and goodness; adapting itself with the most exquisite versatility to every devout emotion, melting into the most pathetic tenderness, or swelling out into the most appalling grandeur. The pulpit was then ascended by one of the inferior order, the reader of certain portions or extracts from the sacred volumes, in which God himself spoke to the awe-struck auditory. He was succeeded by an orator of a higher dignity, a presbyter or a bishop, who sometimes addressed the people from the steps which led up to the chancel, sometimes chose the more convenient and elevated position of the ambo.[h] He was a man usually of the highest attainments and eloquence, and instead of the frivolous and subtile questions which the Pagan was accustomed to hear in the schools of rhetoric or philosophy, he fearlessly agitated and peremptorily decided on such eternally and universally awakening topics as the responsibility of man before God, the immortality and future destination of the soul; topics of which use could not deaden the interest to the believer, but which, to an unaccustomed ear, were as startling as important. The mute attention of the whole assembly was broken only by uncontrollable acclamations, which frequently interrupted the more moving preachers. Around the pulpit was the last order of penitents, who prostrated themselves in humble homage during the prayers and the benediction of the bishop.

The preacher.

---

[h] Chrysostom generally preached from the ambo. Socr. vi. 5. Sozomen, viii. 5. Both usages prevailed in the West.

"Seu te conspicuis gradibus venerabilis aræ
Concionaturum plebs sedula circumsistat."
    Sid. Apollon. can. xvi.
"Fronte sub adversâ gradibus sublime tribunal
Tollitur, antistes prædicat unde Deum."
    Prudent. Hymn. ad Hippolyt.

Here the steps of the profane stranger must pause;
an insuperable barrier, which he could not pass without
violence, secluded the initiate from the society of the
less perfect. Yet, till the more secret ceremonial began,
he might behold, at dim and respectful distance, the
striking scene, first of the baptized worshippers in their
order, the females in general in galleries above (the virgins separate from the matrons). Beyond, in still
further secluded sanctity, on an elevated semicircle,
around the bishop, sat the clergy, attended by the sub-
deacons, acolyths, and those of inferior order. Even the
gorgeous throne of the Emperor was below this platform. Before them was the mystic and awful table, the
altar, as it began to be called in the fourth century, over
which was sometimes suspended a richly-wrought canopy
(the ciborium): the altar was covered with fine linen.
In the third century, the simpler vessels of glass or
other cheap material had given place to silver and gold.
In the later persecutions, the cruelty of the Heathen
was stimulated by their avarice; and some of the
sufferers, while they bore their own agonies with patience, were grieved to the heart to see the sacred
vessels pillaged, and turned to profane or indecent uses.
In the Eastern churches, richly embroidered curtains
overshadowed the approach to the altar, or light doors
secluded altogether the Holy of Holies from the profane
gaze of the multitude.

Such was the ordinary Christian ceremonial as it
addressed the mass of mankind. But at a certain time,
the uninitiate were dismissed, the veil was dropped
which shrouded the hidden rites, the doors were closed,
profane steps might not cross the threshold of the baptistery, or linger in the church, when the Liturgy of the
faithful, the office of the Eucharist, began. The veil of

concealment was first spread over the peculiar rites of Christianity from caution. The religious assemblies were, strictly speaking, unlawful, and they were shrouded Secrecy of the in secrecy lest they should be disturbed by the sacraments. intrusion of their watchful enemies;[1] and it was this unavoidable secrecy which gave rise to the frightful fables of the Heathen concerning the nature of these murderous or incestuous banquets. As they could not be public, of necessity they took the form of mysteries, and as mysteries became objects of jealousy and of awe. As the assemblies became more public, that seclusion of the more solemn rites was retained from dread and reverence, which was commenced from fear. Though profane curiosity no longer dared to take a hostile character, it was repelled from the sacred ceremony. Of the mingled multitude, Jews and Heathens, the incipient believers, the hesitating converts, who must be permitted to hear the Gospel of Christ, or the address of the preacher, none could be admitted to the sacraments. It was natural to exclude them, not merely by regulation and by the artificial division of the church into separate parts, but by the majesty which invested the last solemn rites. That which had concealed itself from fear, became itself fearful: it was no longer a timid mystery which fled the light, but an unapproachable communion with the Deity, which would not brook profane intrusion. It is an extraordinary indication of the power of Christianity, that rites in themselves so simple, and of which the nature, after all the concealment, could not but be known, should assume such unquestioned majesty ; that, however significant, the

[1] " Tot hostes ejus, quot extranei . . . quotidiè obsidemur, quotidiè prodimur, in ipsis plurimùm cœtibus et congregationibus opprimimur." Tertull. Apologet. 7.

simple lustration by water, and the partaking of bread
and wine, should so affect the awe-struck imagination,
as to make men suppose themselves ignorant of what
these sacraments really were, and even when the high-
wrought expectations were at length gratified, to experience no dissatisfaction at their plain, and in themselves,
unappalling ceremonies. The mysteriousness was no
doubt fed and heightened by the regulations of the
clergy, and by the impressiveness of the service,[k] but it
grew of itself out of the profound and general religious
sentiment. The baptistery and the altar were closed
against the uninitiate, but if they had been open, men
would scarcely have ventured to approach them. The
knowledge of the nature of the sacraments was reserved
for the baptized; but it was because the minds of the
unbaptized were sealed by trembling reverence, and
shuddered to anticipate the forbidden knowledge. The
hearers had a vague knowledge of these mysteries floating around them, the initiate heard it within.[m] To add
to the impressiveness, night was sometimes spread over
the Christian as over the Pagan mysteries.[n]

---

[k] This was the avowed object of
the clergy. " Catechumenis sacramenta
fidelium non produntur, non ideò fit,
quod ea ferre non possunt, sed ut ab
eis tanto ardentiùs concupiscantur,
quanto honorabiliùs occultantur." Augustin. in Johan. 96. " Mortalium
generi naturâ datum est, ut abstrusa
fortiùs quærat, ut negata magis ambiat,
ut tardiùs adepta plus diligat, et eo
flagrantiùs ametur veritas, quo vel
diutiùs desideratur, vel laboriosiùs
quæritur, vel tardiùs invenitur." Clau-
dius Mamert., quoted by Casaubon in
Baron. p. 497.

[m] The inimitable pregnancy of the

Greek language expresses this by two
verbs differently compounded. Cyril
of Jerusalem, in his Procatechesis,
states the Catechumens περιηχεῖσθαι,
the Faithful ἐνηχεῖσθαι, by the meaning of the mysteries.

[n] " Noctu ritus multi in mysteriis
pergebantur; noctu etiam initiatio
Christianorum inchoabatur." Casaubon, p. 490, with the quotations sub-
joined. This might have originated in
the vigil of Easter being thus prolonged
to midnight. It was an old Jewish
tradition that the Messiah would
come at the Passover at midnight.
" Dicamus aliquid, quod forsitan lectori

At Easter, and at Pentecost,[o] and in some places at
the Epiphany, the rite of Baptism was administered publicly (that is, in the presence of
the Faithful) to all the converts of the year, excepting
those few instances in which it had been expedient to
perform the ceremony without delay, or where the timid
Christian put it off till the close of life ;[p] a practice for
a long time condemned in vain by the clergy. But the
fact of the delay shows how deeply the importance and
efficacy of the rite were rooted in the Christian mind.
It was a complete lustration of the soul. The Neophyte
emerged from the waters of Baptism in a state of
perfect innocence. 'The Dove (the Holy Spirit) was
constantly hovering over the font, and sanctifying the
waters to the mysterious ablution of all the sins of
the passed life. If the soul suffered no subsequent
taint, it passed at once to the realms of purity and bliss ;
the heart was purified ; the understanding illuminated ;
the spirit was clothed with immortality.[q] Robed in

Baptism.

---

utile sit. Traditio Judæorum est
Christum mediâ nocte venturum in
similitudinem Ægyptii temporis, quando Pascha celebratum est, et extermi-
nator venit et Dominus super taber-
nacula transiit et sanguine agni postes
nostrarum frontium consecrati sunt.
Unde reor *traditionem apostolicam* per-
mansisse ut in die vigiliarum paschæ
ante noctis dimidium populos dimittere
non liceat expectantes adventum Christi,
et postquam illud tempus transierit,
securitate præsumta festum cunctis
agentibus diem." Hieron. in Matt. 24.
  [o] At Constantinople, it appears from
Chrysostom, baptism did not take
place at Pentecost. Montfauçon, Diatribe, p. 179.

[p] The memorable example of Constantine may for a time not only have
illustrated but likewise confirmed the
practice. See Gibbon's note (vol. iii.
p. 266) and the author's observations.
  [q] Gregory of Nazianzum almost
exhausts the copiousness of the Greek
language in speaking of Baptism,—
δῶρον καλοῦμεν, χάρισμα, βάπτισμα,
χρίσμα, φώτισμα, ἀφθαρσίας ἔνδυμα,
λοῦτρον παλιγγενεσίας, σφραγίδα,
πᾶν ὅτι τίμιον. Orat. xl. de Baptism.
  Almost all the Fathers of this age,
Basil, the two Gregories, Ambrose (de
Sacram) Augustine, have treatises on
baptism, and vie, as it were, with
each other, in their praises of its
importance and efficacy.

white, emblematic of spotless purity,[r] the candidate
approached the baptistery, in the larger churches a
separate building. There he uttered the solemn vows
which pledged him to his religion.[s] The symbolising
genius of the East added some significant ceremonies.
The Catechumen turned to the West, the realm of
Satan, and thrice renounced his power ; he turned to the
East to adore the Sun of Righteousness,[t] and to pro-
claim his compact with the Lord of Life. The mystic
trinal number prevailed throughout ; the vow was three-
fold, and thrice pronounced. The baptism was usually
by immersion ; the stripping off the clothes was emblematic of "putting off the old man ;" but baptism by
sprinkling was allowed, according to the exigency of the
case. The water itself became, in the vivid language
of the Church, the blood of Christ : it was compared, by
a fanciful analogy, to the Red Sea : the daring metaphors
of some of the Fathers might seem to assert a transmutation of its colour.[u]

The Sacrament of the Lord's Supper imperceptibly
acquired the solemnity, the appellation, of a
sacrifice. The poetry of devotional language   Eucharist.
kindled into the most vivid and realising expressions of
awe and adoration. No imagery could be too bold, no
words too glowing, to impress the soul more profoundly
with the sufferings, the divinity, the intimate union of
the Redeemer with his disciples. The invisible presence

---

[r] "Unde parens sacro ducit de fonte sacerdos
Infantes niveos corpore, corde, habitu."
                              Paulin. ad Sever.

[s] Chrysostom in two places gives
the Eastern profession of faith, which
was extremely simple, "I renounce
Satan, his pomp and worship, and am
united to Christ. I believe in the
resurrection of the dead." See references in Montfauçon, *ubi suprà.*

[t] Cyril. Catech. Mystag. Hieronym.
in Amos, vi. 14.

[u] "Unde rubet Baptismus Christi,
nisi Christi sanguine consecratur." Augustin. Tract. in Johan. Compare
Bingham, xi. 10. 4.

of the Lord, which the devout felt within the whole
church, but more particularly in its more holy and
secluded part, was gradually concentrated as it were
upon the altar. The mysterious identification of the
Redeemer with the consecrated elements was first felt
by the mind, till, at a later period, a material and corporeal transmutation began to be asserted; that which
the earlier Fathers, in their boldest figure, called a
bloodless sacrifice, became an actual oblation of the
body and blood of Christ. But all these fine and subtile
distinctions belong to a later theology. In the dim
vagueness, in the ineffable and inexplicable mystery,
consisted much of its impressiveness on the believer, the
awe and dread of the uninitiate.

These Sacraments were the sole real Mysteries; their
nature and effects were the hidden knowledge which
was revealed to the perfect alone.[x] In Alexandria, where
the imitation or rivalry of the ancient mysteries, in that
seat of the Platonic learning, was most likely to prevail,
the catechetical school of Origen attempted to form
the simpler truths of the Gospel into a regular and
progressive system of development.[y] The works of

---

[x] "Quid est quod occultum est et
non publicum in Ecclesiâ, Sacramentum Baptismi, Sacramentum Eucha-
ristiæ. Opera nostra bona vident et
Pagani, Sacramenta vero occultantur
illis." Augustin., in Psalm, 103. Ordination appears to have been a secret
rite. Casaubon, p. 495. Compare
this treatise of Casaubon, the xivth of
his Exercitationes Anti-Baronianæ,
which in general is profound and
judicious.

[y] Upon this ground rests the famous
Disciplina Arcani, that esoteric doctrine, within which lurked every thing

which later ages thought proper to
dignify by the name of the traditions
of the church. This theory was first
fully developed by Schelstrate, " De
Disciplinâ Arcani," and is very clearly
stated in Pagi, sub Ann. 118. It
rests chiefly on a passage of Origen
(contra Cels. i. 7.) who, after asserting
the publicity of the main doctrines of
Christianity, the incarnation, passion,
and resurrection of Christ, and the
general resurrection to judgement,
admits that Christianity, like Philosophy, had some secret and esoteric
doctrines. Pagi argues that, as the

Clement of Alexandria were progressive, addressed to the Heathen, the Catechumen, the perfect Christian. But the doctrine which was there reserved for the initiate had a strange tinge of Platonic mysticism. In the church in general the only esoteric doctrine, as I have said, related to the Sacraments. After the agitation of the Trinitarian question, there seems to have been some desire to withdraw that holy mystery likewise from the gaze of the profane, which the popular tumults, the conflicts between the Arians and Athanasians of the lowest orders, in the streets of Constantinople and Alexandria, show to have been by no means successful. The apocalyptic hymn, the Trisagion, makes a part indeed of all the older liturgies, which belong to the end of the third or beginning of the fourth century. Even the simple prayer of our Lord, which might seem appropriate to universal man, and so intended by the Saviour himself, was considered too holy to be uttered by unbaptised lips. It was said that none but the baptised could properly address the Almighty as his Father.[z]

That care which Christianity had assumed over the whole life of man, it did not abandon after *Christian* death. In that solemn season it took in *funerals.* charge the body, which, though mouldering into dust, was to be revived for the resurrection. The respect and honour which human nature pays to the remains of the dead, and which, among the Greeks especially, had a strong religious hold upon the feelings, was still more profoundly sanctified by the doctrines and usages of Christianity. The practice of inhumation which prevailed in Egypt and Syria, and in other parts of the

Trinity was not among the public, it must have been among the esoteric tenets. There is no real ground for it. [z] Bingham, i. 4. 7. and x. 5. 9.

East, was gradually extended over the whole western
world by Christianity.[a] The funeral pyre went out of
use, and the cemeteries, which from the earliest period
belonged to the Christians, were gradually enlarged for
the general reception, not of the ashes only in their
urns, but for the entire remains of the dead. The
Eastern practice of embalming was so general,[b] that
Tertullian boasts that the Christians consumed more
of the merchandise of Sabæa in their interments than
the Heathens in their fumigations before the altars of
their Gods.[c] The general tone of the simple inscriptions spoke of death but as a sleep; "he sleeps
in peace" was the common epitaph: the very name
of the inclosure, the *cemetery,* implied the same
trust in its temporary occupancy; those who were
committed to the earth only awaited the summons
to a new life.[d] Gradually the cemetery was, in some
places, closely connected with the church. Where

---

[a] " Nec, ut creditis, ullum damnum
sepulturæ timemus, sed veterem et
meliorem consuetudinem humandi fre-
quentamus." The speaker goes on, in
very elegant language, to adduce the
analogy of the death and revival of
nature,—" Expectandum etiam nobis
corporis ver est." Minuc. Fel. edit.
Ouzel, p. 327.

During the time of the plague in
Alexandria and Carthage, the Christians not only buried their own dead,
but likewise those of the Pagans.
Dion. Alex. apud Euseb. Hist. vii. 22.
Pontius, in Vitâ Cypriani. Compare
a curious Essay in the Vermischte
Schriften of Böttiger, iii. 14. Ver-
brennen oder Beerdigen.

[b] " Titulumque et frigida saxa
    Liquido spargemus odore."
                Prudent. Hym. de Exeq.

" Martyris hi tumulum studeant perfundere
    nardo ;
Et medicata pio referant unguenta se-
    pulcro."
                Paul. Nol. in Nat. S. Fel.

[c] Apologet. c. 42. Boldetti affirms
that these odours were plainly percep-
tible on opening some of the Christian
cemeteries at Rome. See Mamachi,
Costumi dei Christiani, iii. p. 83.
The judge in the acts of Tarachus
(Ruinart, p. 385) says, "you expect
that your women will bury your body
with ointments and spices."

[d] " Hinc maxima cura sepulchris
    Impenditur, hinc resolutos
    Honor ultimus accipit artus
    Et funeris ambitus ornat.
        *   *   *
    Quid nam tibi saxa cavata,
    Quid pulchra volunt monumenta?
    Res quod nisi creditur illis
    Non mortua, sed data somno."
                Prudent. in Exeq. Defunct.

the rigid interdict against burying within the walls
of cities was either inapplicable or not enforced,
the open court before the church became the place
of burial.[e]
Christian funerals began early in their period of
security and opulence to be celebrated with great
magnificence. Jerome compares the funeral procession
of Fabiola to the triumphs of Camillus, Scipio, or
Pompey. The character of this female, who founded
the first hospital in Rome, and lavished a splendid
fortune in alms-giving, may have mainly contributed
to the strong interest excited by her interment. All
Rome was poured forth. The streets, the windows,
the tops of houses, were crowded with spectators.
Processions of youths and of old men preceded the
bier, chaunting the praises of the deceased. As it
passed, the churches were crowded, and psalms were
sung, and their golden roofs rang with the sublime
Alleluia.

The doctrine of the Resurrection of the body
deepened the common and natural feeling of
respect for the remains of the dead:[f] the

Worship of
the Martyrs.

---

[e] There is a law of Gratian, Valentinian and Theodosius, forbidding burial, or the deposition of urns (which shows that cremation was still common), within the walls of Constantinople, even within the cemeteries of the apostles or martyrs. Cod. Theod. ix. 17. 6.

[f] In one of the very curious essays of M. Raoul Rochette, Mémoires de l'Académie, he has illustrated the extraordinary care with which the heathen buried along with the remains of the dead, every kind of utensil, implement of trade, down to the dolls of children; even food and knives and forks. This appears from all the tombs which are opened, from the most ancient Etruscan to the most modern heathen sepulchres. "Il y avait là une notion confuse et grossière sans doute de l'immortalité de l'âme, mais il s'y trouvait aussi la preuve sensible et palpable de cet instinct de l'homme, qui répugne à l'idée de la destruction de son être, et qui y résiste de toutes les forces de son intelligence et de toutes les erreurs même de la raison," p. 689. But it is a more remarkable fact that the Christians long adhered

worship of the relics of saints and martyrs still farther
contributed to the same effect. If the splendid but
occasional ceremony of the apotheosis of the deceased
emperor was exploded, a ceremony which, lavished as
it frequently had been on the worst and basest of
mankind, however it might amuse and excite the
populace, could not but provoke the contempt of the
virtuous; in the Christian world a continual, and in
some respects more rational, certainly more modest,
apotheosis was constantly celebrated. The more distinguished Christians were dismissed, if not to absolute
deification, to immortality, to a state, in which they
retained profound interest in, and some influence over,
the condition of men. During the perilous and gloomy

---

to the same usages, notwithstanding
the purer and loftier notions of another
life bestowed by their religion. " La
première observation qui s'offre à
Boldetti lui-même et qui devra frapper
tous les esprits, c'est qu'en décorant
les tombeaux de leurs frères de tant
d'objets de pur ornement, ou d'usage
réel, les Chrétiens n'avaient pu être
dirigés que par ce motif d'espérance
qui leur faisait considérer le tombeau
comme un lieu de passage, d'où ils
devaient sortir avec toutes les conditions de l'immortalité, et la mort,
comme un *sommeil paisible*, au sein
duquel il ne pouvait leur être indifférent
de se trouver environnés des objets
qui leur avaient été chers durant la
vie ou de l'image de ces objets." Tom.
xiii. p. 692.

The heathen practice of burying
money, sometimes large sums, with
the dead, was the cause of the very
severe laws against the violations of
the tombs. In fact, these treasures
were so great, as to be a source of

revenue, which the Government was
unwilling to share with unlicensed
plunderers. " Et si aurum, ut dicitur,
vel argentum fuerit tuâ indagatione
detectum, compendio publico fideliter
vindicabis, ita tamen ut abstineatis a
cineribus mortuorum. Ædificia tegant
cineres, columnæ vel marmora ornent
sepulcra : talenta non teneant, qui
commercia virorum reliquerunt. Aurum enim justè sepulcro detrahitur,
ubi dominus non habetur ; imò culpæ
genus est inutiliter abdita relinquere
mortuorum, unde se vita potest susten-
tare viventium." Such are the instructions of the minister of Theodoric.
Cassiod. Var. iv. 34.

But it is still more strange, that
the Christians continued this practice,
particularly the piece of money in
the mouth, which the Heathen intended
for the payment of Charon. It continued to the time of Thomas Aquinas,
who, according to M. R. Rochette,
wrote against it.

days of persecution, the reverence for those who
endured martyrdom for the religion of Christ had
grown up out of the best feelings of man's improved
nature. Reverence gradually grew into veneration,.
worship, adoration. Although the more rigid theology
maintained a marked distinction between the honours
shown to the martyrs and that addressed to the
Redeemer and the Supreme Being, the line was too
fine and invisible not to be transgressed by excited
popular feeling. The Heathen writers constantly taunt
the Christians with the substitution of the new idolatry
for the old. The charge of worshipping dead men's
bones and the remains of malefactors, constantly
recurs. A Pagan philosopher, as late as the fourth
century, contemptuously selects some barbarous names
of African martyrs, and inquires whether they are
more worthy objects of worship than Minerva or
Jove.[g]

The festivals in honour of the martyrs were avowedly
instituted, or at least conducted on a sump-
tuous scale, in rivalry of the banquets which   Festivals.
formed so important and attractive a part of the Pagan
ceremonial.[h] Besides the earliest Agapæ, which gave
place to the more solemn Eucharist, there were other

---

[g] " Quis enim ferat Jovi fulmina
vibranti præferri Mygdonem ; Junoni,
Minervæ, Veneri, Vestæque Sanaem,
et cunctis (prô nefas) Diis immortali-
bus archimartyrem Nymphanionem,
inter quos Lucitas haud minore cultu
suscipitur atque alii interminato nu-
mero ; Diisque hominibusque odiosa
nomina." See Augustin. Epist. xvi.
p. 20.

[h] "Cum factâ pace, turbæ Gentilium
in Christianum nomen venire cupien-
tes, hoc impedirentur, quod dies festos
cum idolis suis solerent in abundantiâ
epularum et ebrietate consumere, nec
facilè ab his perniciosissimis et tam
vetustissimis voluptatibus se possent
abstinere, visum fuisse majoribus nostris, ut huic infirmitatis parti interim
parceretur, diesque festos, post eos,
quos relinquebant, alios in honorem
sanctorum martyrum vel non simili
sacrilegio, quamvis simili luxu cele-
brarent." Augustin. Epist. xxix. p. 52.

κinds of banquets, at marriages and funerals, called likewise Agapæ;[1] but those of the martyrs were the most costly and magnificent. The former were of a more private nature; the poor were entertained at the cost of the married couple or the relatives of the deceased. The relationship of the martyrs extended to the whole Christian community, and united all in one bond of piety. They belonged, by a new tie of spiritual kindred, to the whole Church.

By a noble metaphor, the day of the martyrs' death was considered that of their birth to immortality; and their birthdays became the most sacred and popular festivals of the Church.[k] At their sepulchres,[m] or more frequently, as the public worship became more costly, in stately churches erected either over their sepulchres, or in some more convenient situation but dedicated to their honour, these holy days commenced with the most impressive religious service. Hymns were sung in their praise (much of the early Christian poetry was composed for these occasions); the history of their lives and martyrdoms was read [n] (the legends which

---

[1] Gregory Nazianzen mentions the three kinds.

Οὐδ' ἱερὴν ἐπὶ δαῖτα γενέθλιον, ἠὲ θανόντος,
Η τινα νυμφιδίην σὺν πλεονέσσι θέων. Carm. x.

[k] Γενέθλια, natalitia. This custom was as early as the time of Polycarp. The day of his martyrdom was celebrated by the Church of Antioch. Euseb. lib. iv. 15. Compare Suicer, in voce γενέθλιον. Tertullian instances the offerings for the dead, and the annual celebration of the *birthdays* of the martyrs as of Apostolic tradition. "Oblationes pro defunctis, in natalibus annuâ die facimus." De

Coron. Mil. c. 2. Compare Exhortat. ad Cast. c. 11. In the treatise de Monogamiâ, he considers it among the sacred duties of a faithful widow, "offert annuis diebus dormitionis ejus."

[m] At Antioch, the remains of St. Juventinus and St. Maximinus were placed in a sumptuous tomb, and honoured with an annual festival. Theodoret, E. H. iii. 15.

[n] The author of the Acts of Ignatius wrote them, in part that the day of his martyrdom might be duly honoured. Act. Martyr. Ign. apud Cotelerium, vol. ii. p. 161. Compare Acta St. Polycarpi.

grew up into so fertile a subject for Christian mythic fable) ; panegyrical orations were delivered by the best preachers.[o] The day closed with an open banquet, in which all the worshippers were invited to partake. The wealthy Heathens had been accustomed to propitiate the Manes of their departed friends by these costly festivals ; the banquet was almost an integral part of the Heathen religious ceremony. The custom passed into the Church ; and with the Pagan feeling, the festival assumed a Pagan character of gaiety and joyous excitement, and even of luxury.[p] In some places, the confluence of worshippers was so great that, as in the earlier, and indeed the more modern religions of Asia, the neighbourhood of the more celebrated churches of the martyrs became marts for commerce, and fairs were established on those holidays.[q]

As the evening drew in, the solemn and religious

---

[o] There is a law of Theodosius the Great against selling the bodies of martyrs. Cod. Theod. ix. 17. 7.

[p] Lipsius considered these Agapæ derived from the Silicernium of the ancients. Ad Tac. Ann. vi. 5. " Quod illa parentalia superstitioni Gentilium essent similia." Such is the observation of Ambrose apud Augustin. Conf. vi. 2. Boldetti, a good Roman Catholic and most learned antiquarian, observes on this and other usages adopted from Paganism,—" Fu anchè sentimento de' prelati di chiesa di condescendere con ciò alla debolezza de' convertiti dal Gentilesimo, per istaccarli più soavemente dell' antichi superstizioni, non levando loro affetto ma bensì convertendo in buoni i loro divertimenti." Osservazioni, p. 46. Compare Marangoni's work " dei Cose Gentilesche."

[q] Already had the Montanist asceticism of Tertullian taken alarm at the abuse of the earlier festival, which had likewise degenerated from its pious use, and with his accustomed vehemence denounced the abuse of the Agapæ among the Catholics. " Apud te Agape in sæculis fervet, fides in culinis calet, spes in ferculis jacet. Sed major his est Agape, quia per hanc adolescentes tui cum sororibus dormiunt, appendices scilicet gulæ lascivia atque luxuria est." De Jejun. c. xvii.
There are many paintings in the catacombs representing Agapæ. Raoul Rochette, Mém. des Inscrip. p. 141. The author attributes to the Agapæ held in the cemeteries, many of the cups, glasses, &c. found in the catacombs.

thoughts gave way to other emotions; the wine flowed freely, and the healths of the martyrs were pledged, not unfrequently, to complete inebriety. All the luxuries of the Roman banquet were imperceptily introduced. Dances were admitted, pantomimic spectacles were exhibited,[r] the festivals were prolonged till late in the evening, or to midnight, so that other criminal irregularities profaned, if not the sacred edifice, its immediate neighbourhood.

The bishops had for some time sanctioned these pious hilarities with their presence; they had freely partaken of the banquets, and their attendants were accused of plundering the remains of the feast, which ought to have been preserved for the use of the poor.[s]

But the scandals which inevitably arose out of these paganised solemnities awoke the slumbering vigilance of the more serious prelates. The meetings were gradually suppressed: they are denounced, with the strongest condemnation of the luxury and license with which they were celebrated in the church of Antioch, by Gregory of Nazianzum[t] and by Chrysostom. They were autho-

---

[r] Böttiger, in his prolusion on the four ages of the drama (Opera Lat. p. 326), supposed, from a passage of St. Augustine, that there were scenic representations of the deaths of martyrs. Müller justly observes that the passage does not bear out this inference; and Augustine would scarcely have used such expressions unless of dances or mimes of less decent kind. "Sanctum locum invaserat pestilentia et *petulantia* saltationis; per totam noctem cantabantur *nefaria*, et cantantibus saltabatur." Augustin. in Natal.

Cyprian. p. 311.

[s] See the poem of Greg. Naz. de Div. Vit. Gener. Jerome admits the gross evils which took place during these feasts, but ascribes them to the irregularities of a youthful people, which ought not to raise a prejudice against the religion, or even against the usage. The bishops were sometimes called νεκροβόροι, feasters on the dead.

[t] Carm. ccxviii., ccxix., and Oratio vi. Chrysostom, Hom. in. S. M. Julian.

ritatively condemned by a canon of the Council of
Laodicea.[u] In the West, they were generally held in
Rome, and in other Italian cities, to a later period.
The authority of Ambrose had discountenanced, if not
entirely abolished them, in his diocese of Milan.[x] They
prevailed to the latest time in the churches of Africa,
where they were vigorously assailed by the eloquence of
Augustine. The Bishop of Hippo appeals to the example of Italy and other parts of the West, in which
they had never prevailed, and in which, wherever they
had been known, they had been suppressed by common
consent. But Africa did not surrender them without a
struggle. The Manichean Faustus, in the ascetic spirit
of his sect, taunts the orthodox with their idolatrous
festivals. " You have but substituted your Agapæ for
the sacrifices of the Heathen ; in the place of their idols
you have set up your martyrs, whom you worship with
the same ceremonies as the Pagans their gods. You
appease the Manes of the dead with wine and with
meat-offerings." The answer of Augustine indignantly
repels the charge of idolatry, and takes refuge in the
subtile distinction in the nature of the worship offered
to the martyrs. " The reverence paid to martyrs is the
same with that offered to holy men in this life, only
offered more freely, because they have finally triumphed
in their conflict. We adore God alone, we offer sacrifice
to no martyr, or to the soul of any saint, or to any
angel. * * Those who intoxicate themselves by the
sepulchres of the martyrs are condemned by sound
doctrine. It is a different thing to approve, and to
tolerate till we can amend. The discipline of Christians

---

[u] Conc. Harduin. t. i. p. 786.   gustin. Confessiones, vi. 2 ; see like-
[x] Ambros. de Jejun. c. xvii. Au-   wise Augustin. Epist. xxii. p. 28.

is one thing, the sensuality of those who thus indulge in drunkenness and the infirmity of the weak is another." [y]

So completely, however, had they grown into the habits of the Christian community, that in many places they lingered on in obstinate resistance to the eloquence of the great teachers of Christianity. Even the Councils pronounced with hesitating and tardy severity the sentence of condemnation against these inveterate usages, to which the people adhered with such strong attachment. That of Carthage prohibited the attendance of the clergy, and exhorted them to persuade the people, as far as possible, to abstain from these festivals; that of Orleans condemns the singing, dancing, or dissolute behaviour, in churches; that of Agde (Sens) condemns secular music, the singing of women, and banquets, in that place of which " it is written that it is a house of prayer;" finally, that in Trullo, held at Constantinople, as late as the beginning of the eighth century, prohibits the decking of tables in churches (the prohibition indicates the practice): and at length it provoked a formal sentence of excommunication.[z]

A.D. 397.

A.D. 533.

A.D. 578.

---

[y] Cont. Faust. lib. xx. c. xxi. One of the poems of St. Paulinus of Nola describes the general concourse to these festivals, and the riots which arose out of them.

" Et nunc ecce frequentes
Per totam et vigiles extendunt gaudia noctem,
Lætitiâ somnos, tenebras funalibus arcent.
Verum utinam sanis agerent hæc gaudia votis,
Nec sua liminibus miscerent gaudia sanctis.
. . . . ignoscenda tamen puto talia parcis
Gaudia quæ ducant epulis, quia mentibus error
Irrepit rudibus, nec tantæ conscia culpæ

Simplicitas pietate cadit, male credula Sanctos
Perfusis halante mero gaudere sepulcris."
      Carmen ix. in St. Felicem Martyrem.

[z] It is high time that the catacombs should be withdrawn from the domain of Polemics and, if not of Poetry, of Romance, to that of sober History. According to the language of many modern writers, it would be supposed that for the first three centuries the Catacombs were the ordinary dwellings, the only places of divine worship for the Christians of

But notwithstanding all its efforts to divert and preoccupy the mind by these graver or at least Profane
primarily religious spectacles, the passion for spectacles.
theatrical amusements was too strong to be repressed by

Rome. A noble author, never to be
mentioned without respect, writes
about a whole population living in
these dens and caves of the earth (Lord
Lindsay, 'Christian Art,' i. pp. 4, 5).
Even M. de Pressensé writes of the
Church of the Catacombs, (i. 367).
Cardinal Wiseman, though he has pru-
dently laid the scene of his romance
in the time of Diocletian, leads to
the inference that those days represent
the ordinary life of the Roman Christians of the first three centuries. It
is assumed, or insinuated, that the
whole period was a continuous persecution, that the Christians were (luci-
fugæ) obliged to shroud themselves
from the eye of day; to conceal their
ordinary worship and their mysteries
alike under the earth. It might be
supposed that Dodwell's unanswered
and unanswerable Treatise de Paucitate
Martyrum had never been written.
In truth there was no general persecution of the Christians in Rome, from the
reign of Nero, A.C. 65, to that of Decius,
249-251. During that period the Christians were in general as free and secure
as other inhabitants of Rome. Their
assemblies were no more disturbed than
the synagogues of the Jews, or the rites
of other foreign religions. How much
earlier we know not, but we know
that they had churches in the reign of
Alexander Severus. The first Martyr-
Pope, after apostolic times, was Fabianus in the reign of Decius. From this
first terrible but brief onslaught under
Decius, in which Cornelius, the succes-

sor of Fabianus also perished, to the general, and more merciless persecution
under Diocletian and Galerius (A.C.
303) there were periods of local and
very barbarous trial in many parts of
the empire; the Roman Christians may
not have escaped in the times of Clau-
dius and Aurelian: but of any Roman
persecution there is no trustworthy
record; nor of any martyr-pope.
Though it may have been occasionally
interrupted, the public worship of
Christ disdained concealment, lurked
not in secret places, but confronted
authority, and asserted its privilege of
Roman citizenship.

No doubt from the profound reverence for the dead (deepened by the
belief in perhaps the speedy resurrection of the body) there were in all the
catacombs, what we may call mortuary
chapels (one has been found in one
of the Jewish catacombs) in which
some funeral ceremony was performed;
and to which the bereaved Christian
would resort to mourn over the remains of the parent, the wife, or
husband, or the child prematurely laid
to rest. Sorrow would find its consolation in prayer. Natural grief, the quiet
assurance of the peace in which the departed slept, the hope, the confidence in
their immortality, all which the submissive, or rather rejoicing faith expresses so simply and so beautifully in
all the earlier epitaphs, would lead to
the more devout worship of God in these
holy places. Nor would that be the
natural and spontaneous offering of

Christianity. It succeeded in some humane improve-
ments, but, in some parts, it was obliged to yield to
the ungovernable torrent. The populace of an empire
threatened on all sides by dangerous enemies, oppressed
by a remorseless tyranny, notwithstanding the remonstrances of a new and dominant religion, imperiously
demanded, and recklessly enjoyed, their accustomed
diversions.[a] In some places, that which had been a
delight became a madness; and it was a Christian city
which first broke out in sedition and insurrection, whose
streets ran with blood, from the rivalry of two factions
in the circus. The Heathen World was degenerate even in
its diversions. It was not the nobler drama of Greece,
or even that of Rome; neither the stately tragedy, nor
even the fine comedy of manners, for which the mass
of the people endured the stern remonstrances of the
Christian orator; but spectacles of far less intellectual
pretensions, and far more likely to be injurious to
Christian morals. The higher drama, indeed, was not,

---

private sorrow alone. The sepulchres
of distinguished Christians, distinguished for Christian virtues of holiness and charity, would assemble the
sad but at the same time triumphant
Christians to celebrate the departure
of such men from the sinful world—
their departure to their Redeemer,
Christ. Out of this reverent sorrow
would grow, in times like the Decian
persecution, over the graves of martyred bishops, like Fabianus and
Cornelius, or in the more terrible
persecution under Diocletian, that
which in later times became the worship of the martyrs themselves. By
the time of Jerome, this worship had
become more common. To visit the
tombs of the martyrs became a kind

of pilgrimage. It is but in the course
of things that martyr-worship multiplied the martyrs; till, after centuries, the whole line of Popes which
are now deduced from St. Peter, become, according to some not very scrupulous or authentic lists, excepting
one unfortunate Greek, honoured by
this holy title.

[a] In the fifth century, Treves, four
times desolated by the barbarians, no
sooner recovered its freedom, than it
petitioned for the games of the circus.
" Ubique facies captæ urbis, ubique
terror captivitatis, ubique imago mortis, jacent reliquiæ infelicissimæ plebis
super tumulos mortuorum suorum, et
tu circenses rogas." Compare the whole
passage, Salvian, de Gub. Dei, vi.

as I shall show hereafter, entirely obsolete, but comparatively rare and unattractive.

The Heathen calendar still regulated the amusements of the people.[b] Nearly 100 days in the year were set apart as festivals; the commencement of every month was dedicated to the public diversions. Besides these, there were extraordinary days of rejoicing, a victory, the birthday of the reigning Emperor, or the dedication of his statue by the prefect or the provincials of any city or district. On the accession of a new Emperor, processions always took place, which ended in the exhibition of games.[c] The dedication of statues to the Emperors by different cities, great victories, and other important events, were always celebrated with games. The Christians obtained a law from Theodosius, that games should be prohibited on the Lord's day. The African bishops, in the fifth Council of Carthage, petitioned that this prohibition might be extended to all Christian holidays. They urged that many members of the corporate bodies were obliged

Heathen calendar.

---

[b] The ordinary calendar of holidays, on which the courts of law did not sit, at the close of the fourth century, is given by Godefroy (note on the Cod. Theodos. lib. ii. viii. 11.).

Feriæ æstivæ (harvest)	-	-	-	xxx
Feriæ autumnales (vintage)	-	-	-	xxx
Kalendæ Januarii	-	-	-	iii
Natalitia urbis Romæ	-	-	-	i
urbis Constantin.	-	-	-	1
Paschæ	-	-	-	xv
Dies Solis,[1] circiter	-	-	-	xli
Natalitia Imperatorum	-	-	-	iv

cxxv

Christmas-day, Epiphany, and Pentecost, were not as yet general holidays.

[c] The Constantinian Calendar (Græ- vii Thesaur. viii.) reckons ninety-six days for the games, of which but few were peculiar to Rome. Müller, ii. p. 49.

[1] The other Sundays were comprised in the summer, autumnal, and Easter holidays.

officially to attend on these occasions, and prevented from
fulfilling their religious duties. The law of Theodosius
the Elder had inhibited the celebration of games on Sundays,[d] one of the Younger Theodosius added, at Christmas,
the Epiphany, Easter, and Pentecost, and directed that
on those days the theatres should be closed, not only to
the Christians, but to the impious Jews and superstitious
Pagans.[e] But, notwithstanding this law, which must have
been imperfectly carried into execution, the indignant
preachers still denounce the rivalry of the games, which
withdrew so many of their audience.[f] The Theoretica
The Theo-   or fund for the expenses of public shows and
retica.   amusements, which existed not only in the two
capitals, but in all the larger cities of the Empire, was
first confiscated to the imperial treasury by Justinian.
Up to that time, the imperial policy had sanctioned and
enforced this expenditure; and it is remarkable that this
charge, which had been so long voluntarily borne by the
ambition or the vanity of the higher orders, was first
imposed as a direct tax on individuals by a Christian
Emperor. By a law of Constantine, the Senate of Rome
and of Constantinople were empowered to designate
any person of a certain rank and fortune for the costly
function of exhibiting games in these two great cities.[g]
These were in addition to the spectacles exhibited
by the consuls. In the other cities decemvirs were
nominated to this office.[h] The only exemptions were

[d] Cod. Theod. xv. v. 2.
[e] Cod. Theod. xv. t. 5. l. 5. A.D.
425. Müller, p. 50.
[f] See, for the earlier period, Apostolic Constit. ii. 60, 61, 62 ; Theophyl.
ad Autolyc. iii. p. 396 ; for the later,
Chrysostom, pæne passim, Hom. contra
Ant.; Hom. in princip. Act i. 58 ;

Hom. in Johann.
[g] Zosim. lib. ii. c. 38.
[h] See various laws of Constantius,
regulating the office, the expenses, the
fines imposed on the prætors, Cod.
Theodos. vi. 3 ; Laws i. 1-33. This
shows the importance attached to the
office. These munerarii, as well as

nonage, military or civil service, or a special indulgence
from the Emperor. Men fled from their native cities
to escape this onerous distinction. But if the charge
was thrown on the treasury, the treasury could recover
from the prætor or decemvir, besides assessing heavy
fines for the neglect of the duty; and they were liable
to be condemned to serve two years instead of one. In
the Eastern provinces, this office had been joined with
a kind of high-priesthood, such were the Asiarchs, the
Syriarchs,[i] the Bithyniarchs. The most distinguished
men of the province had been proud of accepting the
station of chief minister of the gods, at the expense of
these sumptuous festivities. The office remained under
the Christian Emperors,[k] but had degenerated into a
kind of purveyorship for the public pleasures. A law
of Theodosius enacted that this office should not be imposed on any one who refused to undertake it.[m] Another
law, from which, however, the Asiarchs were excluded,

---

the actors, were to do penance all their
lives. Act. Conc. Illeb. can. 3. Compare Bingham, xvi. 4. 8. This same
council condemned all who took the
office of decemvir to a year's exclusion
from the communion. Bingham, ubi
supra.

[i] Malala, Chronograph. lib. xii. in
art. Codex Theodos. vi. 3. 1.

[k] The "tribunus voluptatum" appears as a title on a Christian tomb.
Bosio, Roma Sotteranea, p. 106. Compare the observations of Bosio.

[m] Cod. Theodos. xii. l. 103. Compare the quotations from Libanius, in
Godefroy's Commentary. There is a
sumptuary law of Theodosius II.
limiting the expenses: " Nec inconsulta
plausorum insania curialium vires,
fortunas civium, principalium domus,

possessorum opes, reipublicæ robur
evellant." The Alytarchs, Syriarchs,
Asiarchs, and some others, are exempted
from this Law. C. T. xv. 9. 2. In
Italy, at a later period, the reign of
Theodoric, the public games were
provided by the liberality of the
Gothic sovereign : " Beatitudo sit tem-
porum lætitia populorum." Cassio-
dorus, epist. i. 20. The Epistles of
Theodoric's minister are full of provisions and regulations for the celebration of the various kinds of games.
Lib. i. epist. 20, 27, 30, 31, 32, 33,
iii. 51, iv. 37. Theodoric espoused
the green faction; he supported the
pantomime. There were still tribuni
voluptatum at Rome, vi. 6. Stipends
were allowed to scenici, ix. 21.

attempted to regulate the expenditure between the
mean parsimony of some, and the prodigality of others.[n]
Those who voluntarily undertook the office of exhibiting
games were likewise exempted from this sumptuary law,
for there were still some, ambitious of this kind of
popularity. They were proud of purchasing at this
enormous price, the honour of seeing their names displayed on tablets to the wondering multitude,[o] and of
being drawn in their chariots through the applauding
city on the morning of the festival.

Throughout the empire, this passion prevailed in every
city,[p] and in all classes. From early morning to late
in the evening, the theatres were crowded in every
part.[q] The artisan deserted his work, the merchant
his shop, the slaves followed their masters, and were
admitted into the vast circuit. Sometimes, when the
precincts of the circus or amphitheatre were insufficient
to contain the thronging multitudes, the adjacent hills
were crowded with spectators, anxious to obtain a glimpse
of the distant combatants, or to ascertain the colour of
the victorious charioteer. The usages of the East and
of the West differed as to the admission of women to
these spectacles. In the East, they were excluded by
the general sentiment from the theatre.[r] Nature itself,

---

[n] Symmachus, lib. x. epist. 28, 42.
Compare Heyne, Opuscula, vi. p. 14.

[o] Basil, in Psal. 61. Prudent.
Hamartigenia.

[p] Müller names the following cities,
besides the four great capitals, Rome,
Constantinople, Antioch, and Alexandria, in which the games are alluded
to by ancient authors, Gortyna, Nicomedia, Laodicea, Tyre, Berytus, Cæsarea, Heliopolis, Gaza, Ascalon,
Jerusalem, Berea, Corinth, Cirta,

Carthage, Syracuse, Catania, Milan,
Aquileia, Ravenna, Mentz, Cologne,
Treves, Arles. p. 53.

[q] Augustine, indeed, asserts, "per
omnes ferè civitates cadunt theatra
caveæ turpitudinum, et publicæ pro-
fessiones flagitiorum." De Cons. Evan-
gelist. c. 51.

[r] There are one or two passages of
the Fathers opposed to this opinion.
Tatian says, τοὺς ὅπως δεῖ μοιχεύειν
ἐπὶ τῆς σκήνης σοφιστεύοντας αἱ

observes St. Chrysostom, enforces this prohibition.[s] It arose, not out of Christianity, but out of the manners of the East; it is alluded to not as a distinction, but as a general usage.[t] Chrysostom laments that women, though they did not attend the games, were agitated by the factions of the circus.[u] In the West, the greater freedom of the Roman women had long asserted and still maintained this privilege.[x] It is well known that the vestal virgins had their seats of honour in the Roman spectacles, even those which might have been supposed most repulsive to feminine gentleness and delicacy; and the Christian preachers of the West remonstrate as strongly against the females as against the men, on account of their inextinguishable attachment to the public spectacles.

The more austere and ascetic Christian teachers condemned alike all these popular spectacles. From the avowed connection with Paganism, as to the time of their celebration,[y] their connection with the worship of Pagan deities, according to the accredited notion that

---

θυγάτερες ὕμων καὶ οἱ παῖδες θεωροῦσι. c. 22. Clemens Alex. Strom. lib. iii.

[s] Chrys. Hom. 12 in Coloss. vol. ii. p. 417.

[t] Procop. de Bell. Pers. l. c. 42.

[u] It was remarked as an extraordinary occurrence that, on the intelligence of the martyrdom of Gordius, matrons and virgins, forgetting their bashfulness, rushed to the theatre. Basil, vol. ii. p. 144, 147.

[x] " Quæ pudica forsitan ad spectaculum matrona processerat, de spectaculo revertitur impudica." Ad Donat. Compare Augustine, de Civ. Dei, ii. 4. " Quid juvenes aut virgines faciant, cum hæc et fieri sine pudore, et spectari

libenter ab omnibus cernunt, admonentur, quid facere possent, inflammantur libidines, ac se quisque pro sexu in illis imaginibus præfigurat, corruptiores ad cubicula revertuntur." Lact. Div. Instit. xv. 6. 31.

[y] " Dubium enim non est, quod lædunt Deum, utpote idolis consecratæ. Colitur namque et honoratur Minerva in gymnasiis, Venus in theatris, Neptunus in circis, Mars in arenis, Mercurius in palæstris." Salvian, lib. vi.

A fair collection of the denunciations of the Fathers against theatrical amusements may be found in Mamachi, de' Costumi de' Primitivi Cristiani, ii. p. 150, et seqq.

all these deities were dæmons permitted to delude mankind, the theatre was considered a kind of temple of the
Evil Spirit.[z]   There were some, however, who openly
vindicated these public exhibitions, and alleged the
chariot of Elijah, the dancing of David, and the quotations of St. Paul from dramatic writers, as cases
in point.

Four kinds of spectacles.
These public spectacles were of four kinds, independent of the common and more vulgar exhibitions, juggling, rope-dancing, and tumbling.[a]

Gymnastic games.
I. The old gymnastic games. The Olympic games
survived in Greece till the invasion of Alaric.[b]
Antioch likewise celebrated this quinquennial
festivity; youths of station and rank exhibited themselves as boxers and wrestlers.   These games were also
retained at Rome and in parts of Africa:[c] it is uncer-
tain whether they were introduced into Constantinople.
The various passages of Chrysostom which allude to
them probably were delivered in Antioch.   Something
of the old honour adhered to the wrestlers and performers in these games: they either were, or were
supposed to be, of respectable station and unblemished
character.   The herald advanced into the midst of the
arena and made his proclamation, " that any man should

---

[z] See the book de Spect., attributed
to St. Cyprian.   The author calls
Idolatry, " Ludorum omnium mater."
" Quod enim spectaculum sine idolo,
quis ludus sine sacrificio (De specta-
culis). Ludorum celebrationes deorum
festa sunt." Lactant. Inst. Div. vi. 20.

[a] Compare the references to Chrysostom's works on the rope dancers,
jugglers, &c. in Montfaucon, Diatribe,
p. 194.

[b] Liban. de Vocat. ad Festa Olympiæ.

"Cuncta Palæmoniis manus explorata co-
      ronis
   Adsit, et Eleo pubes laudata Tonanti."
         Claudian, de Fl. Mal. Cons. 288.
This, however, may be poetic remini-
scence.   These exhibitions are described
as conducted with greater decency and
order (probably because they awoke
less passionate interest) than those of
the circus or theatre.

[c] They were restored in Africa, by
a law of Gratian, A.D. 376. Cod.
Theod. xv. 7. 3.

come forward who had any charge against any one
of the men about to appear before them, as a thief,
a slave, or of bad reputation."[d]

II. Theatrical exhibitions, properly so called. The
higher tragedy and comedy were still repre- Tragedy and
sented on the inauguration of the consuls at comedy.
Rome. Claudian names actors of the sock and buskin,
the performers of genuine comedy and tragedy, as exhibiting on the occasion of the consulship of Mallius.[e]
During the triumph of the Christian Emperors Theodosius and Arcadius, the theatre of Pompey was filled by
chosen actors from all parts of the world. Two actors
in tragedy and comedy[f] are named as standing in the
same relation to each other as the famous Æsopus
and the comic Roscius. Prudentius speaks of the tragic
mask as still in use; and it appears that females acted
those parts in Terence which were formerly represented
by men.[g] The youthful mind of Augustine took delight
in being agitated by the fictitious sorrows of the stage.[h]
Nor was this higher branch of the art extinct in the
East : tragic and comic actors are named, with other
histrionic performers, in the orations of Chrysostom,[i]
and there are allusions in Libanius to mythological
tragic fables and to the comedies of Menander.[k] But as
these representations, after they had ceased to be integral
parts of the Pagan worship, were less eagerly denounced
by the Christian teachers,[m] the comparatively slight and

---

[d] Compare Montfaucon's Diatribe, p. 194.

[e] " Qui pulpita socco
Personat, aut altè graditur majore cothurno."
                                In Cons. Mall. 313.
" Pompeiana proscenia delectis actoribus
personarent." Symmach. lib. x. ep. 29.

[f] Publius Pollio and Ambivius.
Symmach. epist. x. 2.

[g] Donatus in Andriam, act. iv. sc. 3.

[h] Confess. iii. 2.

[i] Chrysostom, Hom. 10 in Coloss. v. ii. p. 403 ; Hom. 6 in Terræ mot. i. 780. i. p. 38. i. 731.

[k] Liban. vol. ii. p. 375.

[m] Lactantius inveighs with all the

scanty notices in their writings, almost our only records of the manners of the time, by no means prove the infrequency of these representations; though it is probable, for other reasons, that the barbarous and degraded taste was more gratified by the mimes and pantomimes, the chariot races of the circus, and the wild-beasts in the amphitheatre.[n] But tragedy and comedy, at this period, were probably maintained rather to display the magnificence of the consul or prætor, who prided himself on the variety of his entertainments, and were applauded, perhaps,[o] by professors of rhetoric, and a few faithful admirers of antiquity, rather than by the people at large. Some have supposed that the tragedies written on religious subjects in the time of Julian were represented on the stage; but there is no ground for this notion; these were intended as school books, to supply the place of Sophocles and Menander.

In its degeneracy, the higher Drama had long been supplanted by,—1st, the Mimes. Even this kind of drama, perhaps of Roman, or even of earlier Italian origin, had degenerated into the coarsest scurrility, and, it should seem, the most repulsive indecency. Formerly it had been the representation of some incident in common life, extemporaneously dramatised by the mime, ludicrous in its general character,

Mimes.

---

energy of the first ages against tragedy and comedy:—"Tragicæ historiæ subjiciunt oculis patricidia et incesta regum malorum, et cothurnata scelera demonstrant. Comicæ de stupris virginum et amicitiis meretricum, et quo magis sunt eloquentes, eo magis persuadent, faciliùs inhærent memoriæ versus numerosi et ornati." Instit. vi. 20.

[n] Augustine, however, draws a distinction between these two classes of

theatric representations and the lower kind:—" Scenicorum tolerabiliora ludorum, comœdiæ scilicet et tragœdiæ, hoc est fabulæ poëtarum, agendæ in spectaculo multâ rerum turpitudine, sed nullâ saltem, sicut aliæ multæ, verborum obscenitate compositæ, quas etiam inter studia, quæ liberalia vocantur, pueri legere et discere coguntur a senibus." De Civ. Dei, lib. ii. c. 8.

[o] Müller, p. 139.

mingled at times with sharp or even grave and sententious satire. Such were the mimes of Laberius, to
which republican Rome had listened with delight. It
was now the lowest kind of buffoonery. The mime,
or several mimes, both male and female, appeared in
ridiculous dresses, with shaven crowns, and, pretending
still to represent some kind of story, poured forth their
witless obscenity, and indulged in all kinds of practical
jokes and manual wit, blows on the face and broken
heads. The music was probably the great charm, but
that had become soft, effeminate, and lascivious. The
female performers were of the most abandoned character,[p] and scenes were sometimes exhibited of the
most abominable indecency, even if we do not give
implicit credit to the malignant tales of Procopius concerning the exhibitions of the Empress Theodora, when
she performed as a dancing girl in these disgusting
mimes.[q]

2nd. The Pantomime was a kind of ballet in action.[r]
It was the mimic representation of all the old
tragic and mythological fables, without words,[s]   Pantomimes.

---

[p] Many passages of Chrysostom
might be quoted, in which he speaks
of the naked courtesans, meaning
probably with the most transparent
clothing (though women were exhibited at Antioch swimming in an
actual state of nudity), who performed in these mimes. The more
severe Christian preacher is confirmed
by the language of the Heathen Zosimus, whose bitter hatred to Christianity induces him to attribute their
most monstrous excesses to the reign
of the Christian Emperor. Μῖμοί τε
γὰρ γελοίων, καὶ οἱ κακῶς ἀπολού-
μενοι ὀρχησταὶ, καὶ πᾶν δ᾽ τι πρὸς

αἰσχρότητα κα᾽ τὴν ἄτοπον ταύτην
καὶ ἐκμελῆ συντελεῖ μουσικὴν, ἠσ-
κήθη τε ἐπὶ τούτου. Lib. iv. c. 33.
[q] Müller, 92. 103.
[r] Libanius is indignant that men
should attempt to confound the or-
chestæ or pantomimes with these degraded and infamous mimes. Vol. iii.
p. 350. The pantomimes wore masks,
the mimes had their faces uncovered,
and usually had shaven crowns.
[s] The pantomimi or dancers represented their parts,—

"Clausis faucibus et loquente gestu
Nutu, crure, genu, manu, rotatu."
                              Sid. Apoll.

z 2

or intermingled with chants or songs.[t] These exhibitions
were got up at times with great splendour of scenery,
which was usually painted on hanging curtains, and with
musical accompaniments of the greatest variety. The
whole cycle of mythology,[n] both of the gods and heroes,
was represented by the dress and mimic gestures of the
performer. The deities, both male and female,—Jupiter,
Pluto, and Mars; Juno, Proserpine, Venus; Theseus
and Hercules; Achilles, with all the heroes of the
Trojan war; Phædra, Briseis, Atalanta; the race of
Œdipus; these are but a few of the dramatic personages
which, on the authority of Libanius,[x] were personated by
the pantomimes of the East. Sidonius Apollinaris[y] fills
twenty-five lines with those represented in the West by
the celebrated dancers Caramalus and Phabaton.[z] These
included the old fables of Medea and Jason, of the house
of Thyestes, of Tereus and Philomela, Jupiter and
Europa, and Danae, and Leda, and Ganymede, Mars
and Venus, Perseus and Andromeda. In the West, the
female parts thus exhibited were likewise represented by
women[a] of whom there were no less than 3000 in
Rome:[b] and so important were these females considered to the public amusement, that, on the expulsion
of all strangers from the city during a famine, an excep-

[t] There was sometimes a regular chorus, with instrumental music. Sid. Apoll. xxiii. 268, and probably poetry composed for the occasion. Müller, p. 122.

[n] Greg. Nyssen. in Galland. Bibliothec. Patrum, vi. p. 610. Ambrose, in Hexaem. iii. 1. 5. Synes. de Prov. ii. p. 128, ed. Petav. Symmach. i. ep. 89.

[x] Liban. pro Salt. v. iii. 391.

[y] Sidon. Apoll. carm. xxiii. v. 267, 299.

[x] Claudian mentions a youth, who, before the pit, which thundered with applause,—

"Aut rigidam Nioben aut flentem Troada fingit."

[a] Even in Constantinople, women acted in the pantomimes. Chrysostom, Hom. 6 in Thessalon., denounces the performance of Phædra and Hippolytus, by women: Ὥσπερ σώματος τύπῳ φαινομένας.

[b] Ammian. Marcell., xiv. 6.

tion was made by the prætor, in deference to the popular wishes, in favour of this class alone. The profession, however, was considered infamous, and the indecency of their attire upon the public stage justified the low estimate of their moral character. Their attractions were so dangerous to the Roman youth, that a special law prohibited the abduction of these females from their public occupation, whether the enamoured lover withdrew one of them from the stage as his mistress, or, as not unfrequently happened, with the more honourable title of wife.[c] The East, though it sometimes endured the appearance of women in those parts, often left them to be performed by boys, with any thing but advantage to general morality. The aversion of Christianity to the subjects exhibited by the pantomimes, almost invariably moulded up as they were with Paganism, as well as its high moral sense (united, perhaps, with something of the disdain of ancient Rome for the histrionic art, which it patronised nevertheless with inexhaustible ardour), branded the performers with the deepest mark of public contempt. They were, as it were, public slaves, and could not abandon their profession.[d] They were considered unfit to mingle with respectable society; might not appear in the forum or basilica, or use the public baths; they were excluded even from the theatre as spectators, and might not be attended by a slave, with a folding-stool for their use. Even Christianity appeared to extend its mercies and its hopes to this devoted race with some degree of rigour and jealousy. The actor baptized in the apparent agony of death, if he should recover, could not be forced

---

[c] Cod. Theodos. xv. 7. 5.

[d] Cod. Theodos. xv. 13. Compare Chastel, p. 211, concerning the laws which inflicted dishonour and incapacity on actors.

back upon the stage; but the guardian of the public
amusements was to take care, lest, by pretended sick-
ness, the actor should obtain this precious privilege
of baptism, and thus exemption from his servitude.
Even the daughters of actresses partook of their mothers'
infamy, and could only escape being doomed to their
course of life by the profession of Christianity, ratified
by a certain term of probationary virtue. If the actress
relapsed from Christianity, she was invariably condemned
to her impure servitude.[e]

Such was the general state of the theatrical exhibitions in the Roman empire at that period.   The
higher drama, like every other intellectual and inventive art, had to undergo the influence of Christianity
before it could revive in its splendid and prolific energy.
In all European countries, the Christian mystery, as it
was called, has been the parent of tragedy, perhaps of
comedy.   It reappeared as a purely religious representation, having retained no remembrance whatever
of Paganism; and was at one period, perhaps, the most
effective teacher, in times of general ignorance and
total scarcity of books, both among priests and people,
of Christian history as well as of Christian legend.[f]

But at a later period, the old hereditary hostility of
Christianity to the theatre has constantly revived.   The
passages of the Fathers have perpetually been repeated
by the more severe preachers, whether fairly applicable
or not to the dramatic entertainments of different
periods; and in general it has had the effect of keeping
the actor in a lower caste of society; a prejudice often
productive of the evil which it professed to correct;
for men whom the general sentiment considers of

---

[e] Cod. Theodos. de Scenicis, xv. 7.   [f] The subject is reviewed in Latin
2. 4. 8. 9.   Christianity, Book xiv. c. 4.

a low moral order will rarely make the vain attempt at raising themselves above it : if they cannot avoid contempt, they will care little whether they deserve it.

III. The Amphitheatre, with its shows of gladiators and wild-beasts. The suppression of those bloody spectacles, in which human beings slaughtered each other by hundreds for the diversion of their fellow men, is one of the most unquestionable and proudest triumphs of Christianity.

Amphitheatre. Gladiatorial shows.

The gladiatorial shows, strictly speaking, that is, the mortal combats of men, were never introduced into the less warlike East, though the combats of men with wild-beasts were exhibited in Syria and other parts. The former were Roman in their origin, and to their termination.   It might seem that the pride of Roman conquest was not satisfied with the execution of her desolating mandates, unless the whole city witnessed the bloodshed of her foreign captives ; and in her decline she seemed to console herself with these sanguinary proofs of her still extensive empire : the ferocity survived the valour of her martial spirit. Barbarian life seemed, indeed, to be of no account, but to contribute to the sports of the Roman.   The humane Symmachus, even at this late period,[g] reproves the *impiety* of some Saxon captives, who, by strangling themselves in prison, escaped the ignominy of this public exhibition.[h]   It is an humiliating consideration to find how little Roman civilisation had tended to

---

[g] "Quando prohibuisset privatâ custodiâ desperatæ gentis *impias* manus, cum viginti novem fractas sine laqueo fauces primus ludi gladiatorii dies viderit." Symmach. lib. ii. epist. 46.

[h] It is curious that at one time the exposure to wild beasts was considered a more ignominious punishment than fighting as a gladiator. The slave was condemned to the former for kidnapping ; the freeman to the latter. Codex Theod. iv. 18. 1.

mitigate the ferocity of manners and of temperament. Not merely did women crowd the amphitheatre during the combats of these fierce and almost naked savages or criminals, but it was the especial privilege of the vestal virgin, even at this late period, to give the signal for the mortal blow, to watch the sword driven deeper into the palpitating entrails.[i] The state of uncontrolled frenzy worked up even the most sober spectators. The manner in which this contagious passion for bloodshed engrossed the whole soul is described with singular power and truth by St. Augustine. A Christian student of the law was compelled by the importunity of his friends to enter the amphitheatre. He sat with his eyes closed, and his mind totally abstracted from the scene. He was suddenly startled from his trance by a tremendous shout from the whole audience. He opened his eyes, he could not but gaze on the spectacle. Directly he beheld the blood, his heart imbibed the common ferocity; he could not turn away; his eyes were riveted on the arena; and the interest, the excitement, the pleasure, grew into complete intoxication. He looked on, he shouted, he was inflamed; he carried away from the amphitheatre an irresistible propensity to return to its cruel enjoyments.[k]

Christianity began to assail this deep-rooted passion of the Roman world with caution, almost with timidity. Christian Constantinople was never defiled with the blood of gladiators. In the same year as that of the Council of Nicæa, a local edict was issued, declaring

---

i   "Virgo—consurgit ad ictus,
Et quotiens victor ferrum jugulo inserit, illa
Delicias ait esse suas, pectusque jacentis
Virgo modesta jubet, converso pollice,
     rumpi;

Ni lateat pars ulla animæ vitalibus imis,
Altius impresso dum palpitat ense secutor."
        Prudent. adv. Sym. ii. 1095.

k   August. Conf. vi. 8.

the Emperor's disapprobation of these sanguinary
exhibitions in time of peace, and prohibiting the
volunteering of men as gladiators.[m] This was a considerable step, if we call to mind the careless apathy
with which Constantine, before his conversion, had
exhibited all his barbarian captives in the amphitheatre
at Treves.[n] This edict, however, addressed to the
prefect of Phœnicia, had no permanent effect, for
Libanius, several years after, boasts that he had not
been a spectator of the gladiatorial shows still regularly
celebrated in Syria. Constantius prohibited soldiers,
and those in the imperial service (Palatini), from hiring
themselves out to the Lanistæ, the keepers of gladiators.[o] Valentinian decreed that no Christian or
Palatine should be condemned for any crime whatsoever
to the arena.[p] An early edict of Honorius prohibited
any slave who had been a gladiator [q] from being
admitted into the service of a man of senatorial dignity.
But Christianity now began to speak in a more
courageous and commanding tone.[r] The Christian poet
urges on the Christian Emperor the direct prohibition
of these inhuman and disgraceful exhibitions.[s] But
a single act often affects the public mind much more
strongly than even the most eloquent and reiterated
exhortation. An Eastern monk, named Telemachus,
travelled all the way to Rome, in order to protest
against those disgraceful barbarities. In his noble

---

[m] Codex Theodos. xv. 12. 1.
[n] See vol. ii. p. 320.
[o] Codex Theodos. xv. 12. 2.
[p] Ibid. ix. 40. 8.
[q] Codex Theodos. ix. 40. 8.
[r] Ibid. xv. 12. 3.
[s] " Arripe dilatam tua, dux, in tempora
famam,

Quodque patri superest, successor laudis
habeto.
Ille urbem vetuit taurorum sanguine tingi,
Tu mortes miserorum hominum prohibeto
litari :
Nullus in urbe cadat, cujus sit pœna
voluptas,
Nec sua virginitas oblectet cædibus ora.
Jam solis contenta feris infamis arena,
Nulla cruentatis homicidia ludat in armis."
Prudent. adv. Sym. ii. 1121.

enthusiasm, he leaped into the arena to separate the combatants; either with the sanction of the prefect, or that of the infuriated assembly, he was torn to pieces, the martyr of Christian humanity.[t] The impression of this awful scene, of a Christian, a monk, thus murdered in the arena, was so profound, that Honorius issued a prohibitory edict, putting an end to these bloody shows. This edict, however, only suppressed the mortal combats of men;[u] the less inhuman, though still brutalising, conflicts of men with wild-beasts seems scarcely to have been abolished[x] till the diminution of wealth, and the gradual contraction of the limits of the empire, cut off both the supply and the means of purchasing these costly luxuries.[y] The revolted or conquered provinces of the South, the East, and the North, no longer rendered up their accustomed tribute of lions from Libya, leopards from the East, dogs of remarkable ferocity from Scotland, of crocodiles and bears, and every kind of wild and rare animal. The Emperor Anthemius prohibited the lamentable spectacles of wild-beasts on the Sunday; and Salvian still inveighs against those bloody exhibitions. And this

---

[t] Theodoret, v. 26.

[u] The law of Honorius is not extant in the Theodosian code, which only retains those of Constantine and Constantius. For this reason, doubts have been thrown on the authority of Theodoret; but there is no recorded instance of gladiatorial combats *between man and man* since this period. The passage of Salvian, sometimes alleged, refers to combats with wild-beasts.— " Ubi summum deliciarum genus est mori homines, aut quod est mori gravius acerbiùsque, lacerari, expleri ferarum alvos humanis carnibus, comedi

homines cum circumstantium lætitiâ, conspicientium voluptate." De Gub. Dei, lib. vi. p. 51.

[x] " Quicquid monstriferis nutrit Gætulia campis,
Alpinâ quicquid tegitur nive, Gallica quicquid
Silva timet, jaceat. Largo ditescat arena
Sanguine, consumant totos spectacula montes."
Claud. in Cons. Mall. 306.

[y] A law of Honorius provides for the supply of wild beasts for the amphitheatre at Constantinople. It is a very curious provision. Cod. Theodos. xv. xi., 2.

amusement gradually degenerated, if the word may be used, not so much from the improving humanity, as from the pusillanimity of the people. Arts were introduced to irritate the fury of the beast, without endangering the person of the combatant. Such arts would have been contemptuously exploded in the more warlike days of the Empire. It became a mere exhibition of skill and agility. The beasts were sometimes tamed before they were exhibited. In the West, those games seem to have sunk with the Western empire; [z] in the East, they lingered on so as to require a special prohibition by the Council in Trullo at Constantinople, at the close of the seventh century.

IV. The chariot race of the circus. If these former exhibitions were prejudicial to the modesty *The circus.* and humanity of the Roman people, the *Chariot races* chariot races were no less fatal to their peace. This frenzy did not, indeed, reach its height till the middle of the fifth century, when the animosities of political and religious difference were outdone by factions enlisted in favour of the rival charioteers in the circus. As complete a separation took place in society; adverse parties were banded against each other in as fierce opposition; an insurrection as destructive and sanguinary took place; the throne of the Emperor was as fearfully shaken in the collision of the Blue and Green factions, as ever it had been in defence of the sacred rights of liberty or of faith. Constantinople seemed to concentre on the circus all that absorbing interest, which at Rome was divided by many spectacles. The

---

[z] Agincourt, Histoire de l'Art, is of opinion that Theodoric substituted military games for theatrical shows, and that these military games were the origin of the tournaments. The wild beast shows were still celebrated at Rome. Cassiod. Epist. v. 42.

Christian city seemed to compensate to itself for the excitement of those games which were prohibited by the religion, by the fury with which it embraced those which were allowed, or rather against which Christianity remonstrated in vain. Her milder tone of persuasiveness, and her more authoritative interdiction, were equally disregarded, where the sovereign and the whole people yielded to the common frenzy. But this consolation remained to Christianity, that when it was accused of distracting the imperial city with religious dissension, it might allege, that this at least was a nobler subject of difference; or rather, that the passions of men seized upon religious distinctions with no greater eagerness than they did on these competitions for the success of a chariot driver in a blue or a green jacket, in order to gratify their inextinguishable love of strife and animosity.

CHAPTER III.

Christian Literature.

CHRISTIANITY was extensively propagated in an age in which Greek and Latin literature had fallen into hopeless degeneracy; nor could even its spirit awaken the dead. Both these languages had already attained and passed their complete developement; they had fulfilled their part in the imaginative and intellectual advancement of mankind; and it seems, in general, as much beyond the power of the genius of a country, as of an individual, to renew its youth. It was not till it had created new languages, or rather till languages had been formed in which the religious notions of Christianity were an elementary and constituent part, that Christian literature assumed its free and natural dignity.

The genius of the new religion never coalesced in perfect and amicable harmony with either the Greek or the Latin tongue. In each case it was a foreign dialect introduced into a fully-formed and completely organised language. The Greek, notwithstanding its exquisite pliancy, with difficulty accommodated itself to the new sentiments and opinions. It had either to endure the naturalisation of new words, or to deflect its own terms to new significations. In the latter case, the doctrines were endangered, in the former, the purity of the language; more especially since the Oriental writers were in general alien to the Grecian mind. The Greek language had indeed long before yielded to the conta-

minating influences of Barbarism. From Homer to
Demosthenes, it had varied in its style and

character, but had maintained its admirable
perfection, as the finest, the clearest, and
most versatile instrument of poetry, oratory,
or philosophy. But the conquests of Greece were as
fatal to her language as to her liberties. The Mace-
donian, the language of the conquerors, was not the
purest Greek,[a] and in general, by the extension over a
wider surface, the stream contracted a taint from every
soil over which it flowed. Alexandria was probably
the best school of foreign Grecian style, at least in
literature; in Syria it had always been infected in some
degree by the admixture of Oriental terms. The
Hellenistic style, as it has been called, of the New
Testament, may be considered a fair example of the
language, as it was spoken in the provinces among
persons of no high degree of intellectual culture.

The Latin seemed no less to have fulfilled its
mission and to have passed its culminating
point, in the verse of Virgil and the prose of

Of Roman.

Cicero. Its stern and masculine majesty, its plain and
practical vigour, seemed as if it could not outlive the
republican institutions, in the intellectual conflicts of
which it had been formed. The impulse of the old
freedom carried it through the reign of Augustus, but
no further; and it had undergone rapid and progressive
deterioration before it was called upon to discharge its
second office of disseminating and preserving the
Christianity of the West; and the Latin, like the
Greek, had suffered by its own triumphs. Among
the more distinguished Heathen writers, subsequent to

---

[a] Compare the dissertation of Sturz | the prolegomena to Valpy's edition of
on the Macedonian dialect, reprinted in | Stephens' Thesaurus.

Augustus, the largest number were of provincial origin; and something of their foreign tone still adhered to their style. Of the best Latin Christian writers, it is remarkable that not one was a Roman, not one, except Ambrose, an Italian. Tertullian, Cyprian, Arnobius (perhaps Lactantius), and Augustine were Africans; the Roman education, and superior understanding of the last, could not altogether refine away that rude provincialism which darkened the whole language of the others. The writings of Hilary are obscured by another dialect of Barbarism. Even at so late a period, whatever exceptions may be made to the taste of his conceptions and of his imagery, with some limitation, the *Roman* style of Claudian, and the structure of his verse, carries us back to the time of Virgil; in Prudentius, it is not merely the inferiority of the poet, but something foreign and uncongenial refuses to harmonise with the adopted poetic language.[b]

Yet it was impossible that such an enthusiasm could be disseminated through the empire without in some degree awakening the torpid languages. The mind could not be so deeply stirred without expressing itself with life and vigour, even if with diminished elegance and dignity. No one can compare the energetic sentences of Chrysostom with the prolix and elaborate, if more correct, periods of Libanius, without acknowledging that a new principle of vitality has been infused into the language. *Christian literature.*

But in fact the ecclesiastical Greek and Latin are new dialects of the ancient tongue. Their literature

---

[b] Among the most remarkable productions as to Latinity are the Ecclesiastical History and Life of St. Martin of Tours, by Sulpicius Severus; the legendary matter of which contrasts singularly with the perspicuous and almost classical elegance of the style. See post, on Minucius Felix.

stands entirely apart from that of Greece or Rome. The Greek already possessed the foundation of this literature in the Septuagint version of the Old, and in the original of the New Testament. The Vulgate of Jerome, which almost immediately superseded the older imperfect or inaccurate versions from the Greek, supplied the same groundwork to Latin Christendom. There is something singularly rich and, if I may so speak, picturesque in the Latin of the Vulgate; the Orientalism of the Scripture is blended up with such curious felicity with the idiom of the Latin, that, although far removed either from the colloquial ease of the comic poets, or the purity of Cicero, it both delights the ear and fills the mind. It is an original and somewhat foreign, but nevertheless an expressive and harmonious dialect.[c] It has no doubt powerfully influenced the religious style, not merely of the later Latin writers, but those of the modern languages of which Latin is the parent. Constantly quoted, either in its express words, or in terms approaching closely to its own, it contributed to form the dialect of ecclesiastical Latin, which became the religious language of Europe; and as soon as religion condescended to employ the modern languages in its service, was transfused as a necessary and integral part of that which related to religion. Christian literature was as yet purely religious in its scope; though it ranged over

---

[c] There appears to me more of the Oriental character in the Old Testament of the Vulgate than in the LXX. That translation having been made by Greeks, or by Jews domiciled in a Greek city, the Hebrew style seems subdued, as far as possible, to the Greek. Jerome seems to have endeavoured to Hebraise or Orientalise his Latin.

The story of Jerome's nocturnal flagellation for his attachment to profane literature rests (as we have seen) on his own authority; but his later works show that the offending spirit was not effectively scourged out of him.

the whole field of ancient poetry, philosophy, and history, its sole object was the illustration or confirmation of Christian opinion.

For many ages, and indeed as long as it spoke the ancient languages, the new religion was barren of poetry in all its loftier departments, at least of that which was poetry in form as well as in spirit. *Poetry.*

The religion itself was the *poetry* of Christianity. The sacred books were to the Christians what the national epic and the sacred lyric had been to the other races of antiquity. They occupied the place, and proscribed in their superior sanctity, or defied by their unattainable excellence, all rivalry. The Church succeeded to the splendid inheritance of the Hebrew temple and synagogue. The Psalms and the Prophets, if they departed somewhat from their original simple energy and grandeur in the uncongenial and too polished languages of the Greeks and Romans, still, in their imagery, their bold impersonations, the power and majesty of their manner, as well as in the sublimity of the notions of divine power and wisdom with which they were instinct, stood alone in the religious poetry of mankind.

The religious books of Christianity, though of a gentler cast, and only in a few short passages (and in the grand poetic drama of the Revelation) poetical in their form, had much, especially in their narratives, of the essence of poetry; the power of awakening kindred emotions; the pure simplicity of truth, blended with imagery and with language which kindled the fancy. Faith itself was constantly summoning the imagination to its aid, to realise, to impersonate those scenes which were described in the sacred volume, *Sacred writings.*

and which it was thus enabled to embrace with greater fervour and sincerity. All the other early Christian poetry was pale and lifeless in comparison with that of the sacred writers. Some few hymns, as the noble Te Deum ascribed to Ambrose, were admitted, with the Psalms, and the short lyric passages in the New Testament, the Magnificat, the Nunc Dimittis, and the Alleluia, into the services of the Church. But the sacred volume commanded exclusive adoration not merely by its sanctity, but by its unrivalled imagery and sweetness. Each sect had its hymns; and those of the Gnostics, with the rival strains of the orthodox churches of Syria, attained great popularity. But in general these compositions were only a feebler echo of the strong and vivid sounds of the Hebrew psalms. The epic and tragic form into which, in the time of Julian, the scripture narratives were cast, in order to provide a Christian Homer and Euripides for those schools in which the originals were interdicted, were probably but cold paraphrases, the Hebrew poetry expressed in an incongruous cento of the Homeric or tragic phraseology. The garrulous feebleness of Gregory's own poem does not awaken any regret for the loss of those writings either of his own composition or of his age.[d] Even in the martyrdoms, the noblest unoccupied subjects for Christian verse, the poetry seems to have forced its way into the legend, rather than animated the writer of verse. Prudentius—whose

---

[d] The Greek poetry after Nazianzen was almost silent; some perhaps, of the hymns are ancient (one particularly in Routh's Reliquiæ). See likewise Smith's account of the Greek church. The hymns of Synesius are very interesting as illustrative of the state of religious sentiment, and by no means without beauty. But may we call these dreamy Platonic raptures Christian poetry?

finest lines (and they are sometimes of a very spirited, sententious, and eloquent, if not poetic cast) occur in his other poems, on these which would appear at first far more promising subjects is sometimes pretty and fanciful, but scarcely more.[e]

[e] One of the best, or rather perhaps *prettiest*, passages, is that which has been selected as a hymn for the Innocents' day :—

"Salvete flores martyrum
Quos lucis ipso in limine,
Christi insecutor sustulit
Ceu turbo nascentes rosas.
Vos, prima Christi victima,
Grex immolatorum tener,
Aram ante ipsam simplices
Palma et coronis luditis."

But these are only a few stanzas out of a long hymn on the Epiphany. The best verses in Prudentius are to be found in the books against Symmachus; but their highest praise is that, in their force and energy, they *approach* to Claudian. With regard to Claudian, I cannot refrain from repeating what I have stated in another place, as it is so closely connected with the subject of Christian poetry. M. Beugnot has pointed out one remarkable characteristic of Claudian's poetry and of the times—his extraordinary religious indifference. Here is a poet writing at the actual crisis of the complete triumph of the new religion, and the visible extinction of the old : if we may so speak, a strictly historical poet, whose works, excepting his mythological poem on the rape of Proserpine, are confined to temporary subjects, and to the politics of his own eventful times ; yet, excepting in one or two small and indifferent pieces, manifestly written by a Christian and interpolated among Claudian's poems, there is no allusion whatever to the great religious strife. No one would know the existence of Christianity at that period of the world by reading the works of Claudian. His panegyric and his satire preserve the same religious impartiality ; award their most lavish praise or their bitterest invective on Christian or Pagan : he insults the fall of Eugenius, and glories in the victories of Theodosius. Under the child of Theodosius, —and Honorius never became more than a child,—Christianity continued to inflict wounds more and more deadly on expiring Paganism. Are the gods of Olympus agitated with apprehension at the birth of their new enemy ? They are introduced as rejoicing at his appearance, and promising long years of glory. The whole prophetic choir of Paganism, all the oracles throughout the world, are summoned to predict the felicity of the reign of Honorius. His birth is compared to that of Apollo, but the narrow limits of an island must not confine the new *deity*—

"Non littora nostro
Sufficerent angusta Deo."

Augury, and divination, the shrines of Ammon and of Delphi, the Persian magi, the Etruscan seers, the Chaldæan astrologers, the Sibyl herself, are described as still discharging their poetic functions, and celebrating the natal day of this Christian prince. They are noble lines, as well as curious illustrations of the times :—

2 A 2

There is more of the essence of poetry in the simpler
and unadorned Acts of the Martyrs, more pathos, oc-

" Quæ tunc documenta futuri?
Quæ voces avium? quanti per inane volatus?
Quis vatum discursus erat? Tibi corniger Ammon,
Et dudum taciti rupêre silentia Delphi.
Te Persæ cecinêre Magi, te sensit Etruscus
Augur, et inspectis Babylonius horruit astris:
Chaldæi stupuêre senes, Cumanaque rursus
Intonuit rupes, rabidæ delubra Sibyllæ."
Note on Gibbon, v. 249.

But *Roman* poetry expired with Claudian. In the vast mass of the Christian Latin poetry of this period, independent of the perpetual faults against metre and taste, it is impossible not to acknowledge that the subject matter appears foreign, and irreconcileable with the style of the verse. Christian images and sentiments, the frequent biblical phrases and expressions, are not yet naturalised; and it is almost impossible to select any passage of considerable length from the whole cycle, which can be offered as poetry. I except a few of the hymns, and even, as to the hymns (setting aside the Te Deum), paradoxical as it may sound, I cannot but think the later and more barbarous the best. There is nothing in my judgement to be compared with the monkish " Dies iræ, Dies illa," or even the " Stabat Mater."

I am inclined to select, as a favourable specimen of Latin poetry, the following almost unknown lines (they are not in the earlier editions of Dracontius). I have three reasons for my selection : 1. The real merit of the verses compared to most of the Christian poetry ; 2. Their opposition to the prevailing tenet of celibacy, for which cause they are quoted by Theiner ; 3. The interest which early poetry on this subject (Adam in Paradise) must possess to the countrymen of Milton.

" Tunc oculos per cuncta jacit, miratur amœnum
Sic florere locum, sic puros fontibus amnes,
Quatuor undisonas stringenti gurgite ripas,
Ire per arboreos saltus, camposque virentes
Miratur ; sed quid sit homo, quos factus ad usus
Scire cupit simplex, et non habet, unde requirat ;
Quo merito sibimet data sit possessio mundi,
Et domus alma nemus per florea regna paratum :
Ac procul expectat virides jumenta per agros ;
Et de se tacitus, quæ sint hæc cuncta, requirit,
Et quare secum non sint hæc ipsa, volutat :
Nam consorte carens, cum quo conferret, egebat.
Viderat Omnipotens, hæc illum corde moventem,
Et miseratus ait : Demus adjutoria facto ;
Participem generis : tanquam si diceret auctor,
Non solum decet esse virum, consortia blanda
Noverit, uxor erit, quum sit tamen ille maritus,
Conjugium se quisque vocet, dulcedo recurrat
Cordibus innocuis, et sit sibi pignus uterque
Velle pares, et nolle pares, stans una voluntas,
Par animi concors, paribus concurrere votis.
Ambo sibi requies cordis sint, ambo fideles,
Et quicunque datur casus, sit causa duorum.
Nec mora, jam venit alma quies, oculosque supinat
Somnus, et in dulcem solvuntur membra soporem.

Sed

casionally more grandeur, more touching incident and
expression, and even, we may venture to say, happier
invention than in the prolix and inanimate strains of the
Christian poet. For the awakened imagination was not
content with feasting in silence on its lawful nutriment,
the poetry of the Bible ; it demanded and received perpetual stimulants, which increased, instead of satisfying,
the appetite. That peculiar state of the human mind
had now commenced, in which the imagination so far

> Sed quum jure Deus, nullo prohibente valeret
> Demere particulam, de quo plus ipse pararat,
> Ne vi oblata daret juveni sua costa dolorem,
> Redderet et tristem subitò, quem lædere nollet,
> Fur opifex vult esse suus ; nam posset et illam
> Pulvere de simili princeps formare puellam.
> Sed quo plenus amor toto de corde veniret,
> Noscere in uxore voluit sua membra maritum,
> Dividitur contexta cutis, subducitur una
> Sensim costa viro, sed mox reditura marito.
> Nam juvenis de parte brevi formatur adulta
> Virgo, decora, rudis, matura tumentibus annis,
> Conjugii, sobolisque capax, quibus apta probatur,
> Et sine lacte pio crescit infantia pubes.
> Excutitur somno juvenis, videt ipse puellam
> Ante oculos astare suos, pater, inde maritus.
> Non tamen ex costâ genitor, sed conjugis auctor.
> Somnus erat partus, conceptus semine nullo,
> Materiem sopita quies produxit amoris,
> Affectusque novos blandi genuêre sopores.
> Constitit ante oculos nullo velamine tecta,
> Corpore nuda simul niveo, quasi nympha profundi,
> Cæsaries intonsa comis, gena pulchra rubore,
> Omnia pulchra gerens, oculos, os, colla, manusque,
> Vel qualem possent digiti formare Tonantis.
> Nescia mens illis, fieri quæ causa fuisset ;
> Tunc Deus et princeps ambos conjunxit in unum,
> Et remeat sua costa viro ; sua membra recepit ;
> Accipit et fœnus, quum non sit debitor ullus.
> His datur omnis humus, et quicquid jussa creavit,
> Aëris et pelagi fœtus, elementa duorum,
> Arbitrio commissa manent. His, crescite, dixit
> Omnipotens, replete solum de semine vestro,
> Sanguinis ingeniti natos nutrite nepotes,
> Et de prole novos iterum copulate jugales.
> Et dum terra fretum, dum cœlum sublevat aër,
> Dum solis micat axe jubar, dum luna tenebras
> Dissipat, et puro lucent mea sidera cœlo ;
> Sumere, quicquid habent pomaria nostra licebit ;
> Nam totum quod terra creat, quod pontus et aër
> Protulit, addictum vestro sub jure manebit,
> Deliciæque fluent vobis, et honesta voluptas ;
> Arboris unius tantum nescite saporem."

Dracontii Presbyt. Hispani Christ. | F. Arevalo. Romæ, 1791. Carmen de
secul. v. sub Theodos. M. Carmina, à | Deo, lib. i. v. 348. 415.

predominates over the other faculties, that truth cannot
help arraying itself in the garb of fiction; credulity
courts fiction, and fiction believes its own fables.   That
some of the Christian legends were deliberate
Legends. forgeries can scarcely be questioned; the principle of pious fraud appeared to justify this mode of
working on the popular mind; it was admitted and
avowed.   To deceive into Christianity was so valuable
a service, as to hallow deceit itself.   But the largest
portion was probably the natural birth of that imaginative excitement which quickens its day-dreams and
nightly visions into reality.   The Christian lived in a
supernatural world; the notion of the divine power, the
perpetual interference of the Deity, the agency of the
countless invisible beings which hovered over mankind,
was so strongly impressed upon the belief, that every
extraordinary, and almost every ordinary incident became a miracle, every inward emotion a suggestion
either of a good or an evil spirit.   A mythic period was
thus gradually formed, in which reality melted into
fable, and invention unconsciously trespassed on the
province of history.   This invention had very early let
itself loose, in the spurious gospels, or accounts
Spurious Gospels. of the lives of the Saviour and his Apostles,
which were chiefly, I conceive, composed among, or
rather against, the sects which were less scrupulous in
their veneration for the sacred books.   Unless Antido-
cetic, it is difficult to imagine any serious object in
fictions, in general so fantastic and puerile.[f]   This example had been set by some, probably, of the foreign
Jews, whose apocryphal books were as numerous and

---

[f] Compare what has been said on the Gospel of the Infancy, vol. i. page 127; though I would now observe that the antiquity of this gospel is very dubious.

as wild as those of the Christian sectaries. The Jews had likewise anticipated them in the interpolation or fabrication of the Sibylline verses. The fourth book of Esdras, the Shepherd of Hermas,[g] and other prophetic works, grew out of the Prophets and the book of Revelation, as the Gospels of Nicodemus, and that of the Infancy, and the various spurious acts of the different Apostles,[h] out of the Gospels and Acts. The Recognitions and other tracts which are called the Clementina, partake more of the nature of religious romance. Many of the former were obviously intended to pass for genuine records, and must be proscribed as unwarrantable fictions; the latter may rather have been designed to trace, and so to awaken religious feelings, than as altogether real history. The Lives of St. Anthony by Athanasius and of Hilarion by Jerome are the Lives of Saints. prototypes of the countless biographies of saints ; and with a strong outline of truth, became impersonations of the feeling, the opinions, the belief of the time. We

---

[g] The Shepherd of Hermas, as Bunsen has well shown, is a kind of ancient Pilgrim's Progress.—Christianity and Mankind, i. 182.

[h] Compare the Codex Apocryphus Novi Testamenti, by J. A. Fabricius, and Jones on the Canon. A more elaborate collection of these curious documents has been commenced (I trust not abandoned) by Dr. Thilo, Lipsiæ, 1832. Of these, by far the most remarkable in its composition and its influence, was the Gospel of Nicodemus. The author of this work was a poet, and of no mean invention. The latter part, which describes the descent of the Saviour to hell, to deliver "the spirits in prison," according to the hint in the epistle of St. Peter, (1 Peter iii. 19), is extremely striking and dramatic. This "harrowing of hell," as it is called in the old mysteries, became a favourite topic of Christian legend, founded on, and tending greatly to establish the popular belief in, a purgatory, and to open, as it were, to the fears of man, the terrors of the penal state. With regard to these spurious gospels in general, it is a curious question in what manner, so little noticed as they are in the higher Christian literature, they should have reached down, and so completely incorporated themselves, in the dark ages, with the superstitions of the vulgar. They would never have furnished so many subjects to painting, if they had not been objects of popular belief.

have no reason to doubt that the authors implicitly
believed whatever of fiction embellishes their own
unpremeditated fables; the colouring, though fanciful
and inconceivable to our eyes, was fresh and living to
theirs.

History itself could only reflect the proceedings of
the Christian world, as they appeared to that
world. We may lament that the annals of
Christianity found in the earliest times no historian
more judicious and trustworthy than Eusebius; the
heretical sects no less prejudiced and more philosophical
chronicler than Epiphanius: but in them, if not scru-
pulously veracious reporters of the events and characters
of the times, we possess almost all that we could reasonably hope; faithful reporters of the opinions entertained,
and the feelings excited by both. Few Christians of
that day would not have considered it the sacred duty
of a Christian to adopt that principle, avowed and
gloried in by Eusebius, but now made a bitter reproach,
that he would relate all that was to the credit, and pass
lightly over all which was to the dishonour of the faith.[1]

History.

---

[1] " In addition to these things (the appointment of rude and unfit persons to episcopal offices, and other delin-quencies), the ambition of many; the precipitate and illegitimate ordinations; the dissensions among the confessors; whatever the younger and more se-ditious so pertinaciously attempted against the remains of the Church, introducing innovation after innova-tion, and unsparingly, in the midst of the calamities of the persecution, adding new afflictions, and heaping evil upon evil; all these things I think it right to pass over, as unbefitting my history, which, as I stated in the beginning, declines and avoids the re-lation of such things. But whatsoever things, according to the sacred Scrip-ture, are ' honest and of good report:' if there be any virtue, and if there be any praise, these things I have thought it most befitting the history of these wonderful martyrs, to speak and to write and to address to the ears of the faithful." On this passage, de Martyr. Palæst. cxii., and that to which it alludes, E. H. viii. 2, the honesty and impartiality of Eusebius, which were not above suspicion in his own day (Tillemont, M. E. tom. i. part i. p. 67), have been severely questioned.

The historians of Christianity were credulous, but of that which it would have been considered impiety to disbelieve, even if they had the inclination.

The larger part of Christian literature consists in controversial writings, valuable to posterity as records of the progress of the human mind, and of the gradual developement of Christian opinions ; at times worthy of admiration for the force, the copiousness, and the subtlety of argument ; but too often repulsive from their solemn prolixity on insignificant subjects, and above all, the fierce, the unjust, and the acrimonious spirit with which they treat their adversaries. The Christian literature in prose (excluding the history and hagiography), may be distributed under five heads :—I. Apologies, or defences of the Faith, against Jewish, or more frequently Heathen adversaries. II. Hermeneutics, or commentaries on the sacred writings. III. Expositions of the principles and doctrines of the Faith. IV. Polemical works against the different sects and heresies. V. Orations.

I. I have already traced the manner in which the apology for Christianity, from humbly defen-
sive, became vigorously aggressive. The calm   Apologies.
appeal to justice and humanity, the earnest deprecation

Gibbon's observations on the subject gave rise to many dissertations. Müller, de Fide Euseb. Cæs. Havniæ, 1813. Danzius, de Euseb. Cæs. H. E. Scriptore, ejusque Fide Historicâ rectè æstimandâ. Jenæ, 1815. Kestner, Comment. de Euseb. H. E. Conditoris Auctoritate et Fide. See also Reuterdahl, de Fontibus H. E. Eusebianæ. Lond. Goth. 1826, and various passages in the Excursus of Heinichen. In many passages it is clear that Eusebius did not adhere to his own rule of partiality. His Ecclesiastical History, though probably highly coloured in many parts, is by no means an uniform panegyric on the early Christians. Strict impartiality could not be expected from a Christian writer of that day ; and probably Eusebius erred more often from credulity than from dishonesty. Yet the unbelief produced, in later times, by the fictitious character of early Christian History, may show how dangerous, how fatal, may be the least departure from truth. On pious fraud read Mosheim, Diss. i. 206, *et seqq.*

of the odious calumnies with which the Christians were charged, the plea for toleration, gradually rise to the vehement and uncompromising proscription of the folly and guilt of idolatry. Tertullian marks, as it were, the period of transition, though his fiery temper may perhaps have anticipated the time when Christianity, in the consciousness of strength, instead of endeavouring to appease or avert the wrath of hostile Paganism, might defy it to deadly strife. The earliest extant apology, that of Justin Martyr, is by no means severe in argument or vigorous in style, and though not altogether abstaining from recrimination, is still rather humble and deprecatory in its tone. The short apologetic orations—as the Christians had to encounter not merely the general hostility of the Government or the people, but direct and argumentative treatises, written against them by the philosophic party—gradually swelled into books. The first of these is perhaps the best, that of Origen against Celsus. The intellect of Origen, notwithstanding its occasional fantastic aberrations, appears to me more suited to grapple with this lofty argument than the diffuse and excursive Eusebius, whose Evangelic Preparation and Demonstration heaped together vast masses of curious but by no means convincing learning, and the feebler, more violent, and less candid Cyril of Alexandria, in his Books against Julian. I have already noticed the great work which perhaps might be best arranged under this head, the "City of God" of St. Augustine; but there was one short treatise which may vindicate the Christian Latin literature from the charge of barbarism: perhaps no late work, either Pagan or Christian, reminds us of the golden days of Latin prose so much as the Octavius of Minucius Felix.

II. The Hermeneutics, or the interpretation of the sacred writers, might be expected to have _{Hermeneu-} more real value and authority than can be ^{tics.} awarded them by sober and dispassionate judgement. But it cannot be denied that almost all these writers, including those of highest name, are fanciful in their inferences, discover mysteries in the plainest sentences, wander away from the clear historical, moral, or religious meaning, into a long train of corollaries, at which we arrive we know not how. Piety, in fact, read in the Scripture whatever it chose to read, and the devotional feeling it excited was at once the end and the test of the biblical commentary. But the character of the age and the school in which the Christian teachers were trained, must here, as in other cases, be taken into account. The most sober Jewish system of interpretation (setting aside the wild cabalistic notions of the significance of letters, the frequency of their recurrence, their collocation, and all those strange theories which were engendered by a servile veneration of the very form and language of the sacred writings) allowed itself at least an equal latitude of authoritative inference. The Platonists spun out the thoughts or axioms of their master into as fine and subtle a web of mystic speculation. The general principle of an esoteric or recondite meaning in all works which commanded veneration, was universally received; it was this principle upon which the Gnostic sects formed all their vague and mystic theories; and if in this respect the Christian teachers did not bind themselves by much severer rules of reasoning than prevailed around them on all sides, they may have been actuated partly by some jealousy, lest their own plainer and simpler sacred writings should appear dry and barren, in comparison with the rich and imaginative freedom of their adversaries.

III. The expositions of faith and practice may com-
Expositions prehend all the smaller treatises on particular
of Faith. duties ; prayer, almsgiving, marriage, and celibacy. They depend, of course, for their merit and authority on the character of the writer.

IV. Christianity might appear, if we judge by the
Polemical proportion which the controversial writings
writings. bear to the rest of Christian literature, to have introduced an element of violent and implacable discord. Nor does the tone of these polemical writings, by which alone we can judge of the ancient heresies, of which the heretics' own accounts have almost entirely perished, impress us very favourably with their fairness or candour. But it must be remembered that, after all, the field of literature was not the arena in which the great contest between Christianity and the world was waged; it was in the private circle of each separate congregation, which was constantly but silently enlarging its boundaries : it was the immediate contact of mind with mind, the direct influence of the Christian clergy and even the more pious of the laity, which were tranquilly and noiselessly pursuing their course of conversion.[k]

[k] I might perhaps have made another and a very interesting branch of the prose Christian literature, the epistolary. The letters of the great writers form one of the most valuable parts of their works. The Latin Fathers, however, maintain that superiority over the Greek, which in classical times is asserted by Cicero and Pliny. The letters of Cyprian and Ambrose are of the highest interest as historical documents; those of Jerome, for manners; those of Augustine, perhaps, for style. They far surpass those of Chrysostom, which we must, however, recollect were written from his dreary and monotonous place of exile. Yet Chrysostom's are superior to that dullest of all collections, the huge folio of the letters of Libanius.

These treatises, however, were principally addressed to the clergy, and through them worked downward into the mass of the Christian people: even with the more rapid and frequent communication which took place in the Christian world, they were but partially and imperfectly disseminated; but that which became another considerable and important part of their literature, their oratory, had in the first instance been directly addressed to the popular mind, and formed the chief part of the popular instruction. Christian preaching had opened a new field for eloquence.

V. Oratory, that oratory at least which communicates its own impulses and passions to the heart, which not merely persuades the reason, but sways the whole soul of man, had suffered a long and total silence. It had everywhere expired with the republican institutions. The discussions in the senate had been controlled by the imperial presence; and even if the Roman senators had asserted the fullest freedom of speech, and allowed themselves the most exciting fervour of language, this was but one assembly in a single city, formed out of a confined aristocracy. The municipal assemblies were alike rebuked by the awe of a presiding master, the provincial governor, and of course afforded a less open field for stirring and general eloquence. The perfection of jurisprudence had probably been equally fatal to judicial oratory; we hear of great lawyers, but not of distinguished advocates. The highest flight of Pagan oratory which remains is in the adulatory panegyrics of the Emperors, pronounced by rival candidates for favour. Rhetoric was taught, indeed, and practised as a liberal, but it had sunk into a mere, art; it was taught by salaried professors in all the great towns to the higher youth; but they were mere exer-

cises of fluent diction, on trite or obsolete subjects, the
characters of the heroes of the Iliad, or some subtle
question of morality.[m]

It is impossible to conceive a more sudden and total
change than from the school of the rhetorician to a
crowded Christian church. The orator suddenly emerged
from a listless audience of brother scholars, before whom
he had discussed some one of those trivial questions according to formal rules, and whose ear could require no
more than terseness or elegance of diction, and a just
distribution of the argument: emotion was neither
expected nor could be excited. He found himself
among a breathless and anxious multitude, whose
eternal destiny might seem to hang on his lips, catching
up and treasuring his words as those of divine inspiration, and interrupting his more eloquent passages
by almost involuntary acclamations.[n] The orator, in
the best days of Athens, the tribune, in the most turbulent periods of Rome, had not such complete hold upon
the minds of his hearers; and—but that the sublime
nature of his subject usually lay above the sphere of immediate action, but that, the purer and loftier its tone,
if it found instantaneous sympathy, yet it also met the
constant inert resistance of prejudice, and ignorance, and
vice to its authority,—the power with which this privilege of oratory would have invested the clergy would
have been far greater than that of any of the former
political or sacerdotal dominations. Wherever the

---

[m] The declamations of Quintilian
are no doubt favourable specimens both
of the subjects and the style of these
orators.

[n] These acclamations sometimes re-
warded the more eloquent and successful teachers of rhetoric. Themistius
speaks of the ἐκβοήσεις τε καὶ κρό-
τους, οἴων θαμὰ ἀπολαύουσι παρ'
ὑμῶν οἱ δαιμόνιοι σοφισταί. Ba-
sanistes, p. 236, edit. Deindorf. Compare the note. Chrysostom's works
are full of allusions to these acclamations.

oratory of the pulpit coincided with human passion, it
was irresistible, and sometimes when it resolutely encountered it, it might extort an unwilling triumph:
when it appealed to faction, to ferocity, to sectarian
animosity, it swept away its audience like a torrent,
to any violence or madness at which it aimed; when
to virtue, to piety, to peace, it at times subdued the
most refractory, and received the homage of devout
obedience.

The bishop in general, at least when the hierarchical
power became more dominant, reserved for himself
an office so productive of influence and so liable to
abuse.[o] But men like Athanasius or Augustine were
not compelled to wait for that qualification of rank.
They received the ready permission of the bishop to
exercise at once this important function. In general, a
promising orator would rarely want opportunity of distinction; and he who had obtained celebrity would

---

[o] The laity were long permitted to
address the people in the absence of
the clergy. It was objected to the
Bishop Demetrius, that he had permitted an unprecedented innovation in
the case of Origen: he had allowed a
layman to teach when *the bishop was
present.* Euseb. E. H. vi. 19. Ὁ δι-
δάσκων, εἰ καὶ λαϊκὸς ᾖ, ἔμπειρος δὲ
τοῦ λόγου, καὶ τὸν τρόπον σεμνὸς,
διδασκέτω. Constit. Apost. viii. 32.
23. "Laicus, præsentibus clericis, nisi
illis jubentibus, docere non audeat."
Conc. Carth. can. 98. Jerome might
be supposed, in his indignant remonstrance against the right which almost
all assumed of interpreting the Scriptures, to be writing of later days.

" Quod medicorum est, promittunt me-
dici, tractant fabrilia fabri. Sola
Scripturarum ars est, quam sibi omnes
passim vindicant. Scribimus, indocti
doctique poëmata passim. *Hanc gar-
rula anus,* hanc delirus senex, hanc
sophista verbosus, hanc universi præ-
sumunt, lacerant, *docent antequam dis-
cant.* Alii addicto supercilio, grandia
verba trutinantes, inter mulierculas
de sacris literis philosophantur. Alii
discunt, proh pudor! à feminis, quod
viros doceant: et ne parum hoc sit
quadam facilitate verborum, imò au-
daciâ, edisserunt aliis quod ipsi non
intelligunt." Epist. l. ad Paulinum,
vol. iv. p. 571.

frequently be raised by general acclamation, or by a·
just appreciation of his usefulness by the higher clergy,
to an episcopal throne.[p]

But it is difficult to conceive the general effect
produced by this devotion of oratory to its new office.
From this time, instead of seizing casual opportunities
of working on the mind and heart of man, it was constantly, regularly, in every part of the empire, with
more or less energy, with greater or less commanding
authority, urging the doctrines of Christianity on awe-
struck and submissive hearers. It had, of course, as
it always has had, its periods of more than usual excitement, its sudden paroxysms of power, by which it
convulsed some part of society. The constancy and
regularity with which, in the ordinary course of things,
it discharged its function, may in some degree have
deadened its influence; and in the period of ignorance
and barbarism, the instruction was chiefly through the
ceremonial, the symbolic worship, the painting, and even
the dramatic representation.

Still, this new moral power, though intermitted at
times, and even suspended, was almost continually operating, in its great and sustained energy, throughout the
Christian world; though of course strongly tempered
with the dominant spirit of Christianity, and, excepting
in those periods either ripe for or preparing some great
change in religious sentiment or opinion, the living and
general expression of the prevalent Christianity, it was
always in greater or less activity, instilling the broader
principles of Christian faith and morals; if superstitious,
rarely altogether silent; if appealing to passions which

---

[p] But compare Latin Christianity. Pope Leo I., vol. i. p. 168.

ought to have been rebuked before its voice, and exciting those feelings of hostility between conflicting sects which it should have allayed,—yet even then in some hearts its gentler and more Christian tones made a profound and salutary impression, while its more violent language fell off without mingling with the uncongenial feelings. The great principles of the religion,—the providence of God, the redemption by Christ, the immortality of the soul, future retribution,—gleamed through all the fantastic and legendary lore with which the faith was encumbered and obscured in the darker ages. Christianity first imposed it as a duty on one class of men to be constantly enforcing moral and religious truths on all mankind. Though that duty, of course, was discharged with very different energy, judgement, and success, at different periods, it was always a strong counteracting power, an authorised, and in general respected, remonstrance against the vices and misery of mankind. Man was perpetually reminded that he was an immortal being under the protection of a wise and all-ruling Providence, and destined for a higher state of existence.

Nor was this influence only immediate and temporary: Christian oratory did not cease to speak when its echoes had died away upon the ear, and its expressions faded from the hearts of those to whom it was addressed. The orations of the Basils and Chrysostoms, the Ambroses and Augustines, became one of the most important parts of Christian literature. That eloquence which, in Rome and Greece, had been confined to civil and judicial affairs, was now inseparably connected with religion. The oratory of the pulpit took its place with that of the bar, the comitia, or the senate, as the historical record of that which once had powerfully moved the minds of multitudes. No part of Christian literature so vividly reflects the times, the tone of religious doctrine or sentiment, in many cases the manners, habits, and character of the period, as the sermons of the leading teachers.

CHAPTER IV.

Christianity and the Fine Arts.

As in literature, so in the fine arts, Christianity had to await that period in which it should become completely interwoven with the feelings and moral being of mankind, before it could put forth all its creative energies, and kindle into active productiveness those new principles of the noble and the beautiful, which it infused into the human imagination. The dawn of a new civilisation must be the first epoch for the full developement of Christian art. The total disorganisation of society, which was about to take place, implied the total suspension of the arts which embellish social life. The objects of admiration were swept away by the destructive ravages of Barbarian warfare ; or, where they were left in contemptuous indifference, the mind had neither leisure to indulge, nor refinement enough to feel, that admiration, which belongs to a more secure state of society, and of repose from the more pressing toils and anxieties of life.

Fine arts.

This suspended animation of the fine arts was of course different in degree in the various parts of Europe, in proportion as they were exposed to the ravages of war, the comparative barbarism of the tribes by which they were overrun, the station held by the clergy, the security which they could command by

the sanctity of their character, and their disposable
wealth. At every period, from Theodoric, who dwelt
with vain fondness on the last struggles of decaying
art, to Charlemagne, who seemed to hail, with prophetic
taste, the hope of its revival, there is no period in which
the tradition of art was not preserved in some part of
Europe, though obscured by ignorance, barbarism, and
that still worse enemy, if possible, false and meretricious
taste. Christianity, in every branch of the arts, preserved something from the general wreck, and brooded
in silence over the imperfect rudiments of each, of
which it was the sole conservator. The mere mechanical skill of working stone, of delineating the human
face, and of laying on colours so as to produce something like illusion, was constantly exercised in the works
which religion required to awaken the torpid emotions
of an ignorant and superstitious people.[a]

In all the arts, Christianity was at first, of course,
purely imitative, and imitative of the prevalent degenerate style. It had not yet felt its strength, and dared
not develope, or dreamed not of those latent principles
which lay beneath its religion, and which hereafter
were to produce works, in its own style, and its own
department, rivalling all the wonders of antiquity; when
the extraordinary creations of its proper architecture
were to arise, far surpassing in the skill of their construction, in their magnitude more than equalling those
wonders, and in their opposite indeed, but not less
majestic, style, vindicating the genius of Christianity:
when Italy was to transcend ancient Greece in painting
as much as the whole modern world is inferior to Greece
in the rival art of sculpture.

[a] The Iconoclasts had probably more the Barbarians themselves in the
influence in barbarising the East than West.

I. Architecture was the first of these arts which was summoned to the service of Christianity. The devotion of the earlier ages did not need, and could not command, this subsidiary to pious emotion, —it imparted sanctity to the meanest building; now it would not be content without enshrining its triumphant worship in a loftier edifice. Religion at once offered this proof of its sincerity by the sacrifice of wealth to this hallowed purpose; and the increasing splendour of the religious edifices reacted upon the general devotion, by the feelings of awe and veneration which they inspired. Splendour, however, did not disdain to be subservient to use; and the arrangements of the new buildings, which arose in all quarters, or were diverted to this new object, accommodated themselves to the Christian ceremonial. In the East, I have already shown, in the church of Tyre, described by Eusebius, the ancient temple lending its model to the Christian church; and the basilica, in the West, adapted with still greater ease and propriety for Christian worship.[b] There were many distinctive points which materially affected the style of Christian architecture. The simplicity of the Grecian temple, as it has been shown,[c] harmonised perfectly only with its own form of worship; it was more of a public place, sometimes, indeed, hypæthral, or open to the air. The Christian worship demanded more complete enclosure; the church was more of a chamber, in which the voice of an individual could be distinctly heard; and the whole assembly of worshippers, sheltered from the change or inclemency of the weather, or the intrusion of unauthorised persons, might listen in undisturbed devotion to the prayer, the reading of the scripture, or the preacher.

Architecture.

[b] Vol. ii. pp. 239, 240.   [c] Vol. ii. pp. 340, 344.

One consequence of this was the necessity of regular
apertures for the admission of light;[d] and these
imperatively demanded a departure from the
plan of temple architecture.

Windows.

Windows had been equally necessary in the basilicæ
for the public legal proceedings; the reading legal
documents required a bright and full light; and
in the basilicæ the windows were numerous and large.
The nave, probably from the earliest period, was lighted
by clerestory windows, which were above the roof of
the lower aisles.[e]

Throughout the West, the practice of converting the
basilica into the church continued to a late period;
the very name seemed appropriate : the royal hall was
changed into a dwelling for the GREAT KING.[f]

---

[d] In the fanciful comparison (in H. E. x. 4) which Eusebius draws between the different parts of the church and the different gradations of catechumens, he speaks of the most perfect as " shone on by the light through the windows:"—τοὺς δὲ πρὸς τὸ φῶς ἀνοίγμασι καταυγάζει. He seems to describe the temple as full of light, emblematical of the heavenly light diffused by Christ, — λαμπρὸν καὶ φωτὸς ἔμπλεω τά τε ἔνδοθεν καὶ τὰ ἐκτὸς : but it is not easy to discover where his metaphor ends and his fact begins. See Ciampini, vol. i. p. 74.

[e] The size of the windows has been disputed by Christian antiquaries : some asserted that the early Christians, accustomed to the obscurity of their crypts and catacombs, preferred narrow apertures for light; others that the services, especially reading the Scriptures, required it to be both bright and equally diffused. Ciampini, as an Italian, prefers the latter, and sarcastically alludes to the narrow windows of Gothic architecture, introduced by the "Vandals," whose first object being to exclude the cold of their northern climate, they contracted the windows to the narrowest dimensions possible. In the monastic churches, the light was excluded, " quia monachis meditantibus fortasse officiebat, quominùs possent intento animo soli Deo vacare." Ciampini, Vetera Monumenta. This author considers that the parochial or cathedral churches may, in general, be distinguished from the monastic by this test.

[f] " Basilicæ priùs vocabantur regum habitacula, nunc autem ideo basilicæ divina templa nominantur, quia ibi Regi omnium Deo cultus et sacrificia offeruntur." Isidor. Orig. lib. v. " Basilicæ olim negotiis pæne, nunc votis pro tuâ salute susceptis." Auson. Grat. Act. pro Consul.

The more minute subdivision of the internal arrangement contributed to form the peculiar character of Christian architecture. The different orders of Christians were distributed according to their respective degrees of proficiency. But besides this, the church had inherited from the synagogue, and from the general feeling of the East, the principle of secluding the female part of the worshippers. Enclosed galleries, on a higher level, were probably common in the synagogues; and this arrangement appears to have been generally adopted in the earlier Christian churches.[g] *Subdivision of the building.*

This great internal complexity necessarily led to still farther departure from the simplicity of design in the exterior plan and elevation. The single or the double row of columns, reaching from the top to the bottom of the building, with the long and unbroken horizontal line of the roof reposing upon it, would give place to rows ot unequal heights, or to the division into separate stories.

The same process had probably taken place in the palatial architecture of Rome. Instead of one order of columns, which reached from the top to the bottom of the buildings, rows of columns, one above the other, marked the different stories into which the building was divided.

Christianity thus, from the first, either at once assumed, or betrayed its tendency to, its peculiar character. Its harmony was not that of the Greek, arising from the breadth and simplicity of one design, which, if at times too vast for the eye to contemplate at a single glance, was comprehended and felt at once by the mind; of which the lines were all horizontal and regular, and the

---

[g] " Populi confluunt ad ecclesias castâ celebritate, honestâ utriusque sexûs discretione." Augustin. de Civ. Dei, ii. 28. Compare Bingham, viñ. 5, 5.

general impression a majestic or graceful uniformity, either awful from its massiveness or solidity, or pleasing from its lightness and delicate proportion.

The harmony of the Christian building (if in fact it attained, before its perfection in the mediæval Gothic, to that first principle of architecture) consisted in the combination of many separate parts, duly balanced into one whole; the subordination of the accessories to the principal object; the multiplication of distinct objects coalescing into one rich and effective mass, and pervaded and reduced to a kind of symmetry by one general character in the various lines and in the style of ornament.

This predominance of complexity over simplicity, of variety over symmetry, was no doubt greatly increased by the buildings which, from an early period, arose around the central church, especially in all the monastic institutions. The baptistery was often a separate building, and frequently, in the ordinary structures for worship, dwellings for the officiating priesthood were attached to, or adjacent to, the church. The Grecian temple appears often to have stood alone, on the brow of a hill, in a grove, or in some other commanding or secluded situation. In Rome, many of the pontifical offices were held by patricians, who occupied their own palaces; but the Eastern temples were in general surrounded by spacious courts, and with buildings for the residence of the sacerdotal colleges. If these were not the models of the Christian establishments, the same ecclesiastical arrangements, the institution of a numerous and wealthy priestly order attached to the churches, demanded the same accommodation. Thus a multitude of subordinate buildings would crowd around the central or more eminent house of God. At first, where mere

convenience was considered, and where the mind had
not awakened to the solemn impressions excited by
vast and various architectural works, combined by a
congenial style of building, and harmonised by skilful
arrangement and subordination, they would be piled
together irregularly and capriciously, obscuring that
which was really grand, and displaying irreverent confusion rather than stately order. Gradually, as the
sense of grandeur and solemnity dawned upon the mind,
there would arise the desire of producing one general
effect and impression; but this no doubt was the later
developement of a principle which, if at first dimly perceived, was by no means rigidly or consistently followed
out. We must wait many centuries before we reach the
culminating period of genuine Christian architecture.

II. Sculpture alone, of the fine arts, has been faithful
to its parent Paganism. It has never cordially
imbibed the spirit of Christianity. The second   Sculpture.
creative epoch (how poor, comparatively, in fertility and
originality!) was contemporary and closely connected
with the revival of classical literature in Europe. It
has lent itself to Christian sentiment chiefly in two
forms; as necessary and subordinate to architecture,
and as monumental sculpture.

Christianity was by no means so intolerant, at least
after its first period, of the remains of ancient sculpture,
or so perseveringly hostile to the art, as might have
been expected from its severe aversion to idolatry. The
earlier fathers, indeed, condemn the arts of sculpture
and of painting as inseparably connected with Paganism.
Every art which frames an image is irreclaimably idolatrous;[h] and the stern Tertullian reproaches Hermogenes

---

[h] " Ubi artifices statuarum et imaginum et omnis generis simulachrorum
diabolus sæculo intulit—caput facta
est idololatriæ ars omnis quæ idolum

with the two deadly sins of painting and marrying.[1]
The Council of Elvira proscribed paintings on the walls
of churches,[k] which nevertheless became a common
usage during the two next centuries.

In all respects, this severer sentiment was mitigated
by time. The civil uses of sculpture were generally
recognised. The Christian emperors erected, or permitted the adulation of their subjects to erect, their
statues in the different cities. That of Constantine on
the great porphyry column, with its singular and unchristian confusion of attributes, has been already noticed.
Philostorgius indeed asserts that this statue became an
object of worship even to the Christians; that lights and
frankincense were offered before it, and that the image
was worshipped as that of a tutelary god.[m] The sedition in Antioch arose out of insults to the statues of
the emperors,[n] and the erection of the statue of the
empress before the great church in Constantinople gave
rise to the last disturbance, which ended in the exile of
Chrysostom.[o] The statue of the emperor was long the
representative of the imperial presence; it was reve-
renced in the capital and in the provincial cities with
honours approaching to adoration.[p] The modest law of

---

quoque modo edit." Tertull. de Idol.
c. iii. He has no language to express
his horror that makers of images
should be admitted into the clerical
order.

[1] " Pingit illicitè, nubit assiduè, legem Dei in libidinem defendit, in artem
contemnit ; bis falsarius et cauterio et
stylo." In Hermog. cap. i. "Cauterio"
refers to encaustic painting. The
Apostolic Constitutions reckon a maker
of idols with persons of infamous character and profession. viii. 32.

[k] " Placuit picturas in ecclesiâ esse
non debere, ne quod colitur et adoratur,
in parietibus depingatur." Can. xxxvi.
[m] Vol. ii. p. 337. Philostorg.
ii. 17.
[n] Vol. iii. p. 123.
[o] Vol. iii. p. 144.
[p] Εἰ γὰρ βασιλέως ἀπόντος εἰκὼν
ἀναπληροῖ χώραν βασιλέως, καὶ
προσκυνοῦσιν ἄρχοντες ·καὶ ἱερομη-
νίαι ἐπιτελοῦνται, καὶ ἄρχοντες
ὑπαντῶσι, καὶ δῆμοι προσκυνοῦσιν
οὐ πρὸς τὴν σάνιδα βλέποντες ἀλλὰ

Theodosius, by which he attempted to regulate these
ceremonies, of which the adulation bordered at times
on impiety, expressly reserved the excessive honours,
sometimes lavished on these statues at the public games,
for the supreme Deity.[q]

The statues even of the gods were condemned with
some reluctance and remorse. No doubt iconoclasm,
under the first edicts of the emperors, raged in the provinces with relentless violence. Yet Constantine, we
have seen, did not scruple to adorn his capital with
images both of gods and men, plundered indiscriminately
from the temples of Greece. The Christians, indeed,
asserted that they were set up for scorn and contempt.

Even Theodosius exempts such statues as were admirable as works of art from the common sentence of
destruction.[r] This doubtful toleration of profane art
gradually gave place to the admission of Art into the
service of Christianity.

Sculpture, and, still more, Painting, were after no long
time received as the ministers of Christian piety, and
allowed to lay their offerings at the feet of the new
religion.

But the commencement of Christian art was slow,
timid, and rude. It long preferred allegory to repre-

πρὸς τὸν χαρακτῆρα τοῦ βασιλέως,
οὐκ ἐν τῇ φύσει θεωρουμένου ἀλλ'
ἐν γραφῇ παραδεικνυμένου. Joann.
Damascen. de Imagin. orat. 9. Jerome, however (on Daniel), compared
it to the worship demanded by Ne-
buchadnezzar. " Ergo judices et prin-
cipes sæculi, qui imperatorum statuas
adorant et imagines, hoc se facere in-
telligent quod tres pueri facere no-
lentes placuêre Deo."

[q] They were to prove their loyalty
by the respect which they felt for the
statue in their secret hearts :—" exce-
densc ultura hominum dignitatum su-
pernonumini reservetur." Cod. Theod.
xv. 4, 1.

[r] A particular temple was to remain
open, " in quâ simulachra feruntur
posita, artis pretio quam divinitate
metienda." Cod. Theod. xvi. 10, 8.

sentation, the true and legitimate object of art.[5] It expanded but tardily during the first centuries, from the significant symbol to the human form in colour or in marble.

The Cross was long the primal, and even the sole, symbol of Christianity—the cross in its rudest and its most artless form; for many centuries elapsed before the image of the Saviour was wrought upon it. It was the copy of the common instrument of ignominious execution in all its nakedness; and nothing, indeed, so powerfully attests the triumph of Christianity as the elevation of this, which to the Jew and the Heathen was the basest, the most degrading, punishment of the lowest criminal,[t] the proverbial terror of the wretched slave, into an object for the adoration of ages, the reverence of

---

[5] Rumohr. Italienische Forschungen, i. p. 158. We want the German words *andeutung* (allusion or suggestion, but neither conveys the same forcible sense), and *darstellung*, actual representation or placing before the sight. The artists who employ the first can only address minds already furnished with the key to the symbolic or allegoric form. Imitation (the genuine object of art) speaks to all mankind.

[t] The author has expressed in a former work his impression on this most remarkable fact in the history of Christianity.

"In one respect it is impossible now to conceive the extent to which the Apostles of the *crucified* Jesus shocked all the feelings of mankind. The public establishment of Christianity, the adoration of ages, the reverence of nations, has thrown around the Cross of Christ an indelible and inalienable sanc-tity. No effort of the imagination can dissipate the illusion of dignity which has gathered round it; it has been so long dissevered from all its coarse and humiliating associations, that it cannot be cast back and desecrated into its state of opprobrium and contempt. To the most daring unbeliever among ourselves it is the symbol—the absurd and irrational, he may conceive, but still the ancient and venerable symbol —of a powerful and influential religion. What was it to the Jew and the Heathen?—the basest, the most degrading, punishment of the lowest criminal, the proverbial terror of the wretched slave! It was to them what the most despicable and revolting instrument of public execution is to us. Yet to the Cross of Christ men turned from deities, in which were embodied every attribute of strength, power, and dignity," &c. Milman's Bampton Lectures, p. 279.

nations. The glowing language of Chrysostom expresses the universal sanctity of the Cross in the fourth century. "Nothing so highly adorns the imperial crown as the Cross, which is more precious than the whole world: its form, at which, of old, men shuddered with horror, is now so eagerly and emulously sought for, that it is found among princes and subjects, men and women, virgins and matrons, slaves and freemen; for all bear it about, perpetually impressed on the most honourable part of the body, or on the forehead as on a pillar,. This appears in the sacred temple, in the ordination of priests; it shines again on the body of the Lord, and in the mystic supper. It is to be seen everywhere in honour, in the private house and the public market-place, in the desert, in the highway, on mountains, in forests, on hills, on the sea, in ships, on islands, on our beds, and on our clothes, on our arms, in our chambers, in our banquets, on gold and silver vessels, on gems, in the paintings of our walls, on the bodies of diseased beasts, on human bodies possessed by devils, in war and peace, by day, by night, in the dances of the feasting, and the meetings of the fasting and praying." In the time of Chrysostom the legend of the Discovery of the True Cross was generally received. "Why do all men vie with each other to approach that true Cross, on which the sacred body was crucified? Why do many, women as well as men, bear fragments of it set in gold as ornaments round their necks, though it was the sign of condemnation. Even emperors have laid aside the diadem to take up the Cross." [u]

---

[u] Chrysost. Oper. vol. i. p. 57. 569. See in Munter's work (p. 68, et seq.) the various forms which the Cross assumed, and the fanciful notions concerning it.

"Ipsa species crucis quid est nisi forma quadrata mundi? Oriens de vertice fulgens; Arcton dextra tenet;

A more various symbolism gradually grew up, and
extended to what approached nearer to works
of art. Its rude designs were executed in
engravings on seals, or on lamps, or glass vessels, and
before long in relief on marble, or in paintings on
the walls of the cemeteries. The earliest of these were
the seal rings, of which many now exist, with Gnostic
symbols and inscriptions. These seals were considered
indispensable in ancient housekeeping. The Christian
was permitted, according to Clement of Alexandria,
to bestow on his wife one ring of gold, in order that,
being entrusted with the care of his domestic concerns,
she might seal up that which might be insecure. But
these rings must not have any idolatrous engraving,
only such as might suggest Christian or gentle thoughts,
the dove, the fish,[x] the ship, the anchor, or the Apostolic fisherman fishing for men, which would remind
them of children drawn out of the waters of baptism.[y]
Tertullian mentions a communion cup with the image of
the Good Shepherd embossed upon it. But Christian
symbolism soon disdained these narrow limits, extended
itself into the whole domain of the Old Testament
as well as of the Gospel, and even ventured at times

Symbolism.

Auster in lævâ consistit; Occidens sub
plantis formatur. Unde Apostolus
dicit : ut sciamus, quæ sit altitudo, et
latitudo, et longitudo, et profundum.
Aves quando volant ad æthera, formam
crucis assumunt; homo natans per
aquas, vel orans, formâ crucis vehitur.
Navis per maria antennâ cruci similatâ
sufflatur. Thau litera signum salutis
et crucis describitur." Hieronym. in
Marc. xv.

[x] The 'ΙΧΘΥΣ, according to the
rule of the ancient anagram, meant
'Ιησοῦς Χριστὸς Θεοῦ Υἱὸς Σωτήρ.

It is remarkable, according to the
high authority of the Cavalier de
Rossi, that after Constantine the
ΙΧΘΥΣ as an anagram and as a symbol almost entirely disappears. It
was a secret symbol used for the purpose of what we may venture to call
Christian Freemasonry in early and
dangerous times.—See the long and
very curious letter addressed to Dom
Pitra, Editor of the Spicilegium So-
lesmense, t. iii. ; especially p. 498.

[y] Clem. Alex. Pædagog. iii. 2.

over the unhallowed borders of Paganism. The persons
and incidents of the Old Testament had all a typical or
allegorical reference to the doctrines of Christianity.[x]
Adam asleep, while Eve was taken from his side, represented the death of Christ; Eve, the mother of all who
are born to new life; Adam and Eve with the serpent
had a latent allusion to the new Adam and the Cross.
Cain and Abel, Noah and the ark with the dove and the
olive branch, the sacrifice of Isaac, Joseph sold by his
brethren as a bondslave, Moses by the burning bush,
breaking the tables of the law, striking water from the
rock, with Pharaoh perishing in the Red Sea, the ark of
God, Samson bearing the gates of Gaza, Job on the
dung-heap, David and Goliah, Elijah in the car of fire,
Tobias with the fish, Daniel in the lion's den, Jonah
issuing from the whale's belly or under the gourd, the
three children in the fiery furnace, Ezekiel by the valley
of dead bones, were favourite subjects, and had all their
mystic significance.   They reminded the devout worshipper of the Sacrifice, Resurrection, and Redemption
of Christ.   The direct illustrations of the New Testament showed the Lord of the Church on a high mountain, with four rivers, the Gospels, flowing from it; the
Good Shepherd bearing the lamb,[a] and sometimes
the Apostles and Saints of a later time appeared in the
symbols.   Paganism lent some of her spoils to the conqueror.[b]   The Saviour was represented under the

---

[x] See Mamachi, Dei Costumi de' primitivi Christiani, lib. i. c. iv.

[a] There is a Heathen prototype (see
R. Rochette) even for this good shepherd, and one of the earliest images is
encircled with the "Four Seasons"
represented by Genii with Pagan attributes.   Compare Munter, p. 61.

Tombstones, and even inscriptions,
were freely borrowed. One Christian
tomb has been published by P. Lupi,
inscribed "Diis Manibus."

[b] In three very curious dissertations
in the last volume of the Memoirs of
the Academy of Inscriptions on works
of art in the catacombs of Rome, M.

person and with the lyre of Orpheus, either as the
civiliser of men, or in allusion to the Orphic poetry,
which had already been interpolated with Christian
images. Hence also the lyre was the emblem of truth.
Other images, particularly those of animals, were not
uncommon.[c] The Church was represented by a ship,
the anchor denoted the pure ground of faith; the stag
implied the hart which thirsted after the water-brooks;
the horse the rapidity with which men ought to run and
embrace the doctrine of salvation; the hare the timid
Christian hunted by persecutors; the lion prefigured
strength, or appeared as the emblem of the tribe of
Judah; the fish was an anagram of the Saviour's name;
the dove indicated the simplicity, the cock the vigilance, of the Christian; the peacock and the phœnix
the Resurrection.

But these were simple and artless memorials to which
devotion gave all their value and significance; in them-

Raoul Rochette has shown how much,
either through the employment of
Heathen artists, or their yet imperfectly unheathenised Christianity, the
Christians borrowed from the monumental decorations, the symbolic
figures, and even the inscriptions, of
Heathenism. M. Rochette says, " La
physionomie presque payenne qu'offre
la décoration des catacombes de Rome,"
p. 96. The Protestant travellers,
Burnet and Misson, from the singular
mixture of the sacred and the profane
in these monuments, inferred that
these catacombs were common places
of burial for Heathens and Christians.
The Roman antiquarians, however,
have clearly proved the contrary. M.
Raoul Rochette, as well as M. Rostelli
(in an Essay in the Roms Beschreibung), consider this point conclusively
made out in favour of the Roman
writers. M. R. Rochette has adduced
monuments in which the symbolic
images and the language of Heathenism and Christianity are strangely
mingled together. Munter had observed
the Jordan represented as a river god.

[c] The catacombs at Rome are the
chief authorities for this symbolic
school of Christian art. They are represented in the works of Bosio, Roma
Sotteranea, Aringhi, Bottari, and Boldetti. But perhaps the best view of
them, being in fact a very judicious
and well-arranged selection of the most
curious works of early Christian art,
may be found in the Sinnbilder und
Kunstvorstellungen der alten Christen,
by Bishop Munter.

The

selves they neither had, nor aimed at grandeur or
beauty. They touched the soul by the reminiscences
which they awakened, or the thoughts which they suggested; they had nothing of that inherent power over
the emotions of the soul which belongs to the higher
works of art.[d]

Art must draw nearer to human nature and to the

The recent discoveries in the Catacombs add some curious facts to the
history of the symbolism of Christian
art. In the catacomb of Callistus discovered and explored by the Cav.
de Rossi, which contains according to
his statement the remains of eleven
Roman Pontiffs, from Pontianus to
Melchiades, as well as those of St.
Cæcilia, appear, in I fear fading colours,
symbolic representations of the Rite of
Baptism and of the Holy Eucharist.
There is a man with a cloak or pallium over a tunic, laying hands on a
naked child, just emerged from a
stream of running water; on the other
side is a seated figure, with a pallium,
like the dress of a philosopher, apparently in the act of preaching.

The symbolism of the Eucharist is
more various, in more than one picture, and therefore more obscure.
In one is a table with loaves of bread,
and a fish in a platter. On one wall
is a man stretching out his naked
arm over the bread, as if, according to
De Rossi, in the act of consecrating
it; on the other is a woman in the
act of prayer—it is conjectured that
she symbolises the Church. The fish
(the 'Ιχθύς), according to De Rossi,
symbolises the Saviour; the real presence (or if I understand Cav. de Rossi,
more than the real presence); but

how a symbol can be more than symbolic, I am at a loss to comprehend.
C. de Rossi's connection of the remarkable representation of the scene in John
xxi. 9 and 19, with the Eucharist seems
to me a very perilous interpretation,
especially to a devout Roman Catholic.
Letter to Dom Pitra, quoted above.
Note, p. 328.

[d] All these works in their different
forms are in general of coarse and inferior execution. The funereal vases
found in the Christian cemeteries are
of the lowest style of workmanship.
The senator Buonarotti, in his work,
"De' Vetri Cemeteriali," thus accounts
for this:—"Stettero sempre lontane
da quelle arti, colle quali avessero po-
tuto correr pericolo di contaminarsi
colla idolatria, e da ciò avvenne, che
pochi, o niuno di essi si diede alla pit-
tura e alla scultura, le quali aveano
per oggetto principale di rappresentare
le deità, e le favole de' gentili. Sicche,
volendo i fedeli adornar con simboli
devoti i loro vasi, erano forzati per lo
più a valersi di artefici inesperti, e che
professavano altri mestieri." See Mamachi, vol. i. p. 275. Compare
Rumohr, who suggests other reasons
for the rudeness of the earliest Christian relief, in my opinion, though by no
means irreconcileable with this, neither
so simple nor satisfactory. Page 170.

truth of life, before it can accomplish its object. The
elements of this feeling, even the first sense of external
grandeur and beauty, had yet to be infused into the
Christian mind. The pure and holy and majestic
inward thoughts and sentiments had to work into form,
and associate themselves with appropriate visible images.
This want and this desire were long unfelt.

The person of the Saviour was a subject of grave dispute among the older fathers. Some took the
expressions of the sacred writings in a literal
sense, and insisted that his outward form was mean and
unseemly. Justin Martyr speaks of his want of form
and comeliness.[e] Tertullian, who could not but be in
extremes, expresses the same sentiment with his accustomed vehemence. The person of Christ wanted not
merely divine majesty, but even human beauty.[f] Clement of Alexandria maintains the same opinion.[g] But
the most curious illustration of this notion occurs in the
work of Origen against Celsus. In the true spirit of
Grecian art and philosophy, Celsus denies that the
Deity could dwell in a mean form or low stature.
Origen is embarrassed with the argument; he fears to
recede from the literal interpretation of Isaiah, but
endeavours to soften it off, and denies that it refers to
lowliness of stature, or means more than the absence of
noble form or pre-eminent beauty. He then triumphantly adduces the verse of the forty-fourth Psalm, " Ride
on in thy loveliness and in thy beauty."[h]

*Person of
the Saviour.*

---

[e] Τὸν ἀειδῆ καὶ ἄτιμον φάνεντα.
Dial. cum Tryph. 85 and 88, 100.

[f] " Quodcumque illud corpusculum
sit, quoniam habitum, et quoniam con-
spectum sit, si inglorius, si ignobilis, si
inhonorabilis ; meus erit Christus. . .
— Sed species ejus inhonorata, defi-
ciens ultra omnes homines." Contr.

Marc. iii. 17. " Ne aspectu quidem ho-
nestus." Adv. Judæos, c. 14. " Etiam
despicientium formam ejus hæc erat
vox. Adeo nec humanæ honestatis corpus fuit, nedum cœlestis claritatis." De
Carn. Christi, c. 9.

[g] Pædagog. iii. 1.

[h] 'Αμήχανον γὰρ ὅτῳ θεῖον τι

But as the poetry of Christianity obtained more full
possession of the human mind, these debasing and
inglorious conceptions were repudiated by the more
vivid imagination of the great writers in the fourth
century. The great principle of Christian art began to
awaken; the outworking as it were, of the inward
purity, beauty, and harmony, upon the symmetry of the
external form, and the lovely expression of the countenance. Jerome, Chrysostom, Ambrose, Augustine, with
one voice, assert the majestic and engaging appearance
of the Saviour. The language of Jerome first shows
the sublime conception which was brooding, as it were,
in the Christian mind, and was at length slowly to
develope itself up to the gradual perfection of Christian
art. "Assuredly that splendour and majesty of the
hidden divinity, which shone even in his human
countenance, could not but attract at first sight all
beholders." "Unless he had something celestial in his
countenance and in his look, the Apostles would not
immediately have followed him."[1] "The Heavenly
Father poured upon him in full streams that corporeal
grace, which is distilled drop by drop upon mortal
man." Such are the glowing expressions of Chrysostom.[k]
Gregory of Nyssa applies all the vivid imagery of the
Song of Solomon to the person as well as to the
doctrine of Christ; and Augustine declares that "He

πλέον τῶν ἄλλων προσῆν, μηδὲν
ἀλλοῦ διαφέρειν· τοῦτο δὲ οὐδὲν
ἄλλου διέφερεν, ἀλλ' ὡς φασὶ, μικ-
ρὸν, καὶ δυσειδὲς, καὶ ἀγενὲς ἦν.
Celsus, apud Origen. vi. 75. Origen
quotes the text of the LXX., in which
it is the forty-fourth, and thus translated : Τῇ ὡραιότητί σου, καὶ τῷ
κάλλει σου καὶ ἔντεινον, καὶ κα-
τευοδοῦ, καὶ βασίλευε.

[1] "Certe fulgor ipse et majestas divi-
nitatis occultæ, quæ etiam in humanâ
facie relucebat, ex primo ad se veni-
entes trahere poterat aspectu." Hieronym. in Matth. c. ix. 9.
"Nisi enim habuisset et in vultu
quiddam et in oculis sidereum, nunquam eum statim secuti fuissent Apo-
stoli." Epist. ad Princip. Virginem.
[k] In Psalm xliv.

2 c 2

was beautiful on his mother's bosom, beautiful in the
arms of his parents, beautiful upon the Cross, beautiful
in the sepulchre."

There were some, however, who even at this, and to
a much later period, chiefly among those addicted to
monkish austerity, adhered to the older opinion, as
though human beauty were something carnal and
material. St. Basil interprets even the forty-fourth
Psalm in the more austere sense. Many of the painters
among the Greeks, even in the eighth century, who were
monks of the rule of St. Basil, are said to have been too
faithful to the judgement of their master, or perhaps
their rude art was better qualified to represent a mean
figure, with harsh outline and stiff attitude and a
blackened countenance, rather than majesty of form or
beautiful expression. Such are the Byzantine pictures
of this school. The harsh Cyril of Alexandria repeats
the assertion of the Saviour's mean appearance, even
beyond the ordinary race of men, in the strongest
language.[m] This controversy proves decisively that
there was no traditionary type, which was admitted to
represent the human form of the Saviour. The distinct
assertion of Augustine, that the form and countenance
of Christ were entirely unknown, and painted with
every possible variety of expression, is conclusive as to
the West.[n] In the East we may dismiss at once as a

---

[m] Ἀλλὰ τὸ εἶδος αὐτοῦ ἄτιμον,
ἐκλεῖπον παρὰ πάντας τοὺς υἱοὺς
τῶν ἀνθρώπων. De Nud. Noe, lib. ii.
t. i. p. 43.

[n] "Qua fuerit ille facie nos penitus
ignoramus: nam et ipsius Dominicæ
facies carnis innumerabilium cogitationum diversitate variatur et fingitur,
quæ tamen una erat, quæcunque erat."
De Trin. lib. vii. c. 4, 5.
The Christian apologists uniformly

acknowledge the charge, that they have
no altars or *images*. Minuc. Fel.
Octavius, x. p. 61. Arnob. vi. post
init. Origen, contrà Celsum, viii. p.
389. Compare Jablonski (Dissertatio
de Origine Imaginum Christi, opuscul.
vol. iii. p. 377) who well argues that,
consistently with Jewish manners, there
could not have been any likeness of the
Lord. Compare Pearson on the Creed,
vol. ii. p. 101.

manifest fable, probably of local superstition, the statue of Christ at Cæsarea Philippi, representing him in the act of healing the woman with the issue of blood.[o] But there can be no doubt that paintings, purporting to be actual resemblances of Jesus, of Peter, and of Paul, were current in the time of Eusebius in the East,[p] though I am disinclined to receive the authority of a later writer, that Constantine adorned his new city with likenesses of Christ and his Apostles.

The earliest images emanated, no doubt, from the Gnostic sects, who not merely blended the Christian and Pagan, or Oriental notions on their gems and seals, engraved with the mysterious Abraxas; but likewise, according to their eclectic system, consecrated small golden or silver images of all those ancient sages whose doctrines they had adopted, or had fused together in their wild and various theories. The image of Christ appeared with those of Pythagoras, Plato, Aristotle, and probably some of the eastern philosophers.[q] The Carpocratians had painted portraits of Christ; and Marcellina,[r] a celebrated female heresiarch, exposed to the view of the Gnostic church in Rome, the portraits of Jesus and St. Paul, of Homer,

Earliest images Gnostic.

----

[o] Euseb. H. E. vii. 18, with the Excursus of Heinichen. These were, probably, two bronze figures, one of a kneeling woman in the act of supplication; the other, the upright figure of a man, probably of a Cæsar, which the Christian inhabitants of Cæsarea Philippi transformed into the Saviour and the woman in the Gospels: Τοῦτον δὲ τὸν ἀνδριάντα εἰκόνα τοῦ Ἰησοῦ φέρειν ἔλεγον. Eusebius seems desirous of believing the story. Compare Munter.

[p] Ὅτε καὶ τῶν Ἀποστόλων τῶν αὐτοῦ τὰς εἰκόνας Παύλου καὶ Πέτρου καὶ αὐτοῦ δὴ τοῦ Χριστοῦ διὰ χρωμάτων ἐν γραφαῖς σωζομένας ἱστορήσαμεν. Ibid. loc. cit.

[q] Irenæus de Hær. i. c. 84 (edit. Grabe). Epiphan. Hæres. xxvii. 6. Augustin. de Hæresib. c. vii. These images of Christ were said to have been derived from the collection of Pontius Pilate. Compare Jablonski's Dissertation.

[r] Marcellina lived about the middle of the second century, or a little later.

and of Pythagoras. Of this nature, no doubt, were the images of Abraham, Orpheus, Pythagoras, Apollonius, and Christ, set up in his private chapel by the Emperor Alexander Severus. These small images,[a] which varied very much, it should seem, in form and feature, could contribute but little, if in the least, to form that type of superhuman beauty, which might mingle the sentiment of human sympathy with reverence for the divinity of Christ. Christian art long brooded over such feelings as those expressed by Jerome and Augustine, before it could even attempt to embody them in marble or colour.[t]

---

[a] Of these Gnostic images of Christ there are only two extant which seem to have some claim to authenticity and antiquity. Those from the collection of Chifflet are now considered to represent Serapis. One is mentioned by M. Raoul Rochette (Types Imitatifs de l'Art du Christianisme, p. 21); it is a stone, a kind of tessera with a head of Christ, young and beardless, in profile, with the word ΧΡΙΣΤΟΣ in Greek characters, with the symbolic fish below. This is in the collection of M. Fortia d'Urban, and is engraved as a vignette to M. R. Rochette's essay. The other is adduced in an " Essay on Ancient Coins, Medals and Gems, as illustrating the Progress of Christianity in the Early Ages, by the Rev. R. Walsh." This is a kind of medal or tessera of metal, representing Christ as he is described in the apocryphal letter of Lentulus to the Roman senate. (Fabric. Cod. Apoc. Nov. Test. p. 301, 302.) It has a head of Christ, the hair parted over the forehead, covering the ears, and falling over the shoulders; the shape is long, the beard short and thin. It has the name of Jesus in Hebrew, and has not the *nimbus*, or glory. On the reverse is an inscription in a kind of cabalistic character, of which the sense seems to be, " The Messiah reigns in peace ; God is made man." This may possibly be a tessera of the Jewish Christians ; or modelled after a Gnostic type of the first age of Christianity. See Discours sur les Types Imitatifs de l'Art du Christianisme, par M. Raoul Rochette.

[t] I must not omit the description of the person of our Saviour in the spurious Epistle of Lentulus to the Roman Senate (see Fabric. Cod. Apoc. N. T. i. p. 301), since it is referred to constantly by writers on early Christian art. But what proof is there of the existence of this epistle previous to the great æra of Christian painting ? " He was a man of tall and well-proportioned form ; the countenance severe and impressive, so as to move the beholders at once to love and awe. His hair was of the colour of wine (vinei coloris), reaching to his ears,

The earliest pictures of the Saviour seem formed on one type or model. They all represent the oval countenance, slightly lengthened; the grave, soft, and melancholy expression; the short thin beard; the hair parted on the forehead into two long masses, which fall upon the shoulders.[u]   Such are the features which characterise the earliest extant painting, that on the vault of the cemetery of St. Callistus, in which the Saviour is represented as far as his bust, like the images on bucklers in use among the Romans.[x]   A later painting, in the chapel of the cemetery of St. Pontianus, resembles this;[y] and a third was discovered in the catacomb then called that of St. Callistus by Boldetti, but unfortunately perished while he was looking at it, in the attempt to remove it from the wall.   The same countenance appears on some, but not the earliest, reliefs on the sarcophagi, five of which may be referred, according to M. Rochette, to the time of Julian.   Of one, that of Olybrius, the date appears certain—the close of the fourth century.   These, the paintings at least, are no doubt the work of Greek artists; and this head may be considered the archetype,

The earliest portraits of the Saviour.

---

with no radiation (sine radiatione, without the nimbus), and standing up, from his ears, clustering and bright, and flowing down over his shoulders, parted on the top according to the fashion of the Nazarenes. The brow high and open; the complexion clear, with a delicate tinge of red; the aspect frank and pleasing; the nose and mouth finely formed; the beard thick, parted, and the colour of the hair; the eyes blue, and exceedingly bright. . . His countenance was of wonderful sweetness and gravity; no one ever saw him laugh, though he was seen to weep; his stature was tall; the hands and arms finely formed. . . . He was the most beautiful of the sons of men." Compare Latin Christianity. The unanswerable proof that this description is of late date is that it was not produced at the second Council of Nicea, at which time Christendom was ransacked to find proofs, good or bad, of early image worship.

[u] Raoul Rochette, p. 26.

[x] Bottari, Pitture e Sculture Sacre, vol. ii. tav. lxx. p. 42.

[y] This, however, was probably re-painted in the time of Hadrian I.

the Hieratic model, of the Christian conception of the
Saviour, imagined in the East, and generally adopted in
the West.[z]

Reverential awe, diffidence in their own skill, the
The Father still dominant sense of the purely spiritual
rarely re-
presented. nature of the Parental Deity,[a] or perhaps the
exclusive habit of dwelling upon the Son as the direct
object of religious worship, restrained early Christian
art from those attempts to which we are scarcely
reconciled by the sublimity and originality of Michael
Angelo and Raffaelle. Even the symbolic representation
of the Father was rare. Where it does appear, it is
under the symbol of an immense hand issuing from a
cloud, or a ray of light streaming from heaven, to
imply, it may be presumed, the creative and all-
enlightening power of the Universal Father.[b]

---

[z] Rumohr considers a statue of the
Good Shepherd in the Vatican collection, from its style, to be a very early
work; the oldest monument of Christian sculpture, prior to the urn of
Junius Bassus, which is of the middle
of the fourth century.   Italienische
Forschungen, vol. i. p. 168.   In that
usually thought the earliest, that of
Junius Bassus, Jesus Christ is represented between the Apostles, beardless,
seated in a curule chair, with a roll
half unfolded in his hand, and under
his feet a singular representation of the
upper part of a man holding an inflated
veil with his two hands, a common
symbol or personification of heaven.
See R. Rochette, p. 43, who considers
these sarcophagi anterior to the formation of the ordinary type.

[a] Compare Munter, ii. p. 49: "Nefas habent docti ejus (ecclesiæ Catholicæ) credere Deum figurâ humani
corporis terminatum." August. Conf.
vi. 11.

[b] M. Emeric David (in his Discours
sur les Anciens Monumens, to which I
am indebted for much information),
says that the French artists had first
the *heureuse hardiesse* of representing
the Eternal Father under the human
form.   The instance to which he
alludes is contained in a Latin Bible
(in the Cabinet Impérial) cited by
Montfaucon, but not fully described.
It was presented to Charles the Bald
by the canons of the church of Tours,
in the year 850.   This period is far
beyond the bounds of our present
history.   See therefore E. David, pp.
43. 46.

The Virgin Mother could not but offer herself to the imagination, and be accepted at once as the subject of Christian art.

As respect for the mother of Christ deepened into reverence, reverence bowed down to adoration ; as she became the mother of God, and herself a deity in popular worship, this worship was the parent, and, in some sense, the offspring of art. Augustine, indeed, admits that the real features of the Virgin, as of the Saviour, were unknown.[c] But the fervent language of Jerome shows that art had already attempted to shadow out the conception of mingling virgin purity and maternal tenderness, which as yet probably was content to dwell within the verge of human nature, and aspired not to mingle a divine idealism with these more mortal feelings. The outward form and countenance could not but be the image of the purity and gentleness of the soul within : and this primary object of Christian art could not but give rise to one of its characteristic distinctions from that of the ancients, the substitution of mental expression for purely corporeal beauty. As reverential modesty precluded all exposure of the form, the countenance was the whole picture. This reverence, indeed, in the very earliest specimens of the art, goes still further, and confines itself to the expression of composed and dignified attitude. The artists did not even venture to expose the face. With one exception, the Virgin appears veiled on the reliefs on the sarcophagi, and in the earliest paintings. The oldest known picture of the Virgin is in the catacomb, once so called, of St. Callistus,

---

[c] " Neque enim novimus faciem Virginis Mariæ." Augustin. de Trin. c. viii. " Ut ipsa corporis facies simula- crum fuerit mentis, figura probitatis." Ambros. de Virgin. lib. ii. c. 2.

in which she appears seated in the calm majesty, and in
the dress, of a Roman matron. It is the transition, as
it were, from ancient to modern art, which still timidly
adheres to its conventional type of dignity.[d] But in
the sarcophagi, art has already more nearly approximated to its most exquisite subject—the Virgin Mother
is seated, with the divine child in her lap, receiving the
homage of the Wise Men. She is still veiled,[e] but with
the rounded form and grace of youth, and a kind of
sedate chastity of expression in her form, which seems
designed to convey the feeling of gentleness and
holiness. Two of these sarcophagi, one in the Vatican
collection, and one at Milan, appear to disprove the
common notion that the representation of the Virgin
was unknown before the Council of Ephesus.[f] That
council, in its zeal against the doctrines of Nestorius,
established, as it has been called, a Hieratic type of the
Virgin, which is traced throughout Byzantine art, and
on the coins of the Eastern empire. This type,
however, gradually degenerates with the darkness of
the age, and the decline of art. The countenance,
sweetly smiling on the child, becomes sad and severe.
The head is bowed with a gloomy and almost sinister
expression, and the countenance gradually darkens, till
it assumes a black colour, and seems to adapt itself in
this respect to an ancient tradition. At length even
the sentiment of maternal affection is effaced, both the
mother and child become stiff and lifeless, the child is

---

[d] Bottari, Pitture e Sculture Sacre,
t. iii. p. 111, tav. 218. See Mémoire
de M. Raoul Rochette, Académ. In-
script.

[e] In Bottari there is one picture of
the Virgin with the head naked, t. ii.

tav. cxxvi. The only one known to
M. Raoul Rochette.

[f] A.D. 431. This opinion is maintained by Basnage and most Protestant
writers.

swathed in tight bands, and has an expression of pain rather than of gentleness or placid infancy.[g]

The apostles, particularly St. Peter and St. Paul, were among the earlier objects of Christian art. Though in one place, St. Augustine asserts that the persons of the Apostles were equally unknown with that of the Saviour, in another he acknowledges that their pictures were exhibited on the walls of many churches for the edification of the faithful.[h] In a vision ascribed to Constantine, but of very doubtful authority, the Emperor is said to have recognised the apostles by their likeness to their portraits.[i] A picture known to St. Ambrose pretended to have come down by regular tradition from their time : and Chrysostom, when he studied the writings, gazed with reverence on what he supposed an authentic likeness of the apostle.[k] Paul and Peter appear on many of the oldest monuments, on the glass vessels, fragments of which have been discovered, and on which Jerome informs us that they were frequently painted. They are found, as we have seen, on the sarcophagus of Junius Bassus, and on many others. In one of these, in which the costume is Roman, St. Paul is represented bald, and with the high nose, as

The Apostles.

---

[g] Compare Raoul Rochette, page 35. M. R. Rochette observes much similarity between the pictures of the Virgin ascribed to St. Luke, the tradition of whose painting ascends to the sixth century, and the Egyptian works which represent Isis nursing Horus. I have not thought it necessary to notice further these palpable forgeries, though the object, in so many places, of popular worship.

[h] St. Augustin in Genesin, cap. xxii. "Quod pluribus locis simul eos (apostolos) cum illo (Christo) pictos viderint · · · · in pictis parietibus." Augustin. de Cons. Evang. i. 16.

[i] Hadrian I. Epist. ad Imp. Constantin. et Iren. Concil. Nic. ii. art. 2.

[k] These two assertions rest on the authority of Joannes Damascenus, de Imagin.

he is described in the Philopatris,[m] which, whatever its
age, has evidently taken these personal peculiarities of
the Apostle from the popular Christian representations.
St. Peter has usually a single tuft of hair on his bald
forehead.[n] Each has a book, the only symbol of his
apostleship. St. Peter has neither the sword nor the
keys. In the same relief, St. John and St. James are
distinguished from the rest by their youth; already,
therefore, this peculiarity was established which pre-
vails throughout Christian art. The majesty of age,
and a kind of dignity of precedence, are attributed to
Peter and Paul, while all the grace of youth, and the
most exquisite gentleness, are centered in John. They
seem to have assumed this peculiar character of
expression, even before their distinctive symbols.

It may excite surprise that the acts of martyrdom
Martyrdom did not become the subjects of Christian art,
not repre-
sented. till far down in the dark ages. That of St.
Sebastian, a relief in terra-cotta, which formerly existed
in the cemetery of St. Priscilla, and that of Peter and
Paul in the Basilica Siciniana, assigned by Ciampini
to the fifth century, are rare exceptions, and both
of doubtful date and authenticity. The martyrdom of
St. Felicitas and her seven children, discovered in
1812, in a small oratory within the baths of Titus,
cannot be earlier, according to M. R. Rochette, than
the seventh century.[o]

The absence of all gloomy or distressing subjects
is the remarkable and characteristic feature in the

---

[m] Γαλιλαῖος ἀναφαλαντίας ἐπίρρι-
νος. Philop. c. xii.

[n] Munter says the arrest of St. Peter
(Acts xii. 1, 3) is the only subject
from the Acts of the Apostles among

the monuments in the catacombs.
ii. p. 104.

[o] Raoul Rochette, in Mém. de l'Académie, tom. xiii. p. 165.

catacombs of Rome and in all the earliest Christian art. A modern writer, who has studied the subject with profound attention, has expressed himself in the following language:[p]—" The catacombs destined for the sepulture of the primitive Christians, for a long time peopled with martyrs, ornamented during times of persecution, and under the dominion of melancholy thoughts and painful duties, nevertheless everywhere represent in all the historic parts of these paintings only what is noble and exalted,[q] and in that which constitutes the purely decorative part only pleasing and graceful subjects, the images of the good shepherd, representations of the vintage, of the agape, with pastoral scenes: the symbols are fruits, flowers, palms, crowns, lambs, doves, in a word nothing but what excites emotions of joy, innocence, and charity. Entirely occupied with the celestial recompense which awaited them after the trials of their troubled life, and often of so dreadful a death, the Christians saw in death, and even in execution, only a way by which they arrived at this everlasting happiness ; and far from associating with this image that of the tortures or privations which opened heaven before them, they took pleasure in enlivening it with smiling colours, or presented it under agreeable symbols, adorning it with flowers and vine leaves; for it is thus that the asylum of death appears to us in the Christian catacombs. There is no sign of mourning, no token of resentment, no expression of vengeance ; all breathes softness, benevolence, charity."[r]

---

[p] M. D'Agincourt says, " Il n'a rencontré lui-même dans ces souter-rains aucune trace de nul autre tableau (one of barbarian and late design had before been noticed) représentant une martyre."   Hist. de l'Art.

[q] Des traits héroiques.

[r] Gregory of Nyssa, however, de-

It may seem even more singular, that the passion of our Lord himself remained a subject inter-dicted, as it were, by awful reverence. The cross, it has been said, was the symbol of Christianity many centuries before the crucifix.[s] It was rather a cheerful and consolatory than a depressing and melancholy sign; it was adorned with flowers, with crowns and precious stones, a pledge of the resurrection, rather than a memorial of the passion. The catacombs of Rome, faithful to their general character, offer no instance of a crucifixion, nor does any allusion to such a subject of art occur in any early writer.[t] Cardinal Bona gives the following as the progress of the gradual change. I. The simple cross.[u] II. The cross with the lamb at the foot of it.[x] III. Christ clothed, on the cross, with hands uplifted in prayer, but not nailed to it. IV. Christ fastened to the cross with four nails,

The crucifix.

---

scribes the heroic acts of St. Theodorus as painted on the walls of a church dedicated to that saint. " The painter had represented his sufferings, the forms of the tyrants like wild beasts. The fiery furnace, the death of the athlete of Christ—all this had the painter expressed by colours, as in a book, and adorned the temple like a pleasant and blooming meadow. The dumb walls speak and edify."

[s] See, among other authorities, Munter, page 77. " Es ist unmöglich das alter der Crucifixe genau zu bestimmen. Von dem Ende des siebenten Jahrhunderts kannte die Kirche sie nicht."

[t] The decree of the Quinisextan Council, in 695, is the clearest proof that up to that period the Passion had been usually represented under a symbolic or allegoric form.

[u] There is an interesting description by the Cav. de Rossi in the Spicilegium Solemnense, iv. p. 505, et seqq., on the form of the cross, as usually found in the catacombs. Before the beginning of the fourth century the simple cross + occurs rarely if at all. It is " dissembled," according to de Rossi's phrase, in various ways, as X, so as to be confounded with the initial letter of Christ, and takes other monogrammatic forms. Under Constantine and after Constantine it is generally the monogram with the Labarum. See pp. 329, 331 at the bottom, and 322.

[x] " Sub cruce sanguineâ niveo stat Christus in agno,
Agnus ut innocua injusto datur hostia letho."
Paull. Nolan, Epist. 32.

still living, and with open eyes.   He was not represented as dead till the tenth or eleventh century.[y]
There is some reason to believe that the bust of the
Saviour first appeared on the cross, and afterwards the
whole person ; the head was at first erect, with some
expression of divinity ; by degrees it drooped with the
agony of pain, the face was wan and furrowed, and
death, with all its anguish, was imitated by the utmost
power of coarse art—mere corporeal suffering without
sublimity, all that was painful in truth, with nothing
that was tender and affecting.   This change took place
among the monkish artists of the Lower Empire.
Those of the order of St. Basil introduced it into the
West; and from that time these painful images, with
those of martyrdom, and every scene of suffering which
could be imagined by the gloomy fancy of anchorites, who
could not be moved by less violent excitement, spread
throughout Christendom.   It required all the wonderful
magic of Italian art to elevate them into sublimity.

But early Christian art, at least that of painting, was
not content with these simpler subjects; it endeavoured
to represent designs of far bolder and more intricate
character.   Among the earliest descriptions   Paintings at Nola.
of Christian painting is that in the Church of
St. Felix, by Paulinus of Nola.[z]   In the colonnades

---

[y] De cruce Vaticanâ. | [z] The lines are not without merit:

"Quo duce Jordanes suspenso gurgite fixis
Fluctibus, a facie divinæ restitit arcæ.
Vis nova divisit flumen ; pars amne recluso
Constitit, et fluvii pars in mare lapsa cucurrit,
Destituitque vadum : et validus qui forte ruebat
Impetus, adstrictas altè cumulaverat undas,
Et tremulâ compage minax pendebat aquæ mons
Despectans transire pedes arente profundo;
Et medio pedibus siccis in flumine ferri
Pulverulenta hominum duro vestigia limo."

If this description is drawn from the | composition and for landscape, as well
picture, not from the book, the painter | as for the drawing of figures.
must have possessed some talent for |

of that church were painted scenes from the Old
Testament: among them were the Passage of the Red
Sea, Joshua and the Ark of God, Ruth and her Sister-
in-law, one deserting, the other following her parent
in fond fidelity;[a] an emblem, the poet suggests, of
mankind, part deserting, part adhering to the true
faith. The object of this embellishment of the churches
was to beguile the rude minds of the illiterate peasants
who thronged with no very exalted motives to the altar
of St. Felix—to preoccupy their minds with sacred
subjects, so that they might be less eager for the
festival banquets, held with such munificence and with
such a concourse of strangers, at the tomb of the
martyr.[b] These gross and irreligious desires led them
to the church; yet, gazing on these pictures, they
would not merely be awakened by these holy examples
to purer thoughts and holier emotions; they would

---

[a] " Qnum geminæ scindunt sese in diversa sorores ;
Ruth sequitur sanctam, quam deserit Orpa, parentem :
Perfidiam nurus una, fidem nurus altera monstrat.
Præfert una Deum patriæ, patriam altera vitæ."

[b] " Forte requiratur, quanam ratione gerendi
Sederit hæc nobis sententia, pingere sanctas
Raro more domos animantibus adsimulatis.
    *   *   *   turba frequentior hic est
Rusticitas non casta fide, neque docta legendi.
Hæc adsueta diù sacris servire profanis,
Ventre Deo, tandem convertitur advena Christo,
Dum sanctorum opera in Christo miratur aperta.
Propterea visum nobis opus utile, totis
Felicis domibus picturâ illudere sanctâ :
Si forte attonitas hæc per spectacula mentes
Agrestum caperet fucata coloribus umbra,
Quæ super exprimitur literis—ut littera monstret
Qnod manus explicuit : dumque omnes picta vicissim
Ostendunt releguntque sibi, vel tardius escæ
Sunt memores, dum grata oculis jejunia pascunt :
Atque ita se melior stupefactis inserat usus,
Dum fallit pictura famem ; sanctasque legenti
Historias castorum operum subrepit honestas
Exemplis inducta piis; potatur hianti
Sobrietas, nimii subeunt oblivia vini :
Dumque diem ducunt spatio majore tuentes,
Pocula rarescunt, quia per mirantia tracto
Tempore, jam paucæ superant epulantibus horæ."

In Natal. Felic., Poema xxiv.

feast their eyes instead of their baser appetites ; an involuntary sobriety and forgetfulness of the wine flagon would steal over their souls; at all events, they would have less time to waste in the indulgence of their looser festivity.

Christianity has been the parent of music, probably as far surpassing in skill and magnificence the compositions of earlier times, as the cathedral organ the simpler instruments of the Jewish or Pagan religious worship.   But this perfection of the art belongs to a much later period in Christian history. Like the rest of its service, the music of the Church no doubt grew up from a rude and simple, to a more splendid and artificial form.   The practice of singing hymns is coeval with Christianity ; the hearers of the Apostles sang the praises of God; and the first sound which reached the Pagan ear from the secluded sanctuaries of Christianity was the hymn to Christ as God.[c]   The Church succeeded to an inheritance of religious lyrics as unrivalled in the history of poetry as of religion.[d]   The Psalms were introduced early into the public service ; but at first, apparently, though some psalms may have been sung on appropriate occasions—the 73rd, called the morning, and the 141st, the evening psalm—the whole Psalter was introduced only as part of the Old Testament, and read in the course of the service.[e]   With the poetry did they borrow the music of the Synagogue?   Was this music the same which had filled the spacious courts of

----

[c] See the famous Epistle of Pliny.

[d] The Temple.Service, in Lightfoot's works, gives the Psalms which were appropriate to each day.   The author has given a slight outline of this hym-nology of the Temple in the Quarterly Review, xxxviii. page 20.

[e] Bingham's Antiquities, vol. xiv. 1, 5.

the Temple, perhaps answered to those sad strains
which had been heard beside the waters of the
Euphrates, or even descended from still earlier times
of glory, when Deborah or when Miriam struck their
timbrels to the praise of God? This question it must
be impossible to answer; and no tradition, as far as
I am aware, indicates the source from which the
Church borrowed her primitive harmonies, though
the probability is certainly in favour of their Jewish
parentage.

The Christian hymns of the primitive churches seem
to have been eucharistic and confined to the glorifica-
tion of their God and Saviour.[f] Prayer was considered
the language of supplication and humiliation; the soul
awoke, as it were, in the hymn to more ardent expressions of gratitude and love. Probably, the music
was nothing more at first than a very simple accompaniment, or no more than the accordance of the
harmonious voices; it was the humble subsidiary of
the hymn of praise, not itself the soul-engrossing art.[g]
Nothing could be more simple than the earliest
recorded hymns ; they were fragments from the
Scripture—the doxology, " Glory be to the Father, and
to the Son, and to the Holy Ghost ;" the angelic hymn,
" Glory be to God on high ;" the cherubic hymn from
Revel. iv. 12.—"Holy, holy, holy ;" the hymn of
victory, Revel. xv. 3., " Great and marvellous are thy
works." It was not improbably the cherubic hymn, to
which Pliny alludes, as forming part of the Christian

---

[f] Gregory of Nyssa defines a hymn
—ὕμνος ἐστὶν ἡ ἐπὶ τοῖς ὑπάρχουσιν
ἡμῖν ἀγαθοῖς ἀνατιθεμένη τῷ Θεῷ
εὐφημία. See Psalm ii.

[g] Private individuals wrote hymns
to Christ, which were generally sung.
Euseb. H. E. v. 28 ; vii. 24.

worship. The "Magnificat" and the "Nunc dimittis" were likewise sung from the earliest ages; the Halleluia was the constant prelude or burden of the hymn.[h] Of the character of the music few and imperfect traces are found. In Egypt the simplest form long prevailed. In the monastic establishments one person arose and repeated the psalm, the others sate around in silence on their lowly seats, and responded, as it were, to the psalm within their hearts.[i] In Alexandria, by the order of Athanasius, the psalms were repeated with the slightest possible inflection of voice; it could hardly be called singing.[k] Yet, though the severe mind of Athanasius might disdain such subsidiaries, the power of music was felt to be a dangerous antagonist in the great religious contest. Already the soft and effeminate singing, begun by Paul of Samosata, had estranged the hearts of many worshippers, and his peculiar doctrines had stolen into the soul, which had been melted by the artificial melodies, introduced by him into the service. The Gnostic hymns of Bardesanes and Valentinus,[m] no doubt, had their musical accompaniment. Arius himself had composed hymns which were sung to popular airs; and the streets of Constantinople, even to the time of Chrysostom, echoed at night to those seductive strains which denied or imperfectly expressed the Trinitarian doctrines.

---

[h] "Alleluia novis balat ovile choris."
    Paulin. Epist. ad Sev. 12.

"Curvorum hinc chorus helciariorum,
    Responsantibus Alleluia ripis,
    Ad Christum levat amnicum celeusma."
        Sid. Apoll. lib. ii. ep. 10.

[i] "Absque eo qui dicturus in medium Psalmos surrexerit, cuncti sedilibus humillimis insidentes, ad vocem psallentis omni cordis intencione dependent." Cassian. Instit. ii.1 2. Compare Euseb. H. E. ii. 17. Apostol. Constit. H. E. ii. 17. Apostol. Constit. xx. 57.

[k] "Tam modico flexu vocis faciebat sonare lectorem Psalmi, ut pronuncianti vicinior esset quam canenti." August. Confess. x. 33.

[m] Tertull. de Carn. Christi, 17.

2 D 2

Chrysostom arrayed a band of orthodox choristers, who hymned the coequal Father, Son, and Holy Ghost. The Donatists in Africa adapted their enthusiastic hymns to wild and passionate melodies, which tended to keep up and inflame, as it were, with the sound of the trumpet, the fanaticism of their followers.[n]

The first change in the manner of singing was the substitution of singers,[o] who became a separate order in the Church, for the mingled voices of all ranks, ages, and sexes, which was compared by the great reformer of church music to the glad sound of many waters.[p]

The antiphonal singing, in which the different sides of the choir answered to each other in responsive verses, was first introduced at Antioch by Flavianus and Diodorus. Though, from the form of some of the psalms, it is not improbable that this system of alternate chanting may have prevailed in the Temple service, yet the place and the period of its appearance in the Christian Church seems to indicate a different source. The strong resemblance which it bears to the chorus of the Greek tragedy, might induce a suspicion, that as it borrowed its simple primitive music from Judaism, it may, in turn, have despoiled Paganism of some of its lofty religious harmonies.

This antiphonal chanting was introduced into the West[q] by Ambrose, and if it inspired, or even fully

[n] "Donatistæ nos reprehendunt, quod sobriè psallimus in ecclesia divina cantica Prophetarum, cum ipsi ebrietates suas ad canticum psalmorum humano ingenio compositorum quasi tubas exhortationis inflammant." Augustin. Confess.

[o] Compare Bingham. The leaders were called ὑποβολεῖς.

[p] "Responsoriis psalmorum, cantu mulierum, virginum, parvularum consonans undarum fragor resultat." Ambros. Hexam. l. iii. c. 5.

[q] Augustin. Confess. ix. 7. 1. How indeed could it be rejected, when it had received the authority of a vision of the blessed Ignatius, who was said to have heard the angels singing in the antiphonal manner the praises of the Holy Trinity. Socr. H. E. vi. 8.

accompanied the Te Deum, usually ascribed to that
prelate, we cannot calculate too highly its effect upon
the Christian mind. So beautiful was the music in the
Ambrosian service, that the sensitive conscience of the
young Augustine took alarm, lest, when he wept at
the solemn music, he should be yielding to the luxury
of sweet sounds, rather than imbibing the devotional
spirit of the hymn.[r] Though alive to the perilous
pleasure, yet he inclined to the wisdom of awakening
weaker minds to piety by this enchantment of their
hearing. The Ambrosian chant, with its more simple
and masculine tones, is still preserved in the Church of
Milan; in the rest of Italy it was superseded by the
richer Roman chant, which was introduced by the Pope,
Gregory the Great.[s]

---

[r] " Cum reminiscor lachrymas meas
quas fudi ad cantus ecclesiæ tuæ, in
primordiis recuperatæ fidei meæ, et
nunc ipsum cum moveor, non cantu
sed rebus quæ cantantur, cum liquidâ
voce et convenientissimâ modulatione
cantantur: magnam instituti hujus
utilitatem rursus agnosco. Ita fluc-
tuo inter periculum voluptatis et ex-
perimentum salubritatis ; magisque
adducor, non quidem irretractabilem
sententiam proferens cantandi consuetudinem approbare in ecclesiâ : ut per ob-
lectamenta aurium, infirmior animus in
affectum pietatis assurgat." Augustin.
Confess. x. 33, 3. Compare ix. 7, 2.

[s] The cathedral chanting of England
has probably almost alone preserved the
ancient antiphonal system, which has
been discarded for a greater variety of
instruments, and a more complicated
system of music, in the Roman Catholic service. This, if I may presume
to offer a judgement, has lost as much
in solemnity and majesty as it has
gained in richness and variety. " Ce
chant (le Plain Chant) tel qu'il sub-
siste encore aujourd'hui est un reste
bien défiguré, mais bien précieux de
l'ancienne musique, qui après avoir
passé par la main des barbares n'a pas
perdu encore toutes ses premières
beautés." Millin, Dictionnaire des
Beaux Arts.

CHAPTER V.

Conclusion.

THUS, then, Christianity had become the religion of the Roman world : it had not, indeed, confined its adventurous spirit of moral conquest within these limits ; yet it is in the Roman world that its more extensive and permanent influence, as well as its peculiar vicissitudes, can alone be followed out with distinctness and accuracy.

Paganism was slowly expiring ; the hostile edicts of the emperors, down to the final legislation of Justinian, did but accelerate its inevitable destiny. Its temples, where not destroyed, were perishing by neglect and peaceful decay, or, where their solid structures defied these less violent assailants, stood deserted and overgrown with weeds ; the unpaid priests ceased to offer, not only sacrifice, but prayer, and were gradually dying out as a separate order of men. Its philosophy lingered in a few cities of Greece, till the economy or the religion of the Eastern Emperor finally closed its schools.

The doom of the Roman empire was likewise sealed : the horizon on all sides was dark with overwhelming clouds ; and the internal energies of the empire, the military spirit, the wealth, the imperial power, had crumbled away. The external unity was dissolved ; the provinces were gradually severed from the main body ; the Western empire was rapidly sinking, and the

Eastern falling into hopeless decrepitude. Yet though her external polity was dissolved, though her visible throne was prostrate upon the earth, Rome still ruled the mind of man, and her secret domination maintained its influence, until it assumed a new outward form. Rome survived in her laws, in her municipal institutions, and in that which lent a·new sanctity and reverence to her laws, and gave strength by their alliance with its own peculiar polity to the municipal institutions—in her adopted religion. The empire of Christ succeeded to the empire of the Cæsars.

When it ascended the throne, assumed a supreme and universal dominion over mankind, became the legislator, not merely through public statutes, but in all the minute details of life, discharged, in fact, almost all the functions of civil as well as of religious government, Christianity could not but appear under a new form, and wear a far different appearance than when it was the humble and private faith of a few scattered individuals, or of only spiritually connected communities. As it was about to enter into its next period of conflict with barbarism, and to undergo the temptation of unlimited power, however it might depart from its primitive simplicity, and indeed recede from its genuine spirit, it is impossible not to observe how wonderfully (those who contemplate human affairs with religious minds may assert how providentially) it adapted itself to its altered position, and the new part which it was to fulfil in the history of man. We have already traced this gradual change in the formation of the powerful Hierarchy, in the development of Monasticism, the establishment of the splendid and imposing Ritual; we must turn our attention, before we close, to the new modification of the religion itself.

Its theology now appears wrought out into a regular, multifarious, and, as it were, legally established system. It was the consummate excellence of Christianity, that it blended in apparently indissoluble union religious and moral perfection. Its essential doctrine was, in its pure theory, inseparable from humane, virtuous, and charitable disposition. Piety to God, as he was impersonated in Christ, worked out, as it seemed, by spontaneous energy, into Christian beneficence.

Christian theology of this period.

But there has always been a strong propensity to disturb this nice balance : the dogmatic part of religion, the province of faith, is constantly endeavouring to set itself apart, and to maintain a separate existence. Faith, in this limited sense, aspires to be religion. This, in general, takes place soon after the first outburst, the strong impulse of new and absorbing religious emotions. At a later period morality attempts to stand alone, without the sanction or support of religious faith. One half of Christianity is thus perpetually striving to pass for the whole, and to absorb all the attention, to the neglect, to the disparagement of, at length to a total separation from, its heaven-appointed consort. The multiplication and subtle refinement of theologic dogmas, the engrossing interest excited by some dominant tenet, especially if associated with, or embodied in, a minute and rigorous ceremonial, tend to satisfy and lull the mind into complacent acquiescence in its own religious completeness. But directly religion began to consider itself something apart, something exclusively dogmatic or exclusively ceremonial, an acceptance of certain truths by the belief, or the discharge of certain ritual observances, then the transition from separation to hostility was rapid and un-

Separation of Christian faith and Christian morals

impeded.[a] No sooner had Christianity divorced morality
as its inseparable companion through life, than it formed
an unlawful connection with any dominant passion ; and
the strange and unnatural union of Christian faith with
ambition, avarice, cruelty, fraud, and even licence, appeared in strong contrast with its primitive harmony of
doctrine and inward disposition. Thus in a great
degree, while the Roman world became Christian in
outward worship and in faith, it remained Heathen, or
even at some periods worse than Heathenism in its
better times, as to beneficence, gentleness, purity, social
virtue, humanity, and peace. This extreme view may
appear to be justified by the general survey of Christian
society. Yet, in fact, religion did not, except   never
at the darkest periods, so completely insulate   complete.
itself, or so entirely recede from its natural alliance
with morality, though it admitted, at each of its periods,
much which was irreconcileable with its pure and original spirit. Hence the mingled character of its social
and political, as well as of its personal influences. The
union of Christianity with monachism, with sacerdotal
domination, with the military spirit, with the spiritual
autocracy of the papacy, with the advancement at one
time, at another with the repression, of the human mind,
had each their darker and brighter side ; and were in
succession (however they departed from the primal and
ideal perfection of Christianity) to a certain extent
beneficial, because apparently almost necessary to the·
social and intellectual developement of mankind at each
particular juncture. So, for instance, military Christianity, which grew out of the inevitable incorporation
of the force and energy of the barbarian conquerors with
the sentiments and feelings of that age, and which
finally produced chivalry, was, in fact, the substitution

of inhumanity for Christian gentleness, of the love of
glory for the love of peace.   Yet was this indispensable
to the preservation of Christianity in its contest with its
new eastern antagonist.   Unwarlike Christianity would
have been trampled under foot, and have been in danger
of total extermination, by triumphant Mohammedanism.

Yet even when its prevailing character thus stood in
the most direct contrast with the spirit of the
Gospel, it was not merely that the creed of
Christianity in its primary articles was universally accepted, and a profound devotion filled the
Christian mind, there was likewise a constant under-
growth, as it were, of Christian feelings, and even
of Christian virtues.   Nothing could contrast more
strangely, for instance, than St. Louis slaughtering
Saracens and heretics with his remorseless sword, and
the Saviour of mankind by the Lake of Galilee; yet,
when this dominant spirit of the age did not preoccupy
the whole soul, the self-denial, the justice, the purity,
even the gentleness of such a man as St. Louis bore
still unanswerable testimony to the genuine influence of
Christianity.   Our illustration has carried us far beyond
the boundaries of our history, but already the great
characteristic distinction of later Christian history had
begun to be developed, the severance of Christian faith
from Christian love, the passionate attachment, the
stern and remorseless maintenance of the Christian
creed without or with only a partial practice of Christian
virtue, or even the predominance of a tone of mind, in
some respects absolutely inconsistent with genuine
Christianity.   While the human mind, in general,
became more rigid in exacting, and more timid in
departing from, the admitted doctrines of the church,
the moral sense became more dull and obtuse to the

purer and more evanescent beauty of Christian holiness. In truth it was so much more easy, in a dark and unreasoning age, to subscribe, or at least to render passive submission to, certain defined doctrines, than to work out those doctrines in their proper influences upon the life, that we deplore, rather than wonder at, this substitution of one half of the Christian religion for the whole. Nor are we astonished to find those, who were constantly violating the primary principles of Christianity, fiercely resenting, and, if they had the power, relentlessly avenging, any violation of the integrity of Christian faith. Heresy of opinion, we have seen, became almost the only crime against which excommunication pointed its thunders. The darker and more baleful heresy of unchristian passions, which assumed the language of Christianity, was either too general to be detected, or at best encountered with feeble and impotent remonstrance. Thus Christianity became at the same time more peremptorily dogmatic, and less influential; it assumed the supreme dominion over the mind, while it held but an imperfect and partial control over the passions and affections. The theology of the Gospel was the religion of the world: the spirit of the Gospel very far from the ruling influence of mankind.

Yet even the theology maintained its dominion, by in some degree accommodating itself to the human mind. It became to a certain degree *mythic* in its character, and *polytheistic* in its form.

Now had commenced what may be called, neither unreasonably nor unwarrantably, the mythic Mythic age age of Christianity. As Christianity worked tianity. downward into the lower classes of society, as it received the rude and ignorant barbarians within its pale, the

general effect could not but be, that the age would drag
down the religion to its level, rather than the religion
elevate the age to its own lofty standard.

The connection between the world of man and a
higher order of things had been re-established; the
approximation of the Godhead to the human race, the
actual presence of the Incarnate Deity upon earth, was
universally recognised; transcendental truths, beyond
the sphere of human reason, had become the primary
and elemental principles of human belief. A strongly
imaginative period was the necessary consequence of
this extraordinary impulse. It was the reign
of faith, of faith which saw or felt the divine,
or at least supernatural, agency, in every occurrence of
life, and in every impulse of the heart; which offered
itself as the fearless and undoubting interpreter of
every event; which comprehended in its domain the
past, the present, and the future; and seized upon
the whole range of human thought and knowledge,
upon history, and even natural philosophy, as its own
patrimony.

This was not, it could not be, that more sublime
theology of a rational and intellectual Christianity;
that theology which expands itself as the system of the
universe expands upon the mind; and from its wider
acquaintance with the wonderful provisions, the more
manifest and all-provident forethought of the Deity,
acknowledges with more awestruck and admiring, yet
not less fervent and grateful, homage the beneficence
of the Creator; that Christian theology which reveren-
tially traces the benignant providence of God over the
affairs of men—the all-ruling Father—the Redeemer
revealed at the appointed time, and publishing the code
of reconciliation, holiness, peace, and everlasting life—

the Universal Spirit, with its mysterious and confessèd but untraceable energy, pervading the kindred spiritual part of man. The Christian of those days lived in a supernatural world, or in a world under the constant and felt and discernible interference of supernatural power. God was not only present, but asserting his presence at every instant, not merely on signal occasions and for important purposes, but on the most insignificant acts and persons. The course of nature was beheld, not as one great uniform and majestic miracle, but as a succession of small, insulated, sometimes trivial, sometimes contradictory interpositions, often utterly inconsistent with the moral and Christian attributes of God. The divine power and goodness were not spreading abroad like a genial and equable sunlight, enlightening, cheering, vivifying, but breaking out in partial and visible flashes of influence. Each incident was a special miracle, the ordinary emotion of the heart was divine inspiration. Every individual had not merely his portion in the common diffusion of religious and moral knowledge or feeling, but looked for his peculiar and especial share in the divine blessing. His dreams came direct from heaven, a new system of Christian omens succeeded the old; witchcraft merely invoked Beelzebub or Satan instead of Hecate; hallowed places only changed their tutelary nymph or genius for a saint or martyr.

It is not less unjust to stigmatise in the mass as fraud, or to condemn as the weakness of superstition, than it is to enforce as an essential part of Christianity, that which was the necessary developement of this state of the human mind. The case was this,— the mind of man had before it a recent and wonderful revelation, in which it could not but acknow-

Imaginative state of the human mind.

ledge the divine interposition. God had been brought
down, or had condescended to mingle himself with the
affairs of men. But where should that faith, which
could not but receive these high, and consolatory, and
reasonable truths, set limits to the agency of this beneficent power? How should it discriminate between that
which in its apparent discrepancy with the laws of
nature (and of those laws how little was known!) was
miraculous; and that which, to more accurate observation, was only strange or wonderful, or perhaps the
result of ordinary but dimly seen causes? how still more
in the mysterious world of the human mind, of which
the laws are still, we will not say in their primitive, but
in comparison with those of external nature, in profound
obscurity? If the understanding of man was too much
dazzled to see clearly even material objects; if just
awakening from a deep trance, it beheld everything
floating before it in a mist of wonder, how much more
was the mind disqualified to judge of its own emotions,
of the origin, suggestion, and powers, of those thoughts
and emotions, which still perplex and baffle our deepest
metaphysics.

The irresistible current of man's thoughts and feelings
ran all one way. It is difficult to calculate the effect of
that extraordinary power or propensity of the mind to
see what it expects to see, to colour with the preconceived hue of its own opinions and sentiments whatever
presents itself before it. The contagion of emotions or
of passions, which in vast assemblies may be resolved,
perhaps, into a physical effect, acts, it should seem, in a
more extensive manner; opinions and feelings appear
to be propagated with a kind of epidemic force and
rapidity. There were some, no doubt, who saw farther,
but who either dared not, or did not care, to stand across

the torrent of general feeling. But the mass, even of the strongest minded, were influenced, no doubt, by the profound religious dread of assuming that for an ordinary effect of nature, which *might be* a divine interposition. They were far more inclined to suspect reason of presumption than faith of credulity. Where faith is the height of virtue, and infidelity the depth of sin, tranquil investigation becomes criminal indifference, doubt guilty scepticism. Of all charges men shrink most sensitively, especially in a religious age, from that of irreligion, however made by the most ignorant or the most presumptuous. The clergy, the great agents in the maintenance and communication of this imaginative religious bias, the asserters of constant miracle in all its various forms, were themselves, no doubt, irresistibly carried away by the same tendency. It was treason against their order and their sacred duty, to arrest, or to deaden, whatever might tend to religious impression. Pledged by obligation, by feeling, we may add by interest, to advance religion, most were blind to, all closed their eyes against, the remote consequences of folly and superstition. A clergyman who, in a credulous or enthusiastic age, dares to be rationally pious, is a phenomenon of moral courage. From this time, either the charge of irreligion, or the not less dreadful and fatal suspicion of heresy or magic, was the penalty to be paid for the glorious privilege of superiority to the age in which the man lived, or of the attainment to a higher and more reasonable theology.

The clergy.

The desire of producing religious impression was in a great degree the fertile parent of all the wild inventions which already began to be grafted on the simple creed of Christianity. That which was employed avowedly with this end in one generation, be-

Religious impressions.

came the popular belief of the next. The full growth of all this religious poetry (for, though not in form, it was poetical in its essence) belongs to, and must be reserved for, a later period. Christian history would be incomplete without that of Christian popular superstition.

But though religion, and religion in this peculiar form, had thus swallowed up all other pursuits and sentiments, it cannot indeed be said, that this new mythic or imaginative period of the world suppressed the developement of any strong intellectual energy, or arrested the progress of real knowledge and improvement. This, even if commenced, must have yielded to the devastating inroads of barbarism. But in truth, however high in some respects the civilisation of the Roman empire under the Antonines; however the useful, more especially the mechanical, arts must have attained, as their gigantic remains still prove, a high perfection, (though degenerate in point of taste, by the colossal solidity of their structure, the vast buildings, the roads, the aqueducts, the bridges, in every quarter of the world, bear testimony to the science as well as to the public spirit of the age,) still there is a remarkable dearth, at this flourishing period, of great names in science and philosophy, as well as in literature.[b]

Principles may have been admitted, and may have *Effect on natural philosophy.* begun to take firm root, through the authoritative writings of the Christian fathers, which, after a long period, would prove adverse to the free developement of natural, moral, and intellectual philosophy; and, having been enshrined for centuries as a part of religious doctrine, would not easily surrender their claims to divine authority, or be deposed from

---

[b] Galen, as a writer on physic, may be quoted as an exception.

their established supremacy. The church condemned
Galileo on the authority of the fathers as much as of
the sacred writings, at least on their irrefragable
interpretation of the scriptures ; and the denial of the
antipodes by St. Augustine was alleged against the
magnificent, but as it appeared to many no less impious
than frantic, theory of Columbus.[c] The wild cosmo-
gonical theories of the Gnostics and Manicheans, with
the no less unsatisfactory hypotheses of the Greeks,
tended, no doubt, to throw discredit on all kinds of
physical study,[d] and to establish the strictly literal
exposition of the Mosaic history of the creation. The
orthodox fathers, when they enlarge on the works of
the six days, though they allow themselves largely in
allegorical inference, have in general in view these
strange theories, and refuse to depart from the strict
letter of the history ;[e] and the popular language, which

[c] It has been said, that the best
mathematical science which the age
could command was employed in the
settlement of the question about Easter,
decided at the Council of Nicæa. See
on the astronomy and geography of the
fathers, Voss, Kritische Blätter, ii. 155
et seq. ; also Whewell, Hist. of Induc-
tive Sciences, i. 156, &c.

[d] Brucker's observations on the physical knowledge, or rather on the professed contempt of physical knowledge,
of the fathers, are characterised with
his usual plain good sense. Their general language was that of Lactantius : —
" Quanto faceret sapientius ac verius
si exceptione factâ diceret caussas ra-
tionesque duntaxat rerum cœlestium
seu naturalium, quia sunt abditæ, nec
sciri posse, quia nullus doceat, nec
quæri oportere, quia inveniri quærendo
non possunt. Quâ exceptione interpo-

sitâ et physicos admonuisset ne quære-
rent ea, quæ modum excederent cogi-
tationis humanæ ; et se ipsum calum-
niæ invidiâ liberasset, et nobis certe
dedisset aliquid, quod sequeremur."
Div. Instit. iii. 6. See other quotations to the same effect : Brucker,
Hist. Phil. iii. p. 357. The work
of Cosmas Indicopleustes, edited by
Montfaucon, is a curious example
of the prevailing notions of physical
science.

[e] Compare the Hexaemeron of Ambrose, and Brucker's sensible remarks
on the pardonable errors of that great
prelate. The evil was, not that the
fathers fell into extraordinary errors
on subjects of which they were ignorant, but that their errors were ca-
nonised by the blind veneration of
later ages, which might have been
better informed.

was necessarily employed with regard to the earth and the movements of the heavenly bodies, became established as literal and immutable truth. The Bible, and the Bible interpreted by the fathers, became the code not of religion only, but of every branch of knowledge. If religion demanded the assent to a heaven-revealed, or heaven-sanctioned, theory of the physical creation, the whole history of man, from its commencement to its close, seemed to be established in still more distinct and explicit terms. Nothing was allowed for figurative or Oriental phraseology, nothing for that condescension to the dominant sentiments and state of knowledge, which may have been necessary to render each part of the sacred writings intelligible to that age in which it was composed. And if the origin of man was thus clearly revealed, the close of his history was still supposed, however each generation passed away undisturbed, to be imminent and immediate. The Day of Judgement was before the eyes of the Christian, either instant, or at a very brief interval; it was not unusual, on a general view, to discern the signs of the old age and decrepitude of the world; and every great calamity was either the sign or the commencement of the awful consummation. Gregory I. beheld in the horrors of the Lombard invasion the visible approach of the last day; and it is not impossible that the doctrine of a purgatorial state was strengthened by this prevalent notion, which interposed only a limited space between the death of the individual and the final judgement.[f]

---

[f] " Depopulatæ urbes, eversa castra, concrematæ ecclesiæ, destructa sunt monasteria virorum et fœminarum, desolata ab hominibus prædia, atque ab omni cultore destituta; in solitudine vacat terra, occupaverunt bestiæ loca, quæ prius multitudo hominum tenebat. Nam in hâc terrâ, in quâ nos vivimus, finem suum mundus jam non nuntiat sed ostendit." Greg. Mag. Dial. iii. 38.

But the popular belief was not merely a theology in its higher sense.

Christianity began to approach to a polytheistic form, or at least to permit, what it is difficult to call by any other name than polytheistic, Polytheistic form of Christianity. habits and feelings of devotion. It attributed, however vaguely, to subordinate beings some of the inalienable powers and attributes of divinity. Under the whole of this form lay the sum of Christian doctrine; but that which was constantly presented to the minds of men was the host of subordinate, indeed, but still active and influential, mediators between the Deity and the world of man. Throughout (as has already been and will presently be indicated again) existed the vital and essential difference between Christianity and Paganism. It is possible that the controversies about the Trinity and the divine nature of Christ, tended indirectly to the promotion of this worship, of the Virgin, of angels, of saints and martyrs. The great object of the victorious, to a certain extent, of both parties, was the closest approximation, in one sense, the identification, of the Saviour with the unseen and incomprehensible Deity. Though the human nature of Christ was as strenuously asserted in theory, it was not dwelt upon with the same earnestness and constancy as his divine. To magnify, to purify this from all earthly leaven was the object of all eloquence: theologic disputes on this point withdrew or diverted the attention from the life of Christ as simply related in the Gospels. Christ became the object of a remoter, a more awful, adoration. The mind began therefore to seek out, or eagerly to seize, some other more material beings, in closer alliance with human sympathies. The constant propensity of man to humanise his Deity, checked, as

2 e 2

it were, by the receding majesty of the Saviour, readily clung with its devotion to humbler objects.[g] The weak wing of the common and unenlightened mind could not soar to the unapproachable light in which Christ dwelt with the Father ; it dropped to the earth, and bowed itself down before some less mysterious and infinite object of veneration. In theory it was always a different and inferior kind of worship; but the feelings, especially impassioned devotion, know no logic : they pause not ; it would chill them to death if they were to pause for these fine and subtle distinctions. The gentle ascent by which admiration, reverence, gratitude, and love, swelled up to awe, to veneration, to worship, both as regards the feelings of the individual and the general sentiment, was imperceptible. Men passed from rational respect for the remains of the dead,[h] the communion of holy thought and emotion, which might connect the departed saint with his brethren in the flesh, to the superstitious veneration of

Worship of saints and angels.

---

[g] The progress of the worship of saints and angels has been fairly and impartially traced by Shröeck, Christliche Kirchengeschichte, viii. 161, *et seq.* In the account of the martyrdom of Polycarp, it is said, " we love the martyrs as disciples and followers of the Lord." The fathers of the next period leave the saints and martyrs in a kind of intermediate state, the bosom of Abraham or Paradise, as explained by Tertullian, contr. Marc. iv. 34. Apologett. 47. Compare Irenæus adv. Hær. v. c 31. Justin, Dial. cum Tryph. Origen, Hom. vii. in Levit.

[h] The growth of the worship of relics is best shown by the prohibitory law of Theodosius (A.D. 386) against the removal and sale of saints' bodies. " Nemo martyres distrahat, nemo mercetur." Cod. Theodos. ix. 17. Augustine denies that worship was ever offered to apostles or saints. " Quis autem audivit aliquando fidelium stantem sacerdotem ad altare etiam super sanctum corpus martyris ad Dei honorem cultumque constructum, dicere in precibus, offero tibi sacrificium, Petre, vel Paule, vel Cypriane, cum apud eorum memorias offeratur Deo qui eos et homines et martyres fecit, et sanctis suis angelis cœlesti honore sociavit." De Civ. Dei, viii. 27. Compare xvii. 10, where he asserts miracles to be performed at their tombs.

relics, and the deification of mortal men, by so easy a transition, that they never discovered the precise point at which they transgressed the unmarked and unwatched boundary.

This new polytheising Christianity therefore was still subordinate and subsidiary in the theologic creed to the true Christian worship, but it usurped its place in the heart, and rivalled it in the daily language and practices of devotion. The worshipper felt and acknowledged his dependency, and looked for protection, or support, to these new intermediate beings, the intercessors with the great Intercessor. They were arrayed by the general belief in some of the attributes of the Deity,— ubiquity [1] and the perpetual cognisance of the affairs of earth; they could hear the prayer; [k] they could read the heart; they could control nature; they had a power, derivative indeed from a higher source, but still exercised according to their volition, over all the events of the world. Thus each city, and almost each individual, began to have his tutelar saint; the presence of some beatified being hovered over and hallowed particular spots; and thus the strong influence of local and

---

[1] Massuet, in his preface to Irenæus, p. cxxxvi., has adduced some texts from the fathers of the fourth and fifth centuries on the ubiquity of the saints and the Virgin.

[k] Perhaps the earliest instances of these are in the eulogies of the eastern martyrs, by Basil, Greg. Naz. and Greg. Nyssen. See especially the former on the forty Martyrs. ʽΟ θλιβόμενος, ἐπὶ τοὺς τεσσαράκοντα καταφεύγει, ὁ εὐφραινόμενος, ἐπ᾽ αὐτοὺς ἀποτρέχει, ὁ μὲν ἵνα λύσιν εὕρῃ τῶν δυσχερῶν, ὁ δὲ ἵνα φυλαχθῇ αὐτῷ τὰ χρηστότερα· ἐνταῦθα γυνὴ εὐσεβὴς ὑπὲρ τέκνων εὐχομένη καταλαμβάνεται, ἀποδημοῦντι ἀνδρὶ τὸν ἐπάνοδον αἰτουμένη, ἀῤῥωστοῦντι τὴν σωτηρίαν. Oper. vol. ii. p. 155. These and similar passages in Greg. Nazianzen (Orat. in Basil.) and Gregory of Nyssa (in Theodor. Martyr.) may be rhetorical ornaments, but their ignorant and enthusiastic hearers would not make much allowance for the fervour of eloquence. Compare Prudent. in Hippolytum Martyrem. See also Van Dale, p. 230

particular worships combined again with that great universal faith, of which the supreme Father was the sole object, and the Universe the temple.[1]   Still, how-

---

[1] An illustration of the new form assumed by Christian worship may be collected from the works of Paulinus, who, in eighteen poems, celebrates the nativity of St. Felix the tutelary saint of Nola. St. Felix is at least invested in the powers ascribed to the intermediate deities of antiquity. Pilgrims crowded from the whole of the south of Italy to the festival of St. Felix. Rome herself, though she possessed the altars of St. Peter and St. Paul, poured forth her myriads; the Capenian gate was choked, the Appian way was covered with the devout worshippers.[1] Multitudes came from beyond the sea. St. Felix is implored by his servants to remove the impediments to their pilgrimages from the hostility of men or adverse weather; to smooth the seas, and send propitious winds.[2]

There is constant reference, indeed, to Christ[3] as the source of this power, yet the power is fully and explicitly assigned to the saint. He is the prevailing intercessor between the worshipper and Christ. But the vital distinction between this paganising form of Christianity and Paganism itself is no less manifest in these poems. It is not merely as a tutelary deity in this life, that the saint is invoked; the future state of existence and the final judgement are constantly present to the thoughts of the worshipper. St. Felix is entreated after death to bear the souls of his worshippers into the bosom of the Redeemer, and to intercede for them at the last day.[4]

These poems furnish altogether a curious picture of the times, and show how early Christian Italy began to

---

[1] " Stipatam multis unam juvat urbibus urbem
Cernere, totque uno compulsa examina voto.
Lucani coeunt populi, coit Appula pubes;
Et Calabri, et cuncti, quos adluit æstus uterque,
Qui læva, et dextra Latium circumsonat unda.
    *   *   *   *
Et qua bis ternas Campania læta per urbes, &c.
Ipsaque cœlestum sacris procerum monumentis
Roma Petro Pauloque potens, rarescere gaudet
Hujus honore diei, portæque ex ore Capenæ
Millia profundens ad amicæ mœnia Nolæ
Dimittit duodena decem per millia denso
Agmine, confertis longe latet Appia turbis."—Carm. iii.

[2]   " Da currere mollibus undis,
Et famulis famulos a puppi suggere ventos."—Carm. i.

[3] " Sis bonus o felixque tuis, Dominumque potentem
    Exores,———
            Liceat placati munere Christi
Post pelagi fluctus," &c.

[4]   " Positasque tuorum
Ante tuos vultus, animas vectare paterno
Ne renuas gremio Domini fulgentis ad ora.   .   .   .
Posce ovium grege nos statui, ut sententia summi
Judicis, hoc quoque nos iterum tibi munere donet."—Carm. iii.

ever, this new polytheism differed in its influence, as
well as in its nature, from that of Paganism.   It bore
a constant reference to another state of existence.
Though the office of the tutelary being was to avert
and mitigate temporal suffering, yet it was still more so
to awaken and keep alive the sentiments of the religious
being.   They were not merely the agents of the divine
providential government on earth, but indissolubly connected with the hopes and fears of the future state of
existence.

The most natural, most beautiful, and most universal,
though perhaps the latest developed, of these   Worship of
new forms of Christianity, that which tended to   the Virgin.
the poetry of the religion, and acted as the conservator

---

become what it is. The pilgrims
brought their votive offerings, curtains, and hangings, embroidered with
figures of animals, silver plates with
inscriptions, candles of painted wax,
pendent lamps, precious ointments,
and dishes of venison and other meats
for the banquet. The following characteristic circumstance must not be
omitted. The magnificent plans of
Paulinus for building the church of
St. Felix were interfered with by two
wooden cottages, which stood in a
field before the front of the building.
At midnight a fire broke out in these

tenements. The affrighted bishop
woke up in trembling apprehension
lest the splendid "palace" of the saint
should be enveloped in the flames.
He entered the church, armed with a
piece of the wood of the true cross,
and advanced towards the fire. The
flames which had resisted all the
water thrown upon them, retreated
before the sacred wood; and in the
morning every thing was found uninjured except these two devoted
buildings. The bishop, without scruple,
ascribes the fire to St. Felix :—

"Sed et hoc Felicis gratia nobis
Munere consuluit, quod præveniendo laborem
Utilibus flammis, operum compendia nobis
Præstitit."—Carm. x.

The peasant, who had dared to
prefer his hovel, though the beloved
dwelling of his youth, to the house of

God or of his saint, seeing one of the
buildings thus miraculously in flames,
sets fire to the other.

"Et celeri peragit sua damna furore
Dilectasque domos, et inanes plangit amores."

Some of the other miracles at the shrine of St. Felix border close on the
comic.

of art, particularly of painting, till at length it became the
parent of that refined sense of the beautiful, that which
was the inspiration of modern Italy, was the worship of
the Virgin. Directly that Christian devotion expanded
itself beyond its legitimate objects; as soon as prayers or
hymns were addressed to any of those beings who had acquired sanctity from their connection or co-operation with
the introduction of Christianity into the world; as soon
as the apostles and martyrs had become hallowed in
the general sentiment, as more especially the objects of
the divine favour and of human gratitude, the virgin
mother of the Saviour appeared to possess peculiar
claims to the veneration of the Christian world. The
worship of the Virgin, like most of the other tenets
which grew out of Christianity, originated in the lively
fancy and fervent temperament of the East, but was
embraced with equal ardour, and retained with passionate constancy, in the West.[m]

The higher importance assigned to the female sex by
Christianity, than by any other form at least of Oriental

[m] Irenæus, in whose works are
found the earliest of those ardent
expressions with regard to the Virgin,
which afterwards kindled into adoration, may, in this respect, be considered
as Oriental. I allude to his parallel
between Eve and the Virgin, in which
he seems to assign a mediatorial character to the latter. Iren. iii. 33, v.
19.

The earlier fathers use expressions
with regard to the Virgin altogether
inconsistent with the reverence of
later ages. Tertullian compares her
unfavourably with Martha and Mary,
and insinuates that she partook of the
incredulity of the rest of her own
family. "Mater æquè non demon-
stratur adhæsisse illi, cum Marthæ
et Mariæ aliæ in commercia ejus
frequententur. Hoc denique in loco
(St. Luc. viii. 20) apparet incredulitas
eorum cum is doceret viam vitæ," &c.
De Carne Christi, c. 7. There is a
collection of quotations on this subject
in Field on the Church, p. 264, et seqq.
See this subject pursued in Latin
Christianity.

The Collyridians, who offered cakes
to the Virgin, were rejected as heretics.
Epiph. Hær. lxxviii. lxxix.

The perpetual virginity of Mary
was an object of controversy: as
might be expected, it was maintained
with unshaken confidence by Epiphanius, Ambrose, and Jerome.

religion, powerfully tended to the general adoption of the worship of the Virgin, while that worship reacted on the general estimation of the female sex. Women willingly deified (we cannot use another adequate expression) this perfect representative of their own sex, while the sex was elevated in general sentiment by the influence ascribed to their all-powerful patroness. The ideal of this sacred being was the blending of maternal tenderness with perfect purity—the two attributes of the female character which man, by his nature, seems to hold in the highest admiration and love; and this image constantly presented to the Christian mind, calling forth the gentler emotions, appealing to, and giving, as it were, the divine sanction to, domestic affections, could not be without its influence. It operated equally on the manners, the feelings, and in some respect on the inventive powers of Christianity. The gentleness of the Redeemer's character, the impersonation of the divine mercy in his whole beneficent life, had been in some degree darkened by the fierceness of polemic animosity. The religion had assumed a sternness and severity arising from the mutual and recriminatory condemnations. The opposite parties denounced eternal punishments against each other with such indiscriminate energy, that hell had become almost the leading and predominant image in the Christian dispensation. This advancing gloom was perpetually softened; this severity allayed by the impulse of gentleness and purity, suggested by this new form of worship. It kept in motion the genial under-current of more humane feeling; it diverted and estranged the thought from this harassing strife to calmer and less exciting objects. The dismal and the terrible, which so constantly haunted the imagination, found no place during the contemplation of

the Mother and the Child, which, when once it became
enshrined in the heart, began to take a visible and
external form.[n] The image arose out of, and derived its
sanctity from, the general feeling, which in its turn,
especially when, at a later period, real art breathed life
into it, strengthened the general feeling to an incal-
culable degree.

The wider and more general dissemination of the
worship of the Virgin belongs to a later period in Christian history.

Thus under her new form was Christianity prepared
to enter into the darkening period of European history
—to fulfil her high office as the great conservative principle of religion, knowledge, humanity, and of the
highest degree of civilisation of which the age was
capable, during centuries of violence, of ignorance, and
of barbarism.

---

[n] At a later period, indeed, even the Virgin became the goddess of war :—

'Αεὶ γὰρ οἶδε τὴν φύσιν νικᾶν μόνη,
Τόκῳ τὸ πρῶτον, καὶ μάχῃ τὸ δεύτερον.

Such are the verses of George of Pisidia, relating a victory over the Avars.
On the whole subject of this Conclusion, I would venture to refer to the Hist.
of Latin Christianity, especially to the chapters on Iconoclasm, and those in
the Survey, relating to the popular Worship, the Literature, and the Fine Arts
of Christianity.

INDEX.

—◆◇◆—

The Roman numerals refer to the volumes; the Arabic figures denote the pages.

ARLES.

press Justina's futile efforts in its behalf, 158, 159. Arian Council of Antioch, 268 *note*. See ii, 406. 413. 419 *note*, 420. 421–423. 435. 436 *note*, 438. 441. 442 *note*. 443.

ARLES, bishop of, ii, 302. 304. Its Council, 423; iii, 268 *note*. Its ordinance relative to priests' marriages, 280.

ARMENIA, number of Jews (A.D. 367) in, i, 59 *note*. Edicts resisted and worship rejected by its church, ii, 31. War made upon it by Maximin, 235. Magianism forced upon it, 253, 254. The first Christian kingdom, 254. Persecution suffered by it, 254, 255. Authors of its histories, 255. Murder of its king, 255, 256. Its subjugation and establishment as a kingdom, 256. Occasion of its erection into a Christian kingdom, 257, 258. Monumental inscription commemorative of its struggles, 258 *note*. Its apostle, see *Gregory the Illuminator*. See also ii, 222. 235. 235 *note*. iii, 60.

ARNOBIUS, iii, 351. 388 *note*.

ARNUPHIS, elemental manifestation superstitiously attributed to, ii, 143.

ARSACES, vestiges of the deification of kings of the line of, ii, 248.

ARSENIUS, machinations of the accusers of Athanasius defeated by, ii, 378, 379. Modes of self-torture adopted by him, iii, 205, 206.

ART, effect of Christianity on, iii, 247. Portraits of the Father, Saviour, Virgin, Apostles, &c, 389–396.

ARTACES, self-immolations at the funeral of, ii, 257.

ARTAXERXES. See *Ardeschir*.

ARTEMIUS, Duke of Egypt, condemnation and death of, iii, 17.

ARTICLES of Belief, period of the introduction of, ii, 352. See *Church*.

ASCENSIO Isaiæ, an apocryphal book, portions of the Gospel narrative confirmed by the, i, 91 *note*.

ATHANASIUS.

ASCENSION, the, i, 351.

ASCETICISM, source of, ii, 35, 36. Christianity outbidden by Eastern asceticism, 43. Asceticism in Saturnius's system, 63. See *Essenes*.

ASELLA, self-denying devotion of, iii, 231.

ASIA, cause of the rapid rise and fall of the empires in, i, 1. Earthquakes *temp*. Antoninus, ii, 131. Last of the Asiatic martyrs, 140. Marital jealousy of its tribes, 396. Religions of Asia, see *Orientalism*.

ASIATIC hours of the day, Dr. Townson's suggestion relative to the, i, 169 *note*.

ASIA Minor, rescript of Antoninus to the cities of, ii, 110. Its cities the source of poetico-prophetic forgeries, 120, 121. Violence of the persecutions there, 135. See ii, 32. 92. 103. 144. Progress of Maximus through its cities, iii, 2. Results of Chrysostom's visit, 137. See i, 444, 445. 448. 460. ii, 32. 92. 103. 144. 145. iii, 77. 110. 209.

ASIARCHS, functions of the, i, 449, 450, *notes*. Attempt of one to avert the martyrdom of Polycarp, ii, 138. Law from which they were exempted, iii, 333.

ASSOS, Paul takes ship at, i, 451.

ASTARTE, Queen of Heaven, and her attributes, i, 61; ii, 175. See *Dea cœlestis*.

ASTERIUS Amasenus, illustrative citation from, iii, 290 *note* c.

ASTROLOGERS, their influence among the Romans, i, 42, 43.

ASYLUM, right of, restricted by Eutropius, iii, 133. Its original object and gradual abuse, 133–135.

ATHANASIUS, St, controversial point admitted by, ii, 368 *note*. His accusation against Arians and semi-Arians, 370 *note*. His antecedents, 375. Elevated to the Patriarchate of Alexandria, *ibid*. Braves all dangers to establish the

ATHANASIUS.

supremacy of his own opinions, 376.
Ruse by which a charge against
him was disproved, *ibid note* q.
Multiplicity of charges against him,
377. His refutation of a " dead
hand" accusation, 379, 380. Charge
on which he was deposed from his
see, 379. Confronts and demands
justice of Constantine, *ibid.* New
charge against him and sentence
thereon, 379-381. His argument
from the death of Arius, 382 *note.*
Opposition and ultimate consent of
the Emperor to his recall from
banishment, 382, 383. His imperial
and local partisans and opponents,
406, 410. His inflexible pursuit of
his object and triumphant entry
into Alexandria, 410-412. Result
of the councils held at Tyre and
Antioch, 412, 413. Again an exile
and in Rome: his influence there,
413, 414. Effect of the controversy initiated by him, 416. His
accusers summoned to Rome, 416,
417. His case submitted to a council at Sardica : result of same, 417-
419. His triumphal re-entry into
Alexandria in company with Constantius, 419, 420. Constantius
again his enemy and accuser, 423-
425. Orders issued for his removal,
427. Scene in his church on his
attempted arrest: his escape, 428,
429. Treatment of his followers by
the Arians, 430, 431. His asceticism in his forced solitude, 432.
His admiration for Lucifer of Cag-
liari, 434. Contempt for the emperor shown in his Epistle to the
Solitaries, 434, 435. His inflexible
orthodoxy, 436. Style and character
of his writings, 438, 439. His return from exile under and re-banish-
ment by Julian, iii, 19. Received
with favour by Jovian, 32. His
fifth exile and death, 44. His
pause in polemic warfare, 201 *note.*
Not an advocate for church music,
403. See ii, 351. 436. 440. 441-3.
iii, 1, 150. 157. 281. 367.

AUGUSTINE.

ATHANASIUS, Arian bishop of Ana-
zarba, ii, 444.
ATHEISM, Christians charged with, ii,
12. 145. 180.
ATHENAGORAS, principle regarding
clerical marriages laid down by, iii,
279 *note.*
ATHENS, i, 431. Character of its
Paganism, 435. Paul's harangue
to its citizens, 436-441. Impulse
given to its Paganism by Julian, iii,
11. Preserved from Alaric by Minerva, 78 *note.* See ii, 106. 110.
185. 351. iii, 78.
ATLAS of the Greeks, the Homophorus
of Mani, ii, 260. 267, 268 *note.*
ATTALUS, a Phrygian convert, martyred, ii, 146. 148. His vision in
prison, 161 *note.*
ATTALUS, the pagan emperor, iii, 96.
ATTICI of Rome, the, ii, 40.
AUGURS, their " occupation gone," i,
28.
AUGUSTEUM, the, Constantinople, ii,
333.
AUGUSTI, the, sharers of Roman
power, ii, 207. 223. 279. Impolicy
of the system, 242.
AUGUSTINE, Saint, i, 28. Main argument of his *De Civitate Dei,*
ibid note. Its occasion and con-
tents, iii, 182-187. Inference from
his quotation from Seneca, i,
430 *note.* On Nero's expected reappearance as Antichrist, ii, 123
note. Influence of African Christianity upon him, ii, 161 ; iii, 103.
His escape from Manicheanism, ii,
273, 274; iii, 180, 181. His own
words on the subject, ii, 274 *note.*
Pagan rites at which he was present,
iii, 79 *note.* His question to the
Donatists, 91 *note.* Against the
forcible demolition of heathen temples, 94 *note.* At issue with himself on the subject of miracles, 160
note. Most influential of all Christian writers since the apostles, 170,
177. Modern religious systems based

VOL. III.

2 G

456   INDEX.

None

None

dria (see *Alexandria*). Anti-Christian rescript sent to its court, iii, 62. Destruction of its temples and idols, 68-77. Rule of Theophilus, 102. See ii, 32. 64. 76. 104. 113. 120. 133. 159. 228. 277. 360. 374. 378. iii, 105.

EICHHORN on the incidents connected with Stephen's martyrdom, i, 368 *note*. His conjecture relative to the altar " To the unknown God," 439 *note*.

EIRENE, church of, at Constantinople, ii, 333 *note*.

ELAGABALUS, worship imposed on the senate by, ii, 151. Etymology of his name, 173. Celebration of worship to him, 173, 174. His brutal licentiousness, 175. Religious system contemplated by him, *ibid*. His vagaries before his idol and human sacrifices on its altar, 176. Effect of his mother's training, 177.

ELAMITES, ii, 253 *note*.

ELDERS of the Jewish synagogue, ii, 17. Of the Christian church, 21.

ELECT, the, in Mani's system, ii, 273.

ELECTION, Augustine's theory of, iii, 175.

ELEUSIS and Eleusinian mysteries, i, 32 *note*. Their character, 33, 441. Hadrian a worshipper, ii, 105. The nave of the temple, 341 *note*. Its Hierophant, ii, 462. Re-edification of the temple, iii, 12. See iii, 78.

ELIJAH, or Elias, God's revelation to, i, 44. Expectation of his reappearance by the Jews, 88. 137. 149. Why held in reverence by them, 136. Prophetic references to him, 136, 137, *notes*, 138. 238, 239. 336. ii, 306.

ELIZABETH, mother of John the Baptist, i, 89. The angel's declaration regarding her, 92. Incident connected with Mary's visit to her, 95. 97. Degree of relationship be-

tween them, 96 *note*. See *John the Baptist.*

ELSLEY'S ' Annotations on the Gospel,' value of, i, 100 *note.*

ELVIRA, or Illiberis, see, *under Councils, Illiberis.*

ELYMAS, or Bar-Jesus, Jewish wonder-worker, struck blind, i, 389. Consequences of his endeavour to outdo the apostles, 429 *note*. Effect of his influence on Sergius Paulus, 431.

EMANATION system of India, ii, 33, 34. 47. 56. Adopted by Mani, 260. See *Æons.*

EMBLEMS, see *Symbols.*

EMESA, the conical black stone of, ii, 173. Its triumphant conveyance into Rome, 174. Elagabalus consecrated to its service, 177. Massacre of its inhabitants, 223.

EMMAUS, appearance of Jesus to the disciples at, i, 348.

EMPEDOCLES, i, 51 *note.*

ENNIUS, irreligious system translated by, i, 41.

ENNOIA, principles represented in the Gnostic systems by the, ii, 69. 81.

ENOCH in Marcion's Gospel, ii, 79.

EPHESUS, Paul at, i, 398. 415 *note*. 444. Trade reasons for upholding its idolatrous worship, 429 *note*. Its famous temple and silver shrines, 445. Favour shown to the Jews, 445. Effect of Paul's preachings on its Jewish exorcists and Pagan image-mongers, 446-450. Coming over to the new faith, ii, 7. Its Christian church, 15, 16. The scene of the first recorded collision between Christianity and Orientalism, 53. Rise of Gnosticism, 84. See i, 460. ii, 13, 14. 21 *note*, 55. See *Diana of Ephesus.*

EPHRAEM, the Syrian, hymns of, ii, 74. A representative of Syrian mysticism, iii, 102. Sketch of his career, 104-106.

2 H 2

2 K

2 K 2

THE END.

LONDON : PRINTED BY W. CLOWES AND SONS, STAMFORD STREET,
AND CHARING CROSS.